# The Declaration of Independence

# Landmark Events in U.S. History Series

# The Declaration of Independence
## Origins and Impact

*Scott Douglas Gerber, Editor*

CQ PRESS

A Division of Congressional Quarterly Inc.
Washington, D.C.

CQ Press
1255 22nd Street, N.W., Suite 400
Washington, D.C. 20037
202-729-1900; toll-free: 1-866-4CQ-PRESS (1-866-427-7737)

www.cqpress.com

Printed and bound in the United States of America

06  05  04  03  02     5  4  3  2  1

♾ The paper used in this publication meets the minimum requirements of the American National Standard for Information Sciences—Permanence of Paper for Printed Library Materials, ANSI Z39.48-1992.

Cover design: Debra Naylor

**Library of Congress Cataloging-in-Publication Data**

The Declaration of Independence : origins and impact / Scott Douglas
    Gerber, editor.
        p. cm. — (Landmark events in U.S. history)
    Includes bibliographical references and index.
    ISBN 1-56802-705-2 (cloth : alk. paper)
    1. United States. Declaration of Independence.  2. United
States—Politics and government—1775–1783.   3. United States—Politics
and government—1783–1865.   4. United States—Politics and
government—Philosophy.   I. Gerber, Scott Douglas   II. Landmark
events in U.S. history series
    E221 .D35 2002
    973.3′13—dc21
                                                                    2002009634

# Contents

# List of Documents

*(Keyed to relevant chapter)*

# Preface

The founders settled America for a variety of reasons. Some wanted to improve their economic condition, others were recruited by those who saw colonial development as essential to the influence and power of the mother country, and still others sought freedom from religious persecution. As the colonies grew in population and developed economically, the British government enacted and enforced more laws regulating them. Before 1763 regulation was largely confined to colonial trade, and the colonists had grown accustomed to a great degree of self-government in their internal affairs. After 1763 the British government sought to reform its sprawling empire and to extract revenue from the colonies to reduce the national debt resulting from the recently completed French and Indian War. As might be expected, the colonists resented the new British policies.

The road to independence from British rule was, however, cautiously taken. When, for example, in 1764 and 1765 Parliament began taxing the colonies, the colonists objected vigorously, but they also reaffirmed their allegiance to the mother country. As a result of increasingly determined British efforts to bring the colonies under firmer control, a decade-long series of urban riots and violence extended from the Stamp Act riots of 1765 through the Boston Massacre, the Boston Tea Party, and the fighting at Lexington and Concord in 1775. Even so, the prevailing mood in the colonies was one of reconciliation with England. The colonists first tried to work within the system, basing their protests on the rights of Englishmen and on the colonial charters. Finding their conventional appeals unsuccessful, the colonists turned to the underlying doctrine of natural rights, which maintains that all persons possess certain inherent, indefeasible rights by virtue of their humanity.

Much, therefore, had transpired in what is now the United States of America before the issuance of the Declaration of Independence on July 4, 1776, and the colonists made many arguments in opposition to the British oppressions that were to lead to war. But all these struggles culminated in the Declaration of Independence, the founding document of the American regime. It is, then, the Declaration that speaks most fully to America as a nation—its origins, purposes, and ideals. It is, in other words, the Declaration of Independence that articulates the American philosophy of government.

This book examines the Declaration from many perspectives. The objective is to identify both the Declaration's origins and its impact on the course of U.S. history. The chapters in this collection are organized into three parts. The first part explores the text and political theory of the Declaration of Independence. Chapter 1 chronicles how Thomas Jefferson, junior member of the Virginia delegation to the Continental Congress, wrote the most important document in U.S. history. Central to that story are other documents—including the Virginia Declaration of Rights (1776), Jefferson's own *Summary View of the Rights of British America* (1774), and the preamble to the Virginia Constitution (1776)—from which Jefferson drew in drafting the Declaration of Independence. Chapter 2 examines the major political theories that informed the Declaration (Lockean liberalism, Classical Republicanism, Christianity, and the English Ancient Constitution) and discusses how Jefferson blended them in drafting the document. Chapters 3 and 4 investigate how Abraham Lincoln and Clarence Thomas, respectively, have invoked the Declaration of Independence when addressing landmark questions of public policy. The chapter on Lincoln surveys how this icon of U.S. history turned to the Declaration to help abolish slavery and save the Union. The chapter on Thomas explores how the nation's highest-ranking black jurist has relied upon the Declaration when addressing questions of civil rights enforcement.

The second part explores the Declaration's influence on the political architecture and institutions of the American regime. Chapter 5 suggests how closely linked the first constitution of the United States—the Articles of Confederation and Perpetual Union—was to the Declaration of Independence. The two documents formed a completed constitutional covenant offering a set of formative principles and reflecting shared commitments on which America as a nation (a people) and as a state (a government) was founded. Chapter 6 reveals how the U.S. Constitution of 1787, which replaced the Articles of Confederation, and the Bill of Rights that followed are also grounded in the principles of the Declaration of Independence. What some might regard as merely technical, institutional matters—federalism, the rule of law, the content of public policy, and the separation of powers—all have proved to be integral to how the Constitution secures the natural rights of individuals. Chapter 7 explores the Declaration of Independence as viewed from the states. A systematic analysis of the constitutions of the states, the federal enabling acts defining the terms upon which new states were admitted to the Union, and the congressional statutes and presidential proclamations acknowledging admission demonstrate how closely the states identify with—or, in the case of the Southern states following the Civil War, were *forced* to identify with—the principles of the Declaration. Chapter 8 turns to how members of Congress and presidents of the United States have appealed to the Declaration of Independence throughout the course of U.S. history. The chapter describes how members and presidents have participated within—and, therefore, have been influenced by—a political context and tradition whose framework and principles were first articulated in the Declaration, as well as the specific ways in which they have used the nation's founding document. Chapter 9 investigates how U.S. Supreme Court justices have referred to the Declaration of Independence in written opinions. Revealed are two identifiable, and occasionally interrelated, purposes: (1) to determine a formal marker of the independence of the United States of America and (2) to cast light upon the founders' views or the principles underlying the Constitution.

The third part explores how the Declaration of Independence has affected various peoples. Chapter 10 chronicles African Americans' experience with the Declaration, in particular as expressed in the orations of three significant figures in African American history: Frederick Douglass, Martin Luther King Jr., and Malcolm X. Careful consideration is afforded to each leader's most important speech about the Declaration: Douglass's "What to the Slave Is the Fourth of July?" speech (July 5, 1852); King's "I Have a Dream" address (August 28, 1963); and Malcolm X's speech on "Black Revolution" (April 8, 1964). Chapter 11 illustrates how crucial the Declaration of Independence has been to the women's rights movement. From 1776 to the present, the principles of the Declaration have moved generations of women to demand equality. As in the case of African Americans, much has been accomplished to improve the lot of women in the United States, but much remains to be done. Chapter 12 explores how the Declaration of Independence has been received abroad. The chapter illustrates how both the cultural possibilities of different languages and the choices made by individual translators shape the reception of the Declaration in other languages. Chapter 12 closes on

a note that has sounded throughout the book: by explaining how Americans have had difficulty throughout the course of U.S. history putting the Declaration's words into practice.

The volume also contains, in one convenient appendix (which begins on page 213), the text of documents—including book excerpts, speeches, letters, and laws—that help illuminate the thesis of each chapter. The reader should note that original spellings and punctuation have been retained in these documents.

The Declaration of Independence is one of the most valued and sacred political documents in history. The purpose of this collection is to explore, through analytical essays and supporting documents, why this is true.

## Acknowledgments

I would like to thank the contributors for their professionalism throughout the course of this project. I also would like to thank LeAnna Smack for her research assistance, Peg Cain for her secretarial help, and the Claude W. Pettit College of Law at Ohio Northern University for a summer research grant. Thanks also are due to Colleen McGuiness for her fine copyediting. Finally, I am grateful to Bill Casto, Wythe Holt, Paul Marcus, Ellen Frankel Paul, Dan Polsby, Steve Presser, and Walter Wadlington for encouraging me to undertake this important project.

*Scott Douglas Gerber*
*Ada, Ohio*

# About the Contributors

**John C. Eastman** is professor of constitutional law at Chapman University School of Law and director of the Claremont Institute Center for Constitutional Jurisprudence. He has previously served as a law clerk to Supreme Court Justice Clarence Thomas and as the director of congressional and public affairs at the U.S. Commission on Civil Rights.

**Bonnie L. Ford** is professor emeritus of history at Sacramento City College. A founder of the women's studies program, she has contributed to many publications on the history of women.

**Gerard W. Gawalt** is the early American history specialist at the Library of Congress. He has published many books and articles on the founding of the United States, including a new edition of *The Declaration of Independence: The Evolution of the Text.*

**Scott Douglas Gerber** is a law professor at Ohio Northern University. He has published four previous books, including *First Principles: The Jurisprudence of Clarence Thomas* and *To Secure These Rights: The Declaration of Independence and Constitutional Interpretation.*

**Mark David Hall** is associate professor of political science at George Fox University. He is the author of *The Political and Legal Philosophy of James Wilson, 1742–1798.*

**Robert W. Hoffert** is dean of the College of Liberal Arts and professor of political science at Colorado State University. He has published *A Politics of Tensions: The Articles of Confederation and American Political Ideas* and, most recently, "Education in a Political Democracy," in *Developing Democratic Character in the Young.*

**Harry V. Jaffa** is a distinguished fellow of the Claremont Institute and professor emeritus of government at Claremont McKenna College and Claremont Graduate School. He is the author of numerous articles and books, including *Crisis of the House Divided: An Interpretation of the Lincoln-Douglas Debates* and *A New Birth of Freedom: Abraham Lincoln and the Coming of the Civil War.*

**Charles A. Kromkowski** teaches in the Department of Politics at the University of Virginia and currently is a teaching fellow with the Center on Religion and Democracy. He is the author of *Recreating the American Repub-*

*lic: Rules of Apportionment, Constitutional Change, and American Political Development, 1700–1870.*

**Keith D. Miller** is associate professor of English at Arizona State University. He is the author of *Voice of Deliverance: The Language of Martin Luther King, Jr., and Its Sources* and of many scholarly essays, including, most recently, "City Called Freedom: Biblical Metaphor in Spirituals, Gospel Lyrics, and the Civil Rights Movement," which appeared in *African Americans and the Bible,* edited by Vincent Wimbush.

**Garrett Ward Sheldon** is the John Morton Beaty Professor of Political Science at the University of Virginia's College at Wise. He is the author of three books on Thomas Jefferson, including *The Political Philosophy of Thomas Jefferson.*

**David Thelen** is professor of history at Indiana University and author of six books on how Americans have experienced citizenship. As editor of the *Journal of American History* (1985–1999), he coordinated an international collaboration of a dozen scholars to analyze the reception and translation of the Declaration of Independence in different countries over time.

**Thomas G. West** is professor of politics at the University of Dallas and a senior fellow of the Claremont Institute. He is the author of *Vindicating the Founders: Race, Sex, Class, and Justice in the Origins of America.*

# Declaration of Independence

IN CONGRESS, July 4, 1776.

The unanimous Declaration of the thirteen united States of America,

When in the Course of human events, it becomes necessary for one people to dissolve the political bands which have connected them with another, and to assume among the powers of the earth, the separate and equal station to which the Laws of Nature and of Nature's God entitle them, a decent respect to the opinions of mankind requires that they should declare the causes which impel them to the separation.

We hold these truths to be self-evident, that all men are created equal, that they are endowed by their Creator with certain unalienable Rights, that among these are Life, Liberty and the pursuit of Happiness.—That to secure these rights, Governments are instituted among Men, deriving their just powers from the consent of the governed,—That whenever any Form of Government becomes destructive of these ends, it is the Right of the People to alter or to abolish it, and to institute new Government, laying its foundation on such principles and organizing its powers in such form, as to them shall seem most likely to effect their Safety and Happiness. Prudence, indeed, will dictate that Governments long established should not be changed for light and transient causes; and accordingly all experience hath shewn, that mankind are more disposed to suffer, while evils are sufferable, than to right themselves by abolishing the forms to which they are accustomed. But when a long train of abuses and usurpations, pursuing invariably the same Object evinces a design to reduce them under absolute Despotism, it is their right, it is their duty, to throw off such Government, and to provide new Guards for their future security. —Such has been the patient sufferance of these Colonies; and such is now the necessity which constrains them to alter their former Systems of Government. The history of the present King of Great Britain is a history of repeated injuries and usurpations, all having in direct object the establishment of an absolute Tyranny over these States. To prove this, let Facts be submitted to a candid world.

He has refused his Assent to Laws, the most wholesome and necessary for the public good.

He has forbidden his Governors to pass Laws of immediate and pressing importance, unless suspended in their operation till his Assent should be obtained; and when so suspended, he has utterly neglected to attend to them.

He has refused to pass other Laws for the accommodation of large districts of people, unless those people would relinquish the right of Representation in the Legislature, a right inestimable to them and formidable to tyrants only.

He has called together legislative bodies at places unusual, uncomfortable, and distant from the depository of their public Records, for the sole purpose of fatiguing them into compliance with his measures.

He has dissolved Representative Houses repeatedly, for opposing with manly firmness his invasions on the rights of the people.

He has refused for a long time, after such dissolutions, to cause others to be elected;

whereby the Legislative powers, incapable of Annihilation, have returned to the People at large for their exercise; the State remaining in the mean time exposed to all the dangers of invasion from without, and convulsions within.

He has endeavoured to prevent the population of these States; for that purpose obstructing the Laws of Naturalization of Foreigners; refusing to pass others to encourage their migrations hither, and raising the conditions of new Appropriations of Lands.

He has obstructed the Administration of Justice, by refusing his Assent to Laws for establishing Judiciary powers.

He has made Judges dependent on his Will alone, for the tenure of their offices, and the amount and payment of their salaries.

He has erected a multitude of New Offices, and sent hither swarms of Officers to harrass our people, and eat out their substance.

He has kept among us, in times of peace, Standing Armies without the Consent of our legislatures.

He has affected to render the Military independent of and superior to the Civil power.

He has combined with others to subject us to a jurisdiction foreign to our constitution, and unacknowledged by our laws; giving his Assent to their Acts of pretended Legislation:

For Quartering large bodies of armed troops among us:

For protecting them, by a mock Trial, from punishment for any Murders which they should commit on the Inhabitants of these States:

For cutting off our Trade with all parts of the world:

For imposing Taxes on us without our Consent:

For depriving us in many cases, of the benefits of Trial by Jury:

For transporting us beyond Seas to be tried for pretended offences:

For abolishing the free System of English Laws in a neighbouring Province, establishing therein an Arbitrary government, and enlarging its Boundaries so as to render it at once an example and fit instrument for introducing the same absolute rule into these Colonies:

For taking away our Charters, abolishing our most valuable Laws, and altering fundamentally the Forms of our Governments:

For suspending our own Legislatures, and declaring themselves invested with power to legislate for us in all cases whatsoever.

He has abdicated Government here, by declaring us out of his Protection and waging War against us.

He has plundered our seas, ravaged our Coasts, burnt our towns, and destroyed the lives of our people.

He is at this time transporting large Armies of foreign Mercenaries to compleat the works of death, desolation and tyranny, already begun with circumstances of Cruelty & perfidy scarcely paralleled in the most barbarous ages, and totally unworthy the Head of a civilized nation.

He has constrained our fellow Citizens taken Captive on the high Seas to bear Arms against their Country, to become the executioners of their friends and Brethren, or to fall themselves by their Hands.

He has excited domestic insurrections amongst us, and has endeavoured to bring on the inhabitants of our frontiers, the merciless Indian Savages, whose known rule of warfare, is an undistinguished destruction of all ages, sexes and conditions.

In every stage of these Oppressions We have Petitioned for Redress in the most humble terms: Our repeated Petitions have been answered only by repeated injury. A Prince whose character is thus marked by every act which may define a Tyrant, is unfit to be the ruler of a free people.

Nor have We been wanting in attention to our Brittish brethren. We have warned them from time to time of attempts by their legislature to extend an unwarrantable jurisdiction over us. We have reminded them of the circumstances of our emigration and settlement here. We have appealed to their native justice and magnanimity, and we have conjured them by the ties of our common kindred to disavow these usurpations, which, would inevitably interrupt our connections and correspondence. They too have been deaf to the voice of justice and of consanguinity. We must, therefore, acquiesce in the necessity, which denounces our Separation, and hold them, as we hold the rest of mankind, Enemies in War, in Peace Friends.

We, therefore, the Representatives of the united States of America, in General Congress, Assembled, appealing to the Supreme Judge of the world for the rectitude of our intentions, do, in the Name, and by Authority of the good People of these Colonies, solemnly publish and declare, That these United Colonies are, and of Right ought to be Free and Independent States; that they are Absolved from all Allegiance to the British Crown, and that all political connection between them and the State of Great Britain, is and ought to be totally dissolved; and that as Free and Independent States, they have full Power to levy War, conclude Peace, contract Alliances, establish Commerce, and to do all other Acts and Things which Independent States may of right do. And for the support of this Declaration, with a firm reliance on the protection of divine Providence, we mutually pledge to each other our Lives, our Fortunes and our sacred Honor.

John Hancock.

*New Hampshire:*
Josiah Bartlett, William Whipple, Matthew Thornton.

*Massachusetts:*
Samuel Adams, John Adams, Robert Treat Paine, Elbridge Gerry.

*Rhode Island:*
Stephen Hopkins, William Ellery.

*Connecticut:*
Roger Sherman, Samuel Huntington, William Williams, Oliver Wolcott.

*New York:*
William Floyd, Philip Livingston, Francis Lewis, Lewis Morris.

*Pennsylvania:*
Robert Morris, Benjamin Harris, Benjamin Franklin, John Morton, George Clymer, James Smith, George Taylor, James Wilson, George Ross.

*Delaware:*
Caesar Rodney, George Read, Thomas McKean.

*Georgia:*
Button Gwinnett, Lyman Hall, George Walton.

*Maryland:*
Samuel Chase, William Paca, Thomas Stone, Charles Carroll of Carrollton.

*Virginia:*
George Wythe, Richard Henry Lee, Thomas Jefferson, Benjamin Harrison, Thomas Nelson, Jr., Francis Lightfoot Lee, Carter Braxton.

*North Carolina:*
William Hooper, Joseph Hewes, John Penn.

*South Carolina:*
Edward Rutledge, Thomas Heyward, Jr., Thomas Lynch, Jr., Arthur Middleton.

*New Jersey:*
Richard Stockton, John Witherspoon, Francis Hopkinson, John Hart, Abraham Clark.

# The Declaration of Independence

# 1

# Drafting the Declaration

## Gerard W. Gawalt

May it be to the world, what I believe it will be, (to some parts sooner, to others later, but finally to all,) the Signal of arousing men to burst the chains, under which Monkish ignorance and superstition had persuaded them to bind themselves, and to assume the blessings and security of self-government. that form which we have substituted, restores the free right to the unbounded exercise of reason and freedom of opinion. all eyes are opened, or opening, to the rights of man. the general spread of the light of science has already laid open to every view the palpable truth, that the mass of mankind has not been born with saddles on their backs, nor a favored few booted and spurred, ready to ride them legitimately, by the grace of god. these are grounds of hope for others. for ourselves, let the annual return of this day for ever refresh our recollections of these rights, and an undiminished devotion to them.

Thomas Jefferson wrote these evocative phrases on his deathbed to Washington, D.C., mayor Roger C. Weightman, as he looked back five decades to July 4, 1776, when "that host of worthies, who joined with us on that day, in the bold and doubtful election we were to make for our country, between submission, or the sword." The drafting and adoption of the Declaration of Independence has become the defining moment of the American Revolution. The Declaration of Independence has become the most important document in American history. And Thomas Jefferson, who drafted the Declaration, has become one of the most important personal icons in American history.

Understanding the drafting of the Declaration of Independence is far more complicated than envisioning a single patriotic American, sitting down to write a document to declare independence from an oppressive foreign government ruled by a tyrannical monarch. For more than 225 years Thomas Jefferson has remained the central figure in the drafting of the Declaration of Independence. However, the importance of his role on occasion has been challenged. Political opponents of Jefferson have attacked his authorship. Scholars have examined in detail the influential precedents, the process, and various surviving drafts of the document. The actions of Jefferson, the committee appointed by Congress to draft the document, and Congress itself have been chronicled in as much detail as meager resources allow. Still what remains is that Thomas Jefferson, junior member of the Virginia delegation to the Continental Congress, wrote the most important document for the American Revolution and the American nation.

## Dreams of the Future

Thomas Jefferson was only thirty-three years old when he traveled to Philadelphia in May

1

1776. A member of the Virginia House of Burgesses since 1769, he had achieved a modicum of notoriety in August 1774 by writing provocative instructions for the Virginia delegation to the First Continental Congress. These instructions were soon published as *A Summary View of the Rights of British America*. Elegantly written, Jefferson's pamphlet was a radical, some said intemperate, condemnation of Britain's oppressive treatment of the colonies. Jefferson argued that "[s]ingle acts of tyranny may be ascribed to the accidental opinion of a day; but a series of oppressions, begun at a distinguished period, and pursued unalterably through every change of ministers, too plainly prove a deliberate and systematical plan of reducing us to slavery."

However, Jefferson's *Summary View* went beyond the standard condemnation of the British to an innovative contention that the American colonies had become an independent nation. Jefferson asserted that "the British parliament has no right to exercise authority over us" because Americans had established "new societies" by the act of emigration, just as the Saxons and Danes had established centuries before in Great Britain. He argued that "our ancestors, before their emigration to America, were the free inhabitants of the British dominion in Europe, and possessed a right which nature has given to all men, of departing from the country in which chance, not choice, has placed them, of going in quest of new habitations, and of there establishing new societies, under such laws and regulations as to them shall seem most likely to promote public happiness." But an oppressive British government had violated their natural rights (see Chapter 2), denied them the fruits of laws passed by

their legislatures, heaped illegal taxes upon them, banned American manufactures, and prevented free trade. Many of these charges were familiar to American revolutionaries and appeared in many pamphlets.

One of the charges stood out for its boldness, especially coming from an aristocratic Virginia planter and slaveholder. Jefferson called for an end to domestic slavery and he condemned the British government's negation of a Virginia law prohibiting the foreign importation of slaves. He wrote:

The abolition of domestic slavery is the great object in those colonies, where it was unhappily introduced in their infant state. But previous to the enfranchisement of the slaves we have, it is necessary to exclude all further importations from Africa; yet our repeated attempts to effect this by prohibitions, and by imposing duties which might amount to a prohibition, have been hitherto defeated by his majesty's negative: Thus preferring the immediate advantages of a few African [changed to "British" by Jefferson on his personal copy] corsairs to the lasting interest of the American states, and to the rights of human nature, deeply wounded by this infamous practice.

When this charge appeared in Jefferson's draft of the Declaration of Independence, along with many more acceptable charges against the "abuse of power" by the British monarch found in the *Summary View,* Congress was forced to confront the apparent paradox of slaveholders seeking to cast off the chains of political bondage while keeping those of personal bondage tightly fastened.

On March 27, 1775, Jefferson was chosen a member of the Virginia delegation to the Second Continental Congress in Philadelphia. He took his seat on June 21, just in time for his fellow Virginian, George Washington, to march off to Boston as commander in chief of

America's new Continental Army. Jefferson was content to seize the opportunities to assist Congress and enhance his reputation with his writing talents and radical thinking. At six feet two inches, he made an impressive appearance, but he showed a reticent public demeanor. No recorded incidence exists of Jefferson speaking in the Congress, although he served on many committees and often drafted the reports. Massachusetts delegate John Adams, his collaborator in drafting the Declaration of Independence, later wrote in his autobiography that "Mr. Jefferson had been now about a Year a Member of Congress, but had attended his Duty in the House but a very small part of the time and when there had never spoken in public: and during the whole Time I satt with him in Congress, I never heard him utter three Sentences together." But he could write, and write he did. Jefferson played a leading role in drafting the fiery congressional document *A Declaration of the Causes and Necessity for Taking Up Arms,* dispatched to Great Britain in 1775.

Jefferson cast his draft along the theme of the innocent Americans assaulted by the aggressive Britishers—of innocent virtue versus entrenched, aggressive corruption. Like the *Summary View* before it, the rhetoric of the *Declaration of the Causes and Necessity* found a place in Jefferson's Declaration of Independence. This was the view of Henry St. John Bolingbroke, Thomas Gordon, James Burgh, and other British Whigs. But, as historian Joseph Ellis has written, "Jefferson's embrace of the Whig rhetoric and the Whig story line was utterly sincere. His draft of *Causes and Necessity,* then his subsequent draft of the Declaration, were not undertaken as self-conscious polemics or exaggerated pieces of propaganda. What he wrote actually reflected his understanding of the forces swirling through Anglo-America."

Jefferson, as always, seemed eager to return to his wife, Martha, family, and Monticello, his home in Charlottesville, Virginia. So at the end of July 1775, he left Philadelphia, only to be reelected to Congress on August 11 and to return in October. He again departed quickly at the end of December. However, an American army met defeat at the gates of Quebec. Another American army forced the British from occupied Boston. Native Americans joined the British, their traditional commercial and military allies. Thomas Paine wrote and published his ringing call for American independence—*Common Sense.* Jefferson lingered at Monticello until late spring of 1776 once again brought him north to Philadelphia and fame.

Jefferson was the junior member of the Virginia delegation when he arrived at Congress on May 14. The next day, Congress called for states to erect their own governments and write new constitutions. While Virginia voted to form its own government and George Mason drafted the Virginia Declaration of Rights, Jefferson longed to be in Williamsburg and assist in drafting a constitution for his "country"—Virginia. On May 16, Jefferson wrote to Thomas Nelson, a former congressional compatriot, "Should our Convention propose to establish a new form of government perhaps it might be agreeable to recall for a short time their delegates. It is a work of the most interesting nature and such as every individual would wish to have his voice in. In truth it is the whole object of the present controversy; for should a bad government be instituted for us in future, it had been as well to have accepted at first the bad one offered to us from beyond the water without the risk and expence of contest." Even while serving as a delegate to the Continental Congress, Jefferson wrote three drafts of a new constitution for Virginia. Parts were conveyed to Edmund Pendleton, president of the Virginia Convention. George Wythe, a mentor and friend of Jefferson's, carried a draft with him when he left Congress on June 13 for the convention.

In the introduction, or preamble, to his Virginia constitution, Jefferson charged the British king, George III, with a long list of abuses. Drawing on his knowledge of the English Declaration of Rights (1688–1689), his own *Summary View,* and *A Declaration of the Causes and Necessity of Taking Up Arms,* Jefferson maintained that the British Crown had forfeited all rights to govern by its acts of misrule. Nearly all of the twenty acts of oppression and "crimes" listed by Jefferson in his draft were adopted by the Virginia Convention as a preamble to the Virginia constitution.

Jefferson was well into this third and final draft of the Virginia constitution when Virginia's senior delegate to Congress, Richard Henry Lee, acting on instructions adopted on May 15 by the Virginia Convention, introduced in Congress on June 7, 1776, the Virginia resolutions calling on Congress

to declare that these United colonies are & of right ought to be free and independent States, that they are absolved from all allegiance to the British Crown, and that all political connection between them and the State of Great Britain is, and ought to be totally dissolved. That it is expedient forthwith to take the most effectual measures for forming foreign Allegiances. That a plan of confederation be prepared and transmitted to the respective Colonies for their consideration and approbation.

Beset by divisions in Congress and the country, a vote on independence was postponed "to this day three weeks." But an aggressive Congress pushed forward toward independence even though events were not favorable for the American cause. For example, the war was not going well. The army in Canada was in full retreat. British fleets and armies were hovering around New York and Charleston. Native Americans were attacking the American frontier from New England to Georgia. Nevertheless, Congress appointed a five-man committee to "prepare a Declaration" of independence for its consideration.

Richard Henry Lee undoubtedly would have been Virginia's representative on this committee had he not wished to return home to Virginia to help write the state's constitution. Jefferson, too, wanted to return to Williamsburg, but his junior status and the desire "to keep out" Benjamin Harrison, a conservative, led to his inclusion. Not only was Jefferson put on the committee, but he also was deliberately given the most votes to exclude Harrison. Jefferson became the chairperson by virtue of his vote count. He was joined on the committee by John Adams of Massachusetts, Roger Sherman of Connecticut, Benjamin Franklin of Pennsylvania, and Robert R. Livingston of New York.

## Drafting the Document

So far the road to the Declaration of Independence has been open and well documented. However, from the June 11 appointment of the committee until the final approval on July 4, 1776, the course of activity is more secretive (partly as required by Congress) and less well chronicled. Much of the contemporary or near contemporary evidence and testimony is in the hand of Jefferson. Later memories of the event no doubt suffered from natural deterioration and time compression that all memories are subject to and from a natural desire to inflate one's role or simply the tendency to remember one's own role and not those of one's colleagues in what became the defining event of the American Revolution.

Jefferson's Notes of the Proceedings in Congress, June 7–August 1, 1776, are the closest to a contemporary account. Although they were almost certainly not notes taken day by day, they were probably taken in June and July 1776 and possibly refined shortly before they were transmitted to James Madison seven years later. However, in an accompanying letter Jefferson indicates that they were at least based on contemporary records: "I send you inclosed the debates in Congress on the subjects of Independence, Voting in Congress, and the Quotas of money to be required from the states. I found on looking that I had taken no others save only in one trifling case. as you were desirous of having a copy of the original of the declaration of Independence I have inserted it at full length distinguishing the alterations it underwent." Although the notes add many details about the debate on the Virginia resolution for independence, few details were provided about the appointment of the committee and the subsequent operation of the committee. Jefferson wrote about the basic structure of the committee as follows.

It appearing in the course of these debates that the colonies of N.York, New Jersey, Pennsylvania, Delaware, Maryland & South carolina were not yet matured for falling from the parent stem, but that they were fast advancing to that state, it was thought most prudent to wait a while for them, to postpone the final decision to July 1. but that this might occasion as little delay as possible, a committee was appointed to prepare a declaration of independence. the committee were J. Adams, Dr. Franklin, Roger Sherman, Robert R. Livingston & myself. committees were also appointed at the same time to prepare a plan of confederation for the colonies, and to state the terms proper to be proposed for foreign alliance. the committee for drawing the Declaration of Independence desired me to do it.

Unfortunately, the committee kept no minutes, or the minutes Adams later said the committee had kept have not survived. Adams, while minister to France in 1779, recorded in his diary a succinct conversation he had with Francois Chevalier de Marbois, which supports Jefferson's contention that he was appointed as the only member of the committee to draft the declaration: "Whom, said the Chevalier, made the Declaration of Independence? Mr. Jefferson of Virginia, said I, was the Draughtsman. The Committee consisted of Mr. Jefferson, Mr. Franklin, Mr. Harrison, Mr. R. and myself, and We appointed by Jefferson a subcommittee to draw it up." If Adams's memory about the appointment of Jefferson is to be believed, one has to overlook his mistakes. For example, Benjamin Harrison and "Mr. R" were not on the committee.

Adams, in his autobiography, wrote a more vibrant account of Jefferson's selection.

It will naturally be enquired, how it happened that he was appointed on a Committee of such importance. There were more reasons than one. Mr. Jefferson had the Reputation of a masterly Pen. He had been chosen a Delegate in Virginia, in consequence of a very handsome public Paper which he had written for the House of Burgesses, which had given him the Character of a fine Writer.

Another reason was that Mr. Richard Henry Lee was not beloved by the most of his Colleagues from Virginia and Mr. Jefferson was sett up to rival and supplant him. . . . The Committee had several meetings, in which were proposed the Articles of which the Declaration was to consist, and minutes made of them. The Committee then appointed Mr. Jefferson and me, to draw them up in form, and cloath them in a proper Dress. The Sub Committee met, and considered the Minutes, making such Observations on them as then occured: when Mr. Jefferson desired me to take them to my Lodgings and make the Draught. This I declined and gave several reasons for declining. 1. That he was a Virginian and I a Massachusettensian. 2. That he was a southern Man and I a northern one. 3. That I had been so obnoxious for my early and constant Zeal in promoting the Measure, that any draught of mine, would undergo a more severe Scrutiny and criticism in Congress, than one of his composition. 4thly and lastly and that would be reason enough if there were no other, I had a great Opinion of the Elegance of his pen and none at all of my own. I therefore insisted that no hesitation should be made on his part. He accordingly took the Minutes and in a day or two produced to me his Draught.

What seems to be the most reasonable explanation is that Jefferson was elected to the committee because Richard Henry Lee wanted to return to Virginia. Jefferson received the most votes and, under the prevailing rules in Congress, was designated the chairperson. Because he was the chairperson and because he had a known gift and flair for writing, he was often appointed to draft important congressional reports and documents. This case was no different. Jefferson was given the task of translating ideas into words. As Jefferson later recalled in an 1825 letter to Henry Lee:

this was the object of the Declaration of Independence. Not to find out new principles, or new arguments, never before thought of, not merely to say things which had never been said before; but to place before mankind the common sense of the subject; in terms so plain and firm as to command their assent, and to justify ourselves in the independent stand we are compelled to take, neither aiming at originality of principle or sentiment, nor yet copied from any particular and previous writing, it was intended to be an expression of the american mind, and to give to that expression the proper tone and spirit called for by the occasion. all its authority rests then on the harmonizing sentiments of the day, whether expressed in conversation, in letters, printed essays, or in the elementary books of public right, as Aristotle, Cicero, Locke, Sidney, &c.

Possibly before the committee could meet for the first time, one of the most influential documents in the writing of the Declaration of Independence appeared in the public print. The Virginia Declaration of Rights as drafted by George Mason and Thomas Ludwell Lee was published in the *Pennsylvania Gazette* on June 12. Mason had presented it to the Virginia Convention in May, where it underwent further amendment by Lee and the convention before its final adoption on June 12. It is even possible that Jefferson brought a copy of Mason's draft with him to Philadelphia or one was sent to him by Mason, Lee, or Edmund Pendleton, the convention president.

Jefferson undoubtedly read Mason's draft language and molded it into his own distinctive style in the Declaration of Independence. Mason had written these striking words:

That all Men are born equally free and independant, and have certain inherent natural Rights, of which they can not by any Compact, deprive or divest their Posterity; among which are the Enjoyment of Life and Liberty, with the Means of acquiring and possessing Property, and pursueing and obtaining Happiness and Safety.
    That Power is, by God and Nature, vested in, and consequently deprived from the People; that

Magistrates are their Trustees and Servants, and at all times amenable to them.

That Government is, or ought to be, instituted for the common Benefit and Security of the People, Nation, or Community. Of all the various Modes and Forms of Government, that is best, which is capable of producing the greatest Degree of Happiness and Safety, and is most effectually secured against the Danger of mal-administration. And that whenever any Government shall be found inadequate, or contrary to these Purposes, a Majority of the Community had an indubitable, inalienable and indefeasible Right to reform, alter or abolish it, in such Manner as shall be judged most conducive to the Public Weal.

## Self-Evident Truths

After the committee organized itself, discussed the Declaration, and assigned the task of writing it, Jefferson settled into his room at the home of the brick mason Jacob Graff at the southwest corner of Market and Seventh Streets with his Windsor chair and portable writing desk made by Benjamin Randolph. Of the surviving drafts or fragments of drafts of the Declaration of Independence, all but the one in John Adams's hand were written by Jefferson. First is the fragment of the earliest known composition draft, which contains only one heavily edited paragraph accusing the British people of supporting George III's use of "not only soldiers of our common blood but Scotch & foreign mercenaries." Second is John Adams's copy of Jefferson's original draft made between June 11 and June 21 when Jefferson brought a copy of the Declaration to Franklin "to peruse it and suggest such alterations as his more enlarged view of the subject will dictate." Third is Jefferson's "original Rough draught," which incorporates nearly all of the eighty-six changes made in the document after it was first

shown to Adams and Franklin. Several small changes also were made in the hands of Adams and Franklin. The fourth, fifth, and sixth are copies Jefferson made for Richard Henry Lee, George Wythe, and an unidentified third person, either Edmund Pendleton or John Page, and sent to them between July 4 and 10. All are useful in determining which changes were made in Congress. The seventh is the copy Jefferson made as early as 1776 and inserted in his autobiography in 1821. The eighth is the copy made by Jefferson for Madison in the spring of 1783 as part of his Notes of the Proceedings in Congress, which was sent to Madison on June 1, 1783. Here again Jefferson was careful to deliberately mark the changes made by Congress. Ninth is the first printed broadside of the Declaration composed by John Dunlap on July 4 and later inserted into the Journals of Congress by Charles Thomson as the official copy of the Declaration. Finally, there is the signed, engrossed copy of the Declaration of Independence on vellum.

No one knows what documents, books, or pamphlets Jefferson had in his room when he sat down to write. He surely had access to Mason's Virginia Declaration of Rights, his own drafts for a Virginia constitution, his own *A Summary View of the Rights of British America,* and his own draft of *A Declaration of the Causes and Necessity for Taking Up Arms.* Thomas Paine's *Common Sense* also was readily available. Many of Jefferson's ideas and even phrases can be found in the works of John Locke, Algernon Sidney, and Henry Home, Lord Kames (see Chapter 2). But whether Jefferson relied on his detailed knowledge of these works or whether he turned to them in the drafting process is not known.

However, Adams, in an August 6, 1822, letter to Timothy Pickering, referred to the ideas as "commonplace" and the phrases as "hackney'd"—surely not the level of work that would require reference materials. And Jefferson himself later claimed that he turned "to neither book nor pamphlet" while writing it. Both these views may be correct to a large extent. Jefferson was undoubtedly so familiar with the common radical Whig sentiments of the day, with Mason's recent Declaration of Rights, and certainly with his own writings that he may have dashed off the first composition draft without recourse to secondary sources. But the Declaration of Independence has more than its roots in some of these documents.

As in the *Summary View* and *A Declaration of the Causes and Necessity for Taking Up Arms,* Jefferson sought to demonstrate in precise detail that George III was a tyrant unfit to rule the Americans or any free people. He did so by declaring that the denial of certain inalienable rights by a ruler justified an act of revolution. To prove the tyrannical nature of George III, Jefferson listed a long series of charges and indictments against the king that justified the assertion of natural rights. If the people had a right to revolution, they had a right to institute new governments based on the authority of the people. Congress, acting as the people's representative, could and must end American allegiance to the British Crown to preserve the rights of life, liberty, and the pursuit of happiness. These were not ideas new to Jefferson or the other American revolutionaries, but the expression and form that Jefferson was about to present was a unique, elegant, and powerful declaration of natural and revolutionary rights.

The only surviving fragment of Jefferson's composition draft of the Declaration offers clues into his drafting process. Using the technique of writing one paragraph on a page with room for editing, Jefferson seemingly moved quickly through his first draft before returning again and again to edit and recast his thoughts. Eventually, he must have produced a complete fair copy, which he then began to show committee members starting with Adams and Franklin. Analysis of the surviving fragment indicates that Jefferson continued to edit his draft even as Adams, Franklin, Sherman, and Livingston offered suggestions and made editorial changes.

To look at the Declaration of Independence as it emerged from Jefferson's pen requires turning to John Adams's copy. Jefferson's fair copy (now encompassed in the Rough Draft) was so encumbered with alterations that it is only by examining the other copies made by Adams and Jefferson that one can hope to decipher the order of changes.

Adams's copy is the earliest surviving unedited draft. Adams seems to have made this copy shortly after the Declaration was shown to Franklin on June 21, because the phrase "self-evident," which appears to have been written by Franklin to replace "sacred & undeniable" in paragraph two of the Rough Draft, appears in the Adams copy. Historian Julian Boyd has credited Jefferson with the insertion of the phrase.

At least forty-seven changes were made in the document between Jefferson's first fair copy and the submission to Congress on June 28. It is not known, however, who made the changes except for a very few in the handwriting of Adams and Franklin on the Rough Draft or those changes identified by Jefferson late in life as belonging to Adams and Franklin. Franklin's role had to be limited because he had been confined to his house with gout for most of June and Jefferson had to send a draft of the Declaration to him on June 21. The draft may not have reached Franklin until late in the day or even the next day, because on the twenty-first, Franklin had clearly not seen it when he wrote to George Washington that "I am just recovering from a severe Fit of the Gout, which has kept me from Congress & Company almost ever since you left us, so that I know little of what has pass'd there, except that a Declaration of Independence is preparing." Jefferson may have continued editing the document himself, or the changes may have been made at the suggestion of Franklin, Adams, Sherman, or Livingston. In any event, Jefferson planned to have the committee reexamine the document. He wrote Franklin asking for a preliminary assessment of his work: "Will Doctr. Franklin be so good as to peruse it, and suggest such alterations as his more enlarged view of the subject will dictate? The paper having been returned to me to change a particular sentiment or two, I propose laying it again before the committee tomorrow morning, if Doctr. Franklyn can think of it before that time." Given that almost all the corrections are recorded in the handwriting of Jefferson, there is no conclusive way of knowing what was the "particular sentiment or two" of Jefferson and what was the work of the other members of the committee.

Yet a number of significant changes can be identified as having been made at this point. Without considering the complex analyses conducted by Julian Boyd, the former editor of the most recent documentary edition of Jefferson's papers, of the mostly verbal changes, some of the more important or more interesting ones are worth mentioning. First, "advance from that subordination in which they have hitherto remained, & to" was replaced with "dissolve the political bands which have connected them with another, and to." Second, "equal & independent" was changed to "separate and equal." Third, "from that equal creation they derive rights" was changed to "they are endowed by their creator with inalienable rights." Fourth, a paragraph was inserted (on page 2 of the Rough Draft): "he has called together legislative bodies at places unusual, uncomfortable, & distant from the depository of their public records, for the sole purpose of fatiguing them into compliance with his measures." Fifth, a paragraph was inserted (on page 2 of the Rough Draft): "for abolishing the free system of English law in a neighboring province, establishing therein an arbitrary government and enlarging its boundaries so as to render it at once an example & fit instrument for introducing the same absolute rule into these colonies." Sixth, the committee inserted a paragraph (on page 3 of the Rough Draft): "he has constrained others taken captive on the high seas to bear arms against their country to become the executioners of their friends & brethen or to fall themselves by their hands."

Later in life, perhaps as late as 1823, when his authorship was criticized by Timothy Pickering and Adams, Jefferson identified the authorship of six editorial insertions by writing the names of Franklin (four) and Adams (two) in the margin. All of these changes in the handwriting of Franklin and Adams were, as Jefferson claimed, merely verbal.

On June 28 the committee submitted its draft to Congress, where it would remain until after the July 2 vote "That these United Colonies are, and of Right ought to be Free and Independent States." Later that day Congress began the process of editing the Declaration of Independence that would result in thirty-nine additional changes that would alter nearly a quarter of the document. At the end of the first day Benjamin Harrison reported that the Committee of the Whole "not having had time to go through" the Declaration "desired leave to sit again." Congress met again on July 3. Then in the morning of July 4 Benjamin Harrison reported that "the committee of the whole Congress have agreed to a Declaration," which was then read again and adopted for the public record. This is the bare skeleton of the events.

Jefferson provides some details in his Notes of the Proceedings in Congress. The dearth of direct contemporary testimony (neither Adams or any other delegate left contemporary information) makes an extensive quotation from Jefferson worthwhile.

Congress proceeded the same day to consider the declaration of Independence, which had been reported & laid on the table the Friday preceding, and on Monday referred to a commee. of the whole. the pusillanimous idea that we had friends in England worth keeping terms with, still haunted the minds of many. for this reason those passages which conveyed censures on the people of England were struck out, lest they should give them offence. the clause too, reprobating the enslaving the inhabitants of Africa, was struck out in complaisance to South Carolina & Georgia, who had never attempted to restrain the importation of slaves, and who on the contrary still wished to continue it. our Northern brethren also I believe felt a little tender under those censures; for tho' their people have very few slaves themselves yet they had been pretty considerable carriers of them

to others. the debates having taken up the greater parts of the 2d 3d & 4th days of July were, in the evening of the last closed. the declaration was reported by the commee. agreed to by the house, and signed by every member present except Mr. Dickinson.

Jefferson's testimony not only details the legislative path of the Declaration, but it also describes two of the major changes made by Congress and the reasons Jefferson believed influenced members of Congress to delete two critical paragraphs.

## 'Mangled as It Is'

With this testimony, the combined fair draft of the Declaration as it was presented to Congress on June 28 and the changes made to the document by unidentified members of Congress can be profitably read. As Jefferson wrote: "As the sentiments of men are known not only by what they receive, but what they reject also, I will state the form of the declaration as originally reported."

Once again all proof is in the hand of Jefferson, who busily took notes and inserted changes on his "original Rough draught." Adams carried the burden of the public defense of the resolution for independence and the Declaration of Independence. In his autobiography Adams simply explained that for the Declaration "in substance at least it was reported to Congress where, after a severe Criticism, and striking out several of the most oratorical Paragraphs it was adopted on the fourth of July 1776, published to the World." Beyond Jefferson's Notes of the Proceedings in Congress, Jefferson later stated in an 1823 letter to James Madison that "this however I will say for Mr. Adams, that he supported the Declaration with zeal and ability, fighting fearlessly for every word of it. As to myself, I thought it a duty to be, on that occasion, a passive auditor of the opinions of others, more impartial judges than I could be, of its merits or demerits. During the debate I was sitting by Dr. Franklin, and he observed that I was writhing a little under the acrimonious criticisms on some of its part; and it was on that occasion that, by way of comfort, he told me the story of John Thompson, the Hatter, and his new sign." As the story goes, a hatter proposed a sign that read "John Thompson, hatter, makes and sell hats for ready money," which became simply "John Thompson" with a figure of a hat subjoined.

Jefferson's draft of the Declaration upon which he overlaid changes made during the debates has become the most intriguing document to survive from this crucible. Jefferson tried to incorporate all of the changes made from first draft through final editing. This "original Rough draught" has provided in one document the full editorial record. But it is a virtually indecipherable story without the aid of other contemporary and noncontemporary documents.

What emerged from Congress was essentially Jefferson's draft of the Declaration, but in a shorter, simpler form. Gone were the paragraph denouncing the British people for supporting the monarch in his oppression of America—the only surviving fragment of the original composition draft of the Declaration of Independence that Jefferson had clearly labored over in his own editing process—and the paragraph denouncing the king for continuing to allow the enslavement of Africans and the continued importation of African slaves by

negating provincial laws forbidding the foreign importation of slaves. Then there was the replacement of his final gothic paragraph, with words from the Virginia resolution calling for independence. At this point in his "Rough draught," Jefferson, worn out by the ordeal of Congress having "mangled" his document, could only write in the margin "a different phraseology inserted." Most of the editorial changes were meritorious verbal corrections that only served to tighten the language and focus the view of the reader.

Historian Pauline Maier concludes in *American Scripture* that "Congress's achievement was remarkable" and that "by exercising their intelligence, political good sense, and a discerning sense of language, the delegates managed to make the Declaration at once more accurate and more consonant with the convictions of their constituents, and to enhance both its power and its eloquence."

The adoption of the Declaration by an equally overwhelmed Congress came in the morning of July 4. Even though Jefferson wrote in his notes that debates on the Declaration were "in the evening of the" fourth of July "closed" and that it was then "signed by every member present except Mr. Dickinson," the direct contemporary evidence points to a slightly different scenario. An examination of the records of Congress indicates that the Declaration of Independence was approved in the morning, not the evening, of July 4. After Congress adjourned in the early afternoon of July 4, Jefferson and Charles Thomson took a corrected copy of the Declaration to the printer John Dunlop, who produced the first printed copies of the document later that day. Adams, in a letter to his wife, Abigail, advanced the notion that July the second, not the fourth, would be "the most memorable Epocha, in the History of America . . . celebrated by succeeding Generations, as the great anniversary Festival" of the day Congress passed an act of independence. But it has been the approval of the Declaration of Independence on the fourth that has become the cause of celebration, just as the nation has come to celebrate Jefferson, the person who drafted the Declaration, not Richard Henry Lee, the person who introduced the resolution for independence.

The first public reading of the Declaration was not until July 6, when Pennsylvania militia colonel John Nixon read it in Philadelphia. John Hancock, the president of Congress, then sent copies of the Dunlop broadside of the Declaration to army and state leaders. General Washington did not receive his until July 9, when he had it read to the American army in New York. Members of Congress did not approve an engrossed copy of the Declaration until July 19—after New York's delegates were authorized to approve it, when it became entitled "the unanimous declaration of the thirteen united states of america." The general signing of the engrossed copy of the Declaration of Independence by "all members of Congress" as directed by Congress began on August 2 and continued even after Congress had fled Philadelphia for Baltimore in December 1776. Not until January 18, 1777, did Congress vote that authenticated copies with "the names of the members subscribing the same . . . be sent to each of the United States, and that they be desired to have the same put upon the record." Despite all of the changes wrought on Jefferson's draft of the document, the Declaration of Independence as it was engrossed by Timothy Matlack, a Pennsylvania lawyer and scribe, and signed by fifty-six members of Congress, remained very much the product of Thomas Jefferson.

Jefferson was impatient and disappointed in many of the changes made by Congress to his revolutionary declaration. By his own testimony, he complained during the debates in Congress to Franklin. Furthermore, not only did Jefferson sharply comment on congressional actions in his Notes of the Proceedings in Congress, but he also immediately sent marked copies of the Declaration to many friends in Virginia, including George Wythe, Edmund Pendleton, and Richard Henry Lee. After the receipt of the Declaration with Jefferson's comments, Lee made this consoling response in a July 21 letter to Jefferson: "I wish sincerely, as well for the honor of Congress, as for that of the States, that the Manuscript had not been mangled as it is. It is wonderful, and passing pitiful, that the rage of change should be so unhappily applied. However the *Thing* is in its nature so good, that no Cookery can spoil the Dish for the palates of Freemen."

Eager to return to Virginia, disappointed by the criticisms of his writing, and worried about the health of his wife now in the midst of her third difficult pregnancy, Jefferson urged Richard Henry Lee to rescue him: "[F]or god's sake, for your country's sake, and for my sake, come. I receive every post such accounts of the state of Mrs. Jefferson's health, that it will be impossible for me to disappoint her expectation of seeing me at the time I have promised, . . . I pray you to come. I am under a sacred obligation to go home." Jefferson left for Virginia on September 2.

# The Prism of Time

As the fiftieth anniversary of the Declaration of Independence came closer, political opponents of the Jeffersonian Republicans sought to minimize Jefferson's role in its writing. Timothy Pickering was the most vocal. Pickering, a former Federalist secretary of state and an ancient political enemy of Jefferson, led the attack in a July 4, 1823, address. Based on an August 6, 1822, letter from John Adams, Pickering charged that the ideas of the Declaration were "hackneyed" by 1776 and had been first clearly stated by James Otis of Massachusetts in his pamphlet *The Rights of the British Colonies Asserted and Proved* (1764). Acting on a request from Pickering, Adams had written at length about the drafting of the Declaration in which he referred to Jefferson as "the author of the Declaration of Independence." The aged Adams wrote:

You inquire why so young a man as Mr. Jefferson was placed at the head of the Committee for preparing a Declaration of Independence? I answer; it was the Frankfort advice to place Virginia at the head of every thing. Mr. Richard Henry Lee might be gone to Virginia, to his sick family, for aught I know, but that was not the reason of Mr. Jefferson's appointment. There were three committees appointed at the same time. One for the Declaration of Independence, another for preparing articles of confederation, and another for preparing a treaty to be proposed to France. Mr. Lee was chosen for the Committee of confederation, and it was not thought convenient that the same person should be upon both. Mr. Jefferson came into Congress, in June, 1775, and brought with him a reputation for literature, science, and a happy talent of composition. Writings of his were handed about, remarkable for the peculiar felicity of expression. Though a silent member in Congress, he was so prompt, frank, explicit, and decisive upon committees and in conversation, not even Samuel Adams was more so, that he soon seized upon my heart; and upon this occasion I gave him my vote, and did all in my power to procure the votes of others. I think he had one more vote than any other, and that placed him at the head of the committee. I had the next highest number, and that placed me the second. The committee met, discussed the subject, and then appointed Mr. Jefferson and me to make the draught, I suppose because we were the two first on the list.

The sub-committee met. Jefferson proposed me to make the draught. I said 'I will not.' 'You shall do it.' 'Yo! No.' 'Why will you not? You ought to do it.' 'I will not.' 'Why.' 'Reasons enough.' 'What can be your reasons?' 'Reason 1st—You are a Virginian, and a Virginian ought to appear at the head of this business. Reason 2d—I am obnoxious, suspected, and unpopular. You are very much otherwise. Reason 3d—You can write ten times better than I can.' 'Well,' said Jefferson, 'if you are decided, I will do as well as I can.' 'Very well. When you have drawn it up. We will have a meeting.' A meeting we accordingly had, and conned the paper over. I was delighted with its high tone and the flights of oratory with which it abounded, especially that concerning Negro slavery, which, though I knew his Southern brethren would never suffer to pass in Congress, I certainly never would oppose. There were other expressions which I would not have inserted, if I had drawn it up, particularly that which called the King a Tyrant; I thought this too personal, for I never believed George to be a tyrant in disposition and in nature; I always believed him to be deceived by his courtiers on Both sides of the Atlantic, and in his official capacity only, cruel. I thought the expression too passionate, and too much like scolding, for so grave and solemn a document; but as Franklin and Sherman were to inspect it afterwards, I thought it would not become me to strike it out. I consented to report it, and do not now remember that I made or suggested a single alteration. We reported it to the committee of five. It was read, and I do not remember that Franklin or Sherman criticized any thing. We were all in haste. Congress was impatient, and the instrument was reported, as I believe, in Jefferson's handwriting, as he first drew it. Congress cut off about a quarter of it, as I expected they would; but they obliterated some of the best of it, and left all that was exceptionable, if any thing in it was. I have long wondered that the original draught has not been published. I suppose the reason is, the vehement philippic against negro slavery. As you justly observe, there is not an idea in it but what has been hackney'd in Congress for two years before. The substance of it is contained in the declaration of rights and the violation of those rights, in the Journals of Congress, in 1774. Indeed, the essence of it is contained in a pamphlet, voted and printed by the town of Boston, before the first Congress met, composed by James Otis, and I suppose, in one of his lucid intervals, and pruned and polished by Samuel Adams.

Jefferson did not respond directly to Pickering or Adams, but in an August 30, 1823, letter he poured out his thoughts to his best friend and confidant, James Madison.

You have doubtless seen Timothy Pickering's 4th of July Observations on the Declaration of Independence. if his principles and prejudices personal and political, gave us no reason to doubt whether he had truly quoted the information he alledges to have received from Mr. Adams, I should then say that, in some of the particulars, Mr. Adams' memory has led him into unquestionable error. at the age of 88., and 47. years after the transactions of Independence, this is not wonderful. nor should I, at the age of 80., on the small advantage of that difference only, venture to oppose my memory to his, were it not supported by written notes, taken by myself at the moment and on the spot. he says, 'the committee (of 5. to wit, Dr. Franklin, Sherman, Livingston, and ourselves) met, discussed the subject, and then appointed him and myself to make the draught; that we, as a subcommittee, met, and after the urgencies of each on the other, I consented to undertake the task; that the draught being made, we, the subcommittee, met, and conned the paper over, and he does not remember that he made or suggested a single alteration.' now these details are quite incorrect. the committee of 5. met, no such thing as a subcommittee was proposed, but they unanimously pressed on myself alone to undertake

the draught. I consented; I drew it; but before I reported it to the committee, I communicated it *separately* to Dr. Franklin and Mr. Adams, requesting their corrections, because they were the two members of whose judgments and amendments I wished most to have the benefit, before presenting it to the Committee; and you have seen the original paper now in my hands, with the corrections of Doctor Franklin and Mr. Adams interlined in their own hand writings. their alterations were two or three only, and merely verbal. I then wrote a fair copy, reported it to the Committee, and from them, unaltered to Congress. this personal communication and consultation with Mr. Adams, he has misremembered into the actings of a sub-committee. Pickering's observations, and Mr. Adams' in addition, 'that it contained no new ideas, that it is a commonplace compilation, it's sentiments hackneyed in Congress for two years before, and its essence contained in Otis's pamphlet' may all be true. of that I am not to be the judge. Richard Henry Lee charged it as copied from Locke's treatise on government. Otis's pamphlet I never saw, and whether I had gathered my ideas from reading or reflection I do not know. I know only that I turned to neither book or pamphlet while writing it. I did not consider it as any part of my charge to invent new ideas altogether and to offer no sentiment which had ever been expressed before. had Mr. Adams been so restrained, Congress would have lost the benefit of his bold and impressive advocations of the rights of revolution. for no man's confident and fervid addresses, more than Mr. Adams's encouraged and supported us thro' the difficulties surrounding us, which, like the ceaseless action of gravity, weighed on us by night and by day. yet, on the same ground, we may ask what of these elevated thoughts was new, or can be affirmed never before to have entered the conceptions of man?

Whether also the sentiments of independence, and the reasons for declaring it which make so great a portion of the instrument, had been hacknied in Congress for two years before the 4th. of July '76, or this dictum also of Mr. Adams be another slip of memory, let history say. this however I will say for Mr. Adams, that he supported the Declaration with zeal and ability, fighting fearlessly for every word of it. As to myself, I thought it a duty to be, on that occasion, a passive auditor of the opinions of others, more impartial judges than I could be, of its merits or demerits. During the debate I was sitting by Dr. franklin, and he observed that I was writhing a little under the acrimonious criticisms on some of its part; and it was on that occasion that, by way of comfort, he told me the story of John Thompson, the Hatter, and his new sign.

Timothy thinks the instrument the better for having a fourth of it expunged. he would have thought it still better had the other three-fourths gone out also, all but the single sentiment (the only one he approves), which recommends the friendship to his dear England, whenever she is willing to be at peace with us. his insinuations are that altho' 'the high tone of the instrument was in unison with the warm feelings of the times, this sentiment of habitual friendship to England should never be forgotten, and that the duties it enjoins should *especially* be borne in mind on every celebration of this anniversary.' in other words, that the Declaration, as being a libel on the government of England, composed in times of passion, should now be buried in utter oblivion to spare the feelings of our English friends and Angloman fellow citizens. But it is not to wound them that we wish to keep it in mind; but to cherish the principles of the instrument in the bosoms of our own citizens: and it is a heavenly comfort to see that these principles are yet so strongly felt, as to render a circumstance so trifling as this little lapse of memory of Mr. Adams worthy of being solemnly announced and supported at an anniversary assemblage of the nation on its birthday. In opposition however to Mr. Pickering, I pray God that these principles may be eternal.

Despite their differing viewpoints, an essential core of agreement exists: Thomas Jefferson was the author of the Declaration of Independence. In reality and in the minds of most contemporaries and subsequent generations throughout the world, Jefferson would remain the author of the Declaration. Despite periodic efforts to dilute Jefferson's role in producing this defining document of American history, he has been rightly hailed as the draftsman of this "signal" for equality, liberty, pursuit of happiness, and the right of revolution from Europe in the 1790s to China in the twenty-first century.

## Bibliography

Boyd, Julian P. *The Declaration of Independence: The Evolution of the Text*. Rev. ed. Ed. Gerard W. Gewalt. Washington, D.C.: Library of Congress and Thomas Jefferson Memorial Foundation, 1999.

Ellis, Joseph J. *American Sphinx: The Character of Thomas Jefferson*. New York: Knopf, 1997.

[Gerard W. Gawalt and Amy Pastan.] *Thomas Jefferson: Genius of Liberty*. New York: Viking Studio in association with the Library of Congress, 2000.

Maier, Pauline. *American Scripture: Making the Declaration of Independence*. New York: Knopf, 1997.

Wills, Garry. *Inventing America: Jefferson's Declaration of Independence*. New York: Doubleday, 1978.

# 2

# The Political Theory of the Declaration of Independence

## GARRETT WARD SHELDON

The political theory contained in the Declaration of Independence reflects the three dominant ideologies present during the American Revolution and the founding of the American republic. These political philosophies were British liberalism (after *The Second Treatise of Government* by John Locke), Classical Republicanism (drawn from ancient Greek and Roman political thinkers, such as Aristotle and Cicero), and Christianity (especially the Reformed theology of John Calvin, prevalent in most of the colonial churches). Each of these theoretical strains in early American political thought had distinctive views of human nature, politics, ethics, history, and justice. Although different in many ways, these three philosophical schools possessed enough in common to be successfully combined into a coherent political worldview—a worldview that united the revolutionary North American colonists against Great Britain.

In the past, historians tended to emphasize one or the other of these philosophies in the Declaration of Independence, as well as in subsequent American political thought. But, by the end of the millennium, the historiographic scholarship had reached a basic consensus on the presence of all three theories in this revolutionary document and in Jefferson's later political writings. By viewing the ideas of the Declaration of Independence through Lockean liberalism, Classical Republicanism, and Christianity, the real meaning of the document, in its historical context, can be illuminated.

## Lockean Liberalism

Most studies of the political theory of the Declaration of Independence (notably Carl Becker in *The Declaration of Independence: A Study of the History of Political Ideas*) focus on Lockean liberalism, or natural rights philosophy. The British philosopher John Locke (1632–1704) developed the most influential theory of modern liberalism. The son of an officer in Oliver Cromwell's Puritan army, Locke was imbued with antimonarchy ideology at an early age. His exposure to royalist and Anglican culture at Oxford University further instilled populist and Calvinist sensibilities in his mind and ideas. He penned, in his famous *The Second Treatise of Government*, the classic social contract and natural rights theory of politics as well as the justification for revolution that prompted both the British Glorious Revolution of 1688 and the American Revolution of 1776. Locke's philosophical liberalism animates the Declaration of

Independence more than any other theory and provides the most striking verbal parallels of any thinker in the document.

### Political Equality

Locke begins by discussing the various social groups that humans naturally occupy, from the family, to economic relationships, to, finally, political society. At the beginning of Chapter VII of his *Second Treatise,* Locke writes, "God, having made man such a creature that, in His own judgment, it was not good for him to be alone [*Genesis* 2:18], put him under strong obligations of necessity, convenience, and inclination, to drive him in to society. . . . The first society was between man and wife . . . to which, in time, that between master and servant came to be added . . . [and then] political society." The familial and business societies are not between equals, for Locke, but the citizens of a political society enjoy basic equality. This political equality, for Locke, is based in humans' shared species, interests, and physical powers. "A State of Equality, wherein all the Power and Jurisdiction is reciprocal, . . . there being nothing more evident, than that Creatures of the same species and rank promiscuously born to all the same advantages of Nature, and the use of the same faculties, should also be equal one amongst another." This viewpoint of Locke's flows into the most famous phrase in the Declaration of Independence: "all men are created equal." People are equal, politically speaking, in all being members of the human race, with the attendant shared physical, rational, and spiritual faculties.

### Liberty and Freedom

From Locke's perspective of human equality based in physical "faculties," he maintains that

such "free equal and independent" individuals will learn by private sensory perception and follow their material self-interest. His empirical, or biological, approach (Locke studied medicine at Oxford University) leads to an appreciation of human social competition for goods, property, and status and, therefore, of the potential conflict amongst people aggravated by human pride. However, Locke ascribes a moral and spiritual dimension to human reason, or the "Law of Nature," that tells each person that he or she can exercise liberty only so far as it does not harm the rights of other people. By nature, for Locke, individuals have rights to those things needed to survive (or "self-preservation") as humans and these "natural rights" include "Life, Liberty and Property." But that natural liberty or freedom is restricted by the similar rights of other human beings (and their physical, intellectual, and spiritual rights). "But though this be a State of Liberty, yet it is not a State of License. . . . The State of Nature has a Law of Nature to govern it, which obliges everyone: And Reason, which is that Law, teaches all Mankind, who will but consult it, that being all equal and independent, no one ought to harm another in his Life, Health, Liberty, or Possessions." Locke ascribes this Golden Rule to a divinely ordained conscience, which shows everyone that it is wrong to kill, steal, or enslave anyone. St. Paul's description in Romans 2:14–15 says: "For when the Gentiles, which have not the law, do by nature the things contained in the law . . . the law written in their hearts, their conscience also bearing witness." This makes human society fairly peaceful and orderly, because, for Locke, most people respect others' lives, property, and freedom. If everyone was law abiding, no state would be necessary. But Locke asserts that some people either do not have a conscience or choose to ignore it and so violate the rights of others—murdering, stealing, and enslaving. Such people are like wild beasts, injuring others, and, as Locke says, "such Men are not under the ties of the Common Law of Reason, have no other Rule, but that of Force and Violence, and so may be treated as Beasts of Prey . . . a Wolf or a Lyon." In short, one can defend oneself against oppression by others who do not respect one's rights in the state of nature.

### Instituting Government

In the state of nature in Lockean theory, everyone must protect his or her own rights, punishing criminals who assault or rob people. But, this inevitably leads to the creation of government because the way humans are made disqualifies them from being judges in their own cases. From Locke's Calvinist Christianity, he sees people as naturally sinful and self-interested. When hurt, their pride causes them to seek extreme vengeance. He writes: "[I]t is unreasonable to Men to be Judges in their own Cases, that Self-Love will make Men partial to themselves. . . . And, on the other side, that Ill nature, Passion and Revenge will carry them too far in punishing others." Human pride and sin disqualifies people from fairly judging injuries to their own rights. As a consequence, government is created by the consent of the governed to provide an impartial judge to protect individual natural rights and adjudicate violations of life, property, and liberty. As Locke puts it, the state is to "preserve his Property, that is his Life, Liberty and Estate, against the Injuries of other men; but to judge of, and pun-

ish the breaches of that Law . . . for the mutual preservations of their Lives, Liberties and Estates." This natural rights view of the origins of government is reflected in the Declaration of Independence's evocative words "all men are created equal; that they are endowed by their Creator with certain inalienable rights, that among these are Life, Liberty and the pursuit of Happiness. That to secure these rights, Governments are instituted among Men, deriving their just powers from the consent of the governed." Jefferson's substitution of "pursuit of Happiness" for Locke's "property" or "Estate" may reflect his Classical Republicanism as Aristotle in his *Nicomachean Ethics* identifies happiness as the ultimate end of human life. But in Locke's *Questions Concerning the Law of Nature* he states that the Law of Nature, like government, secures peace, security, property, "and, to embrace all these in a single word happiness."

From this Lockean political theory, government is instituted by people as a necessary protector and preserver of natural, God-given rights of individuals to continued existence and happiness. This state has power delegated from the people and is limited to that charge to protect life, liberty, and property. It is basically a court function or the state qua judiciary: adjudicating and punishing violations of private rights. Most of society (family, business, education, religion) will be conducted privately—in nongovernmental associations or civil society.

Given this Lockean view of the government's proper authority and purpose, a change or political revolution will occur if the state deviates from that legitimate role, especially if it becomes a criminal itself, by invading the citizens' natural rights to life, liberty, and property. If a government murders people, steals their possessions, or denies them freedom (beyond the Law of Nature) without due process of law (or accepted judicial procedures) it ceases to be a legitimate state and forfeits its authority. This justifies the people in abolishing that government and establishing another one that will properly perform its function. This constitutes John Locke's famous "Right to Revolution."

### The Right to Alter the Government

When any government no longer protects the natural rights for which it was formed and violates the rights of citizens itself, the people can appropriately replace that deficient state with a proper one. As Locke insists: "The Reason why Men enter into Society is the preservation of their Property. . . . [W]henever the Legislature endeavors to take away, and destroy the Property of the People, or reduce them to Slavery under Arbitrary Power, they put themselves into a state of war with the People, who are thereupon absolved from any farther Obedience." Locke ascribes irregular actions by a state or ruler to the sins of "Ambition, Revenge, Covetousness, or any other irregular Passion." Such a government is a tyranny and citizens are no longer under allegiance to it. This kind of state rules not by common consent but by brutal force. As the Declaration summarizes Locke's theory of revolution: "[W]henever any form of Government becomes destructive of these ends, it is the Right of the People to alter or to abolish it, and to institute new Government, laying its foundation on such principles and organizing its powers in such form, as to them shall seem most likely to effect their Safety and Happiness." Many of the words in the Declaration of Independence specifically reflect the ideas of John Locke.

However, these Lockean ideals were expanded and modified by the prevailing Classical Republican and Christian ideals of the American colonists' time and worldview.

## Classical Republicanism

The Classical Republican ideology expressed in many colonial pamphlets, sermons, and letters derives from ancient Greek and Roman political thinkers, especially Aristotle, Cicero, and Polybius. This strain of political thought emphasizes man's social nature, the need for direct citizen democracy and participation (as in Athens), an economically and educationally qualified populace, and the dangers of political corruption. Discovered in early American writers by Harvard historian Bernard Bailyn (in his book *The Ideological Origins of the American Revolution*) and Professor J. G. A. Pocock of Johns Hopkins University (in the book *The Machiavellian Moment*), this paradigm greatly influenced many revolutionaries in eighteenth-century North America. From the classical world, this political theory spread to Renaissance republicanism, Cromwell's Puritan Commonwealthsmen, and seventeenth-century philosopher James Harrington. Its ideology provided a lens through which the American colonists could interpret the politics and policies of the British government and British Empire, and with which they could justify independence.

### Public Virtue

Classical Republican political theory begins with a view of human nature as social and political. Aristotle asserts in *The Politics* that "[m]an is by nature a social and political animal; it is his nature to live in the state." For

Aristotle, this naturally political humanity derives from two distinctive faculties: reasoned speech and moral choice. Both of these human faculties require direct involvement in governing to be developed and exercised. A true citizen must participate in politics. A citizen, from this classical perspective, is "one who has a share both in ruling and being ruled." And a direct democracy such as that requires a small, local government (like the Greek *polis*) in which every citizen knows every other one over a long period of time and has a chance to make and administer laws. A large or populous country makes such direct participation by every citizen impossible. Active participation in common rule also requires an economic self-sufficiency in the citizens, both to provide the leisure from work to spend time in governing and to render everyone's judgment independent from economic coercion. A republic of well-educated, middle-class citizens is the ideal. It will produce an ethic of public virtue, or individual sacrifice, for the common good, whether contributing one's time or money to a public project or serving in the government or military. Defense of one's nation is a strong value in Classical Republicanism, so a citizen militia is favored and patriotism expected of everyone. As Cicero idealized the sturdy Roman citizen-soldier, the classical view valued honor, integrity, and sacrifice for the common good. A simplicity of lifestyle; a healthy, athletic citizenry; military discipline; and economic frugality were held up as the best standards of society. A strong sense of honor and duty existed in these societies.

### Decentralized Authority

The Classical Republican worldview of sturdy honest yeoman, farmer-citizen-soldiers, appealed to the agrarian, independent, Protestant society of colonial America. It eschewed centralized imperial power (which was monarchical and undemocratic), economic luxury and extravagance (which were vain and decadent), political pride and corruption (which violated the simple dignity and honesty of the people), and worldly prestige and power (which denigrated ordinary virtue and common folk). Sometimes the English republicans framed this distinction between "court" politics (of kingly patronage employment, mercenary standing armies, pomp and pride, and financial manipulation and corruption) and "country" politics (elected common leaders accountable to average people, a citizen army, simple decent morals, and honest hard work). The "city" was the seedbed of moral corruption and financial intrigue; the "country" was the refuge of simple manners, Godly morality, and connection with the land. During the height of imperial power (whether the Roman Empire, the medieval Catholic empire, or the eighteenth-century British Empire), an emphasis was placed on high society—an overconcern with appearance (elegant clothes, expensive jewelry, powered wigs, perfumes—and that was the men), gaudy display of luxury and wealth (large houses, carriages, artwork), moral decadence (sexual infidelity and license, drunkenness, perversion), and a prideful insistence on official titles, prestige, and pomp. The simple, frugal morality of the Classical Republican ideal regarded such imperial society as perverted vanity and corrupted morality. Like the fifteenth-century Italian reformer Girolamo Savonarola's attack on refined Florence, the republican ethos expressed disgust over the pretenses of decadent imperial lifestyles. But more dangerous for classical thinkers was the political corruption and tyranny that accompanied this social and economic condition. A government run by the city elite would cheat and rob the good people through high taxes, fiscal trickery, and corruption. A centralized regime would inevitably lead to tyranny, impoverishing the common people and destroying their rights while feeding the vice and extravagance of a decadent elite. Instead of noble independence, the citizens in a rich, centralized empire would be enslaved and degraded by dependence upon the central state and economy. Everyone would be dependent on others and enslaved by commercialism. Cicero lamented the decline of the virtuous Roman republic with its manly citizen-soldiers and the rise of imperial luxury, tyranny, and moral depravity. He wrote: "[W]hen . . . the State begins to be ruled by the riches, instead of the virtue, of a few men[,] . . . [w]hen they lack wisdom and knowledge of how to live and to rule over others, are full of dishonor and insolent pride[,] . . . is there any more depraved type of State . . . ?" The English Puritan republicans of Cromwell's day contrasted their simple Christian faith, plain church architecture, and honest piety with the established church's wealth, finery, sophistication, and immorality. Instead of an honest, healthy society, all the Classical Republicans saw in imperialism was the rise of worldly power, economic extravagance, and moral decline.

## Historical Cycles

The Roman historian Polybius developed a theory of historical cycles of politics. Like animals, states are born, grow, reach maturity, and then go into decline and death. Republics go through the same life cycle. Signs of age, decay, and dying are reflected in growing selfishness, privatism, lack of honor, and moral decadence. Concern with luxury and privilege, pride and elaborate ceremony mark the decline of a republic. Soon the absence of public virtue will lead to political apathy and lack of patriotism. The overweight, lazy, morally decadent populace will gladly turn over the state to dictators, the military over to hired soldiers, and the economy to whoever will give them the goods for which they lust. A weak, foolish people addicted to pleasure will emerge as ignorant slaves fattened for the slaughter. The people will be controlled by a few clever, deceitful leaders, who impoverish, degrade, and use them. Politics will be dominated by groveling, effete officials dependent on royal favor and patronage. Instead of strong, self-respecting citizens, the people will be reduced to pathetic, weak, slothful slaves. Instead of intelligent virtuous rule, government will be dominated by fear, vice, vanity, intrigue, and cowardice. The later Athenian and Roman empires attested to this frightening prospect. The American colonists saw the British Empire showing the same tendencies. Only separation from it would save them from destruction. *The Pilgrim's Progress* by John Bunyan, a widely read novel in the colonies, depicted the lead character "Christian" fleeing this immoral city.

The American Revolution, in this Classical Republican perspective, was a war to preserve republican virtue, economic integrity, and simple Christian morality from the corruption and tyranny of the British Crown and British Empire. England's increasing wealth and luxury, finery and pomp, authoritarian policies (for example, the Intolerable Acts), fiscal manipulations (bank, trade and tax laws), and ecclesiastical domination (the established Anglican Church) all evinced the downward spiral of the British realm. To not separate from this decadent empire would doom the American colonies to oppression and slavery. Breaking with Great Britain would end the evils of a decaying empire and protect republican virtue in the Western world. The American Revolution and national independence, in this view, took on enormous, almost apocalyptic, proportions. It was not merely a battle between two countries but a war between real civilization and freedom, and social destruction, enslaved to vice, and spiritual darkness. Like "Christian" in *The Pilgrim's Progress,* Americans had to flee the City of Destruction to gain political independence.

### Preventing Tyranny

The list of "injuries and usurpations" of Great Britain and King George III in the Declaration of Independence reveals Classical Republican sensibilities. Several deal with the British Crown and Parliament destroying the democratic institutions of the North American colonies. The king has "refused his Assent to laws" passed by colonial legislatures for "the public good" and has "forbidden his Governors to pass Laws of immediate and pressing importance." He has "dissolved Representative" institutions to be formed or to operate, and he "refused . . . others to be elected." He has "obstructed the Administration of Justice" and "made Judges dependent on his Will alone." The move to concentrated, centralized political power is aggravated by new royal patronage appointments ("a multitude of New Offices" and "swarms of Officers"). These authoritarian, unpopular officials undermine the

political and economic independence of the American republic by harassing the people and eating their substance. The British Empire further shows its corruption and tyranny by stationing "Standing Armies" (contrary to the citizen militia) and by making the military authority "independent of and superior to the Civil Power"—that is, establishing a police state. The imposition of new taxes and severe regulation of trade destroys the economic foundation of the republic and enriches a dishonorable party of usurers and financial imperialists. The "abolishing" of "the free System of English laws in a neighboring Province" refers to the Quebec Act of 1774, which allowed the French to resume their Catholic state church and control the territory west of the Allegheny Mountains, a terrifying specter of ecclesiastical tyranny to North American Protestants. The Roman Church represented, to the English Calvinists, the Antichrist and the "whore of Babylon" of the Bible's book of Revelation. Britain's accommodation with French Canadian Catholics was another alarming sign of its decadence. The inciting of enslaved Africans and "Indian Savages" similarly alarmed the American populace. Employment of "foreign mercenaries" to "compleat the works of death, desolation and tyranny" rounded out the British crimes against noble American republicanism. Jefferson's original draft of the Declaration of Independence includes a typically classical reference to the "manly spirit" with which the American cause is fought (against the cowardly, effeminate British aristocracy). This, along with the reference to "honor" in the last sentence of the final version of the Declaration, reflects the Classical Republican ideological worldview in this document.

The American Revolution thus was seen as saving the Western (Greek, Roman, Renaissance, English) heritage of free, representative government from suppression by absolutist, imperial tyranny. The presence of Classical Republican ideology in the Declaration of Independence means the preservation of human dignity and decency from annihilation by human enslavement, poverty, and degradation. And because North America was the last remnant of republicanism in the world, its preservation had worldwide, historic ramifications. This Messianic quality of American democracy continues in the American democratic ethos to the present day.

## Christianity

Although not an orthodox Christian believer himself, Jefferson's words in the Declaration of Independence reflect the prevalent Calvinist Christian culture in the North American colonies. From New England Puritans to Mid-Atlantic Presbyterians, Reformed Dutch, and Southern Baptists and Anglicans, the predominant theology of early America was Protestant Christianity. Its view of God, God's law, and historical Providence imbued the Revolutionary cause with religious and cosmic significance.

### God's Will and the American Revolution

Since the earliest Christian political thought (St. Augustine's *City of God*), history has been seen as governed by God's divine plan, order, or "providence." John Calvin emphasizes the sovereign will of God in human affairs throughout his Reformed theology. He describes it in his *Institutes of the Christian Religion* as that agency "by which, as keeper of

the keys, he [God] governs all events. . . . [T]he universe is ruled by God, not only because he watches over the order of nature set by himself, but because he exercises especial care over each of his works." The most important of God's works is his church, the body of Christian believers, so the faithful can especially rely on God's loving protection of their lives and cause. As Calvin writes: "God so attends to the regulation of individual events, and they all so proceed from his set plan, that nothing takes place by chance . . . especially his vigilance in ruling the church, which he deigns to watch more closely." This faith in God's power and help for his people led the American Christian colonists to believe that the Lord would bring them victory in the American Revolution because it was his will that they be free, unabused, and able to practice their Protestant faith unencumbered or oppressed by the hierarchical and heretical English or Roman Catholic Church. Remembering that the original meaning of "Protestant" was not "protesting" against the Catholic Church but derived from the Latin *pro testa* or "to testify" to the truth of the Gospel, the liberty that American churches enjoyed (and which they saw threatened by the British Empire and French Canada) was perceived as the light of Christ in the world and deserving of God's protection.

The New England colonies had been settled by Puritans who subscribed to a covenant or federal theology that held that they had made a contract with God, like the people of ancient Israel, promising to obey his laws. In return, God would bless them with peace, happiness, and prosperity. The Revolutionary movement was seen as an extension of that faithfulness to God's ordinances, preserving the liberty of his church and reverence for his moral law. The colonists thus could expect God's favor in the war for independence. Preservation of the true teachings of scripture and republican structure of the church (against the heresies and authoritarian hierarchy of bishops in the Anglican and Catholic churches) was a prime example of obedience to Christ, worthy of divine protection within God's providence. The reference to "reliance on the Protection of Divine Providence" in the Declaration of Independence was not a merely casual or rhetoric flourish. It was stating a truth that most American colonists believed and cherished.

### Laws of Nature and of Nature's God

The Declaration's use of the phrase "Laws of Nature and of Nature's God" reflects a long tradition of Christian teachings on the place of law and government within God's order and universe. The basic idea in this Christian natural law perspective is that all human laws and governments must conform to God's law to succeed. A person or regime may resist the divinely ordained natural order for a while, but eventually any such scheme will fail. By violating the colonists' "unalienable" God- (not state-) given rights (of self-governance, Christian liberty) the British realm was resisting the Almighty's law and would suffer the consequences (of losing the empire in North America). Conformance to God's justice (as revealed in the Bible) was necessary for God's continued blessings and favor. While the English had championed Christ's cause in their Reformation and the Puritan and Glorious Revolutions in the 1600s, they had slipped into moral decadence and political corruption in the 1700s and were losing God's favor and protection. As long as Americans

obeyed God's law and his laws of nature (and made governmental laws that conform with them), they would be victorious, prosperous, and happy. New England ministers had repeatedly warned their flocks that they, too, could bring disasters upon themselves by abandoning or offending God's laws.

The concept of the "Laws of Nature and Nature's God" comes from a Christian legal tradition expressed in the earliest church doctrine, signifying the Lord's divine will and purpose revealed in history, nature, and scripture. In the thirteenth century, St. Thomas Aquinas in his massive *Summa Theologica* divided law into divine or eternal, natural, and human or positive. The higher law, God's law, encompasses the lower laws of nature and humanity. By the eleventh century, Catholic Church doctrine included the term "law of nature or God," signifying the subordinate station of nature and politics to God's law. In English common law this appears in the writings of Lord Bracton (1268) and Sir William Blackstone as "law of Nature" or "creation law." Jurist Blackstone describes this as "[w]hen the Supreme Being formed the universe and created it. . . . [H]e impressed certain principles upon that matter. . . . This will of his maker is called the law of nature." Sir Edward Coke, whom many American lawyers studied along with Blackstone, remarks that "[t]he law of nature is that which God [created]. . . . [T]he law of God and nature is one to all." John Locke follows this reasoning in his lectures on natural law when he states that "[t]his law of nature can, therefore, be so described because it is the command of the divine will."

The American revolutionaries applied this idea to their resistance to British imperial power, as in the 1764 Massachusetts declaration against the Stamp Act: "1. Resolved, That there are certain essential rights of the British constitution and government which are founded in the law of God and nature, and are the common rights of mankind; therefore, 2. Resolved, That the inhabitants of this province are inalienably entitled to those essential rights, in common with all men; and that no law of society can, consistent with the law of God and nature, divest them of those rights."

The Declaration's reference to "unalienable" rights follows from this divine origin of the law of nature. The natural right to self-governance and the individual exercise of reason to read and teach the Scriptures (the basis of Protestant Christian liberty) constitute a "higher law," which neither the king of England nor any state can violate. By threatening these God-given rights, King George III had forfeited his legitimate right to rule the North American colonies and effectively abdicated the throne. Americans believed that obedience to a greater king, God Almighty, would deliver them from this unjust tyranny of the British government and allow them to continue to serve God and Christ with freedom and righteousness. The Lord would honor his covenant with America and miraculously give them victory against a much more powerful worldly adversary, as he had repeatedly delivered the nation of Israel in the Old Testament. In certain extremely Calvinist regions of New England, the Revolutionary War was seen as Armageddon, or the final battle between God (and his servants) and the Antichrist, which would usher in the rule of Christ.

Therefore, to fight fearlessly in this war would bring God's blessings, as they had to King David of Israel. To shrink from the dangers or submit to the Beast of Revelation would bring God's curses and damnation. British political, economic, and religious oppression required heroic resistance to further God's purpose in history (the spreading of the Gospel of Christ) and redemption. Later, this view would show up in American manifest destiny to occupy the entire North American continent for Christian liberty and democratic self-government.

## The Interplay of Theories

The various philosophies contained in the Declaration of Independence were blended and synthesized to accommodate the needs of colonies seeking to justify political independence from a vast and powerful empire. The Classical Republican and Christian perspectives provided a broad background of political and moral corruption from which Americans wished to separate to preserve ancient republican virtue and Reformed Christian liberty. The Lockean liberal rights formed the specific ends to which the revolution would strive, but they were further modified by Jefferson to serve "free, equal and independent" states as well as individuals. This modification of Locke's natural rights theory was expressed in a section of the original draft of the Declaration that for unknown reasons was removed by the committee that revised the Declaration. It read: "[I]n constituting indeed our several forms of government, we had adopted one common King, thereby laying a foundation for perpetual league and amity with them: but that submission to their parliament was no part of our constitution." With these words, Jefferson expressed a theory of the British Empire as a Lockean social compact, each legislature (in London, Virginia, Massachusetts, New York, and so on) being "free, equal and independent," voluntarily associating under the same king, but not dictating to one another. Hence, the Parliamentary Acts regulating the colonial legislatures were invalid. One "free and equal" legislature could not dictate to another one.

This novel theory of the British Empire (more appropriate to the twentieth-century British Commonwealth) was beholden to the British Ancient Constitution, which colonial leaders learned about from various British legal scholars and which was developed in Jefferson's other Revolutionary pamphlets, most notably his *A Declaration of the Causes and Necessity for Taking Up Arms* (1775) and *A Summary View of the Rights of British America* (1774).

The idea of an Ancient Constitution of premonarchy Saxon liberty was invented by seventeenth-century legal scholars such as Sir William Blackstone in their Parliamentary struggles with the Crown. According to this theory of English history, a Golden Age of liberty and representative government existed in England prior to the Norman Conquest of 1066. It was the French who introduced monarchy and feudalism, but these corruptions were not originally English. The Puritan and Glorious Revolutions of the 1600s restored these original rights of the Ancient Constitution, limiting the king and securing liberty and private property. Although probably a legal fiction and historical myth, the Ancient Constitution theory served to undermine a monarchy premised in hereditary privilege by situating representative institutions in a distant past, an-

tedating the royal family. This transferred political legitimacy to Parliament, effectively ending monarchical absolutism in Britain in 1688.

Jefferson took a page from the book of the Ancient Constitution and developed a theory of a federated British Empire in which colonial legislatures were the equal of Parliament in London. He summarized this by stating that "[o]ur Saxon ancestors held their lands, as they did their personal property, in absolute dominion." Then he transferred these ancient rights to the American colonists. "Our ancestors, before their emigration to America, were the free inhabitants of the British dominions in Europe. . . . [They] left their native land to seek on these shores a residence for civil and religious freedom." Once they were comfortably settled in the colonies, these Americans, exercising the ancient rights and liberties of Englishmen, chose to submit themselves and their states to the British Crown. The monarch thus became a kind of umpire over various legislatures throughout the imperial realm. As Jefferson explained it, "That settlements having been thus effected in the wilds of America, the emigrants thought it proper to adopt that system of laws under which they had hither to lived in the Mother Country, and to continue their union with her by submitting themselves to the same common sovereign, who was thereby made the central link connecting the several parts of the empire thus newly multiplied." This king qua link was to serve the same function as any state in a Lockean social contract: to check and punish any violations of natural rights of the member legislatures. When one member legislature (Parliament) violated the rights of other member legislatures (the Virginia House of Burgesses, Massachusetts General Court, and so on), the king should stop it. But King George III failed to arrest these usurpations of authority by the British Parliament, and consequently the Americans rejected him as a ruler. "The true ground on which we declare these [British] acts void," Jefferson wrote, "is that the British Parliament has no right to exercise authority over us." The king not correcting this problem "is thus marked by every act which may define a Tyrant" and "is unfit to be the ruler of a free People." Locke's "Right to Revolution" is applied and the American colonies establish a new government. American independence thus logically rests in an empire viewed through the English Ancient Constitution and Lockean natural rights. Thus, the colonial worldview of the British Ancient Constitution underlies the arguments in the Declaration of Independence.

## Bibliography

Amos, Gary. *Defending the Declaration*. Charlottesville, Va.: Providence Foundation, 1994.

Appleby, Joyce. *Capitalism and a New Social Order*. New York: New York University Press, 1984.

_____. *Liberalism and Republicanism in the Historical Imagination*. Cambridge: Harvard University Press, 1992.

_____. "Republicanism and Ideology." *American Quarterly* 37 (fall 1985): 461–473.

_____. "Republicanism in Old and New Contexts." *William and Mary Quarterly* 3d Ser. 43 (January 1986): 20–34.

_____. "What Is Still American in the Political Philosophy of Thomas Jefferson?" *William and Mary Quarterly* 3d Ser. 39 (April 1982): 287–309.

Aquinas, St. Thomas. *The Political Ideas of St. Thomas Aquinas*. Ed. Dino Bigongiar. New York: Hafner Press, 1981.

Aristotle. *Nicomachean Ethics*. Trans. Martin Ostwald. Indianapolis: Bobbs-Merrill, 1962.

_____. *The Politics*. Trans. T. A. Sinclair. Baltimore: Penguin, 1972.

Bailyn, Bernard. *The Ideological Origins of the American Revolution*. Cambridge: Harvard University Press, 1967.

Banning, Lance. *The Jeffersonian Persuasion*. Ithaca: Cornell University Press, 1978.

Becker, Carl. *The Declaration of Independence: A Study in the History of Political Ideas*. New York: Vintage, 1958.

Boyd, Julian P. *The Declaration of Independence: The Evolution of the Text*. Princeton: Princeton University Press, 1945.

Cicero, Marcus Tullius. *The Republic* and *The Laws*. Trans. Clinton Keyes. Cambridge: Harvard University Press, 1928.

Diggins, John. *The Lost Soul of American Politics*. New York: Basic Books, 1984.

Dworetz, Steven. *The Unvarnished Doctrine: Locke, Liberalism, and the American Revolution*. Durham: Duke University Press, 1990.

Engeman, Thomas. *Thomas Jefferson and the Politics of Nature*. Notre Dame: University of Notre Dame Press, 2000.

Gerber, Scott D. "Whatever Happened to the Declaration of Independence? A Commentary on the Republican Revisionism in the Political Thought of the American Revolution." *Polity* 26 (winter 1993): 207–232.

Harrington, James. *Oceana*. Ed. S.B. Lilijegren. Westport, Conn.: Hyperion Press, 1979.

Hartz, Louis. *The Liberal Tradition in America*. New York: Harcourt Brace, 1955.

Hutson, James H. *Religion and the New Republic*. Lanham, Md.: Rowman and Littlefield, 2000.

Jefferson, Thomas. *Autobiography*. New York: Putnam, n.d.

_____. *The Papers of Thomas Jefferson*. Vol. I. Ed. Julian Boyd. Princeton: Princeton University Press, 1950.

Koch, Adrienne. *The Philosophy of Thomas Jefferson*. New York: Columbia University Press, 1943.

Kramnick, Isaac. *Bolingbroke and His Circle*. Cambridge: Harvard University Press, 1968.

_____. "Republican Revisionism Revisited." *American Historical Review* 87 (June 1982): 629–664.

Lienesch, Michael. *New Order of the Ages*. Princeton: Princeton University Press, 1988.

Locke, John. *Questions Concerning the Law of Nature*. Trans. Robert Horwitz, Jenny Strauss

Clay, and Diskin Clay. Ithaca: Cornell University Press, 1990.

———. *The Two Treatises of Government.* Ed. Peter Laslett. New York: New American Library, 1965.

Lutz, Donald. *A Preface to American Political Theory.* Lawrence: University Press of Kansas, 1992.

Machiavelli, Niccolò. *The Prince and the Discourses.* Trans. Luigi Ricci. New York: Random House, 1950.

Matthews, Richard. *The Radical Politics of Thomas Jefferson.* Lawrence: University Press of Kansas, 1984.

McCoy, Drew. *The Elusive Republic.* Chapel Hill: University of North Carolina Press, 1980.

McDonald, Forrest. *Novus Ordo Seclorum.* Lawrence: University Press of Kansas, 1985.

McWilliams, Wilson Carey. *The Idea of Fraternity in America.* Berkeley: University of California Press, 1973.

Murrin, John M. "The Great Inversion, or Court versus Country." In *Three British Revolutions, 1641, 1688, 1776.* Ed. J. G. A. Pocock. Princeton: Princeton University Press, 1980.

Noll, Mark A. *Religion and American Politics.* New York: Oxford University Press, 1990.

Onuf, Peter. *Jeffersonian Legacies.* Charlottesville: University Press of Virginia, 1993.

Pangle, Thomas. *The Spirit of Modern Republicanism.* Chicago: University of Chicago Press, 1988.

Peterson, Merrill. *Thomas Jefferson and the New Nation.* New York: Oxford University Press, 1970.

Pocock, J. G. A. *The Ancient Constitution and the Feudal Law.* Cambridge: Cambridge University Press, 1951.

———. "Cambridge Paradigms and Scotch Philosophers." In *Wealth and Virtue.* Ed. Istvan Hont and Michael Ignatieff. New York: Cambridge University Press, 1983.

———. "Machiavelli, Harrington, and English Political Ideologies in the Eighteenth Century." *William and Mary Quarterly* 3d Ser. 22 (October 1965): 549–583.

———. *The Machiavellian Moment.* Princeton: Princeton University Press, 1969.

———. ed. *Three British Revolutions, 1641, 1688, 1776.* Princeton: Princeton University Press, 1980.

Robbins, Carolyn. *The Eighteenth-Century Commonwealthsmen.* Cambridge: Harvard University Press, 1959.

Shalhope, Robert E. "Republicanism and Early American Historiography." *William and Mary Quarterly* 3d Ser. 39 (April 1982): 334–356.

Sheldon, Garrett Ward. *The History of Political Theory.* New York: Peter Lang, 1988.

———. *The Political Philosophy of James Madison.* Baltimore: Johns Hopkins University Press, 2001.

———. *The Political Philosophy of Thomas Jefferson.* Baltimore: Johns Hopkins University Press, 1991.

———. *Religion and Politics.* New York: Peter Lang, 1990.

———. *What Would Jefferson Say?* New York: Penguin, 1998.

———. and Daniel Dresibach, eds. *Religion and Political Culture in Jefferson's Virginia.* Lanham, Md.: Rowman and Littlefield, 2000.

Skinner, Quentin. *The Foundations of Modern Political Thought.* New York: Cambridge University Press, 1978.

Wills, Garry. *Inventing America: Jefferson's Declaration of Independence.* New York: Doubleday, 1978.

Wood, Gordon. *The Creation of the American Republic.* Chapel Hill: University of North Carolina Press, 1969.

Yarbrough, Jean. *American Virtues: Thomas Jefferson on the Character of a Free People.* Lawrence: University Press of Kansas, 1998.

Zuckert, Michael P. *Natural Rights and the New Republicanism.* Princeton: Princeton University Press, 1994.

———. *The Natural Rights Republic.* Notre Dame: University of Notre Dame Press, 1996.

# 3

# Abraham Lincoln and the Universal Meaning of the Declaration of Independence

## HARRY V. JAFFA

The long political duel between Stephen A. Douglas and Abraham Lincoln was above all a struggle to determine the nature of the opinion which should form the doctrinal foundation of American government. No political contest in history was more exclusively or passionately concerned with the character of the beliefs in which the souls of men were to abide. Neither the differences which divided Moslem and Christian at the time of the Crusades, nor the differences which divided Protestant and Catholic in sixteenth-century Europe, nor those which arrayed the crowned heads of Europe against the regicides of revolutionary France were believed by the warring advocates to be more important to their salvation, individually and collectively. Vast practical consequences flowed from the differences in all cases, but we could not understand the meaning of the differences if we did not first see them as the men who fought for them saw them, as having absolute intrinsic importance, apart from all external consequences.

"Swinging up and down and back and forth across Illinois, making the welkin ring and setting the prairies on fire, Lincoln and Douglas debated—what? That is the surprising thing," says Professor [James G.] Randall.

With all the problems that might have been put before the people as proper matter for their consideration in choosing a senator—choice of government servants, immigration, the tariff, international policy, promotion of education, westward extension of railroads, the opening of new lands for homesteads, protection against greedy exploitation of those lands[,] . . . encouragement to settlers[,] . . . improving the condition of factory workers, and alleviating those agrarian grievances that were to plague the coming decades—with such issues facing the country, those two candidates for the Senate talked as if there were only one issue.

According to Randall, Lincoln and Douglas ignored any such "representative coverage of the problems of mid-century America" while confining themselves almost exclusively to the question of slavery in the territories. But while slavery in the territories was the single practical issue, it was in large measure subordinated in the course of the debates. For Lincoln there was, indeed, "only one issue," but that issue was whether or not the American people

*Source:* Reprinted from Harry V. Jaffa, *Crisis of the House Divided: An Interpretation of the Issues in the Lincoln-Douglas Debates* (Chicago: University of Chicago Press), 308–329. Copyright © 1959, 1982 by Harry V. Jaffa. Reprinted by permission of Harry V. Jaffa and the University of Chicago Press.

should believe that "all men are created equal" in the full extent and true significance of that proposition. Lincoln did not believe that in concentrating upon this sole and single question he was in any sense narrowing and limiting the range of the discussion. "Our government," Lincoln said before the Dred Scott decision, "rests in public opinion. Whoever can change public opinion, can change the government, practically just so much." But public opinion, according to Lincoln, was not essentially or primarily opinion on a long list of individual topics, such as Professor Randall has enumerated, nor was it the kind of thing that the Gallup poll attempts to measure. "Public opinion, on any subject," said Lincoln, "always has a 'central idea' from which all its minor thoughts radiate." And the " 'central idea' in our political public opinion, at the beginning was, and until recently has continued to be 'the equality of men.' " For Lincoln, then, to debate public lands policy, or the condition of factory workers, when the question of the equality of rights of all the people was in dispute would have been utterly inconsequential. Whether the land would be tilled by freeholders or slaves, and whether factory workers might be permitted to strike, would be vitally affected by a decision concerning that "central idea." Until the matter of that central idea was settled, all peripheral questions were required, by the logic of the situation, to be held in abeyance.

In the first joint debate, at Ottawa, Lincoln affirmed in the strongest language the importance of the contest between himself and Douglas, for capturing the public mind. "In this and like communities," said Lincoln, "public sentiment is everything. With public sentiment,

nothing can fail; without it, nothing can succeed. Consequently, he who molds public sentiment, goes deeper than he who enacts statutes or pronounces decisions. He makes statutes and decisions possible or impossible to be executed. This must be borne in mind, as also the additional fact that Judge Douglas is a man of vast influence, so great that it is enough for many men to profess to believe anything, when they once find out Judge Douglas professes to believe it." These expressions, with minor variations, were repeated over and over. The decision in the Dred Scott case, as we have already noted, Lincoln did not believe would have been "possible . . . to be executed," had it not been for the fact that since 1854 Douglas had been inculcating in the public mind new "general maxims about liberty," as Lincoln put it at Galesburg, maxims such as Douglas's "assertions that he 'don't care whether slavery is voted up or voted down;' and that 'whoever wants slavery has a right to have it;' that 'upon principles of equality it should be allowed to go everywhere;' that 'there is no inconsistency between free and slave institutions.' "

The Kansas-Nebraska Act had said that men might have slavery in the territories if they wished to have it, and the Dred Scott decision had decided that they might not forbid it if they wished to do so, because the Constitution of the United States affirmed the right of property in slaves and forbade either Congress or a territorial legislature to interfere with that right. The common premise of both the act and the decision was, in the words of the chief justice [Roger B. Taney], that the Negro was an "ordinary article of merchandise and traffic," that he "might justly and lawfully be reduced to slavery," and that he was a being "so far inferior that [he] had no rights which the white man was bound to respect." This meant that the proposition that "all men are created equal," upon which the government of the United States was admittedly founded, either could not be understood in its universalistic implications or that the Negro could not be admitted to be a man. Lincoln controverted the Taney-Douglas premise upon the grounds that it was false historically, absurd logically, and immoral politically.

That the Negro was not a man was something that neither Douglas nor Taney would say in so many words; nor was it something that either affirmed to be the opinion of the Fathers. Yet Lincoln insisted that it was an inescapable implication of their denial of the Negro's natural right to freedom. This he demonstrated in the Peoria speech of 1854 when he said, "The law which forbids the bringing of slaves *from* Africa; and that which has so long forbid taking them *to* Nebraska, can hardly be distinguished on any moral principle."

Equal justice to the South, it is said, requires us to consent to the extending of slavery to new countries. That is to say, inasmuch as you do not object to my taking my hog to Nebraska, therefore I must not object to you taking your slave. Now, I admit this is perfectly logical, if there is no difference between hogs and negroes. But while you thus require me to deny the humanity of the Negro, I wish to ask whether you of the south yourselves, have ever been willing to do as much? It is kindly provided that of all those who come into the world, only a small percentage are natural tyrants. That percentage is no larger in the slave states than in the free. The great majority, south as well as north, have human sympathies, of which they can no more divest themselves than they can of their sensibility to physical pain. These sympathies in the bosoms of the southern people,

manifest in many ways, their sense of the wrong of slavery, and their consciousness that, after all, there is humanity in the negro. If they deny this, let me address them a few plain questions. In 1820 you joined the north, almost unanimously, in declaring the African slave trade piracy, and in annexing to it the punishment of death. Why did you do this? If you did not feel that it was wrong, why did you join in providing that men should be hung for it? The practice was no more than bringing wild negroes from Africa, to sell to such as would buy them. But you never thought of hanging men for catching and selling wild horses, wild buffaloes or wild bears.

Lincoln ever maintained that, as there was nothing in logic or morals, neither would there long be anything in politics to forbid the reopening of the slave trade if the legitimacy of the extension of slavery were once accepted by public opinion. If Negroes were nothing but an article of commerce, as Taney contended, then it was certainly an arbitrary infringement on the right of property to compel men to pay upward of fifteen hundred dollars for field hands, when they might be bought upon the coast of Africa for the price of a red pocket handkerchief. But, in fact, it had never been generally believed by Americans that it was just and lawful to reduce Negroes to servitude, as the capital punishment for the slave trade indicated. Moreover, Lincoln continued, the man who engaged in the domestic slave trade, the slave dealer, was generally despised and held in contempt even in the South.

If you are obliged to deal with him, you try to get through the job without so much as touching him. It is common with you to join hands with the men you meet; but with the slave dealer you avoid the ceremony—instinctively shrinking from the snaky contact. . . . Now why is this? You do not so treat the man who deals in corn, cattle or tobacco.

Again, continued Lincoln, there are nearly a half million free blacks, worth over two hundred millions of dollars, at the average prices (in 1854) of five hundred dollars.

How comes this vast amount of property to be running about without owners? We do not see free horses or free cattle running at large. How is this? All these free blacks are the descendants of slaves, or have been slaves themselves, and they would be slaves now, but for *something* which has operated on their white owners, inducing them, at vast pecuniary sacrifices, to liberate them. What is this *something*? Is there any mistaking it? In all these cases it is your sense of justice, and human sympathy, continually telling you, that the poor negro has some natural right to himself—that those who deny it, and make mere merchandise of him, deserve kicking, contempt and death.

Douglas's Nebraska bill, later joined by the Dred Scott decision, instituted a "tendency to dehumanize" the Negro, although the moral sense of the American people, South as well as North, testified to the Negro's humanity, to the moral baseness of treating him as "mere merchandise." Before the contest between Lincoln and Douglas was finally over, Douglas said in a speech at Memphis, as reported by Lincoln in his 1859 Cincinnati speech:

. . . that while in all contests between the negro and white man he was for the white man . . . that in all questions between the negro and the crocodile he was for the negro.

This declaration was not made accidentally, said Lincoln; Douglas had said the same thing many times during the 1858 campaign, although it had not been reported in his speeches then. It indicated an equation, according to Lincoln: as the crocodile is to the Negro, so is the Negro to the white man. Thus it was a calculated attempt to reduce the Negro, from the white man's standpoint, to the level of the brute. "As the negro ought to treat the crocodile as a beast, so the white man ought to treat the negro as a beast."

The attempt to legitimize the extension of slavery was impossible without denying the Negro's humanity or without denying the moral right of humanity or both. Taney, in the Dred Scott decision, had attempted to escape the moral responsibility for such implications by ascribing to the Fathers opinions which he (unlike Douglas) could not bring even himself to espouse. Then he found in the principle of constitutional responsibility a justification for enforcing these opinions.

No one, we presume, supposes that any change in public opinion, or feeling in relation to this unfortunate race . . . should induce the Court to give to the words of the Constitution a more liberal construction in their favor then they were intended to bear when the instrument was framed and adopted . . . Any other rule of construction would abrogate the judicial character of this court, and make it the mere reflex of the popular opinion or passion of the day.

Lincoln agreed wholeheartedly with the foregoing conception of the function of the Supreme Court. But he maintained that Taney was doing exactly what he denied doing; namely, adopting an opinion which had never even been dreamed of until the necessities of the Democratic Party, as indicated by the results of the November 1856 elections, had engendered it. In the course of the joint debates Lincoln finally gave it as his belief that Taney was the first man, and Douglas the second, who had ever denied that the Negro was included in the Declaration. The "fixed and universal" opinion from 1776 until 1857 was, in short, almost the exact opposite of what the Democratic Party, echoing Douglas and Taney, now professed and now said that the Fathers had professed.

At Galesburg, the other day [Lincoln said at Alton], I said, in answer to Judge Douglas, that three years ago there never had been a man, so far as I knew or believed, in the whole world, who had said that the Declaration of Independence did not include negroes in the term "all men". I reassert it today. I assert that Judge Douglas and all his friends may search the whole records of the country, and it will be a great matter of astonishment to me if they shall be able to find that one human being three years ago had ever uttered the astounding sentiment that the term "all men" in the Declaration did not include the negro. Do not let me be misunderstood. I know that more than three years ago there were men who, finding this assertion constantly in the way of their schemes to bring about the ascendancy and perpetuation of slavery, *denied the truth of it.* I know that Mr. [John C.] Calhoun and all the politicians of his school denied the truth of the Declaration. I know that it ran along in the mouth of some Southern men for a period of years, ending at last in that shameful, though rather forcible, declaration of Petit of Indiana, upon the floor of the United States Senate, that the Declaration of Independence was in that respect a "self-evident lie," rather than a self-evident truth. But I say . . . that three years ago there never had lived a man who had ventured to assail it in the sneaking way of pretending to believe it, and then asserting it did not include the negro. I believe the first man who ever said it was Chief Justice Taney in the Dred Scott case, and the next to him was our friend Stephen A. Douglas. And now it has become the catchword of the entire party.

While we would not attest, as a matter of historical record, that no man had ever said what Douglas and Taney were saying, prior to 1857, Lincoln's statement cannot be much of an exaggeration, if it is an exaggeration at all. That [George] Washington, [Thomas] Jefferson, [John] Adams, [James] Madison, [Alexander] Hamilton, [Benjamin] Franklin, Patrick Henry, and all other of their general philosophic persuasion understood the Declaration in its universalistic sense, and as including the Negro, is beyond doubt or cavil. All of them read the Declaration as an expression of the sentiments of Locke's *Second Treatise of Civil Government,* wherein many of them had read, almost from childhood, that all men are naturally in "a state of perfect freedom to order their actions . . . without asking leave, or depending upon the will of any other man. A state also of equality, wherein all power and jurisdiction is reciprocal, no one having more than another; there being nothing more evident than that creatures of the same species and rank . . . should also be equal one amongst another without subordination or subjection . . ." The Declaration of Independence had said that governments are instituted "to secure these rights," which plainly implied that the security, or enjoyment, of the rights which are all men's by nature does not follow from the fact of their unalienability. The Revolution was a great stroke to better secure the unalienable rights of *some* men, but, still more, it was a promise that all men everywhere might *some* day not merely possess but enjoy their natural rights. This promise was to be fulfilled in and through the successful example of a government dedicated to the security of the natural rights of the men who organized that government, the first government in the history of the world so dedicated. If that government had attempted to secure in their fullness the natural rights of all Americans, not to mention all men everywhere, the experiment of such a government would have met disaster before it had been fairly attempted. But the inability of the founders then and there to secure the rights of all the men whom they believed possessed unalienable rights did not in the least mean that they believed that the only people possessed of such rights were those whose rights were to be immediately secured.

"Chief Justice Taney," said Lincoln in his Springfield speech on the Dred Scott decision (June 26, 1857), "admits that the language of the Declaration is broad enough to include the whole human family,

but he and Judge Douglas argue that the authors of that instrument did not intend to include negroes, by the fact that they did not at once, actually place them on the equality with the whites. Now this grave argument comes to just nothing at all, by the other fact, that they did not at once, *or ever afterwards,* actually place all white people on an equality with one another. And this is the staple argument of both the Chief Justice and the Senator, for doing this obvious violence to the plain, unmistakable language of the Declaration. I think the authors of that notable instrument intended to include *all* men, but they did not intend to declare all men equal *in all respects.* They did not mean to say all were equal in color, size, intellect, moral developments, or social capacity. They defined with tolerable distinctness, in what respects they did consider all men created equal—equal in "certain inalienable rights, among which are life, liberty, and the pursuit of happiness." This they said, and this they meant. They did not mean to assert the obvious untruth, that all men were enjoying that equality, nor yet, that they were about to confer it immediately upon them. In fact, they had no power to confer such a boon. They meant simply to declare the *right,* so that the *enforcement* of it might follow as fast as circumstances should permit. They meant to set up a standard maxim for a free society, which should be familiar to all, and revered by all; constantly looked to, constantly labored for, and even though never perfectly attained, constantly approximated, and therefore constantly spreading and deepening its influence, and augmenting the happiness and value of life to all people of all colors everywhere.

We are familiar with Lincoln's conviction of the necessity of a "political religion" for the perpetuation of our political institutions and his tendency, fully matured in the Lyceum speech, but finally consummated in the Second Inaugural, to transform the American story into the moral elements of the Biblical story. We cannot help then perceiving the resemblance, in such expressions as a "standard maxim," "familiar to all," "revered by all," and "constantly looked to," to the words of the greatest of all lawgivers:

And these words, which I command thee this day, shall be in thine heart: And thou shalt teach them diligently unto thy children, and shalt talk of them when thou sittest in thine house, and when thou walkest by the way, and when thou liest down, and when thou risest up.

Nor did Lincoln forget the concept of political salvation when, in the course of the campaign of 1858, he said (July 10, 1858):

It is said in one of the admonitions of the Lord, "As your Father in Heaven is perfect, be ye also perfect." The Savior, I suppose, did not expect that any human creature could be as perfect as the Father in Heaven; but he said, "As your Father in Heaven is perfect, be ye also perfect." He set that up as a standard, and he who did most towards reaching that standard, attained the highest degree of moral perfection. So I say in relation to the principle that all men are created equal, let it be as nearly reached as we can. If we cannot give freedom to every creature, let us do nothing that will impose slavery upon any other creature.

At this point we must obtrude some critical reflections concerning the adequacy of Lincoln's assertions with regard to the meaning of the signers of the Declaration. If we ask, first of all if Lincoln's vindication of the consistency of the Fathers was altogether accurate from an historical standpoint, the answer, we believe, cannot be an unequivocal affirmative. It is true that Lincoln's hypothesis as to the meaning of the Declaration is consistent with the language of that document and is at least superficially consistent with its known philosophic antecedent, whereas the interpretation of Douglas and Taney certainly does the "obvious violence" that Lincoln asserts that it does. We may even supplement Lincoln's indictment by pointing out that Douglas's interpretation transforms the Declaration from a document of natural law to one of positive law. Douglas, in his speech on the Dred Scott decision, had said, as Lincoln quoted him, that when the signers

declared all men to have been created equal . . . they were speaking of British subjects on this continent being equal to British subjects born and residing in Great Britain—that they were entitled to the same inalienable rights . . . The Declaration was adopted for the purpose of justifying the colonists in the eyes of the civilized world in withdrawing their allegiance from the British crown, and dissolving their connection with the mother country.

The last sentence is correct enough as stating *one* purpose of the Declaration. But precisely because the revolutionists appealed to the whole civilized world, to men who were under no obligation to the laws of Great Britain, they did not affirm their rights as Britons but their rights as men, and they appealed not to the laws of Britain for justification but to laws common to themselves and all those to whom they addressed themselves, to the "laws of Nature and of Nature's God." The only logical reconciliation of Douglas's statement with the language of the Declaration would be by means of the proposition that all true men are by nature British! Such a proposition might find its place in some undiscovered operetta by Gilbert and Sullivan, but we cannot imagine the Founding Fathers in the chorus! Still further, the very concept of the unalienability of certain rights is inconsistent with the idea of

there being rights of British subjects. The rights of Britons *as* Britons were rights conferred by British law and hence alienable by the same process which conferred them. The king in Parliament might add to them or subtract from them; but the rights referred to by the Declaration are conceived as properties of man in virtue of his nature and hence unalterable by any mortal power. Douglas and Taney were indeed shamefully ignorant of the distinction between natural law and positive human law, and the obviousness of the violence they did to Jefferson's language cannot be affirmed too strongly.

Yet despite the consistency of Lincoln's alternative rendering of the signers' and founders' meaning, it cannot be endorsed on historical grounds without qualification. For in the passages just quoted Lincoln treats the proposition that "all men are created equal" as a transcendental goal and not as the immanent and effective basis of actual political right. And, in so doing, he transforms and transcends the original meaning of that proposition, although he does not destroy it. His, we might say, is a creative interpretation, a subtle preparation for the "new birth of freedom." Let us try to understand it more precisely.

The idea of the equality of all men, within the eighteenth-century horizon, was connected with the idea of the state of nature, a prepolitical state in which there was no government, no lawful subordination of one man to another man. It was a state which was tolerable but only barely so. Because it was but barely tolerable, "mankind are more disposed to suffer, while evils are sufferable, than to right themselves by abolishing the forms to which they are accustomed." But because it *was* tolerable, it was preferable to "absolute Despotism," which was intolerable. The concept of the state of nature, as a prepolitical state, highly undesirable, yet tolerable, is among the axiomatic premises of the doctrine of the Declaration of Independence. To indicate the departure that Lincoln's interpretation represents we observe that the idea of such a prepolitical state plays no significant role in his thinking. The only use Lincoln ever made of the expression "state of nature" is when he quoted or paraphrased a passage from [Henry] Clay's famous Mendenhall speech. The following is the passage, used by Lincoln in his reply to Douglas at Alton:

I desire no concealment of my opinions in regard to the institution of slavery. I look upon it as a great evil and deeply lament that we have derived it from the parental government, and from our ancestors. I wish every slave in the United States was in the country of his ancestors. But here they are; the question is how they can best be dealt with? If a state of nature existed and we were about to lay the foundation of society, no man would be more strongly opposed than I should be to incorporate the institution of slavery among its elements.

Lincoln likened Kansas and Nebraska to the state of nature, where the political foundations of society were about to be laid. This usage, however, is widely different from the idea of the state of nature presupposed in the Declaration. Lincoln and Clay presuppose a more or less virgin country and conditions which are more or less optimum. They envisage the kind of act of foundation portrayed in the dramatic dialogue of Plato's *Republic,* in which reason chooses the "elements" it would incorporate in a "good" society. The Lockean state of nature, on the other hand, although a normative concept, is normative primarily in a negative way:

it specifies the conditions under which the right of revolution ought to be exercised, and it specifies the purposes for which it ought to be exercised. But because the conditions under which the right ought to be exercised are very bad conditions (although not the worst possible), the purposes for which the right of revolution ought to be exercised are minimal rather than maximal conditions of human welfare. It is true that these minimal conditions, when stated in terms of the political circumstances of the thirteen colonies in 1776, do not appear to us today as so dreadfully undesirable. What the signers termed absolute despotism—forgetting, for the moment, the powerful but overdrawn portrait of the Declaration—would have appeared as a paradise of freedom to the oppressed humanity of the ages. Yet the fact remains that within the range of their experience, and from the point of view of their concept of the state of nature, they were asserting minimal rights, and they claimed they were absolved of their allegiance in the eyes of civilized mankind because of the insecurity which they had come to feel at the hands of the government of Great Britain. On the other hand, Lincoln's interpretation of "all men are created equal" is *not* that it specifies the condition of man in a prepolitical state, a highly undesirable state which marks the point at which men ought to revolt, but that it specifies the optimum condition which the human mind can envisage. It is a condition *toward* which men have a *duty* ever to strive, not a condition *from* which they have a *right* to escape. It is conceived as a political, not a prepolitical, condition, a condition in which—to the extent that it is realized—equality of right is secured to every man not by the natural law (which governs Locke's state of nature, in which all men are equal) but by positive human law. Lincoln's interpretation of human equality, as we have already indicated, is that every man had an equal right to be treated justly, that just treatment is a matter of intrinsic worth, that a man's rewards from society ought to be proportioned to the value of his work and not to any subjective liking or disliking.

In his Springfield speech of July 17, 1858, Lincoln said:

Certainly the negro is not our equal in color—perhaps not in many other respects; still, in the right to put into his mouth the bread that his own hands have earned, he is the equal of every other man, white or black. In pointing out that more had been given you, you can not be justified in taking away the little which has been given him. All I ask for the negro is that if you do not like him, let him alone. If God gave him but little, that little let him enjoy.

Or, as he wrote in a fragment which has survived:

Suppose it is true, that the negro is inferior to the white, in the gifts of nature; is it not the exact reverse justice that the white should, for that reason, take from the negro, any part of the little that has been give him? "*Give* to him that is needy" is the Christian rule of charity; but "Take from him that is needy" is the rule of slavery.

According to Lincoln, as we have said, a man's rewards should be proportioned to his labor, and this is (or should be) a function of his moral and intellectual capacity. Lincoln did not, of course, involve himself in any foolish controversy as to whether the Negro did or did not have the same capacity as the white man; he confined himself to asserting that his claims, *whatever they were,* ought to be determined on the same principle as the white man's. This fol-

lowed from the proposition that all men have an equal claim to just treatment—and that the Negro was a man.

To sum up: in the old, predominantly Lockean interpretation of the Declaration civil society is constituted by a movement away from the state of nature, away from the condition in which the equality of all men is actual. But in Lincoln's subtle reinterpretation civil society (i.e., just civil society) is constituted by the movement *toward* a condition in which the equality of men is actual. In the older view, which Lincoln shared as far as it went, the actual recognition of the equality of all men is really a necessary condition of the legitimacy of the claims of the government upon the governed. But it is also a sufficiency condition. For the language of the Declaration at least permits the view that, if the government of King George III had not been as thoroughly despotic as it is pretended it actually was, the Revolution might not have been justified. In short, the Declaration conceives of just government mainly in terms of the relief from oppression. Lincoln conceives of just government far more in terms of the requirement to achieve justice in the positive sense; indeed, according to Lincoln, the proposition "all men are created equal" is so lofty a demand that the striving for justice must be an ever-present requirement of the human and political condition. While Lincoln most assuredly accepted the Declaration in its minimal, revolutionary meaning, he gave it a new dimension when he insisted that it provided a test not merely of legitimate government—i.e., of government that *may* command our allegiance because it is not despotic—but of *good and just* government—i.e., of a government which may be loved and revered because it augments "the happiness and value of life to all people of all colors everywhere."

Lincoln's interpretation of "all men are created equal" transforms that proposition from a prepolitical, negative, minimal, and merely revolutionary norm, a norm which prescribes what civil society ought *not* to be, into a transcendental affirmation of what it *ought* to be. Lincoln does not, of course, abandon the lower-level Lockean-Jeffersonian demands, yet there is visible a tension between them and the higher ones upon which he insists.

The assertion that "all men are created equal" [he says in the Dred Scott speech] was of no practical use in effecting our separation from Great Britain; and it was placed in the Declaration, not for that, but for future use. Its authors meant it to be, thank God, it is now proving itself, a stumbling block to those who in after times might seek to turn a free people back into the hateful paths of despotism. They knew the proneness of prosperity to breed tyrants, and they meant when such should re-appear in this fair land and commence their vocation they should find left for them at least one hard nut to crack.

Lincoln was trying to perpetuate a government, Jefferson in 1776 to overthrow one, and Lincoln clearly has exaggerated Jefferson's nonrevolutionary purpose. In fact, the equality proposition was indispensable to Jefferson in building his case for the right of revolution upon Lockean ground, but the state-of-nature idea with which it was bound up was alien to Lincoln's whole way of thinking. However, Lincoln was probably right when he said that Jefferson did intend to make a statement which would have future as well as present usefulness, although he may have overstated the degree to which such a thought predominated in Jefferson's consciousness. Yet there is a differ-

ence between the use which Jefferson might have intended and the one Lincoln ascribes to him. Jefferson was always more concerned to remind the people of their rights than of their duties. He emphasized what they should demand of their government rather than what they must demand of themselves. Jefferson feared above all the usurpations which governments might commit if the people became drowsy and did not exercise that eternal vigilance which is the price of freedom. He thought in terms of a perpetual struggle between the governors and the governed, as epitomized in his famous epigrammatic assertions, as "the tree of liberty must be refreshed from time to time with the blood of patriots and tyrants," and "that a little rebellion, now and then, is a good thing, and as necessary in the political world as storms in the physical." The moral horizon of such expressions is markedly different from that of Lincoln's Lyceum speech, with its round condemnation of lawlessness and its conviction that any lawlessness, in such a government as Jefferson himself had helped to found, was an invitation to mob rule and mob rule the prelude to the failure of the entire experiment in popular government. While Lincoln never denied the danger of usurpations by the government, he placed far more emphasis on the danger of usurpations of a lawless people, which might become the usurpations of the government in response to popular pressure. Once the government was established upon a popular basis, the great danger, as Lincoln saw it, was the corruption of the people. Jefferson tended to see the people as sometimes careless of their own rights but as primarily motivated only by the desire not to be oppressed. Lincoln saw in the people, too, the desire to oppress. The Caesarian danger arose because of the coincidence of Caesar's ambitions with the people's desire to oppress; one without the other was powerless.

Jefferson, however, was not wholly unconcerned with the possibilities of popular corruption, as shown by his fear of a propertyless, urban proletariat and his advocacy of agrarianism as a preservative of virtue. Yet Jefferson's position was in this respect in hopeless contradiction with itself, in his simultaneous advocacy of science and an education which was predominantly scientific. For the consequence of science, particularly the emphatically practical science of Jefferson (like that of Franklin), was inevitably such an increase in the productive powers of labor as would necessitate an ever-growing division of labor, ever more commerce, ever improved communications, and the ever-growing urbanization and industrialization of America. Jefferson's agrarianism was a sheer anachronism from its beginning, a vestigial attachment to a world he did as much to destroy as any man. It was a reliance upon external conditions which could not possibly long endure to produce a virtue which he was at least occasionally aware was indispensable to preserve the institutions he so valued. Jefferson's agrarianism, however, was an *ad hoc* remedy for a defect in his theory, a defect of which he was in a confused way conscious, but which he could never overcome. For Jefferson's attempt to conceive of a remedy for the people's corruption was vitiated by his Lockean horizon.[1] All obligation within this horizon is conceived in terms of deductions from the state of nature, the state in which all men are actually equal. In this state, however, in which men have equal and unalienable

rights they have no real duties. The embryonic duties which exist in Locke's state of nature are not genuine duties but only rules which tell us to avoid doing those things which might impel others to injure us. Duties in any meaningful sense arise only in civil society and are conceived as logically required if civil society is to perform well its function of securing our rights. But whether in the state of nature or the state of civil society, men are not instructed, on Lockean grounds, to abstain from injuring others because it is objectively wrong, but because it is foolish: it undermines the security for their own rights. In short, there is little beyond an appeal to enlightened self-interest in the doctrine of universal equality when conceived in its pristine, Lockean form. Whereas for Lincoln, egotism and altruism ultimately coincide, inasmuch the greatest self-satisfaction is conceived as service to others; in the ethics just sketched such altruism as there is is ultimately reduced to egotism. That the patriotism engendered by the struggle for independence gave such an ethics a greater dignity than this suggests cannot be gainsaid, any more than the dignity of the character of Washington or the idealism of Jefferson can be vindicated on such low grounds. Yet it is also true that the widespread lack of concern over the moral challenge of Negro slavery to the doctrine of universal rights in the Declaration in the Revolutionary generation can be traced to the egotistic quality of these rights in their Lockean formulation. For this reason we must concede that Lincoln exaggerated the degree in which the men of the Revolution were concerned with the freedom of all men. And thus there is some color, although it is only the faintest, for Douglas's assertion that the signers would have been inconsistent if they had meant to include the Negroes in "all men" and then had continued to hold slaves themselves. In truth, their principle included the Negroes in "all men," but the Negroes' rights did *not* impose corresponding duties upon the white masters. Lincoln, we believe, gave a greater consistency and dignity to the position of the signers than was theirs originally. Let us try to understand precisely how he did so.

All men admittedly have a *right* to liberty by the doctrine of the Declaration. But so does every man have a right to life. Now, if we conceive these rights as operative within the Lockean state of nature, we will immediately see that no man is under any necessary obligation to respect any other man's rights. For example: because I have a right to life, I have a right to kill any man whom I have reason to believe might kill me. That is, I have no obligation to respect the other man's right to life until he has given me adequate pledges that he will not try to kill me. After I have received such a pledge I have an obligation to him. But I have this obligation then because, and only because, I have a prior concern to preserve myself. By respecting his pledge I increase my own safety. The same holds true of liberty: I have a right to liberty, which right *permits* me to enslave anyone who, I fear, might otherwise enslave me.

Jefferson once remarked, about the Negro's enslavement in America, that justice was in one scale and self-preservation in the other. Or, as he rhetorically asked on another occasion, shall we present our slaves with freedom and a dagger? Jefferson never hesitated in his answer: the Negro must continue to be enslaved so long as, and to the degree that, his freedom might

injure (or, what came to the same thing, might be believed to injure) the white man. Lincoln, of course, was never an abolitionist and always granted the right of the slave states to continue the institution of slavery as long as they felt the kind of dangers that Jefferson (in common with most Southerners) avowedly felt. Yet, when Lincoln said that the policy of the Founding Fathers was to place the institution of slavery where the public mind might rest in the belief that it was in course of ultimate extinction, he was also stretching their attitude to fit *his* theory rather than theirs. It would have been truer to say that they *hoped* it was in course of ultimate extinction than that they believed it was actually in course of extinction. Allan Nevins's observation that "their *expectations* regarding its termination had been much more equivocal than their hopes" is entirely justified. . . . Jefferson's views . . . show how badly he wobbled on the prospect of future conditions favorable to Negro liberty.

To resume the theoretical analysis, we may say that no man, from the strictly Lockean standpoint, is under an obligation to respect any other man's unalienable rights until that other man is necessary to the security of his own rights. Only men bound to each other by the social contract are, in a strict sense, bound to respect each other's unalienable rights. And so far are they from being under the obligation to respect other men's rights that they may kill or enslave other men whenever in their judgment this *adds* to their own security. It would also be true, however, that the enslaved Negroes always had the right to revolt and to kill their masters. But the masters would have had no *obligation* to free them until and unless the Negroes had the physical power to make good their freedom. No one has ever expressed more clearly or candidly this view of the right of revolution than Lincoln, in his speech on the Mexican War, when he said that "any people anywhere, being inclined and having the power, have the *right* to rise up and shake off the existing government, and form a new one that suits them better." A people who are so servile as to lack the desire for freedom, *or who lack* the power, do not in any practical sense have the right. The "appeal to Heaven," the *ultima ratio furis,* in which Locke's right of revolution culminates, and through which the rights to life and liberty alone receive their sanction, is the appeal to *force.* And those who do not have force at their disposal have no effective Lockean argument for denying the assertion of despotic power over them.

But if the foregoing is true, what interest did Jefferson and those minded like him have in ultimate Negro emancipation or, for that matter, in the emancipation of any one whom they could profitably enslave? The answer, we believe, may be found (apart from the matter of mere moral taste) in the concept of long-run as opposed to short-run egotism. The freedom of a free, popular republic depends upon the indoctrination of people *everywhere* in their natural, unalienable rights. Security is a matter of freedom from oppression at home *and* freedom from foreign domination. The great Enlightenment of the eighteenth century, of which Jefferson was such an ornament, was famous for nothing more than for its cosmopolitanism. And the essence of this cosmopolitanism lay in the conviction that only when the rights of man are secured everywhere will they attain their maximum security anywhere. It was expressed typically in the belief that republican governments are unwarlike, because when the government is of the people, when those whose blood and treasure pay for wars must decide between war and peace, there will be no more aggressive wars, no more wars for conquest of dynastic glory.[2] In this vein Jefferson, in . . . the *Notes on Virginia*[,] . . . feared that some day the Negro would rise up to enslave the white man. In short, Jefferson really did believe, as did Lincoln, that he who would not be a slave ought not to be a master. But the Lockean root of Jefferson's conviction—the deepest root for Jefferson's generation—regarded this precept as preeminently a requirement of enlightened self-interest, as a long-run requirement of the security of the rights of the self-regarding, egotistical individual. But in the short run, in the foreseeable future, there could, from this viewpoint, be no pressing conscientious objection to the continued enslavement of those whose slavery was not, but whose emancipation would be, a threat to the masters. Jefferson, it is true, did, in his eighteenth query, state one further objection to slavery. It was that slavery engendered despotic manners, and he implies (although he does not state) that such manners are inimical to the spirit of free republican institutions. But this argument by itself is also a prudential one and is a condemnation of slavery more for its effects upon the whites than for its wrong to the Negroes. How inadequate it is may be seen by recollecting that [Edmund] Burke, in his speech on conciliation with America, observes the same effects that Jefferson does and draws on the opposite conclusion.[3]

Lincoln's morality then extends the full length of Jefferson's, but it also goes further. Jefferson's horizon, with its grounding in

Locke, saw all commands to respect the rights of others as fundamentally hypothetical imperatives: *if* you do not wish to be a slave, then refrain from being a master. Lincoln agreed, but he also said in substance: he who wills freedom for himself must simultaneously will freedom for others. Lincoln's imperative was not only hypothetical; it was categorical as well. Because all men by nature have an equal right to justice, all men have an equal duty to do justice, wholly irrespective of calculations as to self-interest. Or, to put it a little differently, our own happiness, our own welfare, cannot be conceived apart from our well-doing, or just action, and this well-doing is not merely the adding to our own security but the benefiting of others. Civil society, for Lincoln as for Aristotle and Burke, is a partnership "in every virtue and in all perfection." And, while our duties to friends and fellow citizens take precedence over duties to those who are not friends or fellow citizens, the possibility of justice, and of injustice, exists in every relationship with every other human being. Indeed, if it was not possible to do justice to non-fellow citizens, the possibility of justice and friendship with fellow citizens would not exist. For civil society is the realization of a potentiality which must exist whenever man encounters his fellow, or it is not a potentiality anywhere. And that potentiality, for Lincoln, found its supreme expression in the proposition that "all men are created equal."

According to Lincoln, the Douglas-Taney thesis with regard to the Negro was historically false. We cannot but pronounce Lincoln right and his opponents wrong; yet it should be understood that Lincoln's affirmation of the founders' and signers' meaning, as distinct from his contradiction of Douglas and Taney, is not itself impeccable on purely historical grounds. But if it is not impeccable historically, it is superior on logical and moral grounds to the doctrine it purports to interpret. To what extent Lincoln was conscious that his interpretation was "creative" we cannot absolutely say. Yet we cannot forget that in the Lyceum speech Lincoln warned that the Revolution was supported not only by the sense of right but by the passions of the revolutionists, both by the base passions of the people of hatred and revenge and by the noble but dangerous passion of the leaders for fame and distinction. And we cannot help noticing that the Lockean interpretation of unalienable rights, which we have sketched, ultimately views such rights as reducible to *passions*.[4] For the right to life and liberty is held to be indefeasible in Locke just because the passion for life, and for the necessary means thereto, is held to be indefeasible. But when Lincoln said, as he repeatedly did say in the debates, that Douglas's "Don't care" policy with respect to slavery was an absurdity, because it tolerated the notion that there was such a thing as a right to do wrong, he superimposed upon the Lockean doctrine of the unalienable right to liberty a very different conception of right. The Lockean idea of a right to liberty meant that no one can consistently appeal to *my* sense of right to give up *my* liberty, but it does not mean that a man who enslaves another violates the enslaver's sense of *what is right*. Lincoln confounds the meaning of *a right,* meaning an indefeasible desire or passion, with *what is right,* meaning an objective state or condition in which justice is done. Lincoln does not, however, deny that there are natural rights in the Lockean sense; i.e., that there are indefeasible passions which entitle all men to reject allegedly moral claims upon them which are inconsistent with the gratification of these passions. But while the Lyceum speech conceded the adequacy of the notion of natural right as the right of the passions, for the purposes of the Revolutionary generation, it also denied its future utility. "Passion has helped us; but can do so no more . . . Reason . . . must furnish all the materials for our future support . . ." From Lincoln's 1838 criticism of the Revolution we suspect that he was not innocent of the nature of his subsequent "reconstruction" of the meaning of the Fathers. For as passion is subjective so is reason objective. The concept of *what is right* is the concept of an objective condition, a condition discernible by reasons. "All I ask for the negro is that if you do not like him, let him alone," said Lincoln with a pathos which anticipates the war years. But his meaning is that the test of right is not how something agrees with our passions but how it agrees with a discernment of what is due to a man. Right conceived as subjective passion does *not* forbid us to do what is objectively wrong; it only directs us to do whatever we deem necessary for *our* lives and *our* liberty. Right conceived as a state or condition in which every man is rendered his due forbids us to dissociate the value to ourselves of our own lives and liberties and the value to themselves of the lives and liberties of any men who may be affected by our actions.

## Notes

1. Jefferson never remained wholly Lockean. There are passages—for example, in his letter to John Adams, October 28, 1823—in which he speaks of a natural aristocracy and that man is "formed for the social state," which would seem to premise a rejection of the whole egalitarian-state-of-nature theory. It is hard to tell whether such departures are purely *ad hominem* or whether Jefferson simply was unable to make up his mind.

2. Compare Lincoln's letter to [William H.] Herndon, February 15, 1848, especially the following: "The provision of the Constitution giving the war-making power to Congress, was dictated as I understand it, by the following reasons. Kings had always been involving and impoverishing their people in wars, pretending generally, if not always, that the good of the people was the object. This, our convention understood to be the most oppressive of kingly oppressions . . . " Tom Paine's *Rights of Man* is the most famous popular statement of this view of the relation of monarchies and republics.

3. Thus Jefferson, in the aforesaid query XVIII, *Notes on Virginia*: "The whole commerce between master and slave is a perpetual exercise of the most boisterous passions . . . This quality is the germ of all education in him . . . The man must be a prodigy who can retain his manners and morals undepraved by such circumstances. And with what execration should the statesman be loaded, who, permitting one half the citizens thus to trample on the rights of the other, transforms those into despots, and these into enemies, destroys the morals of the one part, and the *amor patriae* of the other . . ." This is an amazing statement for many reasons, perhaps most for the reference to slaves as citizens. Yet Jefferson never wavered in his insistence that these "citizens" should be deported as a price of their freedom. Consider, however, the classic counterpart to the foregoing, from Burke's speech on conciliation with America, paragraph 42: " . . . in Virginia and the Carolinas they have a vast multitude of slaves. Where this is the case in any part of the world, those who are free are by far the most proud and jealous of their freedom. Freedom is to them not only an enjoyment, but a kind of rank and privilege. . . . I do not mean, Sir, to commend the superior morality of this sentiment, which has at least as much pride as virtue in it; but . . . The fact is so: and these

people of the southern colonies are much more strongly, and with a higher and more stubborn spirit, attached to liberty, than those to the northward." Although Burke and Jefferson do not flatly contradict each other—for Burke reserves the difference between pride and virtue—yet the tendency of their evaluations is clearly opposite. Needless to say, the evaluation of the British statesman is the one that became the dominant conviction of the South. Lincoln, of course, accepted fully Jefferson's views in the eighteenth query—except for its optimistic conclusion about the spirit of the master abating, which we have noted above to be a *non sequitur*.

4. For an authoritative exposition of Hobbesian and Lockean natural rights doctrine, with particular reference to the respective roles of reason and passion, see Leo Strauss, *Natural Right and History* (Chicago, 1953), especially Chapter V, "Modern Natural Right."

## Bibliography

Jaffa, Harry V. *Crisis of the House Divided: An Interpretation of the Issues in the Lincoln-Douglas Debates*. Garden City, N.Y.: Doubleday, 1959.

———. *A New Birth of Freedom: Abraham Lincoln and the Coming of the Civil War*. Lanham, Md.: Rowman and Littlefield, 2000.

# 4

# Clarence Thomas, Civil Rights, and the Declaration of Independence

## SCOTT DOUGLAS GERBER

Clarence Thomas fascinates the American people like no other member of the U.S. Supreme Court ever has. A Lexis-Nexis computer search of the major newspapers database reveals that Justice Thomas has been mentioned in twice as many newspapers stories during the past ten years as any other member of the Court.

Much of the public's interest in Justice Thomas stems from 1991's nationally televised confirmation battle, in which he responded to allegations that he had sexually harassed Anita Hill during their tenure together at the U.S. Department of Education and the Equal Employment Opportunity Commission (EEOC). Law professor and journalist Jeffrey Rosen in the summer of 2000 wrote:

After nearly a decade on the Supreme Court, [Clarence Thomas] has developed into a provocative, fiercely independent, and interestingly radical justice, willing to rethink entire areas of the law from the ground up. But in the public mind, he remains nothing more than a dirty joke.

Thomas, however, was a controversial Supreme Court nominee before Hill's allegations became public. Why? Primarily because of the comparisons people made between him and the person whose vacancy on the Court he was nominated to fill: Thurgood Marshall, the first African American appointed to the nation's highest court and one of the most famous and influential civil rights lawyers in American history. Many people objected to Thomas, who is himself black, because he disagreed with the agenda of the modern civil rights movement—especially with the policy of affirmative action.

Thomas believed—and still believes—that the movement's emphasis on groups (especially on African Americans) is inconsistent with the individual rights orientation of the Declaration of Independence. Justice Thomas—the man a major conservative newsmagazine in 1999 named "America's leading conservative"—is without question the nation's leading proponent of the view that the American regime was founded on the principles articulated in the Declaration of Independence and that public policy should be made, and assessed, in light of those principles.

## From Poverty to Power

Clarence Thomas's life could be the basis for a Horatio Alger story. (His critics counter that he is where he is today because of the policy he seeks to dismantle: affirmative action.) Born in

1948 in the dirt-poor town of Pin Point, Georgia, abandoned by his father and then given up by his mother, Thomas was raised by his maternal grandparents in a segregated society. Through hard work, sacrifice, and sheer force of will—both his own and that of his grandfather—he graduated with honors from the College of the Holy Cross in Worcester, Massachusetts, and then from Yale Law School in New Haven, Connecticut. Seven years later, Thomas, who had become active in the black conservative movement after arriving in Washington, D.C., in 1979 to work for U.S. senator John C. Danforth, R-Mo., was named assistant secretary for civil rights in the U.S. Department of Education by President Ronald Reagan. Ten months after that, he was appointed chairman of the EEOC—the federal agency charged with enforcing the nation's equal employment opportunity laws.

During his eight years at the EEOC, Thomas was credited with improving morale in the agency and with making the organization more efficient. However, he was criticized by civil rights groups for shifting the agency away from its traditional group-based approach to civil rights enforcement to an individual-based approach as well as for abandoning the traditional remedies to discrimination—numerical goals and timetables—in the process.

While at the EEOC Thomas became a much sought-after speaker on law school campuses and in conservative circles. In the speeches he made, Thomas began to associate himself publicly with the Declaration of Independence. According to Ken Masugi, a former student of the leading political theorist of the Declaration, Harry Jaffa, and the former EEOC scholar-in-residence who played a major role

in helping to shape Thomas's thinking about the Declaration, Thomas became attracted to the nation's founding document because "he wanted a positive, principled civil rights policy that was also consistent with a political and social agenda that respected individual liberty."

Thomas's most detailed discussions of the Declaration of Independence during his tenure at the EEOC came in two law review articles published in the late 1980s. In a 1987 article in the *Howard Law Journal* titled "Toward a 'Plain Reading' of the Constitution—The Declaration of Independence in Constitutional Interpretation," Thomas maintained that the "founding principles of equality and liberty" set forth in the Declaration "dictate the policy of action towards Black Americans." The EEOC chairman credited Justice John Marshall Harlan for being the first member of the Supreme Court to appreciate the connection between the Declaration and the enforcement of the nation's civil rights laws. In particular, Thomas applauded Justice Harlan's solitary dissent in *Plessy v. Ferguson* (1898)—the case in which the Supreme Court constitutionalized the practice of racial segregation. In that stinging dissent Harlan coined the phrase that would later become closely associated with Thomas himself: "Our Constitution is color-blind, and neither knows nor tolerates classes among citizens." Significantly, Thomas went on in his *Howard Law Journal* article to criticize the most celebrated decision in the history of civil rights law, *Brown v. Board of Education* (1954)—the landmark desegregation decision that overruled *Plessy* and that also played a major role in launching the modern civil rights movement. Thomas wrote:

*Brown* was a missed opportunity, as [are] all its progeny, whether they involve busing, affirmative action, or redistricting. The task of those involved in securing freedom of all Americans is to turn policy toward reason rather than sentiment, toward justice rather than sensitivity, toward freedom rather than dependence—in other words, toward the spirit of the Founding. These steps would validate the *Brown* decision, by replacing the Warren opinion with one resting on reason and moral and political principles, as established in the Constitution and the Declaration of Independence.

Thomas expanded on his views about the Declaration's role in interpreting the Constitution's civil rights provisions in a 1989 article in the *Harvard Journal of Law and Public Policy* titled "The Higher Law Background of the Privileges or Immunities Clause of the Fourteenth Amendment." In that article the EEOC chairman reiterated his position that "the Constitution is a logical extension of the principles of the Declaration of Independence," and he also reaffirmed his belief that Justice Harlan's dissenting opinion in *Plessy* advancing a "color-blind" approach to civil rights enforcement was the proper approach to follow. Thomas wrote:

*Brown v. Board of Education* would have had the strength of the American political tradition behind it if it had relied upon Justice Harlan's arguments instead of relying on dubious social science. . . . The higher-law background of the American Constitution, whether explicitly invoked or not, provides the only firm basis for a just, wise, and *constitutional* decision.

Thomas quoted from the legal briefs of Homer Plessy himself to bring home his point about the importance of turning to the Declaration of Independence if the Constitution's conception of equality is to be truly understood:

The Declaration of Independence . . . is not a fable as some of our modern theorists would have us believe, but the all-embracing formula of personal rights on which our government is based. . . . [This] controlling genius of the American people . . . must always be taken into account in construing any expression of the sovereign will.

Thomas shifted from the ivory-tower abstractions of constitutional theorizing to his daily responsibilities of enforcing the nation's civil rights laws as chairman of the EEOC in a 1985 article in the *Stetson Law Review*. His individual rights approach to civil rights enforcement could not have been more clearly stated. He wrote:

I intend to take EEO enforcement back to where it started by defending the rights of individuals who are hurt by discriminatory practices. To do this, we intend to pursue individual cases as well as pattern and practice cases. . . . Those who insist on arguing that the principle of equal opportunity, the cornerstone of civil rights, means preferences for certain groups have relinquished their roles as moral and ethical leaders in this area. I bristle at the thought, for example, that it is morally proper to protest against minority racial preferences in South Africa while arguing for such preferences here.

Thomas's individual rights orientation to civil rights enforcement was stated with similar clarity in a 1987 article in the *Yale Law and Policy Review*. In that article—"Affirmative Action Goals and Timetables: Too Tough? Not Tough Enough!"—the EEOC chairman criticized the use of numerical goals and timetables in remedying civil rights violations because he believed that those sorts of "group-defined" remedies often failed to provide redress for the "individual" who had suffered the discrimination. "This emphasis on 'systematic' suits led the Commission to overlook many of the individuals who came to our offices to file charges and seek assistance," he maintained. "If an individual's allegations did not involve a priority issue or apply to other members of a class, the

Commission was unlikely to go to bat for the individual in court." Thomas also objected to group-based relief on moral grounds. In language that he would repeat nearly ten years later as a member of the Supreme Court, he stated:

I continue to believe that distributing opportunities on the basis of race or gender, whoever the beneficiaries, turns the law against employment discrimination on its head. Class preferences are an affront to the rights and dignity of individuals—both those individuals who are directly disadvantaged by them, and those who are their supposed beneficiaries. I think that preferential hiring on the basis of race or gender will increase racial divisiveness, disempower women and minorities by fostering the notion that they are in need of handouts, and delay the day when skin color and gender are truly the least important things about a person in the employment context.[1]

## The 'Natural Law Thing'

Clarence Thomas's views about civil rights in general and the Declaration of Independence in particular received much attention in conservative circles. Few were surprised, then, when President George Bush nominated Thomas in 1989 to the U.S. Court of Appeals. Thomas was confirmed in March 1990, after an uneventful confirmation hearing. Less than two years later, President Bush nominated the then forty-three-year-old Thomas to be an associate justice of the Supreme Court of the United States.

Thomas's views about the Declaration of Independence concerned many on the Senate Judiciary Committee. For example, just prior to the commencement of the Judiciary Committee's hearing on Thomas's nomination to the Supreme Court, Sen. Joseph R. Biden Jr., D-Del., chairman of the committee, published a lengthy op-ed in the *Washington Post* titled

"Law and Natural Law: Questions for Judge Thomas." In that op-ed the senator previewed the most important questions he planned to ask the nominee about his views regarding the nation's founding document: "Would he place 'natural law above the Constitution'?" "Is natural law a 'moral code' or is it 'a protector of personal freedom'?" "Is the nominee's vision of natural law a static one or an evolving one?" "Would Judge Thomas employ natural law to limit government's ability to respond in changing circumstances, or does he see it as permitting the government to adjust to new social challenges?" Biden opened Thomas's confirmation hearing by proclaiming that understanding the nominee's views on the Declaration was "the single most important task of this committee."

Thomas clearly knew that his views about the Declaration were controversial. Besides Senator Biden, Laurence H. Tribe, the famous liberal professor at Harvard Law School, wrote the following in the *New York Times* shortly after Thomas was nominated to the Court.

Most conservatives criticize the judiciary for expanding its powers, "creating" rights rather than "interpreting" the Constitution. These critics talk of returning issues like abortion to democratically elected and politically accountable bodies.

Clarence Thomas, judging from his speeches and scholarly writings, seems instead to believe judges should enforce the founders' natural law philosophy—the inalienable rights "given man by his Creator"—which he maintains is revealed most completely in the Declaration of Independence. He is the first Supreme Court nominee in 50 years to maintain that natural law should be readily consulted in constitutional interpretation.

Not surprisingly, then, Thomas was measured in his responses to the flood of questions he received from the Judiciary Committee about the Declaration. When pressed about his speeches and articles that seemed to suggest that, as Thomas phrased it in one of his published articles, "a 'plain reading' of the Constitution . . . puts the fitly spoken words of the Declaration of Independence in the center of the frame formed by the Constitution," the nominee replied that such statements were merely the musings of "a part-time political theorist."

Thomas went on to testify that his approach to judging was, and would continue to be if confirmed to the Supreme Court, unaffected by politics—conservative or otherwise. As he put it in response to a question from Sen. Dennis DeConcini, D-Ariz.:

Senator, I think it is important for judges not to have agendas or to have strong ideology or ideological views. That is baggage, I think, that you take to the Court or you take as a judge.

It is important for us, and I believe one of the Justices, whose name I cannot recall right now, spoke about having to strip down, like a runner, to eliminate agendas, to eliminate ideologies, and when one becomes a judge, it is an amazing process, because that is precisely what you start doing. You start putting the speeches away, you start putting the ideology away. You begin to decline forming opinions in important areas that could come before your court, because you want to be stripped down like a runner. So, I have no agenda, Senator.

How, then, did Thomas avow to remain true to this ideal of nonpartisan judging? By applying, he testified, the "traditional tools of constitutional interpretation or adjudication, as well as statutory construction" (for example, text, framers' intent, precedent). Thomas testified repeatedly that those of his speeches and articles that generated controversy were policy statements and had nothing to do with

his approach to judging. "The only point I am making is that, to the extent that those are political statements or policymaking statements, I don't think they are relevant in my role as a judge," he said in response to a question from Sen. Herbert Kohl, D-Wis.

It is difficult to take seriously Thomas's confirmation hearing attempts to distance himself from his previously articulated approach to constitutional interpretation. The title to one of his law review articles, "Toward a 'Plain Reading' of the Constitution—The Declaration of Independence in Constitutional Interpretation," could not be "plainer" on the matter, nor could his other preconfirmation hearing speeches and articles. However, this does not mean that Thomas underwent a "confirmation conversion" during the hearing, as several of his opponents on the Judiciary Committee proclaimed. He clearly stated during questioning by Senator Biden that the natural rights political philosophy of the Declaration of Independence must play a role in constitutional interpretation:

The Chairman. As a starting point. So at least, Judge will you not acknowledge you conclude that natural law indirectly impacts upon what you think a phrase in the Constitution means?
Judge Thomas. To the extent that it impacts, to the extent that the Framers' beliefs comport with that. . . .
The Chairman. So, you are going to apply, at least in part, the Framers' notion of original intent of natural law, right?
Judge Thomas. As a part of the inquiry.

The exchange between Biden and Thomas on how Thomas would employ the principles of the Declaration in constitutional interpretation continued throughout the hearing. Here is perhaps the most illuminating, not to mention the most colorful, example.

The Chairman. Well, Judge, I don't know why you are so afraid to deal with this natural law thing. I don't see how any reasonable person can conclude that natural law does not impact upon adjudication of a case, if you are a judge, if you acknowledge that you have to go back and look at what the founders meant by natural law, and then at least in part have that play a part in the adjudication of . . .

Judge Thomas. I am admitting that.

The Chairman. Pardon me?

Judge Thomas. I am admitting that.

The Chairman. Oh, you are admitting that?

Judge Thomas. I have. I said that to the extent that the Framers . . .

The Chairman. Good. So, natural law does impact on the adjudication of cases.

Judge Thomas. To the extent the Framers believed.

The Chairman. Good. We both admit, you looking at the Framers and me looking at the Framers, we may come to two different conclusions of what they meant by natural law.

Judge Thomas. But we also agree that the provisions that they chose were broad provisions, that adjudicating through our history and tradition, using our history and tradition evolve.[2]

Many of the questions Thomas was asked during his confirmation hearing attempted to ascertain the specifics of the nominee's views about the Declaration of Independence—to go beyond, in other words, the bare bones of his argument about the use of the Declaration as an exegetical tool. Thomas responded by stating that his concerns for individuals and individual rights were what tied together his speeches and articles on the subject. He made this point unequivocally in response to a question from Sen. Howard M. Metzenbaum, D-Ohio, arguably Thomas's most unwavering opponent on the Judiciary Committee.

Senator, I think that I have not [had] an opportunity to go back and review that speech in detail. I have looked at it and don't know exactly where that quote [that America is "careening with frightening speed toward a statist, dictatorial system"] appears in it. But the point I think throughout these speeches is a notion that we should be careful about the relationship between the Government and the individual and should be careful that the Government itself does not at some point displace or infringe on the rights of the individual. That is a concern, as I have noted here, that runs throughout my speeches.

Thomas made this point elsewhere as well during his confirmation hearing, most notably when he defended a speech in which he had praised Justice Antonin Scalia's controversial dissenting opinion in *Morrison v. Olson* (1988). In that opinion, Scalia called into question on separation of powers grounds the constitutionality of the federal independent counsel law that was passed in response to the Watergate crisis. Thomas responded as follows to a barrage of questions about the law from Sen. Edward M. Kennedy, D-Mass.

The point that I was making was very simply that it wasn't that it should not be determined or that wrongdoing should not be ferreted out, nor did I indicate that perhaps there could not be—that the executive could necessarily totally oversee itself. I don't think that was my point.

My point was that the individual, when an independent body was involved in the investigation and conducted the investigation, that there wasn't that responsiveness directly to either one of the three branches, and that that concern led to a view that an individual—that that lack of accountability could actually undermine the individual freedom of the person who is being investigated. That was the totality of that point. And that is, I think, an important point, and it was one that I made in the context of a speech about individual freedom.

Thomas's commitment to individualism and individual rights is consistent with the classical liberal interpretation of the Declaration that Garrett Ward Sheldon describes in Chapter 2.

The classical liberal orientation of Thomas's interpretation of America's founding document is clear beyond cavil in the following response to a question from Sen. Howell Heflin, D-Ala.

The point there is that, in our regime, if you notice, I speak to the higher law political philosophy of the Founders. Their philosophy was that we were all created equal and that we could be governed only by our consent, and that we ceded to the Government only certain rights, and that, to that extent, the Government had to be and was a limited government.

Nowhere was Thomas's commitment to the classical liberal interpretation of the Declaration of Independence—that government should be a limited government whose primary function is to protect individual rights—more in evidence than in his answers to questions about his approach to civil rights enforcement. Thomas spent most of his public career prior to being appointed to the Supreme Court as chairman of the EEOC. Consequently, he has said more about civil rights than about any other area of the law. Indeed, the initial (that is, pre–Anita Hill) opposition to Thomas's nomination to the high court was motivated primarily by his civil rights views running contrary to those of the traditional civil rights community. However, a nonpartisan analysis of Thomas's pre-Court writings and speeches would have revealed that the nominee's civil rights positions were tied directly to his views about the ideal of inherent equality at the heart of the Declaration of Independence. Thomas himself made this point on several occasions during his confirmation hearing. One such occasion was during an exchange with the strongly pro–Thomas senator, Alan K. Simpson, R-Wyo.

Senator Simpson. . . . So my final question for you, do you believe that that passage that I just

moments ago quoted from the Declaration of Independence has meaning, perhaps the meaning I attached to it? Is the belief that all men are endowed with certain inalienable rights one that you would consider well accepted within the judicial mainstream and consistent with most Americans' values and principles?

Judge Thomas. Senator, I think that most Americans, when they refer to the Declaration of Independence and its restatement of our inherent equality, believe that. And I believe that our revulsion when we think of policies such as apartheid flow from the acceptance of our inherent equality.

Thomas also tied civil rights enforcement to the concept of equality at the heart of the Declaration in a much less friendly exchange with Senator Biden, an exchange—one of many during the hearing—about Thomas's apparent praise for a pro-life article by conservative activist Lewis Lehrman. Thomas testified:

I felt that conservatives would be skeptical about the notion of natural law. I was using that as the underlying approach. I felt that they would be conservative and that they would not—or be skeptical about that concept. I was speaking in the Lew Lehrman Auditorium of the Heritage Foundation. I thought that if I demonstrated that one of their own accepted at least the concept of natural rights, that they would be more apt to accept that concept as an underlying principle for being more aggressive on civil rights. My whole interest was civil rights enforcement.

And Thomas informed Sen. Orrin G. Hatch, R-Utah, that it was his own family's personal experience with racial discrimination that had led him to study the Declaration of Independence in the first place:

Senator, as I noted, my interest particularly in the area of natural rights was as a part-time political theorist at EEOC who was looking for a way to unify and to strengthen the whole effort to enforce our civil rights laws, as well as questions about people like my grandfather being denied opportunities. Those were important questions to me.

## Justice Thomas

Thomas was eventually confirmed to the Supreme Court of the United States, albeit by the narrowest margin in modern history, and "those questions" about how to strengthen civil rights enforcement have continued to occupy him as a member of the nation's highest court. Justice Thomas has emerged as the Court's staunchest defender of individual rights in civil rights cases.

For example, in a much-discussed concurring opinion in *Missouri v. Jenkins* (1995), a school desegregation case, Thomas became the first Supreme Court justice in history to directly criticize *Brown v. Board of Education*.[3] The heart of Justice Thomas's concurring opinion in *Jenkins*, like the heart of EEOC chairman Thomas's speeches and law review articles about civil rights enforcement, was his belief that the Court was wrong in 1954 to rely upon disputable social science evidence to declare segregation unconstitutional and that the Court could have reached the same result by invoking the "constitutional principle" that "the Government must treat citizens as individuals, and not as members of racial, ethnic or religious groups." EEOC chairman Thomas had found that "constitutional principle" most "plainly" stated in the classical liberal political philosophy of the Declaration of Independence.

Justice Thomas's conception of civil rights as an individual, not a group, concern also animates his voting rights jurisprudence. For example, in one of the longest separate opinions in Supreme Court history, his 1994 concurring

opinion in *Holder v. Hall,* Thomas wrote that it is erroneous to read the Voting Rights Act to "cover claims of vote dilution."[4] He argued that racial groups should not "be conceived of largely as political interest groups," that blacks do not all "think alike," and that existing case law should be overturned to eliminate claims for "proportional allocation of political power according to race." In short, Thomas, by way of his "colorblind" approach to civil rights enforcement, seeks to remove the right to group representation from the Voting Rights Act. To him, the act is about ensuring that individuals have access to the electoral process—no matter what the color of a person's skin.

The philosophical foundation for Justice Thomas's individualistic approach to civil rights enforcement was most directly in evidence in a 1995 case involving the area of civil rights law with which he is most closely associated: affirmative action. In a concurring opinion in *Adarand Constructors, Inc. v. Peña,* Thomas maintained that affirmative action programs are inconsistent with the principles of the Declaration of Independence.[5] He wrote:

There can be no doubt that the paternalism that appears to lie at the heart of this [affirmative action] program is at war with the principle of inherent equality that underlies and infuses our Constitution. See Declaration of Independence ("We hold these truths to be self-evident, that all men are created equal, that they are endowed by their Creator with certain unalienable Rights, that among these are Life, Liberty, and the pursuit of Happiness.")

Later in his opinion, the justice explained why he was so committed to the individual rights orientation of the nation's founding document. And it was for the same reason he had articulated in his 1987 *Yale Law and Policy*

*Review* article on the subject. Thomas wrote in *Adarand*:

[Affirmative action] programs not only raise grave constitutional questions, they also undermine the moral basis of the equal protection principle. Purchased at the price of immeasurable human suffering, the equal protection principle reflects our Nation's understanding that such classifications ultimately have a destructive impact on the individual and our society. . . . [T]here can be no doubt that racial paternalism and its unintended consequences can be as poisonous and pernicious as any other form of discrimination. So-called "benign" discrimination teaches many that because of chronic and apparently immutable handicaps, minorities cannot compete with them without their patronizing indulgence. Inevitably, such programs engender attitudes of superiority or, alternatively, provoke resentment among those who believe that they have been wronged by the government's use of race. These programs stamp minorities with a badge of inferiority and may cause them to develop dependencies or to adopt an attitude that they are "entitled" to preferences.

## Conclusion

Clarence Thomas's "colorblind" approach to civil rights enforcement remains as controversial today as it was when he was nominated to the Supreme Court in 1991. For example, A. Leon Higginbotham Jr., a black federal judge and civil rights activist, took the unusual step in 1998 of trying to get Justice Thomas disinvited from the annual meeting of the National Bar Association, the nation's largest black lawyers' group. Judge Higginbotham's efforts were unsuccessful. In fact, Justice Thomas gave perhaps his most powerful speech at that meeting, a speech in which he defended his right to think for himself on all issues of public law, including civil rights. Many in the press agreed. Even the *Washington Post*—which had often criticized

the nation's highest-ranking black judge—defended Justice Thomas's right to disagree with the approach taken by the traditional civil rights community to the vexing problem of civil rights enforcement. The *Post* editorialized:

Justice Thomas's views on issues such as affirmative action are, though certainly conservative, well within the range of accepted American discourse. White people who advocate similar positions are not similarly shunned. . . . This notion that Justice Thomas's proper role on the court is as a representative of an ethnic constituency is nonsense. His job is to interpret the law and the Constitution as faithfully as he can, not to represent anybody. It should be no concession at all to hear his interpretations.

Justice Thomas remains as committed today as he was during his tenure at the EEOC and during his early years on the Supreme Court to the Declaration of Independence when trying to interpret the law and the Constitution—especially with regard to questions involving civil rights. Nowhere was the justice's continuing commitment to the Declaration more in evidence than in his February 9, 1999, Lincoln Day address to the Claremont Institute, a think tank dedicated to advancing the ideals of the nation's founding document. Justice Thomas closed that address with these words:

I began by urging that we learn from Lincoln and from Professor Jaffa, but learn what? Slavery is no longer with us. Yet as we stand on the threshold of the 21st Century, many of our fellow citizens have forgotten—or rather, our modern world has rejected—"the laws of Nature and Nature's God," against which the institution of slavery was so self-evidently wrong and against which we must judge our own generation's assault on the unalienable rights to property, to liberty and to life. . . . I urge you, Professor Jaffa, and others in this room, to be ever vigilant in reminding us—me and everyone else who has the privilege of serving our nation through public office—of the principles of our

Founding and how they apply to the controversies of our time. I challenge each of you to help us with the much more difficult task of charting the course that is most likely to vindicate the principles of the Declaration and to lead to the safety and happiness of this great and blessed people. Recognizing that sometimes the wise and prudent course is to compromise with our principles, and even to make alliance with those who have rejected or misunderstood them, help us know the difference between a prudent compromise that advances the cause of liberty and a capitulation on principle that snuffs it out.

## Notes

1. Thomas criticized at one time or other during his tenure at the EEOC virtually every decision the Supreme Court had issued in favor of affirmative action, including *Regents of the University of California v. Bakke* (1978), *United Steel Workers v. Weber* (1979), *Fullilove v. Klutznick* (1980), *Local 28, Sheet Metal Workers Union v. EEOC* (1986), *Local 93, Firefighters v. Cleveland* (1986), *United States v. Paradise* (1987), and *Johnson v. Transportation Agency, Santa Clara County, California* (1987).

2. Thomas testified in a similar fashion in his less widely publicized U.S. Court of Appeals confirmation hearing: "But recognizing that natural rights is a philosophical, historical context of the Constitution is not to say that I have abandoned the methodology of constitutional interpretation used by the Supreme Court. In applying the Constitution, I think I would have to resort to the approaches that the Supreme Court has used. I would have to look at the texture of the Constitution, the structure. I would have to look at the prior Supreme Court precedents."

3. At issue in *Jenkins* was a district judge's authority to impose the most ambitious and expensive public primary and secondary school desegregation plan in American history—that involving the Kansas City, Missouri, school district. The Supreme Court in a 5 to 4 decision held that the district judge had exceeded his remedial authority.

4. *Holder* involved a challenge by minority black voters to the sole commissioner form of government in Bleckley County, Georgia. The black plaintiffs claimed that Section 2 of the Voting Rights Act of 1965 and the Fourteenth and Fifteenth Amendments required Bleckley County to have a county commission of sufficient size that the county's black citizens would constitute a majority in a single-member district. The Supreme Court in a 5 to 4 decision disagreed.

5. *Adarand* involved an equal protection challenge by a white plaintiff construction subcontractor to a subcontractor compensation clause between a prime contractor and the defendant U.S. Department of Transportation regarding a federal highway project in Colorado. The affirmation action program at issue provided financial incentives to prime contractors to hire subcontractors controlled by "socially and economically disadvantaged individuals" and used race-based assumptions to identify such individuals. The Supreme Court in a 5 to 4 decision sided with the white plaintiff.

## Bibliography

Biden, Joseph R., Jr. "Law and Natural Law: Questions for Judge Thomas." *Washington Post,* September 8, 1991, C1, C4.

Gerber, Scott Douglas. *First Principles: The Jurisprudence of Clarence Thomas.* New York: New York University Press, 1999; exp. ed. 2002.

———. "Judging Thomas: The Politics of Assessing a Supreme Court Justice." *Journal of Black Studies* 27 (November 1996): 224–259.

———. "The Jurisprudence of Clarence Thomas." *Journal of Law and Politics* 8 (fall 1991): 107–141.

———. *To Secure These Rights: The Declaration of Independence and Constitutional Interpretation.* New York: New York University Press, 1995.

"Let Clarence Thomas Speak." *Washington Post,* June 20, 1998, A18.

Masugi, Ken. "Natural Right and Oversight: The Use and Abuse of 'Natural Law' in the Clarence Thomas Hearings." *Political Communication* 9 (October–December 1992): 231–233.

Mersky, Roy M., J. Myron Jacobstein, and Bonnie L. Koneski-White, eds. *The Supreme Court of the United States: Hearings and Reports on Successful and Unsuccessful Nominations of Supreme Court Justices by the Senate Judiciary Committee, 1916–1991.* Vol. 17A: *Clarence Thomas.* Buffalo: William S. Hein, 1995.

Rosen, Jeffrey. "Privacy in Public Places." *Cardozo Studies in Law and Literature* 12 (summer 2000): 167–191.

Thomas, Clarence. "Affirmative Action Goals and Timetables: Too Tough? Not Tough Enough!" *Yale Law and Policy Review* 5 (spring/summer 1987): 402–411.

_____. "Civil Rights as a Principle versus Civil Rights as an Interest." In *Assessing the Reagan Years.* Ed. David Boaz. Washington, D.C.: Cato Institute, 1988, 391–402.

_____. "The Equal Opportunity Commission: Reflections on a New Philosophy. *Stetson Law Review* 15 (fall 1985): 29–36.

_____. "The Higher Law Background of the Privileges or Immunities Clause of the Fourteenth Amendment." *Harvard Journal of Law and Public Policy* 12 (winter 1989): 63–68.

_____. Speech before the National Bar Association, July 29, 1998.

_____. "Toward a 'Plain Reading' of the Constitution—The Declaration of Independence in Constitutional Interpretation." *Howard Law Journal* 30:4 (1987): 983–995.

_____. "The Virtue of Practical Wisdom." Claremont Institute, February 9, 1999, www.claremont.org/publications/thomas2.cfm.

Tribe, Laurence H. " 'Natural Law' and the Nominee." *New York Times,* August 16, 1991, A15.

# 5

# The Declaration of Independence and the Articles of Confederation: A Completed Constitutional Covenant

## ROBERT W. HOFFERT

Taken together, the Declaration of Independence and the Articles of Confederation and Perpetual Union provide a completed constitutional covenant for the American people. They offer a set of formative principles, reflecting shared commitments, on which America as a nation (a people) and as a state (a government) was founded. While the Declaration is studied and revered, the Articles, presented to the American people in the late fall of 1777, is seldom remembered and even less understood. Its political principles are rarely connected with the document, its traditions, or the constitutional covenant it completed with the Declaration.

## The Second Continental Congress

The Second Continental Congress, which convened in Philadelphia in 1776, was the genesis of several actions important to America's political founding. First, in May, it called upon each colony to form its own government. Second, in early July, it issued the formal declaration of the colonies' political autonomy, the Declaration of Independence. Third, by mid-July, it had initiated the formation of a confederation and perpetual union among the newly independent states that was finalized on

November 15, 1777. The second of these actions has been the most remembered and celebrated, often without any reference to the Articles of Confederation. But it is neither irrelevant nor insignificant that the Declaration and the Articles were developed in a shared context of time, place, and circumstances by the same set of willful men. The documents, taken together, create the first constitutional system for the American nation and state.

The Declaration is a powerful statement of what America saw itself to be in 1776, and why Americans did what they did in founding their nation does not exhaust the rhetorical power of that document. The Declaration moves Americans today because in some fundamental ways it expresses what they assume America still is and should be. In this sense, it was in 1776 and remains more than 225 years later a "constitutional" document. Its constitutional character derives from its principles of nationhood and the continuing credibility they have for the American people whenever they interpret their past, whenever they organize their present, and whenever they anticipate their future. The Declaration's lack of explicit legal standing and specificity in describing institutional forms makes its moral and conceptual power more unexpected as well as more significant.

The Declaration of Independence is constitutional vis-à-vis the American nation; that is, it expresses the grounds for constituting the American people. This is especially important for colonial and revolutionary America, even if the document did not stipulate any formal government or state. One of its formative principles is that the state, all states, is to be established within a well-formed community. A proper political society had to be set up before proper political authority in government could be achieved. The Declaration of Independence represents the formation of a people, the American people. It gives form to the American nation. In this sense it is more than an eloquent rationale for specific political, military, and economic actions. It ties those actions to the essential need for a people to constitute themselves properly as a political community. Even as Thomas Jefferson delivered his first inaugural address as president in 1801, his sentiments were focused on the challenges of common purpose and affection central to the constitutional order of the Declaration: "We have called by different names brethren of the same principle. . . . Let us, then, fellow citizens, unite with one heart and one mind. Let us restore to social intercourse that harmony and affection without which liberty and even life itself are but dreary things."

## Constituting the American Nation

The Declaration of Independence asserts the political liberty of the American people. The Declaration describes the shared freedom of the community of Americans, not of its isolated individual members. Frequently, Americans use the proclamation of American national independence as a statement of their individual status as independent Americans, but this is not the constitutional message of the Declaration. The document offers the unambiguous declaration of liberty for a united people in thirteen united states. The unanimous ratification and amendment provisions of the Articles, for example, directly extend the spirit and letter of that principle of national liberty.

The Declaration is eloquent in its directness and simplicity. It presents presuppositions, evidence, and conclusions. In the first two paragraphs, the presuppositions of the American position are expressed. Rebellion involves more than a formal, abstract right to rebel. A mere right of rebellion could be exercised whenever any offenses or violations occur. The Declaration, however, limits itself to those specific circumstances that force a people to take the drastic step of political dissociation—a pattern in the course of human events that leaves a people with only the protections of their natural status. To be sure, "the separate and equal station to which the Laws of Nature and Nature's God entitle them" provides the basis for a right to rebel, but the exercising of that right must be fully warranted by historical conditions and must be readily explainable to all humanity. It should show "a decent respect to the opinions of mankind."

The Declaration assumes the relevance of self-evident truths, which has complex theoretical implications. It suggests a natural order or, more precisely, an accessible natural order. When a people hold to the form and principles of this order as if they were self-evident, they will be committed to making those principles effective in forming the life of their political community.

The holding of self-evident truths by a people also implies an inherent equality. If truths are self-evident, they are knowable because of the shared harmony that exists among nature, human nature, and the nature of all particular humans. Thus, the most fundamental truths are characterized not as the discoveries of esoteric reasonings but as knowledge—equally available to all—of one's own being. As historian Gary Wills has argued, Jefferson was probably attracted to the Scottish Enlightenment's philosophy of moral sense, in part, because egalitarianism was an essential ingredient in its vision. Francis Hutcheson, a leader of the Scottish Enlightenment, for example, believed in universal access to virtue embedded in human nature and based on internal senses of affection, benevolence, and fellow feeling.

The initial self-evident truth asserted by the Declaration is that "all men are created equal." This is not an equality of particular characteristics or of historical circumstances, but of essence or intrinsic worth. Regarding those things that make people human and constitute the essence of their humanity, each is another's equal. This means that no natural basis exists for the authority of some persons over other persons. In historical terms, this natural equality provides the proper basis for democratic authority—the equal empowerment of all members of a political community in constituting the legitimate authority of that community.

Furthermore, the form of equality referred to in the Declaration is substantive, not procedural. It describes something essential about what every human being is. It does not describe the environment or procedural conditions within which they live in nature or civil society. The assertion that people are equal, for example, is a different political claim with different implications than an assertion that each person should have equal opportunity. Politically, equal opportunity is not about persons, but about the circumstances within which people live. The fundamental political value protected by equal opportunity is freedom, not substantive equality. The equal station of all persons, however, asserts a different reality, gives primacy to a different political value, and encourages a different set of practical political implications than does equal opportunity. It asserts something intrinsic and common about every human being.

The Declaration also says that nature has imbued human beings with unalienable rights. The differences between an unalienable right and an alienable right can be seen in the differences between a natural right and a civil right. The former is a direct consequence of humanity; the latter is a consequence of political association and citizenship. The former can be violated, but it never can be legitimately taken away because it is an intrinsic, common part of human nature. The latter can be violated, but it also can legitimately be taken away in the same way it was given—by how a civil society defines itself.

The Declaration does more than grant all persons an equal claim to basic human rights. It identifies a context in which government and politics are to be limited by and answerable to principles beyond their own authority and control. Natural rights define much more than a basis for individual choices. They give form to the most basic characteristics of a proper association of people who are guided by nature. In this sense, natural rights express a framework for order more than for choice. They define options more than they give them. The political community must conform to the authentic principles of nature and must resist and overcome the arbitrariness of power, history, and personal volition.

The specific unalienable rights cited by the Declaration are life, liberty, and the pursuit of happiness. These rights simultaneously express duties. They are not authorizations for personal discretion. They reflect the structure of human nature and identify social responsibilities that correspond with that nature. Humans have a natural duty to honor their life and to stay free in word and deed. Their pursuit of happiness is neither undefined nor self-defined. Jefferson presented natural law in the form of a natural right. When the laws of nature are seen as rights, humans can act freely and purposefully, knowing that their deeds are in concert with the natural order. The discovery of what humans should pursue simultaneously confirms their obligation to pursue it. The pursuit of happiness, therefore, is not a vague or idealistic concept, and it is not rooted in assumptions of atomistic individualism or privacy. The pursuit of happiness is about the public scale of political actions sanctioned by nature.

Governments are empowered by the consent of the governed to protect these natural rights, which is also to say that governments have a duty to serve the common good. Consequently, when a government acts against the will of the people or against the laws of nature, the people must act to alter or abolish it and to institute a new government that will appropriately secure their safety and happiness. In other words, the people should install a government that will protect their rights to life, liberty, and the pursuit of happiness.

For Jefferson, the interplay of transient historical conditions and enduring natural patterns should not invite categorical responses. That is, he does not encourage outrage or authorize reactions to merely accidental, fortuitous, or incidental acts—only to intentional and essential ones. Thus, when a sustained pattern of an unjust intent against a people is evident, "it is their right, it is their duty, to throw off such Government." Jefferson emphasizes the role of patterns, not of mere incidents, in history as well as in nature. And he underscores the intimate relationship between rights and duties that arises within these patterns. Natural rights identify fundamental natural patterns, making them dutiful as well. And as duties they authorize rights. Either way, they express the primary principles, patterned by nature, necessary for personal and communal well-being.

Having developed the presuppositions for his case, Jefferson turns to the relevant evidence—the patterns of abuse by King George III indicating malevolent intentions against the American people. The evidentiary case is not based on any particular offense or even the magnitude constituted by the sum of offenses, but on the intent shown through specific actions and the unjust design of the pattern of behavior that emerges. The despotic intent of England against the colonies had four essential characteristics: (1) the Crown acted against reasonable understandings of the public good; (2) the Crown took no guidance and accepted no restraint from representatives of the people; (3) the Crown assumed authority without consent; and (4) the Crown pursued a strategy of political corruption that denied the colonists the benefits of their own virtuous community. The colonists made repeated requests for redress of these grievances, but they received only renewed injury.

In the penultimate paragraph of the Declaration, Jefferson expresses a radical dimension of the colonial rebellion. He claims that the colonists have an even more fundamental quarrel than the one generated by the pattern of the Crown's governmental abuses. If the abuses of the Crown constituted the full dispute, the colonial rebellion would have been that of Englishmen attempting to reconstitute proper British governmental authority. Instead, the colonists took exception to both the British state and the British nation; that is, its government and its people. They declared themselves to be a new, free people—Americans. The Declaration insists that every kind of appeal to the "native justice and magnanimity" of their "British brethren" was made to no effect. Neither justice nor natural affinity was able to move citizens in England to challenge these abuses. Therefore, the colonists had to separate themselves from the British people every bit as much as from the British government, declaring themselves a new and independent nation—the people of the United States of America.

The Declaration's conclusion is a moving statement of the American national covenant. Appealing to the "Supreme Judge" of the world—nature—Jefferson seeks verification of "the rectitude of their [the colonists'] intentions." The American people as well as their representatives must take the monumental step of declaring independence on a proper moral footing. Their course of action must be designed for the purposes of the common good through the consent of a virtuous people. It was not an assertion of metaphysical presumption for them to claim a firm reliance on the protections of "Divine Providence" because providential intent was fully intelligible in the self-evident truths of the natural order.

The riddle at the center of the Articles of Confederation is how can a perpetually united people (the nation of the Declaration) be formed through fragmented formal authority (the states of the Articles)? By the Declaration, the colonies are declared free and independent states with all the powers properly assigned to sovereign states. The authority that establishes the autonomy of these separate governmental units is one united, virtuous people—"the good People of these Colonies." These independent states are created by a united people and are bound to a perpetual union on the grounds of the most fundamental natural principles.

The Declaration of Independence, by itself, is an incomplete constitutional covenant for American political life. It was, however, a political covenant for the American people; the American nation. It offered principles of virtue tied to human nature through the universal efficacy of natural affections; principles of sociability directed by natural unity, whose test was equal justice; principles of natural rights serving as responsibilities in a society that honors nature and that protects individuals in a community; principles of popular consent; principles of full and proper representation; and principles of civic virtue. These principles were essential to a national covenant that constituted the uncoerced unity of a free people.

## Constituting the American Government: Draft Versions

The American people, through their representatives in the Second Continental Congress, turned to the principles in the Declaration to complete their constitutional covenant by forming a government. Whether or not one agrees with the choices of these representatives, they clearly made decisions with direction and intent and from a full range of political options, including ones closely akin to those that would be in the constitutional document of 1787. For example, Benjamin Franklin drafted a charter of union for the colonies, which he submitted in July 1775, before Congress had appointed a committee to draft articles of confederation. Franklin's draft proposed a government based on centralized sovereign power. The governmental form that would be stipulated in the Constitution of 1787 thus was known, expressed, and preferred by some Americans before the Articles appeared in draft form. The failure of Franklin's proposal to generate support also suggests the strength of an alternative theoretical view that saw centralized, coercive authority as contrary to a proper governmental foundation for the American people.

In 1776, thirteen men were appointed to an official drafting committee charged with proposing a governmental design for the new nation. They presented their document to Congress on July 12, 1776. The balance of power was in the hands of members with more socially and economically conservative interests who preferred formal and centralized organizations of political authority. Two were fence sitters, Roger Sherman of Connecticut and

Josiah Bartlett of New Hampshire, and two represented the dominant popular political perspectives of the revolutionary American nation, Stephen Hopkins of Rhode Island and Samuel Adams of Massachusetts. The other committee members were oriented to views less local, less participatory, less majoritarian, and less consensually based than those that eventually dominated the process.

John Dickinson of Delaware, as chair, was able to steer the committee's proceedings. He was the primary author of the draft proposal, which made the organization of the central government the basis for defining the rights, powers, and duties of the separate states. However, the proposal included a general clause that granted each state "as much of its present Laws, Rights and Customs, as it may think fit, and reserves to itself the sole and exclusive Regulation and Government of its internal police, in all matters that shall not interfere into the Articles of Confederation." States were to maintain militia and appoint commissioned officers for troops serving the common defense, and they could lay imposts if they did not violate any treaty provisions. No other powers were reserved for the states. Moreover, Article III limits state powers to those matters and applications that will not interfere with the operation of the Articles. Thus, in Dickinson's draft, state powers were limited in number, based on grants from the central government, and restricted in their potential range.

The draft contained only one significant restraint on Congress: It could not directly tax citizens. Other restrictions required three-fourth majorities for certain specified actions, such as declaring war, and prohibited congressional interference in a state's internal policing when it was unrelated to the functioning of the Articles' provisions. Congress and the central authority held the stronger grants of power and the theoretical balance of power in the draft proposal. Dickinson's draft is significant because it presented a governmental model balanced much like that of the 1787 Constitution. Thus, together with the effort of Franklin a year earlier, the political options of 1787 were prominent among the political alternatives of 1776. They were knowingly turned aside.

Through the reworking of the draft proposal, the states came to hold fundamental authority and Congress acts by specific grants of power from them. The Continental Congress changed eighteen subject matter areas of the Dickinson draft. Some of these changes enhanced the role of the central government, but most were designed to strengthen accountability or to make adjustments to accommodate the overall diminishment of central authority (for example, treaty and military powers). The most significant changes uniformly weakened the authority and role of the central government and correspondingly strengthened those of the states.

By August 20, 1776, Congress agreed to proceed with the second draft version of the Articles of Confederation. As historian Merrill Jensen noted many years ago, the constitutional process then focused on four unresolved issues: (1) the equal representation of all states in Congress, (2) the basis for the apportionment of common expenses, (3) the grant of powers to the central government over western lands, and (4) the distribution of power between the states and Congress. The fourth issue, regarding sovereignty, was resolved quickly and pointedly. Formal coercive authority was to be held by each individual state.

The issue of state representation in Congress was considerably more complicated than the practical problem of balancing larger and smaller states. What kind of union was the United States to be? If it was to be a single national state, more compromise and experimentation were possible in arranging state representation in Congress. However, if it was to be an alliance of independent states, each state had to be equally represented, regardless of differences in land holdings, populations, or economic strength. Was this to be a perpetual unity of government or, as claimed in the Declaration, a union of the people? In the end, the natural interests of the smaller states and the principles of a group of men committed to keeping coercive powers on a short tether decided the issue. They wanted and got a federal union of sovereign states, not a national government.

The need to determine each state's fiscal obligation to the common treasury was an issue of considerable material interest but one with fewer direct theoretical stakes. The position offered by Dickinson was that the states should pay in proportion to their total populations, excluding Indians, who did not pay taxes. The counterproposal was for an apportionment system based on land values. The New England states, assuming that their lands were much more valuable than the lands of other states, objected to any land-based value system. In the end, a land value criterion was adopted, and it posed no unique stumbling block to ratification in New England.

The genuinely acrimonious disagreements were concentrated in the debates on control of western lands. The states without western lands or land claims wanted authority over these lands to rest with Congress. They wanted to establish the principle that all public lands lying outside the jurisdiction of any state should belong to the United States through Congress. The states holding western lands wanted to continue their control. To them, giving Congress control over these lands was paramount to creating a domestic equivalent of British rule. Dickinson's first draft supported the states lacking western land claims. But by October 1777, in the final draft of the Articles, the states with western lands secured constitutional guarantees against the claims of other states and of land speculators working through land companies.

The debates over these issues were not a pure pursuit of fundamental principles. Yet high principles may have had a role greater than imagined. For example, the western lands issue was one of material interests—landed states fearing the piracy of landless states, and landless states fearing the opportunism of landed states. As a question of self-interest, no clear grounds existed to settle the issue. Neither side had compelling moral leverage, and there was a near stalemate of practical power among them. Both sides used common interest arguments to bolster their claims, and in both cases their rhetoric lacked broadly persuasive credibility. Nevertheless, in one respect the landed states had an argument of theoretical significance to the political covenant initiated by the Declaration. Their position coincided with the strong commitment to limit the formal powers of government beyond the control of the people within each state.

The most fundamental political principle addressed during the writing of the Articles was that of sovereignty. Would it be plural, centered in each state, or singular, centered in

Congress? According to Jensen's classifications, "conservatives" favored a single sovereign with "superintending power over states and citizens." They saw this political form as one that would encourage the more active development of the Union, especially its economic development. "Radicals" saw their political battle as a struggle against coercive, central power, in their conflicts with the British and, equally, with the colonial governing class and economic elites. Their political goal was captured by the Declaration: a union based on consent and trust. For them, governmental decentralization was a noble and inspiring experiment that permitted a large-scale, enduring union to be achieved through persuasion and friendship.

Centralized, coercive authority had been the essence of economic and political life in the colonies. It had moved the American people to rebellion. The most powerful expression of this rebel opposition was the Declaration—the democratic doctrine of a sovereign people. The political base, not the top or, even, the center should be empowered, and governmentally the people should be organized as independent states. Challengers anticipated this arrangement and developed arguments against it. Ever since the United States claimed independence, the issue of the relationship between state governments and a common central government has been and remains at the center of American political disputes.

John Adams argued correctly that the principle of popular sovereignty does not settle the choice between a single sovereign state and a number of confederated sovereign states. The basic division became one between those who called for a federated governmental solution within a confederacy and those who wanted a national governmental solution. Partisans of both options milked the issue of popular sovereignty, but the real choice was how the sovereignty of the people was to be organized governmentally—federally or nationally.

Thomas Burke of North Carolina saw that Article III not only jeopardized the political independence of the states but also threatened to consolidate effective governance in one centralized form. To counter this national government solution, he proposed an amendment giving the Articles the federal character that became so appealing to its eventual supporters. His amendment stated that "all sovereign power was in the states separately, and that particular acts of it, which should be expressly enumerated, would be exercised in conjunction, and not otherwise; but that in all things else each State would exercise all rights and power of sovereignty, uncontrolled." This amendment is expressed as Article II in the final version of the Articles. Its approach authorized two levels of government: original authority vested in the political base and delegated authority in the political center.

## Constituting the American Government: The Articles of Confederation

As is the case with the 1787 Constitution (see Chapter 6), the Articles of Confederation is dominated with discussions of governmental structures and governmental powers. Neither document is theoretically explicit; that is, neither specifies the assumptions and values upon which the organization of those structures and powers is based. Thus, to understand better the theoretical character of the Articles, the fol-

lowing questions are considered: What political assumptions and aspirations in the Articles would serve as a basis for an effective and desirable form of government? What constitutional principles in the Articles would lead to an effective and just political order for the people who had united themselves through the Declaration of Independence?

The Articles establishes a federal system or confederacy that is described as "a firm league of friendship" among sovereign states forming a "perpetual union." A paradoxical interplay exists between Article II and Article XIII. On the one hand, "[e]ach State retains its sovereignty, freedom and independence," and on the other hand, "[e]very State shall abide by the determinations of the United States, in Congress assembled, on all questions which, by this confederation, are submitted to them. And the articles of confederation shall be inviolably observed by every State, and the union shall be perpetual."

The governmental form of this perpetual union is skeletal. The Articles authorizes legislative structures and administrative structures and implies certain judicial-like forms. The primary legislative body is a unicameral Congress. Representatives to this Congress are selected annually by each state. Each state may determine the number of delegates it wishes to send to Congress within a specified range of at least two and no more than seven. No representative may serve for more than three years in any period of six consecutive years. Each state has the authority to recall any of its representatives during his year of appointment and make replacements if it chooses. No state representative may hold a simultaneous office in the U.S. government or receive compensation from the

United States. All representatives enjoy the protections of free speech and debate in Congress and protections from arrest and imprisonment while going to and from sessions of Congress except for reasons of treason, felony, or breach of the peace. Whenever the United States "in Congress assembled" acts to decide a question, each state is limited to one vote.

The Articles also specifies the creation of a secondary legislative body, "a Committee of the States." This committee may be appointed by Congress to sit during congressional recesses and consists of one delegate from each state. The committee shall execute any of Congress's simple majority powers, which has been explicitly invested in the committee by action of at least nine states. One member of the committee shall be appointed to preside as president, but no one shall serve in the office of president for more than one year during any period of three consecutive years.

Although Congress shall be able to adjourn any time within a year and may convene at any place within the United States, no period of adjournment may be longer than six months. Conversely, no period of authorization for a Committee of the State may last longer than six months. Congress must also publish a monthly journal of its proceedings and must include roll-call votes on any question if requested by any delegate.

The Articles creates a quasi-judicial structure to accommodate the responsibilities of Congress in disputes between two or more states. In all such disputes concerning "boundary, jurisdiction or any other cause whatever," Congress is the last resort on appeal. The manner in which Congress's authority shall be exercised in such cases is specified in elaborate detail.

In addition, the Articles contains several other features important to its general form and operation. Canada shall be admitted to full advantages of the Union if it ever wishes to do so. All other colonies shall be admitted only after the agreement of nine states. All bills of credit, borrowed monies, and debts contracted by the Continental Congress will be considered charges against the Union, and a solemn public pledge will be given that they will be fully paid and satisfied. Finally, an amendment procedure is specified that requires the agreement of Congress and confirmation by the legislature of each state.

Although each state is asserted to be sovereign, some general standards of conduct serve as restraints upon the states even though they are not delegated powers to Congress. These restraining, nondelegated standards of conduct are consistent with conditions necessary to honor a perpetual union of friends. For example, Article IV introduces its specifications with a statement of rationale: "The better to secure and perpetuate mutual friendship and intercourse among the people of the different states in this union."

These specified standards of mutual friendship have several dimensions. "Privileges and immunities" protect all free inhabitants of each state; in short, the rights of citizenship are honored from state to state. The people of each state shall have free ingress and regress to any other state, and they shall have the same privileges of trade and commerce as the inhabitants of any particular state. All states must honor extradition requests for persons guilty of or charged with "treason, felony, or other high misdemeanors" in any other state. And "full faith and credit shall be given in each of these states to the records, acts, and judicial proceedings of the courts and magistrates of every other State." Whenever states are authorized to raise land forces, the state legislatures must appoint all officers under the rank of colonel. And all states are charged with maintaining a well-regulated and disciplined militia.

In addition to the delineation of things each state must do, the Articles lists things each state is prohibited from doing. Some of these prohibitions are absolute and others are conditional. The absolute prohibitions include the following: No state may lay imports or duties that interfere with or violate any operative U.S. treaty; no title of nobility may be granted; and no governmental officer may accept any compensation or entitlements from any foreign government. All conditional prohibitions that limit the powers and actions of the states can be modified by explicit actions of the U.S. Congress.

Powers delegated to the United States in Congress assembled are of two types—those consisting of sole and exclusive rights and powers and those of last resort on appeals. Congress is designated as the last resort on appeals regarding all present and future disputes between two or more states. Also, all disputes concerning private rights of soil claimed under the different governments of two or more states will be settled on last resort by appeal of either party to Congress.

Congress is granted sole and exclusive rights and powers to determine the conditions for peace, to declare war, to send and receive ambassadors, to enter into treaties and alliances, to establish rules for legal confiscations and their appropriation, to grant letters of marque and reprisal in peace, to appoint courts to try piracy and high seas felonies, and to determine

appeals in all cases of captures. It has similarly exclusive authorizations in a number of regulatory areas: setting the alloy and value of coins struck through its own action or those of the states, fixing standards of weights and measures, managing trade and other affairs with Indians not residing in any state, establishing a post office and postage system, appointing all officers of land forces excepting regimental officers and all naval officers, and managing the regulation and direction of all land and naval forces.

The most significant and general power granted to Congress is the authority to determine all charges of war, all expenses for common defense, and all expenses for the general welfare. Costs of these authorizations are to be defrayed from a common treasury supplied by the states. The states, in turn, are to be charged in proportion to the value of each state's land. Congress shall specify both the manner by which the value of land shall be estimated and the time period within which states shall raise the tax revenues necessary to establish the common treasury of the United States.

The Articles of Confederation created a truncated set of governmental structures, a somewhat more amplified set of authorizations and processes, and a singular, explicit purpose—to form the governmental basis for a perpetual union of the American people. To make theoretical sense of this order, a process of induction is needed. What are the values, assumptions, and theoretical perspectives necessary to encourage the creation, adoption, and commitment to the constitutional scheme offered by the Articles?

The Articles is simultaneously committed to the pursuit of sovereign statehood and to a perpetual union of these sovereign states. Neither purpose is ingenious or expendable. The challenge is to identify the theoretical basis for sovereign states and for the formation of a perpetual association by members of those states—the Declaration of Independence's unified "good People" organized in "Free and Independent States."

## A Completed Constitutional Covenant: The Declaration and the Articles

The theoretical basis of a completed constitutional covenant is found in the initial constitutional covenant framed by the Declaration. Specifically, the Declaration provides a natural foundation for a national community. As an extension of that covenant from the American people to the American state, the Articles resonates with the assumptions of a covenanted community already in place. The creation of a constitutional state is not the foundation for constituting the nation; rather the constitutional nation is the foundation for constituting an appropriately complementary state.

The sense of community in the Articles is reflected in different forms. Primary communities are represented within the states. States represent the optimal context for meaningful, direct self-definition by the people in communities of natural coherence. Thus, states are, as well, the units of formal sovereignty. Their freedom and independence must be protected not as a telos of the state but as an essential condition for properly constituted communities of the people. Within states, political communities come to life and express themselves, so this is where formal constituting authority is centered as well.

At the same time, the Articles implies that states are not the fullest expression of the people's national unity. A national community is possible and essential. However, the purpose of the national community is not to deny or replace the primary communities of the states, but to organically extend them into broader and more integrative spheres of national life. The evidence in the Articles of a distinction between a state as a community and the nation as a community is keyed to the construction of formal authority: States are the centers of formal authority and coercive powers; the nation has delegated responsibilities and must act largely through informal moral power and persuasion. In other words, the Articles implements the tacit perspective of the Declaration: States do not represent the fullest expression of the desirable national community, but they do constitute the fullest expression of the people attainable through the specifically governmental functions of the people.

In both the Declaration and the Articles, states represent the practical limits of coercive authority and formal structural definition. They are invested with coercive authority not because they are the most extensive form of the national community but because creating a genuinely democratic nation requires limits on coercion. States are the most extensive political structures within which a free people can define themselves without creating a public order indifferent to natural virtue and liberty. In the lexicon of the Articles of Confederation, the most unambiguous expression of formal, coercive authority is "sovereignty." That both the Declaration and the Articles aspire to a perpetual unity beyond the reach of state sovereignty underscores the limits to sovereignty, formal authority, and the devices of state control that framed their constitutional covenant.

The Declaration and the Articles express a vision of and commitment to a national community that will be more integrative than the communities offered by any sovereign state. They thus reflect the assumption that this national community will not be and, by implication, should not be the consequence of formal, coercive authority. Instead, this national community is to be the by-product of natural principles and sentiments. Ultimately, a covenanted people form a community of allies "to secure and perpetuate mutual friendship and intercourse among the people of the different states in this union." Neither the Articles nor the Declaration lacks a vision of a comprehensive national community, and neither lacks a genuine commitment to that vision. However, both expect that the community will be given by the people themselves and not taken from them or imposed on them by governmental power.

This willingness to allow the most comprehensive political goal to evolve within an environment of friendship and trust reflects the basic assumptions about the nature of politics and the nature of humanity articulated in the Declaration. It suggests that an organic order is assumed to underlie history, civilization, and human contrivance. It further suggests that if access to this natural order is not blocked or hidden because of the false and artificial limits imposed by formal authority acting beyond its proper span, a free people will emulate its harmonies. Thus, the fundamental challenge is to establish a constitutional basis for the political principles essential to the vitality of that natural order. Building a democratic, national community is based on the strengthening of per-

suasive power through trust, common purpose, and friendship in the spontaneous life of a virtuous people. From this view, the American state is never the basis for the American people's unity, virtue, and freedom; the American people's unity, virtue, and freedom are the bases for the American state.

The Articles extends the centrality of the Declaration's principle of equality. The inherent natural equality of each person necessitates the equality of primary communities into which these individuals have organized themselves. This is another reason that coercive authority at the national level is not endorsed. There is no substantive basis or procedural technique by which hierarchies of power may be established among the communities of equals in each of the states. In addition to endorsing the value credited to each community that joins together in constituting the nation, egalitarianism and communalism underlie the Articles of Confederation's provisions for annual elections, limited terms, and recalls. True, they reflect suspicion, if not distrust, of persons with formal grants of power. But they also reflect more positive attitudes and possibilities. They imply that the effective defense against the political abuses of power is an attentive, remedial community.

The Declaration's foundation for nationhood becomes the foundation for statehood as well in the Articles. The proper governance of America does not require the special skills of any particular subgroup within society. Neither a class of hereditary rulers nor a natural aristocracy is needed or wanted to supply political leadership. Instead, a vital community guided by nature will provide a continuing supply of able citizens. Exceptional contributions of individuals uncommitted to the community are feared and discouraged. Trust is in the large and self-replenishing stock of persons rooted in and nurtured by a wholesome natural community.

The letter drafted to accompany the Articles to the states highlights the riddle of the Articles, the same riddle initially brought into view through the Declaration: unity based on wholesome intent, not coerced control. The purpose of the Articles was to complete the constitutional covenant initiated by the Declaration by forming an appropriate governmental structure for the "perpetual union" of the American people. Achieving this end among states with so many differences of habit and circumstance requires time, reflection, and a disposition of conciliation, not the heavy hand of authority and coercion. Pleading for support, the letter insists that ratification is "essential to our very existence as a free people, and without it we may soon be constrained to bid adieu to independence, to liberty and safety."

The ratification process reflects the domination of the national covenant articulated by the Declaration and the coherence of the companion governmental covenant offered by the Articles. Ratification was supported, and the most vigorously expressed reservations of principle were those advocating even greater decentralization of government's coercive capacities.

Most states acted expeditiously in ratifying the Articles, suggesting strong popular support for the theoretical basis of its governmental forms. Within about eight months, ten of the states had instructed delegates to support ratification. Maryland, Delaware, and New Jersey were the holdouts united by a concern about the western lands question. The latter two took

exception to the provisions leaving western lands questions to the jurisdiction of individual states. They opposed this specific delegation of state sovereignty, not the principle of state sovereignty itself. In the end, they voluntarily consented and joined in confirming the most fundamental principle of America's national and governmental covenant: confidence in the good will and integrity of the people acting through independent states to reach voluntary agreements about national purpose.

Maryland went through a protracted ratification process, but it never challenged any fundamental constitutional principle central to either the Declaration or the Articles. Its reluctance to ratify expressed a prudent concern of landless states about the unguided intentions and actions of states with extensive western land holdings. Western land claims represented historical accidents that threatened to unbalance the harmonies of nature.

Maryland's inaction did not prevent the de facto implementation of the Articles of Confederation's constitutional order. Between 1776 and 1781 the Continental Congress and the thirteen states conducted American military, economic, and political affairs by the standards and through the forms specified by the Articles. The final ratification of the Articles in 1781, therefore, unlike the contrived ratification of the Constitution of 1787 in 1789, did not initiate divergent governmental processes on the basis of political principles shaped by new assumptions and purposes. Instead, it gave de jure status to the de facto forms of governance and principle already in effect. The fact that ratification represented the formalization of accepted functioning patterns only strengthens the practical credibility of the Articles's commitment to noncoercive governmental solutions. This commitment reflected a high ideal, but not one without known, concrete form and practical everyday successes.

Together, the Declaration of Independence and the Articles of Confederation provide a completed constitutional covenant. They offer a covenant because both documents build on shared commitments; their covenant is constitutional because both documents use these shared commitments to express fundamental formative principles; and their constitutional covenant is completed because together they offer a covenanted constitution of the American nation and the American state.

Articulating what the Articles is not helps distinguish it from the Constitution of 1787 and underscores its direct affinity to the Declaration of Independence. The Articles does not center its attention on autonomous individuals. This does not mean that it does not care about liberty. On the contrary, the Articles specifically mentions the securing of liberties as a primary purpose of the confederated league of friendship. The liberty it wishes to secure, as with the Declaration, is that of the states. Both the Articles and the Declaration pursue traditions of liberty that are available to humans as a consequence of their membership in human communities.

The Declaration does not present a nation beset with the tensions of conflicting interests. Similarly, the Articles does not provide a system of governance well suited to the dominance of competitive self-interests. This is not to say that competitive self-interests will or will not arise and dominate, but if they do the Articles is not designed to govern effectively. The language of friendship, mutuality, and communality sets the document's tone. And the ex-

pectation of cooperative accommodation is assumed to be the basis for operations within the governmental structures and the political authorizations it provides.

James Madison's metaphorical description of the 1787 Constitution as an order-producing machine is a significant departure from the perspectives of the Declaration and Articles. The Articles finds the most fundamental basis for order where Jefferson did in the Declaration—in nature. Order, especially a humanly designed and achieved order, is not at the center of its politics. For better or worse, the Articles is not a project dependent on human artifice and invention. It is better read as an attempt to establish an environment within which the authentic order of nature can be reestablished and properly expressed. It offers a political framework that puts citizens in touch with one another instead of contriving an endless array of isolating and fragmenting contexts for political life. It is more hopeful than fearful. It anticipates the vitalization of a natural order; it does not manufacture an order that will either stabilize naturally destabilizing factors or compensate for natural deficiencies or inconveniences. Consistent with the claims of the Declaration of Independence, the Articles encourages confidence in the ordering possibilities of human life in community as informed by the intrinsic structures of nature.

Both the Declaration and the Articles express a positive and vital nationhood even though both committed themselves to free and independent states. One does not authorize a united, good people, or insist on a perpetual union, or assert an inviolable observation of Congress's acts by sovereign states if one does not invest the national association with great substantive value. Both documents insist that the test of their national commitment cannot be their dependence on centralized, coercive governmental authority, but their deep confidence in a community of friends guided by nature.

Assuming that the Articles was written and supported by people who believed it would result in a proper and workable polity, nothing is more helpful in identifying the coherent values, assumptions, and principles that supported their approach than to remember its direct association with the Declaration of Independence. The completed covenant offered to American politics by these two constitutional documents results in a democratic theory that emphasizes community and community building, the equality of people in community, and the value and validity of intrinsic and spontaneous principles in the pursuit of justice and the common good. The Articles offers a frame-work for the American state focused and balanced differently from the one offered by the 1787 Constitution. Nevertheless, it does represent a practical, governmental extension of the community-focused ideals in America's original national covenant, the Declaration of Independence, and in America's complex, self-conscious process of choosing and shaping political independence.

## Bibliography

Adams, Willi Paul. *The First American Constitutions*. Chapel Hill: University of North Carolina Press, 1980.

Dougherty, Keith L. *Collective Action under the Articles of Confederation*. New York: Cambridge University Press, 2001.

Hoffert, Robert W. *A Politics of Tensions: The Articles of Confederation and American Political Ideas*. Niwot: University Press of Colorado, 1992.

Jensen, Merrill, *The Articles of Confederation*. Madison: University of Wisconsin Press, 1940.

# 6

# The Declaration of Independence, the U.S. Constitution, and the Bill of Rights

## Thomas G. West

American constitutionalism is grounded in the principles of the Declaration of Independence. These principles do not dictate any specific constitutional design. They provide a broad outline of the structure and purposes of government. The ends of government are absolute and unchanging. The means are not. The specifics must be worked out by prudent statesmen. Prudence was evident in the founding era, as state and federal constitutions were written and rewritten. Politicians groped and reasoned their way to a constitutional order that would secure the individual rights of citizens on the basis of government by consent of the governed.

In his letter transmitting the proposed Constitution to the Confederation Congress, George Washington, the presiding officer of the Constitutional Convention of 1787, wrote, "Individuals entering into society, must give up a share of liberty to preserve the rest. . . . It is at all times difficult to draw with precision the line between those rights which must be surrendered, and those which may be reserved." With these words, Washington alluded to the social compact theory of the Declaration, according to which human beings in a state of nature have a natural right to liberty, some of which they conditionally delegate to govern-

ment for the better security of their inalienable rights.

James Wilson was a leading member of the Constitutional Convention of 1787. In a speech in the Pennsylvania Ratifying Convention, he quoted the whole second paragraph of the Declaration (beginning with "We hold these truths to be self-evident") and then said, defending the proposed Constitution, "This is the broad basis on which our independence was placed; on the same certain and solid foundation this system is erected."

Washington's and Wilson's belief that the new Constitution was guided by the principles of the Declaration is widely disputed today. Pauline Maier, in *American Scripture: Making the Declaration of Independence,* asserts: "Not only did its reference to men's equal creation concern people in a state of nature before government was established, but the document's original function was to end the previous regime, not to lay down principles to guide and limit its successor." Maier's view that the Declaration was not meant to guide the government of the newly born United States is contradicted by the leading founders and documents of the period. Most authoritatively, the affirmations of individual rights at the beginning of several state declarations of rights, which echoed and amplified the principles of the Declaration of Independence, were understood as guides and limits to government. The founders agreed with the preamble of the Massachusetts Constitution of 1780, authored by John Adams: "The end of . . . government, is to secure the existence of the body-politic; to protect it; and to furnish the individuals who compose it, with the power of enjoying, in safety and tranquillity, their natural rights, and the blessings of life. The body-politic is formed by a voluntary association of individuals: It is a social compact."

At the time of the Constitutional Convention of 1787, it was accepted that government exists, in the words of the Declaration of Independence, "to secure these rights," namely, the "unalienable Rights" among which "are Life, Liberty, and the pursuit of Happiness." However, unlike some of the state constitutions, the U.S. Constitution of 1787 does not explicitly mention natural rights and the social compact. This was for two reasons.

First, as Edmund Randolph remarked at the convention, a "display of theory, howsoever proper in the first formation of state governments, is unfit here; since we are not working on the natural rights of man not yet gathered into society." Randolph meant that because Americans were already organized into political communities (states), the new federal Constitution would not require any repetition of the theory of government already announced in the state constitutions and the Declaration of Independence.

Second, although plenty of high-sounding talk was heard about first principles in the exhilaration surrounding 1776, too little hard-headed thinking was done about what institutional arrangements would best protect the equal rights of all. The founders were tempted to think that it would be easy to set up a republican government that protects the rights of all. As John Adams wrote in 1774, expressing the extravagant hopes of the day, "a democratical despotism is a contradiction in terms." By the 1780s, Adams and the other founders knew better. A "democratical despotism" had become an embarrassing reality in several states, most notably Rhode Island. Prominent men began to wonder out loud whether democracy—government by elected representatives—could be reconciled with the public order and decency necessary to secure the rights of all citizens. Many of those at the convention shared these concerns. They were alarmed and disgusted by the misconduct of state governments in the 1780s. Yet many of these state constitutions had proclaimed, with all solemnity, the natural rights of mankind. In *The Federalist* (No. 84), Alexander Hamilton sarcastically wrote that "those aphorisms which make the principal figure in several of our state bills of rights . . . would sound much better in a treatise of ethics than in a constitution of government."

Hamilton did not mean to disparage the natural rights of mankind. He was no less their advocate than the other founders. He meant that the state constitutions (see Chapter 7), as well as the Articles of Confederation (see Chapter 5), had not done the job they were supposed to do according to the principles of the Declaration—namely, to secure the equal rights of all on the basis of government by consent of the governed. The whole point of the Constitution of 1787 was to remedy this defect in the governments of the United States. As James Madison wrote on the eve of the Constitutional Convention in his *Vices of the Political System of the United States*, the fundamental problem of government under the Articles of Confederation was "injustice in the laws of states" and "the hands of the federal authority are tied" with regard to the need for a "guaranty to the States of their Constitutions & laws against internal violence." By "injustice" and "internal violence" Madison meant violations of the inalienable rights of the minority by the majority.

*The Federalist* No. 39 and No. 43 noted that the Constitution of 1787 could be justified only if it conformed to "the fundamental principles of the Revolution" and to the "transcendent law of nature and of nature's God" announced in the Declaration of Independence. A lively, sometimes bitter, debate took place between Federalists and Anti-Federalists over whether the Constitution of 1787 should be ratified. But the debate proceeded on the assumption, shared by both sides, that government must be republican (that is, by representatives elected by the people) and that, as Madison wrote, "[j]ustice is the end of government" (that is, securing the rights to life, liberty, and property of all).

## The Principles of the Declaration of Independence

Understanding the principles of the Declaration of Independence today is not easy. Americans have heard the famous phrases so often repeated that their meaning seems obvious and trite. They have been dragged into the service of every imaginable political cause, from conservative to liberal to socialist. Yet the Declaration's principles have a reasonably precise meaning, one that leads to definite conclusions about how government ought to be structured and what it ought to do. The Constitution's deepest debt to the Declaration is not found in phrases (such as the preamble) or provisions (such as the Bill of Rights) that speak explicitly of individual rights or the ends of government. It lies instead in the way in which power is allocated among the parts of the structure and the way in which the parts of government are directed in the exercise of power. The Constitution ensures that government's actions will be most likely to secure the natural rights of everyone, including the minority, when the consent of the governed is its basis.

The central idea of the Declaration of Independence, as Abraham Lincoln frequently said, is equality (see Chapter 3). "All men are created equal" is meant in the sense that no one is so perfect that he may rightfully exercise absolute power over other men for their good or for his own. Nor is anyone so defective that he may rightfully be treated as a "slave by nature," as Aristotle had claimed in his *Politics*. All are rightfully free of the rule of other men, and therefore no one should rule another without that other's consent.

The founders had expressed this argument in a shorthand way by pointing out that human beings are neither God nor angels. For example, in a 1773 document of the Massachusetts Council (Senate), James Bowdoin writes: "Supreme or unlimited authority can with fitness belong only to the sovereign of the universe: And that fitness is derived from the perfection of his nature.—To such authority, directed by infinite wisdom and infinite goodness, is due both active and passive obe-dience: Which, as it constitutes the happiness of rational creatures, should with cheerfulness and from choice be unlimitedly paid by them. —But with truth this can be said of no other authority whatever." Or, as Madison wrote in *The Federalist* No. 51, "But what is govern-ment itself but the greatest of all reflections on human nature? If men were angels, no govern-ment would be necessary. If angels were to gov-ern men, neither external nor internal controls on government would be necessary."

However rational a person might be, a residue of self-interested passion exists to make it imprudent to trust that person with absolute power over another. Just as every human being has enough reason that he can be trusted to govern himself within the standards of public laws, so also every human being has enough nonangelic passion that he cannot be trusted to govern others without their consent.

So when the Declaration announces the equality of men, it means that all possess an equal right to life and liberty. The right to life means that no one has the right to take away the life of another by murdering him. (It does not mean that my neighbor, who needs food to live, has a right to come to my house and de-mand a free dinner.) The right to liberty in-cludes the liberty for people to live as they like, to pursue happiness as they wish, and to use their talents and powers, minds and bodies, to produce through their labor things useful to themselves and their families. Liberty therefore includes the right to the pursuit of happiness, and—as the 1776 Virginia, 1776 Pennsylvania, and 1780 Massachusetts declarations of rights all affirm—the right of "acquiring, possessing, and protecting property." The right to liberty

means that no one has the right to injure an-other in his person or property except as pun-ishment for wrongdoing.

"To secure these rights," says the Declara-tion of Independence, "Governments are insti-tuted among Men." If government is needed to secure people's rights, then they must be inse-cure when no government exists. The founders called the condition of men outside of govern-ment "the state of nature." "[I]n a state of na-ture," Madison writes in *The Federalist* No. 51, "the weaker individual is not secured against the violence of the stronger." In the natural state, people have the natural rights to life, liberty, and property, but predatory and evil men make those rights insecure.

The Declaration continues with the qualify-ing phrase "deriving their just powers from the consent of the governed." This means that if government secures people's rights, but rules without their consent, its powers are not "just." The fundamental self-evident truth is that all men are created equal in the sense that no one has the right to rule another without that other's consent.

Through consent the governed retain, col-lectively, some of their natural liberty, because government's authority over them derives from their free choice to allow it to rule. It is not enough for the people to consent only to the founding of government. Their ongoing con-sent must also be expressed through elections if the government may properly be said to act with the "consent of the governed."

In sum, then, human equality points directly to two conclusions concerning the structure and purpose of government. First, government must "secure these rights." Second, it must be based on "the consent of the governed."

With government limited to these few ends, and with the presumption of individual liberty, a society governed in this way will be characterized by self-rule from top to bottom. The people rule themselves through government policies approved by themselves or their representatives. But perhaps even more important for everyday life, the typical activities and tasks of life are done by self-governing private associations, such as churches, families, businesses, and other voluntary groups. These private groups are all self-governing, with government's role being limited largely to the protection against coercive harm and to the enforcement of contracts; that is, of promises made freely by consenting parties. Separation of church authority from state authority is a part of this scheme. But this separation is only one instance of the overall separation of society from government.

## How Government Secures Rights by Protecting against Injury

Government secures the people's rights by protecting against "the violence of the stronger." There are two ways in which government might do this. The first would be to prescribe in detail the course of everyday life, to regulate choices and actions so minutely that injury can be prevented before it has a chance to happen. In this approach, government should dictate, for example, the construction of factories, including the location and size of exit signs, the horseshoe-shape of the toilet seat, and the location and design of industrial equipment.

This modern way of protecting against injury was rejected by the founders. In their view, when government forbids conduct that is only potentially injurious, it may protect the right to life, but it does so at the expense of the right to liberty. In *The Federalist* No. 10, Madison shows that the right to liberty referred to in the Declaration of Independence means that people have to live with the possibility of misconduct and prejudice. He says that removing liberty to prevent men from acting in ways that may threaten the rights of others is like eliminating air to prevent fire. Just as air is "essential to animal life," so also is liberty "essential to political life." It is essential because people's "faculties"—their minds and talents—are their own, and "[t]he protection of these faculties is the first object of Government." Liberty is the free, noninjurious use of people's "faculties."

Therefore, the founders followed a second approach to prevent injury: punish those who commit injuries only after they have done the deed. That is, no one may be deprived of his liberty unless it is proven that he has done, or is conspiring to do, something that is injurious. This was not an absolute rule, but it was the presumption. Any "prior restraint" on freedom was viewed with suspicion, and the exceptions were few.

How, then, in this second approach, does government protect the citizens' lives, liberties, and properties against injury?

First, government must protect citizens against injuries from foreign enemies. It must raise and organize armed forces to repel force with force in the extreme case. It must conduct diplomacy, form alliances, and make war to enable the nation to survive in a world of potential or actual predators.

Second, government must protect citizens against injuries from other citizens. "The very essence of civil liberty," wrote John Marshall in *Marbury v. Madison* in 1803, "certainly consists in the right of every individual to claim the protection of the laws whenever he receives an injury. One of the first duties of government is to afford that protection." According to Marshall, this is because the principal purpose of government is to secure men's rights to life, liberty, and the pursuit of happiness.

Some injuries are so serious that they threaten the peace and order of the community. Murder, rape, robbery, theft, and other intentional injuries to life, liberty, and property are the most important. Injuries of this severity are crimes. Thomas Jefferson explains the link between punishment of crime and the principles of the Declaration of Independence in his 1779 preamble to the proposed Virginia Bill for Proportioning Crimes: "[W]icked and dissolute men, resigning themselves to the domination of inordinate passions, commit violations on the lives, liberties, and property of others, and, the secure enjoyment of these having principally induced men to enter into society, government would be defective in its principal purpose were it not to restrain such criminal acts, by inflicting due punishments on those who perpetrate them."

The civil law also helps protect people against injury by establishing precise legal definitions of personal injury, property ownership, contracts, and the duties of parents to each other and to their children, and by arranging for appropriate legal means of enforcement. In this way everyone can know what is legally his own, so that he can go to court for redress of injuries.

The third source of injury that government must protect against is its own mistreatment of the people. As Madison writes in *The Federal-* ist No. 51, "In framing a government which is to be administered by men over men, the great difficulty lies in this: you must first enable the government to control the governed; and in the next place oblige it to control itself." Madison continues, "A dependence on the people"—that is, democratic elections—"is no doubt the primary control on the government; but experience has taught mankind the necessity of auxiliary precautions." In the founding era, these included the separation of powers, federalism, and written declarations of rights.

These broad themes of public policy are not part of the written federal or state constitutions. But they are part of America's "constitution" in a deeper sense. They are the minimal things that government must do to secure the rights of the citizens. The question then becomes, what structures of government are most likely to result in the right kind of foreign policy, criminal law, and civil law?

## The Rule of Law

"Law is called a rule, in order to distinguish it from a sudden, a transient, or a particular order: uniformity, permanency, stability, characterize a law." In this way James Wilson, who along with Hamilton and Madison was the most thoughtful of the Constitution's framers, distinguished a law from an ad hoc decision made regarding a particular case. A lawless despot or a lawless assembly may decide whom to send to prison by judging each case according to criteria applied in that case only, in the absence of established rules. In the 1780s, some state legislatures acted lawlessly by condemning or rewarding particular individuals outside of or against the written or common laws. A speaker at the Virginia ratifying convention complained that a man was arbitrarily deprived of his life without trial by the Virginia legislature. This kind of lawless conduct can perhaps be warranted in an exceptional case in which the strict application of the rule might lead to injustice or injury to the public good. But more typically, without rules publicly agreed upon that apply equally to all persons similarly situated, nothing prevents the whims, passions, or private interests of the rulers from having their way. Without laws that have a fair degree of stability, no one would know in advance what was forbidden or permitted. Madison illustrates this point in *The Federalist* No. 62: "Law is defined to be a rule of action; but how can that be a rule, which is little known and less fixed?"

The rule of law helps democratic government to do something that it might seem inherently unable to do. In *The Federalist* No. 15 Hamilton asks: "Why has government been instituted at all? Because the passions of men will not conform to the dictates of reason without constraint." Madison also says: "But it is the reason alone of the public that ought to control and regulate the government. The passions ought to be controlled and regulated by the government." But how can it control their passions when the people themselves elect the government? The answer is that if the government is properly constructed, the people's reason will prevail over and constrain the people's passions. That which is best in the people, their "cool and deliberate sense," will be embodied in their representatives or rather in the laws made and enforced by their representatives. An assembly may wish to exempt themselves, their friends, and their donors from taxes, but a general tax law requires all with the same income

or property to pay the same taxes. Applying equally to all, law inhibits action based on the favoritism or hatred that a government official might have for a friend, relative, political opponent, or personal enemy. As John Locke wrote in a passage quoted in Boston's *Rights of the Colonists* (1772), when laws establish rules that are truly general, there is "one rule for rich and poor, for the favorite at court, and the country man at plow."

Further, rule by law ensures electoral responsibility and therefore effective popular consent, for publicly announced rules can be known and judged by the people better than thousands of discreet particular actions, most of which would necessarily be unknown to the public.

The rule of law, in sum, is a political device designed to make as likely as possible the coincidence of the two requirements of just government laid out in the Declaration of Independence: that it be by consent of the people, and that it secure the safety and happiness of society by protecting the natural rights of the citizens. The law aims to embody the public's reason by requiring the men who govern to act in conformity, at least in principle, with reasoned discussion and a rule of universal application. The idea that law should avoid special favors was regarded as so fundamental to the security of individual rights that it is explicitly stated in several state declarations of rights. For example, the Virginia declaration of 1776 states: "[N]o man, or set of men, are entitled to exclusive or separate emoluments or privileges from the community, but in consideration of public services."

Government, however, must do many things that cannot be regulated by general rules. The most important of these is conduct foreign policy. A government cannot deal with other nations in a framework of laws because citizens and governments of one nation are not subject to the laws of another.

## The Crisis of the 1780s

The principles of the Declaration of Independence, the government's role in securing rights by protecting against injury, and the rule of law were broadly accepted in America after 1776. But by 1787 America had reached a crisis.

Democracy had been established throughout the Union. Every state governed itself through elected representatives. A national government, a Congress, was elected indirectly by the people through their state legislatures. So the second requirement of the equality principle was everywhere achieved: Democracy had won.

But the rights of individuals were not secure. In the area of foreign policy, the government under the Articles of Confederation was ineffectual. When Spain closed the Mississippi to American shipping and refused to acknowledge the boundaries of the United States, little could be done about it by the weak and ineffectual Congress. American ships at sea were likewise vulnerable to foreign depredations. The protection of life and property—the first duty of government—was impossible without a stronger national government.

Domestic policy was in many ways just as bad as foreign policy. The rights of property—sometimes even the rights to life and liberty—were being violated by state governments. State monopolies, for example, frequently prevented market access to those who wished to compete against existing wealth. State tariffs and other commercial barriers to interstate trade were common. State legislatures sometimes overturned state court decisions when someone was able to plead that fairness demanded special treatment, such as nonenforcement of a contract.

A long recession after the Revolutionary War led to increasingly radical measures, including the intentional devaluing of the currency by several states to enable debtors to escape part of their debts. In the worst instance, the state of Rhode Island passed laws requiring merchants to accept almost worthless currency for their goods. Business came to a standstill as stores were closed. Mobs attacked businesses and farmers who refused to sell their goods at a loss. Other abuses followed in Rhode Island and, to a lesser degree, in other states. Thoughtful observers concluded that a national power to regulate commerce would help to secure equal opportunity to acquire property as well as to protect existing property.

If the principles of the Declaration were to be fulfilled, a substantial reform was needed.

At least that is what supporters of a stronger national government thought. Many Americans disagreed, but the dispute was largely over implementation. Government by consent and protection of the rights to life, liberty, and property were agreed upon by the founding generation. Hamilton wrote in *The Federalist* No. 22, "The fabric of American empire ought to rest on the solid basis of THE CONSENT OF THE PEOPLE. The streams of national power ought to flow immediately from that pure original fountain of all legitimate authority." How to achieve security of rights on the basis of consent was the question.

The structure of the governments established in America after 1776 had three leading defects. The framers of the Constitution of 1787 traced the foreign and domestic policy failures of the 1780s to these defects.

First, the state legislatures were often dominated by what Madison called factions, groups united by some passion or interest contrary to the rights of others or to the common good. Some device was needed to make it harder for factions to get control of government.

Second, although the state constitutions required separation of the legislative power from the executive and the judiciary, in practice the legislatures often usurped powers belonging to the other branches of government. They routinely took over executive powers such as appointments and administration of the laws. They overrode judicial decisions that were unwelcome to the majority. In his *Notes on Virginia,* Jefferson described the situation in Virginia in this way: "All the powers of government, legislative, executive, and judiciary, result to the legislative body." He went on to say what all the founders believed: "The concentrating [of] these in the same hands is precisely the definition of despotic government."

Third, the nation suffered from the absence of a real national government. The federal government established by the Articles of Confederation was crippled by a fundamental incoherence. On the one hand, the Articles gave Congress substantial powers, especially over foreign affairs and the armed forces. But on the other hand, Congress under the Articles of Confederation had little power. It could not collect taxes; it had to ask and even beg the states for money. It could not enforce its laws, having no system of courts and no executive to

punish individuals who refused to obey. Hamilton summed up the problem: "The great and radical vice in the construction of the existing Confederation is in the principle of legislation for states or governments, in their corporate or collective capacities, and as contradistinguished from the individuals of whom they consist." As Hamilton proved in *The Federalist* with relentless clarity, the Articles of Confederation told Congress to take care of the ends but withheld the means. National weakness and humiliation were the result. The lives and liberties of Americans were in danger.

The founders looked for and found a solution that was consistent with the principles of the Declaration of Independence. Democracy—government by consent expressed through elections—was the basis. Protection of individual rights was the aim. The solution was to redesign the structures that had been implemented in the first years after the Declaration of Independence.

## Federal Powers under the U.S. Constitution

The U.S. Constitution was intended to address the defects in domestic and foreign policymaking under the Articles of Confederation. It did so by creating a genuine national government, with its own executive and judiciary, and with full authority to make laws that could be enforced against individuals. The Constitution listed explicitly the powers of the new Congress. To give it the necessary means to its constitutional ends, Congress was given its own power to raise taxes. In the area of domestic policy, the powers of Congress listed in the Constitution focused on those that would protect the natural right to possess and acquire property, which requires a stable and open market and a reliable currency. Congress had the power to regulate interstate and international commerce, to coin money, to make laws governing bankruptcy, and to encourage inventions by patents. To strengthen the government's ability in foreign policy, the arena in which the right to life is most at risk, Congress had the power to raise and govern the armed forces of the nation and to declare war.

Various limitations on Congress and the states, such as the prohibition of titles of nobility, or of making "anything but gold and silver coin a tender in payment of debts," or of state government restrictions on interstate commerce, were meant to secure the equal rights of all. Other negative provisions also secured fundamental principles of the rule of law, such as the privilege of habeas corpus (forbidding anyone to be imprisoned without being put on trial), prohibitions of bills of attainder (exercise of judicial power of condemnation by a lawmaking body), and ex post facto laws (criminalizing past actions that were legal when committed).

This list of the powers and duties of the federal government would remain mere words on paper, unless the institutions of government, the men and women who exercise power, followed those words conscientiously and capably. The state governments had experienced both defects: lack of conscientiousness, and lack of capacity. There was abuse of power; and there was incompetence, even when officials tried to exercise power with good intentions. The federal constitution tried to remedy those twin defects by dividing the powers of government among and within the three

branches more effectively than the states had done and by arranging elections, term lengths, and responsibilities of office in such a way that capable men of integrity would be more likely to fill them.

All this was necessary to establish a government that would effectively protect the equal rights of all to life, liberty, and property.

## Separation of Powers

In the state of nature, as Madison says, "the weaker individual is not secured against the violence of the stronger." A law of nature governs the state of nature, using Locke's language, which was frequently quoted in the founding era. Locke says this law is reason, which teaches people to refrain from injuring others. In other words, people are obliged to respect in others the rights that they claim for themselves.

But because the law of nature is neither adequately known nor obeyed nor enforced in the state of nature, a well-constructed human government does three things that are lacking in that state. First, it publishes laws that can easily be known and understood by all. Second, it provides some means for impartial judgment of those who violate the laws. Third, it guarantees that wrongdoers judged guilty will be effectively punished.

These distinct powers of government entail different duties, requiring different virtues for good performance. The framers of the U.S. Constitution gave each branch of government—legislative, executive, and judicial—a different mode of appointment, different sizes and tasks, and often different terms of office. The point was to set up each branch in such a way that the people most likely to be put into office (whether by election or appointment) would do their job effectively and honestly, while also being held accountable to the people.

The separation of powers also helps government remain faithful to its trust, which is to protect the people's natural rights without oppressing them. Given that, as *The Federalist* No. 48 says, "power is of an encroaching nature," the branches will tend to keep each other in line if power is divided among them in such a way that each branch has enough constitutional power to resist encroachments by the others. This enables government to control itself by mutual internal constraints, as Madison argues in *The Federalist* No. 51.

## Virtues and Vices of Elected Legislatures

Long before 1776, the most powerful branch of government in America was the legislature, and that did not change under the U.S. Constitution. "In republican government the legislative authority necessarily predominates," writes Madison. The first article of the Constitution is about Congress, because the lawmaking power—the power to make the rules that everyone must live by, or else be punished—is the most comprehensive and most fundamental power of the government. The power to raise and spend taxes also resides there, as does power to set the salaries of the executive and judiciary.

The particular virtue sought from a large legislature is deliberation. Its members must think and reason together about what must be done. Because laws require a majority of both houses of Congress for approval, their passage necessarily involves a consensus of a substantial number of people representing the diverse interests of far-flung constituencies. Composed of a large group, an assembly would be able to act—so it was hoped—only after forming a broad consensus on the merits. Elected assemblies were considered "best adapted to deliberation and wisdom, and best calculated to conciliate the confidence of the people and to secure their privileges and interests." The way a large group acts to promote this quality is described by Hamilton in *The Federalist* No. 70: "In the legislature, promptitude of decision is oftener an evil than a benefit. The differences of opinion, and the jarring of parties in that department of the government, though they may sometimes obstruct salutary plans, yet often promote deliberation and circumspection, and serve to check excesses in the majority. When a resolution is once taken, the opposition must be at an end. That resolution is a law, and resistance to it punishable."

Several constitutional provisions show the way Congress was expected to act as a deliberative body. One is the requirement to publish journals of their proceedings. This provision means lawmakers will be accountable to the public for what they do. Another is the veto clause, which requires the president to give reasons to Congress for his disapproval of legislation. This means that Congress's decision on whether to override should turn in part on the deliberation that follows the veto—a reasoned consideration of why the president refused the bill.

The nature of legislative deliberation will be determined not only by the size and local roots of the members, but also by the quality of the membership. The Constitution's framers worried greatly about this, for they had experienced state governments whose representatives were sometimes irresponsible demagogues, but more often were simply ignorant of public affairs. One of the chief reasons for extending the terms of office for the House and Senate (two- and six-year terms were long for those days; most states had one-year terms) was to enable the members to gain the experience that must underlie intelligent lawmaking. The failure of state governments had been caused by faction and by sheer incompetence— "blunders," Madison says. It was also expected that federal representatives would often be lawyers and other well-informed members of the learned professions. These men, not attached to any particular branch of industry, wrote Hamilton in *The Federalist* No. 35, would "be likely to prove an impartial arbiter between them, ready to promote either, so far as it shall appear to him conducive to the general interests of the society."

However, the framers did not necessarily expect or wish the representatives to be professional politicians. They expected them to be, at their best, men like themselves, who, whatever their profession, would inform themselves conscientiously about matters of public concern.

Because of the poor quality of the state legislators of their day, the framers did not worry about the prospect of a lack of congressional turnover, which is regarded as problematic by many today. Their concern was the opposite, what Madison called, in *The Federalist* No. 62, the "mutability in the public councils, arising from a rapid succession of new members." Shifts of public opinion were sometimes so rapid that some state legislatures, with their annual elections, lost half their members every year. Continuity and experience were indis-

pensable, so the Constitution contained no limitation on the number of terms.

In sum, the proper structure of the legislative body was one of the most difficult challenges facing the framers of the Constitution. To secure the rights of all, government must aim to devise sensible policies and implement them. Prudence and intelligence are indispensable means to that end. Good intentions, while laudable, are not enough. That was one point of the redesign of the legislative branch in the Constitution.

But for all their virtues, representative assemblies also have defects, and the Constitution's framers paid no less attention to these.

When assemblies are too big, they are easily manipulated by their leadership. According to Madison in *The Federalist* No. 55, "In all very numerous assemblies, of whatever characters composed, passion never fails to wrest the scepter from reason. Had every Athenian citizen been a Socrates, every Athenian assembly would still have been a mob." He goes on: "In all legislative assemblies the greater the number composing them may be, the fewer will be the men who will in fact direct the proceedings. . . . The countenance of the government may become more democratic, but the soul that animates it will be more oligarchic." This is because a large group is like a mob, in which few know well what is going on and passion easily communicates itself to the members.

The constitutional limits of the legislature are hard to define, because the scope and nature of law are hard to define. Here is a fertile source of abuse. When does a law become an encroachment? If Congress passed a law forbidding presidential negotiations with a particular country, it would be a violation of the president's authority to conduct such negotiations. But it would be in the form of a law. The framers worried about the natural tendency of legislative bodies to substitute their own will for constitutional law. Speaking of the president, Hamilton warned, in *The Federalist* No. 71, "It is one thing to be subordinate to the laws, and another to be dependent on the legislative body. The first comports with, the last violates, the fundamental principles of good government."

Being elected by the people in local districts, legislators easily form the conviction that they alone speak for the people—even if a president is also elected by the people and is, in fact, the only government official elected by the whole people. Hamilton warned against this tendency explicitly: "The representatives of the people, in a popular assembly, seem sometimes to fancy that they are the people themselves, and betray strong symptoms of impatience and disgust at the least sign of opposition from any other quarter; as if the exercise of its rights, by either the executive or judiciary, were a breach of their privilege and an outrage to their dignity."

Even in the area of deliberation, where an elected assembly would seem to be best suited to act well, there are reasons for worry. Faction, passion, demagogy, ignorance—any or all of these can sour the process.

The Constitution's framers took all these defects into account when they set up the federal government. They tried to remedy them by an improved separation of powers, which required a complex system of legislative checks and balances, and by an improved federalism.

Keeping in mind that the rule of law is the fundamental means by which government secures the natural rights of mankind, the link is clear between these seemingly technical or mechanical institutional questions and the overall purpose of government stated in the Declaration of Independence.

## Legislative Balances and Checks

In 1776 the British king and British royal governors, along with their administrative and judicial appointees, were the principal objects of American fear and suspicion. They had been the source of the most direct threat to the liberty and property of Americans. So the state constitutions generally established weak executives but powerful legislatures. As a result, the legislative body in the state governments became not just predominant, as it must be in a free government resting on the consent of the governed, but also all-powerful—"extending the sphere of its activity and drawing all power into its impetuous vortex," in Madison's memorable phrase in *The Federalist* No. 48.

One of the five key "improvement[s]" in "the science of politics," which appears in *The Federalist* No. 9, is the principle of "legislative balances and checks." Readers often overlook this item, because they have heard the phrase "checks and balances" used so often in connection with separation of powers that they do not notice that the expression refers here only to the legislative part of government.

A separation of statute (or ordinary) lawmaking from constitutional lawmaking properly reduces the legislature to a part of government under the Constitution. It is no longer the legal repository of supreme political power. But constitutionalism in this sense is not enough. Other "legislative balances and checks" had to be devised to prevent the legislature from becoming the de facto or illegal sovereign, threatening the natural rights of the people by its aggression or its incompetence.

These additional checks would have to be discoveries of the founders' own good sense, working within institutions the Americans had become accustomed to. The principles of free government were of little help. The Declaration has nothing to say about whether the legislature should be divided into two houses, or whether the executive should have a veto, or what role the judiciary could play in keeping the legislature in its proper place. In all these instances the colonial and British past furnished examples that provided material for the framers' "auxiliary precautions," which Madison called "inventions of prudence." The framers had to adapt them to serve the "checking" purpose.

Besides the division between ordinary and constitutional lawmaking, ordinary lawmaking is further subdivided in three ways.

First, Congress is to consist of a House of Representatives and a Senate. While both houses are to be representatives of the people, the character of the two bodies is kept as dissimilar as possible. Each has different modes of election (popular for House, by state legislatures for Senate), different terms of office (two years for representatives and six years for senators), different composition (Senate has fewer members from populous states than the House), different sizes (Senate is small, House is large), and different activities (Senate alone shares in some executive powers, for example, making treaties and appointing officials).

Second, the president is to participate in the lawmaking power through the threat or use of the veto and through his constitutional duty of "giv[ing] the Congress information of the state of the union and recommend[ing] to their consideration such measures as he shall judge necessary and expedient."

Third, statute lawmaking for local purposes is to be taken care of by state and local governments.

Finally, Hamilton argued that the judiciary would review ordinary legislation in light of the written Constitution. This feature, later called judicial review, means that when a legislature makes a law that violates the Constitution, the courts will refuse to enforce that law upon individuals who come before them in cases at law.

## The Executive

The chief virtue required of the executive is energy, intelligently directed toward the public good. This active virtue complements the slower deliberative virtue of the legislature. The executive—enforcer and administrator of the laws, prosecutor of crime, and commander of the armed forces—needs to be able to act decisively, forcefully, quickly, and in some cases secretly. These qualities, Hamilton writes, "will generally characterize the proceedings of one man in a much more eminent degree than the proceedings of any greater number." So the executive power in the U.S. Constitution is lodged in a single individual with a term of four years.

The legislature is the heart of democratic government as well as the source of greatest danger to it. Securing the rights of mankind requires a strong legislature, but one that stays within its proper bounds. Therefore, writes Madison in *The Federalist* No. 48, "it is against the enterprising ambition of this department that the people ought to indulge all their jealousy and exhaust all their precautions." The primary institutional means to keep the legislative in its proper place was the presidency.

The U.S. Constitution greatly strengthened the executive branch compared with the existing state constitutions. Under the Constitution the president is a coequal branch, not as a lawmaker, but as a coordinate branch under the Constitution, in the area of executive authority.

In 1776 Americans tended to think of the elected legislature as the "representatives" of the people. The Constitution reflects this early prejudice by calling the lower house of Congress the "House of Representatives," as if the other parts of government do not represent the people. But the executive under a democratic constitution is elected directly or indirectly by the people, and in this sense he is no less "representative" of the people than the legislature. It took Americans several years for this truth to sink in, and the misbehavior of state assemblies helped.

By their growing awareness that an elected executive, even a one-person executive, is a republican institution, the framers of the Constitution made it possible to create a powerful president who could restrain the legislative branch without violating the consent principle. Experience in the states prepared the way. Members of the Constitutional Convention had no problem seeing the president as a representative of the whole people, and therefore worthy of being granted great powers under the Constitution. This was especially true after the hard problem of how to elect him was

solved. The electoral college meant that the people would have a prominent role in the election process and that the president would usually be elected independently of Congress.

Specifically, the president was given a large share of the lawmaking power by the veto (and to a lesser degree by his constitutional duty to recommend measures to Congress). With the veto the president can control the pace of legislation with the support of only one-third of one house of Congress.

Second, the Constitution, by the full grant of executive power to the president alone, gives him supreme authority over the executive branch, although Supreme Court decisions, to say nothing of Congress's laws, have not always recognized this. The Constitution says, "The executive power shall be vested in a president of the United States," not "in a president, subject to such limitations as Congress shall decree." Once officials are appointed, the president has authority to supervise and, if need be, to direct them, to "take care that the laws are faithfully executed." And the Constitution is the supreme law of the land.

Third, the "executive power," as the framers understood it, gives the president extensive but not exclusive powers in the conduct of the nation's foreign policy. To understand the reason for this, it is helpful to reflect on the difference between domestic and foreign affairs. Domestic affairs are generally ruled by law; that is, primarily by the executive and courts acting under Congress's laws. Disputes with other nations, however, can never be resolved by law. All foreign relations are lawless in the sense that there is, to use Locke's language, no common judge to appeal to when one nation claims to be injured by another.

Locke calls this foreign policy power "federative," and he says it naturally belongs to the executive. This is because one man, as opposed to a body of men, can act swiftly, secretly, and flexibly—all necessary in the fast-changing world of international lawlessness. Speed is needed because other nations may attack at any time, and the response may need to be swift. Secrecy is needed because in the absence of a common authority, all devices, including deception, may be needed to prevail in a contest of force. Secrecy conceals one's own vulnerabilities and makes possible exploitation of the weakness of others.

But although the everyday conduct of foreign affairs was recognized as an executive function by the framers, they reserved the declaration of war to Congress. This is the most momentous step a nation can take, and they thought it too important to allow a president alone to do it. But the conduct of war, the "war-making power," belongs to the commander-in-chief. And the president is not required to get congressional approval to "repel sudden attacks," as was said in the Constitutional Convention, or to conduct quick and necessary uses of the nation's force, as presidents have done almost two hundred times since the Constitution went into effect. Even with treaties, the president negotiates and the Senate only ratifies. ("Advise and consent," in the Constitution, is a technical term that does not imply a conegotiating role for the Senate.)

Besides the clauses explicitly listing presidential powers, the Constitution acknowledges the presidential difference in several ways. There is no publicity requirement corresponding to those for Congress (that is, publishing journals and votes). This acknowledges the executive need for secrecy (preserved in the term "executive session," which congressional committees like to invoke). Another textual difference is found in their respective oaths of office. The president alone swears to "preserve, protect, and defend the Constitution." Members of Congress (and other government officials) swear "to support this Constitution." The president, it appears, is the supreme defender of the instrument, in the text as in U.S. history. The example of Lincoln comes foremost to mind.

A government must do many things that cannot be determined by general rules. For example, the location and design of forts and other public buildings; decisions on hiring, firing, and promoting government employees; and the choice of which crimes to prosecute first—all these are by their nature discretionary. That is, they cannot be done, or done well, by general rules. They fall principally under the power of the executive, although Congress is involved in many of them. Under the U.S. Constitution, accountability to the public for such ad hoc actions is best preserved when one person, the president, is responsible for them. The people are then in a position to know whom to praise or blame, and that will inform their votes at the next election.

In sum, the presidential virtue of energy helps secure the natural rights of individuals both by making the rule of law more effective, through vigorous enforcement, and by enabling the nation to respond vigorously and effectively to predatory foreign powers. The rule of law is silent in foreign policy, and only rough justice is possible by the threat and use of force.

## The Judiciary

The virtue of the judiciary is judgment. Its job, as John Marshall wrote in *Marbury*, is "solely to decide on the rights of individuals" in cases at bar. A case is a dispute between two parties, one of whom claims to have suffered an injury for which the law provides redress. In a typical criminal case, for example, one party (the executive branch of the government, speaking for the people) alleges that the other (the accused) has committed some crime. Assume a person has counterfeited money. Congress has passed a law forbidding counterfeiting, which is an injury to the public because it is in effect theft from those who accept the worthless currency. The prosecutor asks the court to find the person guilty and assess the legal punishment. The U.S. Constitution gives judges lifetime appointments. It made the courts independent of elections to promote dispassionate judgment, so that judges will not be easily pressured to reach their decisions in accord with popular whim or anger. The use of juries of ordinary citizens, most of whom will not be government officials, is meant to promote the same goal.

Popular opinion today often holds, mistakenly, that the main job of the federal judiciary is to decide whether laws are constitutional. This is in fact only a tangential part of its work, although it is its most spectacular part. The most important work of the judiciary is to conduct trials, as an integral part of the rule of law, so that those who commit injuries may be punished disinterestedly, according to law, and not arbitrarily. The innocent are to be compensated for their wrongful losses. That is the courts' role in the overall process of government securing citizens' rights.

The "good behavior" term of office for federal judges—in effect, a lifetime appointment—has often been misunderstood as an anti-democratic part of the Constitution. For the founders, however, judges could be trusted to remain in office indefinitely because of their clearly subordinate role. Their job is to judge cases according to the law, meaning under the direction of rules approved by the people's representatives. The founders would have rejected a view often promoted today, that the judicial branch rightly has a lawmaking role coequal with the elected legislature.

The judiciary, unlike the other branches, has very limited power. Having neither will (as the legislative has in lawmaking) nor the power to coerce (as the executive has), it is limited on one side by the law and on the other by the willingness of the executive to carry out its decisions. It continues to be what Hamilton called it, "the least dangerous" of the three branches of government. The inherent weakness of the judicial power became especially clear during the Civil War, when Lincoln ignored several of its decisions, including *Dred Scott v. Sandford* (1856), which had ruled unconstitutional any federal laws limiting slavery in the federal territories. The Republican Congress abolished slavery in the territories in 1862, in direct defiance of the Supreme Court, and the Court could do nothing about it. Because the members of the judiciary are appointed by two of the elected branches of government, the president and the Senate, the courts can always eventually be brought around to the prevailing views of these elected officials.

Which branch of the government protects civil rights? Many would say that is the job of the judiciary. In the founders' understanding, civil rights are natural rights, insofar as natural rights can be embodied in law. In the Constitution, civil rights—legal rights to compensation when life, liberty, or property is injured—are protected only when all three branches of government work together as they were designed to work, passing and enforcing appropriate laws, judging violations of law in trials, and taking executive branch action to protect the nation against foreign governments.

## Large Republic

In the founding era, many doubted that a strong government over a large extent of territory and population could long remain free. But as the early state governments often proved to be ineffectual or worse, and as the Articles of Confederation gradually collapsed after the Revolutionary War was won, the virtues of a large republic were reexamined. In his famous *The Federalist* No. 10, Madison argued that largeness was not only not a problem but also could help provide a solution to the problem of faction that was disrupting state governments. Madison singled out two factors. First, representatives chosen in large districts might prove to be more talented as well as more devoted to the public good. Second, a large country would be better at discouraging the formation of a factious majority that would threaten the rights of the minority. The greater complexity and size of a large society would make it harder to find a common unjust interest and to organize those factious interests into a majority.

Some founders were not entirely convinced by Madison's argument about the multiplicity of factions in a large country. Hamilton, for example, thought that once the representatives met "in one room" in the capital, they would easily find common ground with each other to oppress others if they were so inclined. But all the leading framers saw the usefulness of "filtering" public opinion through an electoral process that chose a government with great responsibilities and longer terms of office. This, it was hoped, would "refine and enlarge the public view" and attract men of large ambitions and unusual devotion to the public good. Hamilton wrote, "[I]t will require other talents and a different kind of merit . . . as would be necessary to make him a successful candidate for the distinguished office of president of the United States. It will not be too strong to say, that there will be a constant probability of seeing the station filled by characters pre-eminent for ability and virtue." In other words, although power can be corrupting, it can also be invigorating. Men moved by "the ruling passion of the noblest minds" will wish to "undertake extensive and arduous enterprises for the public benefit." The fact that the president is the most powerful single person in the system was expected to attract men of talent and grand ambition to the position—as it has, especially in times of crisis such as the Civil War and the Great Depression.

## Federalism and Local Self-Government

Besides the separation of powers, the other chief constitutional device to secure natural rights, and to prevent government oppression by dividing power, is federalism. Under the original Constitution, the national government had authority only over matters of truly national scope, such as foreign policy and national security, regulation of commerce among (but not within) the states, and other "great and national objects." The states, writes Madison in *The Federalist* No. 45, have general authority over "all the objects which, in the ordinary course of affairs, concern the lives, liberties, and properties of the people, and the internal order, improvement, and prosperity of the state."

As with separated powers, federalism has a second purpose apart from preventing tyranny. It makes government work better because, as Madison explains in *The Federalist* No. 10, "local and particular interests" differ from place to place and so are not conducive to regulation by general rules or by a remote body such as Congress. They are handled better by state and local governments, where the representatives are "acquainted with all their local circumstances and lesser interests." That allows "the great and aggregate interests"—which are conducive to laws operating from the center—to be referred to the national government.

The founders' endorsement of federalism must be understood in its proper context. Most of them favored the adoption of the U.S. Constitution of 1787, which greatly increased the power of the national government in comparison to what it had been under the weak government of the Articles of Confederation. But all of them, including the nationalist Hamilton, regarded state and local governments as a leading element of the system. Hamilton approved of the exclusion of state and local matters from the federal mission in *The Federalist* No. 17: "The regulation of the mere domestic police [that is, policy] of a State appears to me to hold out slender allurements to ambition. Com-

merce, finance, negotiation, and war seem to comprehend all the objects, which have charms for minds governed by that passion."

To understand the founders' constitutionalism, then, it is not enough to understand the federal Constitution, *The Federalist,* and the founding principles. It is also necessary to see the state constitutions as part of the overall constitutional order, all of whose parts, in a remarkably effective division of political labor, helped to secure the equal natural rights of all.

## The Bill of Rights

Hardly any of the Constitution's framers cared much about a Bill of Rights. Their view, much misunderstood today, was born of the harsh school of the 1780s. Several of the misbehaving state governments had impressive declarations of rights attached to their constitutions. It was widely noted that these declarations seemed to be of no use whatever in preventing government misconduct. Madison spoke scornfully of the ineffectual "parchment barriers" erected by state constitutions against state violations of the separation of powers.

The framers concluded from these widespread state violations of the rights of individuals that a mere list of rights does little to enable government to secure the rights to life and liberty.

However, the Constitution of 1787 was greeted with considerable suspicion, not only by its Anti-Federalist opponents, but also among some members of state ratification conventions who were in the end willing to support it. Several conventions approved the Constitution with strong recommendations for amendments. So when the First Congress met under the new Constitution, Madison, who was one of those who did not much care about a Bill of Rights, nevertheless supported it, primarily as a means to assure everyone that the new government had no intention of taking away the rights for which the Revolution had been fought.

The rights listed in the first eight amendments of the Bill of Rights were of two kinds. First, the federal government was forbidden to make certain kinds of laws limiting personal liberty, such as limits on freedom of speech and the press, on the free exercise of religion, and on keeping and bearing arms. These had also been listed in some of the state bills of rights.

These liberties were regarded by Americans of the founding era as fundamental. Several were among the "natural rights, retained," as Madison described them when he was preparing his speech introducing the Bill of Rights to the First Congress. Free exercise of religion was the most valuable right, because one's duty to God is higher than any duty one has to other men. Freedom of speech and of the press is indispensable to free discussion of government policy in elections. The right to keep one's own arms, a right denied to Europeans (*The Federalist* No. 46), keeps government from becoming a power independent of the people. Given that Madison and the Federalists favored these rights as much as the Anti-Federalists, they decided that adding them to the Constitution would do little harm and might be of benefit.

Second, the Bill of Rights specified certain legal procedures. These are not natural rights, for there are no courts and juries in the state of nature. These procedural provisions, which also had their parallels in several state constitutions, were thought to be necessary elements

in the impartial judgment of individuals that Locke had said was essential to the enforcement of the law of nature, which prohibits the injury of innocents. This impartial judgment is missing in a state of nature. The procedures for fair trials listed in the Fourth through Eighth Amendments are meant to maximize the chances for the desired impartial judgment. These included the prohibition against being tried twice for the same crime, the guarantee of the right to confront witnesses and have the assistance of counsel, and the broad requirement that no one be deprived of life, liberty, or property without due process of law.

The Ninth Amendment, which says that there are other rights besides those mentioned in the first eight amendments in the Bill of Rights, responds to the complaint, which Hamilton mentions in *The Federalist* No. 84, that a list of specific rights might be taken to mean that the people and the states have no other rights beyond those explicitly named in the Bill of Rights. That is, the Ninth Amendment points back to the enumeration of specific powers of the federal government as the main limitation on the federal government. Beyond those powers, the federal government has no authority over the states or the people.

The Tenth Amendment makes the same point with regard to what is called federalism. It reaffirms the important truth that whatever powers are not delegated by the Constitution to the federal government are retained by the states.

## The Civil War Amendments

Madison thought that majority faction was the greatest danger facing America under its republican form of government. In *The Federalist* No. 10 he argued that factions could be controlled by the right kind of structural improvements. But when Madison presented the same argument behind closed doors at the Constitutional Convention of 1787, he admitted that "[w]e have seen the mere distinction of color made in the most enlightened period of time, a ground of the most oppressive dominion ever exercised by man over man." In other words, America at the time of its birth suffered from a massive majority faction, the enslavement of millions of human beings by the majority.

Slavery proved to be an ugly blemish as well as an almost fatal cancer on the Constitution of 1787. Chief Justice Roger Taney was incorrect when he stated in *Dred Scott* that no blacks had been citizens of any state at the time the Constitution was ratified. But he was right to say that the Constitution supported slavery in any state that chose to allow it. It mandated the continuation of the slave trade until 1808. It required the return of fugitive slaves who had escaped to a free state. It gave the slave states extra clout in the national government by counting three-fifths of their slaves toward the total population that determined the number of seats for each state in the House of Representatives and electors in presidential elections.

These provisions had coexisted uneasily with the principles of the Declaration of Independence and the basic provisions of the Constitution, which provided for government based on consent expressed through elections and outlined duties of government that secured the natural rights of the governed—at least those who were not slaves. Eight states had abolished slavery during the founding era, and the founders had hopes that somehow emancipation would be achieved someday in the others. But as the years rolled by, and as it became increasingly clear that the Southern states were more fiercely attached than ever to their slaves, the consensus of the founding unraveled in the South.

That older view, as Confederate vice president Alexander Stephens correctly described it in 1861, was "that the enslavement of the African was in violation of the laws of nature; that it was wrong in *principle*, socially, morally, and politically. It was an evil they knew not well how to deal with, but the general opinion of the men of that day was that, somehow or other in the order of Providence, the institution would be evanescent and pass away." The South, Stephens proudly insisted, no longer believed in such "fundamentally wrong" ideas, which rested on "the assumption of the equality of races." Instead, "[o]ur new government is founded upon exactly the opposite idea; its corner-stone rests upon the great truth, that the negro is not equal to the white man; that slavery—subordination to the superior race—is his natural and normal condition."

With this Southern repudiation of the principles of the Declaration, the Constitution was imperiled. The South wanted nothing further to do with men who believed that their core institution was profoundly unjust and were prepared to act on that belief to restrict the further spread of slavery. The Civil War did not begin as a war to end slavery, but after Lincoln's Emancipation Proclamation of 1863, that is what it became.

After the war, three amendments to the Constitution were approved. The Thirteenth Amendment outlawed slavery. The Fifteenth gave voting rights to blacks. The Fourteenth made blacks citizens and authorized the federal government to protect their basic civil rights.

Congressional Republicans who supported the Fourteenth Amendment stated explicitly that they intended to bring the Constitution into conformity with the principles of the Declaration of Independence. That is exactly what they did. The basic structure and purpose of government were reaffirmed by these amendments. The federal government was given the responsibility for the enforcement of basic civil rights only when state governments failed to do so. Otherwise, the old presumption prevailed that state governments would have exclusive authority over, in the words of *The Federalist* No. 45, "the objects, which, in the ordinary course of affairs, concern the lives, liberties and properties of the people."

After the statement on citizenship, the Fourteenth Amendment prohibits the states from doing three things. First, they may make no law "which shall abridge the privileges or immunities of citizens." What these privileges are has long been a matter of dispute. Some of those who promoted the Fourteenth Amendment in Congress asserted that among the privileges of citizenship are the first eight amendments of the Constitution. Certainly there was extensive discussion in Congress of free speech and the right to keep and bear arms as a fundamental privilege of citizenship guaranteed by the Fourteenth Amendment. Other privileges of citizenship included the right to travel freely, to buy and sell property, to testify and sue in court, and to engage in a lawful business on equal terms with other citizens.

Second, no state could "deprive any person of life, liberty, or property, without due process of law." This due process requirement includes at least two things. First, no one can be deprived of personal liberty or life unless it can be shown that he has violated a law; that is, a general rule passed by an appropriate elected legislative body. Second, the determination must be through a criminal trial with appropriate safeguards to maximize the probability of impartial judgment. This is the basic Lockean mechanism for impartial judgment of those accused of committing injuries.

The third restriction on state action is that no state may deny to any person the equal protection of the laws. This provision was understood differently when it was passed than it is today. It did not originally mean "equal treatment under the law," for otherwise excluding blacks and women from voting would have become instantly unconstitutional by this clause. Yet Article 2 of the amendment explicitly permits excluding some citizens from voting. What triggered the need for this clause was the Southern practice of government (for example, the white militia) harming blacks or of government failing to prevent private persons, such as the Ku Klux Klan, from harming blacks. "Equal protection" most urgently means that laws against injuring must be enforced equally on all who commit such injuries.

It has been said that the Fourteenth Amendment was badly written and that many of the disputes over its meaning could have been prevented if the drafters had done a better job. I agree with that assessment. But if the amendment is read in light of the social compact theory of the founding, which was the theory of those who wrote and approved the amendment, the most egregious misreadings of it would have been prevented.

## Conclusion

The Declaration of Independence says that securing the inalienable rights of mankind is the main purpose of government. Americans today are accustomed to thinking of civil rights law and the Bill of Rights as the source of their rights. They often assume that the judiciary is the institution that secures their rights.

In the U.S. Constitution, the Bill of Rights is an afterthought. The main protection of rights is to be found in the primary actions of the three branches of the federal and state governments: passing laws, judging cases, and executing the sentence on offenders. The civil rights of Americans, in the framers' view, are protected only when all branches of state and federal government are working together, making and enforcing laws to protect the right of every person to the noninjurious use of his own talents and property, free from the interference of others. This domestic task must be supplemented by a prudent and vigorous foreign policy, to check—and if necessary to repel with violence—aggression from abroad. This is how government secures its citizens' rights.

What some might regard as merely technical, institutional matters—such as the rule of law, the content of public policy, the separation of powers, federalism, and state constitutions—all prove to be central to the question of how the Constitution secures the natural rights of individuals. The connection between the Constitution and the Declaration is only superficially revealed in verbal echoes, lists of rights (such as the Bill of Rights), broad formulas such as the preamble, references in Washington's letter of transmittal to the theory of the social compact, and so on. The deeper connection is found in the complex institutional structures that were meant to correct the errors made in the Articles of Confederation and the early state constitutions. These constitutions did set up governments that rested, more or less, on the consent of the governed. But they did not effectively secure the people's rights to life, liberty, and the pursuit of happiness. Securing rights is not a matter of listing them. It requires tough-minded and detailed thinking about how to arrange elections, set terms of office, allocate responsibilities, grant sufficient authority to government, limit that authority where appropriate, and check power with power. Those who are supposed to secure citizens' rights should have the incentive and the ability to do so, and they should not easily be able to take those rights away.

The Declaration of Independence lays down two markers for just government: (1) it must secure the inalienable rights of the citizens, and (2) it must be based on the consent of the governed. The discouraging experience of the 1780s taught thoughtful Americans that these two criteria are not necessarily in harmony with each other. As Madison notes in *The Federalist* No. 10, the majority is capable of ganging up on a minority and taking away their rights. The majority is also capable of frittering away the rights of everyone through its own ignorance. The solution, insofar as it can be achieved by merely institutional means, is the intricate constitutional structure described and defended in *The Federalist*. The Constitution was needed to save the Revolution.

Constitutionalism as a question of political philosophy is therefore inseparable from the institutional embodiment and implementation of the principles of the Declaration. If the

Constitution's framers had not done such a good job figuring out how to devise offices and elections that helped secure the natural rights of most citizens, the American experiment in government of, by, and for the people might have proved brief and inglorious. The world would perhaps have returned to its old habit of government by the arrogant and the greedy, and responsible popular rule in America might never have seen the light of day.

## Bibliography

Becker, Carl L. *The Declaration of Independence: A Study in the History of Political Ideas.* Orig. pub. 1922. New York: Knopf, 1948.

Curtis, Michael Kent. *No State Shall Abridge: The Fourteenth Amendment and the Bill of Rights.* Durham: Duke University Press, 1986.

Diamond, Martin. *As Far as Republican Principles Will Admit: Essays by Martin Diamond* Ed. William A. Schambra. Washington, D.C.: American Enterprise Institute Press, 1991.

Erler, Edward J. *The American Polity: Essays on the Theory and Practice of Constitutional Government.* New York: Crane Russak, 1991.

Gerber, Scott Douglas. *To Secure These Rights: The Declaration of Independence and Constitutional Interpretation.* New York: New York University Press, 1995.

Goldwin, Robert A. *From Parchment to Power: How James Madison Used the Bill of Rights to Save the Constitution.* Washington, D.C.: American Enterprise Institute Press, 1997.

Goldwin, Robert A., and William A. Schambra, eds. *How Democratic Is the Constitution?* Washington, D.C.: American Enterprise Institute Press, 1980.

_____. *How Does the Constitution Secure Rights?* Washington, D.C.: American Enterprise Institute Press, 1985.

Hamburger, Philip A. "Natural Rights, Natural Law, and American Constitutions." *Yale Law Journal* 102 (January 1993): 907–960.

Hamilton, Alexander, and others. *The Federalist.* Ed. Clinton Rossiter and Charles Kesler. New York: New American Library, Mentor Books, 1998.

Hickok, Eugene, ed. *The Bill of Rights: Original Meaning and Current Understanding.* Charlottesville: University Press of Virginia, 1991.

Jaffa, Harry V. *A New Birth of Freedom: Abraham Lincoln and the Coming of the Civil War.* Lanham, Md.: Rowman and Littlefield, 2000.

Kesler, Charles, ed. *Saving the Revolution: The Federalist Papers and the American Founding.* New York: Free Press, 1987.

Maier, Pauline. *American Scripture: Making the Declaration of Independence.* New York: Knopf, 1997.

Maltz, Earl M. *Civil Rights, the Constitution, and Congress, 1863–1869.* Lawrence: University Press of Kansas, 1990.

McConnell, Michael. "The Fourteenth Amendment: A Second American Revolution or the Logical Culmination of the Tradition?" *Loyola of Los Angeles Law Review* 25 (1992): 1159–1176.

Rahe, Paul. *Republics Ancient and Modern: Classical Republicanism and the American Revolution.* Chapel Hill: University of North Carolina Press, 1992.

West, Thomas G. "Religious Liberty: The View from the Founding." In *On Faith and Free Government,* ed. Daniel Palm. Lanham, Md.: Rowman and Littlefield, 1997, 3–27.

_____. *Vindicating the Founders: Race, Sex, Class, and Justice in the Origins of America.* Lanham, Md.: Rowman and Littlefield, 1997.

# 7 The Declaration of Independence as Viewed from the States

## JOHN C. EASTMAN

The Declaration of Independence is the grand embodiment of the principles upon which the United States was founded, the document that defined what President Abraham Lincoln would describe as his "ancient faith." The first document printed in the *United States Code,* it is described there by Congress as one of the organic laws of the United States. All this majesty, all this reverence, yet its principles are believed to be unenforceable in the courts of law. The Declaration "is not a legal prescription conferring powers upon the courts," U.S. Supreme Court Justice Antonin Scalia wrote in a dissenting opinion in *Troxel v. Granville* (2000). In other words, no matter how self-evidently true the principles articulated in the Declaration of Independence or how much mandated by the "Laws of Nature and of Nature's God," they do not have the status of positive law that can be enforced by the courts of law.

Whether or not Justice Scalia's opinion is correct with respect to the federal government, it is clearly not correct in the state government arena. Beginning with the admission of Nebraska and Nevada into the Union during the Civil War, Congress has specifically required as a condition of admission to statehood that state constitutions conform to the principles of the Declaration of Independence. These enabling acts, the state constitutions drafted in conformity to them, and the statutes or presidential proclamations acknowledging admission together give the Declaration of Independence the sanction of positive law, at least in the eleven states admitted to the Union since the Civil War that were statutorily bound by the principles of the Declaration.

For those states not explicitly bound by the Declaration, the language used in many of their constitutions—the northern state constitutions prior to the Civil War, and the Reconstruction constitutions adopted by the former confederate states after the Civil War—explicitly tracked the principled language of the Declaration of Independence. Thus, these states are also bound by the principles of the Declaration.

More significantly, the historical development of state constitutional provisions that parallel the language of the Declaration demonstrates, or at least strongly suggests, that specific textual provisions of the Constitution were designed to codify the principles of the Declaration and make them enforceable as positive law. The provisions of Article IV (and later of the Fourteenth Amendment) guaranteeing the "privileges and immunities" of citizenship and a "republican" form of government simply cannot be understood apart from the natural law principles of the Declaration from which they were drawn. Although the courts have effectively treated these provisions as nonjusticiable, they are clearly commands of the positive law and not just some vague, philosopher's ideal of higher justice such as is recognized in the Ninth Amendment and parallel state constitutional provisions.

## The Declaration in the Original States

No state was expressly bound by the Declaration of Independence, as such, until Nevada and Nebraska were admitted to the Union during the Civil War. However, most of the original thirteen colonies, in one way or another, relied heavily upon the Declaration's principles to legitimize the revolutionary steps they were taking in writing new constitutions and erecting new governments. And in many, those principles were included in the states' declarations of rights and therefore given the same judicially enforceable status as other provisions found there.

The principles of the Declaration upon which several of the states, in whole or in part, relied are as follows.

- First, all men, all human beings, are created equal, a proposition portrayed in the Declaration as self-evidently true, knowable both by human reason and by divine revelation (the "Nature and Nature's God" of the Declaration's opening paragraph).[1]
- Second, all human beings are endowed by their Creator with certain unalienable rights merely by virtue of the fact that they are

equally created by God as human beings and not as lesser animals.

- Third, among these unalienable rights are the rights of life, liberty, and the pursuit of happiness, which was Thomas Jefferson's eloquent rephrasing of John Locke's statement of the fundamental rights in life, liberty, and property that at once elevated and expanded Locke's conception of rights.
- Fourth, the sole purpose of government is to secure these unalienable rights.
- Fifth, the only just governments are those founded on the consent of the governed, which means that ultimately political power originates from the people.
- Sixth, whenever government becomes destructive of the ends for which it was formed, namely, the securing of the people's unalienable rights, the people have the right to alter or abolish the government, replacing it with a new government that they believe will be most likely to secure their rights.

These principles began appearing in state constitutions even before the Declaration of Independence was issued.

On January 5, 1776, for example—six months before the Declaration of Independence was adopted—New Hampshire became the first of the American colonies to draft its own constitution. The New Hampshire delegates who drafted that constitution pointed out in the preamble that they had been "chosen and appointed by the free suffrages of the people" of New Hampshire "and authorized and empowered by them . . . to establish some form of government . . . for the preservation of peace and good order, and for the security of the lives and properties of the inhabitants of this colony."

They thus demonstrated the same belief in the necessity of the consent of the people that would be articulated in the Declaration of Independence. This was necessary, they asserted, because the British Parliament had deprived the people of New Hampshire of their "natural and constitutional rights and privileges" and because the departure of the governor and legislative council had left the colony "destitute of legislation" and without courts "to punish criminal offenders," so that "the lives and properties of the honest people" of New Hampshire were "liable to the machinations and evil designs of wicked men." That is, because the existing government in England had failed to protect the natural rights of the people in New Hampshire (as well as rights and privileges to which they were entitled as Englishmen), the people of New Hampshire exercised their natural right to alter or abolish that government, and they consented to the establishment of a new government that would more adequately fulfill the fundamental purpose of government.

The Provincial Congress of South Carolina adopted a constitution on March 26, 1776, complaining in the preamble that the British Parliament had imposed taxes "without the consent and against the will of the colonists," a situation that Congress claimed (ironically, given later developments) "would at once reduce them [the colonists] from the rank of freemen to a state of the most abject slavery." New Jersey, too, on the eve of the signing of the Declaration of Independence, adopted a new constitution with a preamble noting that the king's authority, derived from the people by compact, was now dissolved. The state thus subscribed both to the principle of consent and the right to alter or abolish government.

But by far the most influential of the early enactments was the Virginia Declaration of Rights, drafted by George Mason and adopted by the Virginia Constitutional Convention on June 12, 1776. The first three sections of the Virginia Declaration of Rights contain, in substantially similar form, all six principles that three weeks later would appear from the hand of Thomas Jefferson in the Declaration of Independence.

Section 1. That all men are by nature equally free and independent, and have certain inherent rights, of which, when they enter into a state of society, they cannot, by any compact, deprive or divest their posterity; namely, the enjoyment of life and liberty, with the means of acquiring and possessing property, and pursuing and obtaining happiness and safety.

Section 2. That all power is vested in, and consequently derived from, the people; that magistrates are their trustees and servants, and at all times amenable to them.

Section 3. That government is, or ought to be, instituted for the common benefit, protection, and security of the people, nation, or community; of all the various modes and forms of government, that is best which is capable of producing the greatest degree of happiness and safety, and is most effectually securing against the danger of maladministration; and that, when any government shall be found inadequate or contrary to these purposes, a majority of the community hath an indubitable, inalienable, and indefeasible right to reform, alter, or abolish it, in such manner as shall be judged most conducive to the public weal.

Jefferson's explicit references to the "Creator" are missing—all men are "by nature" equal in the Virginia version instead of "created" equal in the Declaration's version. But the elaboration on the equality principle in the Virginia document provides great insight into what Jefferson meant when he described the proposition that all men are created equal as a "self-evident" truth.

Although that great moral truth would later be called a "self-evident lie" by Senator John Pettit of Indiana and disproved using modern science by Confederate vice president Alexander Stephens, both tapped into the obvious fact that human beings are not all equal in outward appearance, physical attributes, or intellectual capacity.[2] Mason's rendition makes clear that such facial inequalities were beside the point. The logical self-evidence of Jefferson's proposition is rooted in the nature of what it is to be a human being, and that nature can only be understood in contrast to the nature from which it is derived (the "Creator," in Jefferson's language) and the nature of lesser animals from which it must be distinguished. In this sense—according to the "nature" of the thing— all men are created equal, which is to say, equally free and independent. Jefferson's proposition is a self-evident truth, not a self-evident lie, once one understands the meaning of the word *man,* which is to say, his "nature."

From this initial, self-evident proposition flows the remaining principles, found in both the Virginia Declaration of Rights and the Declaration of Independence, albeit in slightly different terms. Because human beings are created equally free and independent, they have— inherent in their nature and endowed by their Creator—the fundamental, inalienable right to protect that free and independent nature. That is, they have the right to life and to liberty and the right to acquire property in things that are the fruit of their own free and independent labor and to otherwise pursue their own individual happiness. They do this by establishing governments, whose sole purpose is to protect these equal and unalienable rights of equal human beings. Moreover, that being the purpose of government, the equal human beings for whose benefit the government is instituted must necessarily retain the right to alter or abolish their government whenever, in their judgment, it ceases to fulfill its purpose.

Finally, all such governments, to be legitimate, must be based on consent. Because human beings are equal—that is, neither gods nor beasts—it is impermissible for any human being to rule another without that other's consent (as God may rule man or man may rule beasts) or for one man to take from another the fruit of that other's own labor. Thus, the Virginia Declaration of Rights, Section 2, says, "all power is vested in, and consequently derived from, the people"; the Declaration, the governments that are instituted by men to secure their natural rights "deriv[e] their just powers from the consent of the governed."

Shortly after the Declaration of Independence was adopted, most of the remaining states drafted constitutions that likewise relied upon some or all of the key principles of the Declaration. North Carolina, Maryland, and Delaware all recognized the consent principle in their constitutions: "That all political power is vested in and derived from the people only" (North Carolina Constitution of 1776, Declaration of Rights, Section 1); and "that all government of right originates from the people, is founded in compact only, and instituted solely for the good of the whole" (Maryland Constitution of 1776, Declaration of Rights, Article I; Delaware Constitution of 1776, Declaration of Rights, Section 1). Maryland also explicitly recognized the right of the people "to reform the old or establish a new government . . . whenever the ends of government are perverted, and public liberty manifestly endangered, and all other means of redress are ineffectual" (Article IV). Delaware similarly regarded the right, and the obligation, of the people "to establish a new, or reform the old government" "whenever the ends of government are perverted, and public liberty manifestly endangered by the Legislature singly, or a treacherous combination of both" the legislative and executive branches (Section 5).

Pennsylvania's constitution, also adopted in the fall of 1776, included a more comprehensive reiteration of the Declaration's principles, similar to that which had been adopted by Virginia.

I. That all men are born equally free and independent, and have certain natural, inherent, and inalienable rights, amongst which are, the enjoying and defending life and liberty, acquiring, possessing and protecting property, and pursuing and obtaining happiness and safety. . . .

IV. That all power being originally inherent in, and consequently derived from, the people; therefore all officers of government, whether legislative or executive, are their trustees and servants, and at all times accountable to them.

V. That government is, or ought to be, instituted for the common benefit, protection and security of the people, nation or community; and not for the particular emolument or advantage of any single man, family, or sett of men, who are a part only of that community; And that the community hath an indubitable, unalienable and indefeasible right to reform, alter, or abolish government in such manner as shall be by that community judged most conducive to the public weal.

Massachusetts similarly codified the principles of the Declaration in its Constitution of 1776, and when that constitution was rejected (largely because it was drafted by a convention that had not been elected for the purpose and thus was made without the consent of the people), those principles were carried over to the constitution ultimately adopted in 1780. In the constitution's preamble, Massachusetts acknowledged that "whenever th[e] great objects [of government] are not obtained, the people have a right to alter the government." The document also asserted that government is grounded in consent: "The body politic is formed by a voluntary association of individuals: it is a social compact, by which the whole people covenants with each citizen, and each citizen with the whole people, that all shall be governed by certain laws for the common good." Then, in Article I of its Declaration of Rights, Massachusetts articulated a statement of equality and inalienable rights strikingly similar to the lead sentence of the second paragraph of the Declaration of Independence.

All men are born free and equal, and have certain natural, essential, and unalienable rights; among which may be reckoned the right of enjoying and defending their lives and liberties; that of acquiring, possessing, and protecting property; in fine, that of seeking and obtaining their safety and happiness.

New Hampshire included similar provisions in a Declaration of Rights when it replaced its original, pre–Declaration constitution with new constitutions in 1784 and 1792.

Article I. All men are born equally free and independent; therefore, all government of right originates from the people, is founded on consent, and instituted for the general good.

Article II. All men have certain natural, essential, and inherent rights; among which are—the enjoying and defending life and liberty—acquiring, possessing and protecting property—and in a word, of seeking and obtaining happiness.

Article X. . . . whenever the ends of government are perverted, and public liberty manifestly endangered, and all other means of redress are ineffectual, the people may, and of right ought, to reform the old, or establish a new government.

Thus, the principles of the Declaration were common currency in the early state constitutions, but it was not until Georgia enacted its new constitution in February 1777 that the Declaration was mentioned, and then only with a passing reference, in the preamble, to the fact that independence had been declared. New York went further a couple of months later, reprinting the entire Declaration of Independence in the preamble to the constitution it adopted in April 1777. And South Carolina, like Georgia, mentioned the Declaration in passing when it replaced its temporary constitution of 1776 with a permanent constitution in 1778. In all three cases, though, the Declaration was mentioned in a "whereas" clause, suggesting a mere recitation of fact instead of a judicially enforceable principle. This was much like the recitations of principle in the first constitutions in Maryland, New Hampshire, New Jersey, North Carolina, and South Carolina, which appear simply as a rationale for separation from the existing government.[3] Yet in Massachusetts, Pennsylvania, and Virginia—the most influential of the original states—as well as in Delaware and New Hampshire, the substance of the Declaration's principles appears in those states' declarations of rights, alongside other statements of rights that had customarily been enforceable in the courts, such as the right to trial by jury, the freedom of speech and press, and the free exercise of religion. It is thus likely that these statements of principle were also understood to be judicially enforceable.

What is implicit in the constitutions of Delaware, Massachusetts, New Hampshire, Pennsylvania, and Virginia was explicit in the first constitution enacted by Vermont in 1777 and again in the Vermont Constitutions of 1786 and 1793.[4] The preamble to the Vermont Constitution of 1777 contained the now-familiar statements that governments are formed, by consent, to protect the natural rights of the people and that the people have a right to change their government whenever it fails to meet those ends.

Whereas, all government ought to be instituted and supported, for the security and protection of the community, as such, and to enable the individuals who compose it, to enjoy their natural rights, and the other blessings which the Author of existence has bestowed upon man; and whenever those great ends of government are not obtained, the people have a right, by common consent, to change it, and take such measures as to them may appear necessary to promote their safety and happiness.

But Vermont also reiterated these principles in a separate Declaration of Rights, declaring in Section 1

That all men are born equally free and independent, and have certain, inherent and unalienable rights, amongst which are the enjoying and defending life and liberty; acquiring, possessing and protecting property, and pursuing and obtaining happiness and safety.

And further declaring in Section 6

That government is, or ought to be, instituted for the common benefit, protection, and security of the people, nation or community; and not for the particular emolument or advantage of any single man, family or set of men, who are a part only of that community; and that the community hath an indubitable, unalienable and indefeasible right to reform, alter, or abolish, government, in such manner as shall be, by that community, judged most conducive to the public weal.

As with Delaware, Massachusetts, New Hampshire, Pennsylvania, and Virginia, the sentiments in Vermont's Declaration of Rights were expressed alongside other statements of rights commonly enforced by the courts. But Vermont went further, as if to emphasize the point. Section 43 of the main body of the Vermont Constitution provided: "The declaration of rights is hereby declared to be a part of the Constitution of this State, and ought never to be violated, on any pretense whatsoever." Although Section 43 does not expressly mention judicial review, the fact that it appears in the main body of the Constitution refutes any contention that the Declaration of Rights was designed to be merely a hortatory statement of aspirations.

The Vermont Constitutions of 1777, 1786, and 1793 are significant for another reason. They explicitly drew the conclusion logically compelled by the statement in the Declaration of Independence that "all men are created equal." "All men" meant all human beings, Negro slaves included, and the Vermont constitutions powerfully made the point by concluding the statement of equality and inalienable rights in Section 1 of its Declaration of Rights with the following sentence.

Therefore, no male person, born in this country, or brought from over sea, ought to be holden by law, to serve any person, as a servant, slave or apprentice, after he arrives to the age of twenty-one years, nor female, in like manner, after she arrives to the age of eighteen years, unless they are bound by their own consent, after they arrive to such age, or bound by law, for the payment of debts, damages, fines, costs, or the like.

Not every state subscribed to all of these principles in their own state constitutions, a fact that was the source of a growing discord that culminated in the Civil War. For example, the South Carolina Constitution of 1790 limited due process protections to "freemen." Furthermore, apart from the Virginia Constitution of 1776, penned at the height of devotion to the Declaration's principles, not one of the early southern state constitutions mentioned equality. But the fact that the slave states of the South felt compelled to ignore certain of the Declaration's principles in their constitutions to avoid highlighting the conflict between those principles and their own "peculiar" institution of slavery demonstrates how uniform was the view among the founders—northern and southern alike—that the Declaration meant what it said. It was a statement of universal truth, applicable to all men at all times, not just to white male Europeans of property, as the Supreme Court would hold in the *Dred Scott* case (1856). And it was not a meaningless proposition, as twentieth-century historian Carl Becker would claim in an influential book that would misinform understanding of the Declaration for generations.

## The Declaration in the Northwest Territory

In 1783, after years of wrangling over the disposition of the western lands, Virginia ceded to the United States her claims to all land northwest of the Ohio River, a tract of land that would become the states of Ohio, Indiana, Illinois, Michigan, and Wisconsin. The terms of the Virginia Act of Cession, which were scrupulously followed by Congress in the years to come, included this provision: "that the States so formed shall be distinct republican States, and admitted members of the Federal Union, having the same rights of sovereignty, freedom, and independence as the other States." The two ideas codified in the Act of Cession are extremely important in the historical development of the United States as one nation composed of free and equal states instead of a nation composed of original states and a collection of colonial territories. The first would find its way into the U.S. Constitution of 1787, as the Republican Guaranty Clause of Article IV, Section 4. The second would come to be known as the Equal Footing Doctrine, pursuant to which every new state would be admitted to the Union on an "equal footing" with the original states; see, for example, *United States v. Alaska* (1997) and *Lessee of Pollard v. Hagan* (1845).

The two doctrines expressed in the Virginia Act of Cession shed a great deal of light on the role the Declaration of Independence and its principles—particularly the principle of equality and its derivative, consent—were intended to play in the expansion of the American regime to new territories in the West. The constitutional guaranty of a republican form of government, it was argued by those opposed to slavery, required Congress to deny admission to states that permitted slavery. Those in favor of slavery argued that the Equal Footing doctrine guaranteed to each new state the same constitutional protections of slavery as the original states enjoyed. The actions taken by Congress with respect to the Northwest Territory demonstrate that the former argument was more consistent with the thinking of the founders, but the latter argument would eventually prevail, placing the nation on the road to the Civil War.

"The distinguishing feature" of a republican form of government, according to the Supreme Court in *Duncan v. McCall* (1891), "is the right of the people to choose their own officers for governmental administration, and pass their own laws in virtue of the legislative power reposed in representative bodies, whose legitimate acts may be said to be those of the people themselves." In an extended territory, republican government is the means by which the Declaration's principle of consent by the governed is implemented. And because the principle of consent is mandated by the self-evidence of the proposition that all men are created equal, the constitutional guaranty of a republican form of government is analytically incompatible with the existence of slavery. As James Madison, himself a slaveowner, wrote on the eve of the federal constitutional convention of 1787, "Where slavery exists the republican Theory becomes still more fallacious."

This conclusion was given effect in the Northwest Ordinance, which was adopted by the Continental Congress on July 13, 1787, "for the government of the territory of the United States northwest of the river Ohio" or, in other words, for the territory that had been ceded to the United States by Virginia in 1783. Article VI of that ordinance provided:

There shall be neither slavery nor involuntary servitude in the said territory, otherwise than in the punishment of crime, whereof the party shall have been duly convicted.

Some historians argue that the preamble to the ordinance makes clear that the prohibition on slavery was not adopted because the soil and climate of the region would not support a slave economy. On the contrary, the preamble demonstrates that the antislavery provision was mandated by the principles upon which the nation and existing states had been founded, namely, the principles of the Declaration of Independence.

And for extending the fundamental principles of civil and religious liberty, which form the basis whereon these republics [that is, the existing states], their laws and constitutions, are erected; to fix and establish those principles as the basis of all laws, constitutions, and governments, which forever hereafter shall be formed in the said territory; to provide, also, for the establishment of States, and permanent government therein, and for their admission to a share in the Federal councils on an equal footing with the original States, at as early periods as may be consistent with the general interest: It is hereby ordained and declared, by the authority aforesaid, that the following articles shall be considered as articles of compact, between the original States and the people and States in the said territory, and forever remain unalterable, unless by common consent. . . .

The antislavery article, like the other six articles of the ordinance, was to be considered an "article of compact" that was unalterable unless by the common consent of the original states and the people and states in the new territory because it was mandated by the fundamental principles of civil and religious liberty upon which the existing states were founded and which were to serve as the foundation of government in the new states as well.

The language of the preamble also gives lie to the claim that the Equal Footing Doctrine guaranteed to new states the same right to permit slavery as existed in the original states. The new states to be formed in the Northwest Territory were expressly guaranteed the right to enter the Union on an equal footing with the original states. But the prohibition on slavery was to remain an unalterable principle, established as the basis for "all laws, constitutions, and governments" that would thereafter be formed in the territory.

While the hyper-technical argument might be (and eventually was) advanced that the prohibition applied only to all territorial governments, not to governments formed after admission to statehood, the word *constitutions* undermines that contention. Because the territories were governed by act of Congress until admission to statehood, they did not have separate constitutions. Thus, the word *constitutions* must necessarily have been intended to apply to the constitutions of state governments even after admission to the Union.

Moreover, when the eastern portion of the territory petitioned for statehood in 1802, Congress mandated in the Ohio Enabling Act both that the new state "shall be admitted into the Union upon the same footing with the original States in all respects whatever" and that the new state's constitution and government "shall be republican, and not repugnant to the ordinance of the thirteenth of July, one thousand seven hundred and eighty-seven, between the original States and the people and States of the territory northwest of the river Ohio."[5]

The people of Ohio (and subsequently the people of the other Northwest Territory states) complied with that mandate by incorporating into Article VIII, Section 2 of their new constitution the requirement that "[t]here shall be neither slavery nor involuntary servitude in this State, otherwise than for the punishment of crimes, whereof the party shall have been duly convicted." This provision was necessary, according to the Ohio constitution, so "[t]hat the general, great, and essential principles of liberty and free government may be recognized, and forever unalterably established." Section 1 of Article VIII contained the litany of principles drawn from the Declaration of Independence: the equality of all men; the doctrine of inalienable rights, including the rights to life, liberty, property, and the pursuit of happiness; the requirement of consent; and the right to alter or abolish governments when necessary to effect the legitimate ends of government. Moreover, Section 1 expressly tied these principles to the idea of "republican" government.

That all men are born equally free and independent, and have certain natural, inherent, and unalienable rights, amongst which are the enjoying and defending life and liberty, acquiring, possessing, and protecting property, and pursuing and obtaining happiness and safety; and every free republican government being founded on their sole authority, and organized for the great purpose of protecting their rights and liberties and securing their independence; to effect these ends, they have at all times a complete power to alter, reform, or abolish their government, whenever they may deem it necessary.

Equal footing, then, did not allow new states to avail themselves of the slavery compromises in the Constitution at the expense of the republican principle. Those compromises were to be cabined to the original states.

This conclusion is compelled not just by the theory of the Declaration, but also by the explicit terms of both the Northwest Ordinance and the Constitution themselves. The Northwest Ordinance's antislavery article, Article VI, contains a proviso clause, elided over above.

[P]rovided always, that any person escaping into the same, from whom labor or service is lawfully claimed in any one of the original states, such fugitive may be lawfully reclaimed and conveyed to the person claiming his or her labor or service as aforesaid.

The obligation to return fugitive slaves expressly extended only to slaves escaping from the "original states." Article I, Section 9 of the U.S. Constitution contains a similar limitation: "The migration or importation of such persons as any of the states now existing shall think proper to admit shall not be prohibited by the Congress prior to the year 1808."[6] Thus, the Northwest Ordinance was a large step toward full vindication of the Declaration's principles. The fact that the antislavery provisions in the ordinance were required by the principles upon which the nation was founded and mandated by the requirement of republican government in the Virginia Act of Cession bolsters the contention that those principles were themselves codified as positive law in the U.S. Constitution's Republican Guaranty Clause.

## Provisional Government in the Territories South of the Ohio River

The force and full import of the Northwest Ordinance was not long in coming, particularly in the South. When North Carolina ceded its western lands—present-day Tennessee—to the United States in 1789, it did so on the condition that Congress would govern the area "in a manner similar to that which they support in the government west of the Ohio," protecting "the inhabitants against any enemies" and never barring or depriving them "of any privileges which the people in that territory west of the Ohio enjoy" (Act of April 2, 1790, accepting the North Carolina cession). Unlike the Virginia cession several years earlier, the North Carolina cession contained a proviso: "Provided always, That no regulations made or to be made by Congress shall tend to emancipate slaves." Congress accepted North Carolina's conditions and promptly provided by law for territorial government in the areas south of the Ohio River that followed the Northwest Ordinance "except so far as is otherwise provided in the conditions expressed" in the North Carolina cession—in other words, except for the prohibition on slavery (Act of May 26, 1790, Section 2).[7]

The North Carolina cession condition was repeated by South Carolina and Georgia, when those states ceded land that would eventually become the states of Alabama and Mississippi. The Georgia cession, for example, specifically required that the Northwest Ordinance "shall, in all its parts, extend to the territory contained in the present act of cession, that article only excepted which forbids slavery." Following the South Carolina cession, Congress authorized the president to establish a territorial government for the Mississippi Territory, "in all respects similar to that now exercised in the territory northwest of the Ohio, excepting and excluding the last article of the [Northwest Ordinance]" (Act of April 7, 1798, Section 3).[8]

The states admitted to the Union out of these territories—Alabama, Mississippi, and Tennessee, as well as Kentucky, which was originally part of Virginia—were thus all exempted from the antislavery provision of the Northwest Ordinance. However, they were admitted as though they were in compliance with the Republican Guaranty Clause. Kentucky was admitted to statehood, for example, despite a provision in Article IX of its 1792 constitution restricting the ability of the legislature to emancipate slaves. Kentucky dealt with the facial contradiction with the Declaration's equality principle by simply "declaring" in Article XII, Section 1 that "all men, when they form a social compact, are equal"—a far cry from the

self-evident proposition that all men are created equal contained in the Declaration of Independence.[9] Similarly, the Mississippi and Alabama Enabling Acts of March 1, 1817, and March 2, 1819, respectively, provided that the new government, "when formed, shall be republican, and not repugnant to the principles of the [Northwest Ordinance], so far as the same has been extended to the said territory by the articles of agreement between the United States and the State of Georgia, or of the Constitution of the United States." Both states complied with the terms of their respective enabling acts with constitutions that, like Kentucky's, not only permitted slavery but also severely restricted the ability of the legislature to emancipate slaves. Both states' own Declaration of Rights recognized only that "all freemen, when they form a social compact, are equal in rights."[10]

These subtle restatements of the Declaration's equality principle were made not because slavery was thought compatible with the Declaration, but because it was understood that slavery was not compatible with the proposition that all men are created equal.[11] Alexander Stephens would confirm this point in his Cornerstone Speech, delivered after the South had seceded but before the Civil War had begun with the firing on Fort Sumter.

> The prevailing ideas entertained by [Jefferson] and by most of the leading statesmen of the time of the formation of the old constitution, were that the enslavement of the African was in violation of the laws of nature: that it was wrong in principle, socially, morally, and politically.

Once again, the record from the states proves that Chief Justice Roger B. Taney was wrong in holding in *Dred Scott* that the Declaration's equality clause did not extend to all persons.

Congress promptly admitted Mississippi to statehood on an equal footing with the existing states, noting in the December 10, 1817, Act of Admission that the Mississippi Constitution and state government was "republican and in conformity to the principles of the Northwest Ordinance." Apparently, someone forgot to read all the way through to the end of the Northwest Ordinance, where Article VI expressly prohibited slavery. The mistake was corrected in the December 14, 1819, Alabama Act of Admission, in which Congress recognized that the Alabama Constitution and state government "is republican, and in conformity to the principles of the [Northwest Ordinance], so far as the same have been extended to the said territory by the articles of agreement between the United States and the state of Georgia."

In light of these actions by Congress, it might be contended that Congress simply did not believe that the Republican Guaranty Clause had anything to say about slavery or equality. A better reading, though—given the countervailing precedent in the Northwest Territory—is that these states, carved out of original states, were all entitled to avail themselves of the Constitution's compromises with slavery to the same extent as were the original states from whence they came. Furthermore, they were to that extent exempt from the republican principle that had been applied to the Northwest Territory states. In other words, with respect to these states, Congress was duty bound—constitutionally, as well as contractually, by virtue of the cession agreements—not to consider the conflict between slavery and the constitutional command that each state have a republican form of government.

James Madison makes the same point, albeit obliquely, in *The Federalist* (No. 43). There, he contends that the authority given to Congress by the Republican Guaranty Clause "extends no farther than to a guaranty of a republican form of government, which supposes a pre-existing government of the form which is to be guaranteed. As long as the existing republican forms are continued by the States, they are guaranteed by the Federal Constitution." Congress could not challenge the existing governments' countenance of slavery as unrepublican, but it had to "suppose," or presume, the contrary. The effect of the several cession acts was to extend that presumption to the new states formed from the original beneficiaries of that presumption.

Madison seems to have thought slavery incompatible with the Republican Guaranty Clause, however. In the same *Federalist* paper, he suggests, in language that is a model of studied ambiguity, that the participation of former slaves in the political process would make a government more republican.

I take no notice of an unhappy species of population abounding in some of the States, who during the calm of regular government are sunk below the level of men; but who in the tempestuous scenes of civil violence may emerge into the human character, and give a superiority of strength to any party with which they may associate themselves.

In cases where it may be doubtful on which side justice lies, what better umpires could be desired by two violent factions, flying to arms and tearing a State to pieces, than the representatives of confederate States not heated by the local flame? To the impartiality of Judges they would unite the affection of friends.

Madison leads his readers to believe, without actually saying, that a slave insurrection would allow a state to call on the national government for assistance. He also subtly suggests that "justice," and hence the stronger republican claim, would lie with those who emerged from slavery, a condition in which they were treated "below the level of men," into the "human character." That is, into a position of natural equality, entitled to the same inalienable rights and requirement that they be governed only by their consent as were the people who formed the existing government. In any event, the passage clearly shows Madison applying the Republican Guaranty Clause to the slavery question.

## Admission of New States Carved Out of the Louisiana Territory

If the founders codified the Declaration's principles in the Republican Guaranty Clause, but those principles had limited operation in the original states because of the Constitution's compromises with slavery, then the conflict between the Republican guaranty principle and the slavery compromise should come to a head as slaveholding states that were not carved from original states began seeking admission to the Union. That came about in short order, once the United States purchased the Louisiana Territory from France in 1803. Because this was new territory, not territory ceded to the national government by existing states, it was not entitled to the proslavery contractual presumption, derived from the various deeds of cession by existing states, from which Alabama, Kentucky, Mississippi, and Tennessee had benefited. Instead, its claim to admission was governed by the terms of the treaty of April 30, 1803, between the United States and France, which provided the following.

The inhabitants of the ceded territory shall be incorporated in the Union of the United States, and admitted as soon as possible, according to the principles of the Federal constitution, to the enjoyment of all the rights, advantages and immunities of citizens of the United States.

Just what those principles were would soon give rise to one of the most profound debates in American history.

The first challenge came when the southern portion of the Louisiana Territory, the Orleans district, sought admission in 1811.[12] Section 3 of the Louisiana Enabling Act authorized the people of that district—present-day Louisiana—to adopt a constitution and to form a state government: "*Provided,* The constitution to be formed, in virtue of the authority herein given, shall be republican, and consistent with the constitution of the United States; that it shall contain the fundamental principles of civil and religious liberty." Section 4 provided that "the said state shall be admitted into the Union upon the same footing with the original states."

Here was the conflict presented in textual terms. Louisiana's new constitution was, on the one hand, to be "republican" and to contain the "fundamental principles of civil liberty," and, on the other hand, the state was to be admitted on an equal footing with the existing states. The guaranty of a republican form of government applied to all the existing states (albeit with the slavery presumption). But the guarantees of civil and religious liberty were not imposed on the existing states by the federal Constitution (unless those "fundamental principles" are subsumed under the Republican Guaranty Clause). Was it permissible, then, for Congress to impose such terms as a condition of statehood? Could it impose any terms on new states and still comply with the Equal Footing Doctrine? The admission of Ohio stood as a precedent for the affirmative, but instead of resolving the question, Congress began to question whether the conditions it had imposed on Ohio's admission were themselves constitutional.

During the Louisiana admission debate, the thorny theoretical problem arose not over slavery—which was not addressed in the Louisiana constitution—but over some territory known as West Florida, over which the United States and Spain were having a dispute. Congress wanted to include West Florida in the new state of Louisiana, but it also wanted to keep its options open in the event that the president reached a settlement with Spain that recognized Spain's claim to some or all of West Florida. Thus, Congress sought to impose two conditions on Louisiana's admission: that the title of West Florida would remain subject to future negotiations, and that the people then living in West Florida would, in the meantime, be entitled to representation in the Louisiana legislature.

Perhaps appreciating the full import of the principle that was about to be applied for the first time to a southern slave state, South Carolina representative John C. Calhoun objected. Congress in response shifted gears, imposing the conditions on the grant of land to Louisiana instead of admitting the state to the Union. Although that left the condition regarding civil and religious liberty and others (such as the requirement that the government be conducted in English), and with the immediate issue of concern—the status of West Florida—having been resolved, the more fundamental debate was put off to another day.

Louisiana was admitted in 1812, with a constitution that declared in its preamble that it was adopted "[i]n order to secure to all the citizens thereof the enjoyment of the right of life, liberty and property." In its Act of Admission, Congress stated "[t]hat the said state shall be, and is hereby declared to be one, of the United States of America, and admitted into the Union on an equal footing with the original states, in all respects whatever."

The next portion of the Louisiana Territory to seek admission to statehood was Missouri in 1820. Mississippi and Alabama had by then been admitted, with constitutions permitting slavery that Congress was obligated to recognize because of the terms of the South Carolina and Georgia cessions. Indiana and Illinois had also been admitted, and in the latter case the arguments pro and con about the power of Congress to impose conditions on admission were honed (and brought into line with the politics of slavery).[13]

The Illinois Enabling Act of April 18, 1818, like its predecessors in Ohio and Indiana, mandated that the constitution and state government adopted by Illinois "shall be republican, and not repugnant to the" Northwest Ordinance, including the prohibition on slavery. But Article VI of the Illinois Constitution of 1818 provided only that "[n]either slavery nor involuntary servitude shall hereafter be introduced into this State, otherwise than for punishment of crimes, whereof the party shall have been duly convicted." Moreover, it specifically permitted slave labor to be used in the Shawneetown salt mines for seven years, and it recognized lifelong indentured servitude.

New York representative James Tallmadge Jr. opposed Illinois's admission to statehood because these provisions permitted slavery, in contravention of the condition in the Illinois Enabling Act mandating that the state constitution conform to the principles of the Northwest Ordinance, which he asserted were in turn required by the terms of the Virginia cession in 1783. Mississippi representative George Poindexter provided a threefold response. First, the Illinois provision was not materially different from what had already been approved in Ohio; second, Illinois "virtually" complied with the terms of the Northwest Ordinance; and third, Congress could not prevent a state from altering its constitution, even changing provisions that were enacted because they were required as a condition on admission to statehood.[14] Kentucky representative Richard Clough Anderson Jr. weighed in as well, contending that the antislavery provision was imposed by Congress, not the Virginia cession, and could therefore be altered by the consent of Congress. "The conditions reserved by Virginia on making the cession," he argued, "were that a certain number of States should be erected from the Territory, and all existing rights of the people preserved." Among those rights, he contended, was the right to own slaves, because slavery was already in existence in the Illinois portion of the Northwest Territory at the time of the Virginia cession.

What Representative Anderson failed to mention was that the Virginia cession also required that the states admitted from the territory were to be "distinct republican States." Representative Tallmadge apparently thought that the "republican" condition barred the introduction of slavery or at the very least was a solemn pledge made by Congress so simultaneously given as to amount to a compact with

Virginia. Moreover, he contended "that the interest, honor, and faith of the nation, required it scrupulously to guard against slavery's passing into a territory where they have power to prevent its entrance."

Illinois was ultimately admitted to statehood, but whether it was because Congress believed the Illinois constitution "virtually" complied with the antislavery requirement, the Virginia cession prohibited an antislavery requirement, or Congress was without power to impose any conditions on statehood has not been definitely determined. The conflict between the republican principle and a vested right to own slaves would get a much more complete airing when Missouri knocked at Congress's door.

On February 13, 1819, Representative Tallmadge renewed the effort he had begun during the debate over admission of Illinois with the following amendment to the Missouri Enabling Act.

And provided, That the further introduction of slavery or involuntary servitude be prohibited, except for the punishment of crimes, whereof the party shall have been fully convicted; and that all children born within the said state, after the admission thereof into the Union, shall be free at the age of twenty-five years.

The House accepted Tallmadge's amendment, but the Senate rejected it. The debate over the Missouri bill was held over to the next Congress, during which it centered on a proposal by New York representative John W. Taylor to ban slavery in the new state altogether.

During that debate, Congress explored the full depth of the Equal Footing Doctrine, the doctrine of unconstitutional conditions, and the monumental compromise between the equality principle of the Declaration of Independence and the Republican Guaranty Clause of the Constitution, on the one hand, and the slavery clauses of the Constitution, on the other. Massachusetts representative Timothy Fuller contended that Congress had the power—indeed, was obliged—to require that Missouri prohibit slavery as a condition on its admission to statehood because slavery was itself incompatible with the Republican Guaranty Clause. Taylor added that slavery violated the "principle of the Constitution of the United States, that all men are free and equal." Predictably, the southern delegations strenuously objected. Representative Alexander Smyth articulated the main objection.

It has been questioned by some, whether a constitution can be said to be republican, which does not exclude slavery. But we must understand the phrase, "republican form of government," as the people understood it when they adopted the Constitution. . . . It would be perfidious toward them to put on the Constitution a different construction from that which induced them to adopt it. The people of each of the States who adopted the Constitution, except Massachusetts, owned slaves; yet they certainly considered their own constitutions to be republican. . . .

Sir, if this proposition is adopted, it will be regarded hereafter as an exercise of the power to guaranty a republican form of government to every State in the Union. You are about to admit a State, and you require her to insert in her constitution a clause against slavery. Will it not seem that you have done this by your authority to guaranty a republican form of government? I think it will; for you have no other power that seems to warrant prescribing in part the form of the State constitution. If, in the exercise of this power, you may require of a new State to insert in her constitution a clause against slavery, you may, under the same authority, require an old State to add such a clause to her constitution. Thus you may require of the old States to exclude slavery, or provide for its abolition. The

slaveholding States must make common cause with Missouri; for the recognition of such a power in this Government would be fatal to them.

Representative Smyth's argument ignored Representative Tallmadge's earlier apparent reliance on the "republican" guaranty language in the Virginia Act of Cession to support his claim that the antislavery provision in the Northwest Ordinance was required. His argument also did not respond to the finer distinction involved in the Madisonian supposition. Tragically, Fuller did not issue a rejoinder on either front, and the last great opportunity to reconcile the slavery compromise with the Declaration's principles by limiting the extent of the compromise to the territory of the original states was lost. As a result, the Declaration's self-evident truth of the equality of all human beings and its principle of God-given, inalienable rights took on a decidedly different cast. Responding directly to Taylor's invocation of the Declaration of Independence, Smyth observed, in an argument that unfortunately carried the day:

[The Congress of 1776] asserted [in the Declaration of Independence] that man cannot alienate his liberty, nor by compact deprive his posterity of liberty. Slaves are not held as having alienated their liberty by compact. They are held under the law and usage of nations, from the remotest time of which we have any historical knowledge, and by the municipal laws of the States, over which the Congress of 1776 had not, and this Congress have not, any control. We agree with the Congress of 1776, that men, on entering civil society, cannot alienate their right to liberty and property, and that they cannot, by compact, bind their posterity. And, therefore, we contend that the people of Missouri, cannot alienate their rights, or bind their posterity, by a compact with Congress.

Thus did the great principles of the Declaration get perverted into a defense of the very antithesis of those principles.

## The Declaration and the Civil War

The shift away from the Declaration's principles continued as new states below the Missouri compromise line were admitted to the Union. Texas, Arkansas, and Florida drafted constitutions between 1836 and 1839 protecting slavery and advocating an altered version of the equality principle similar to the language first adopted by Kentucky in 1792. These state constitutions include a similarly subtle shift in the language of inalienable rights, a shift that further allowed some in the South ultimately to make the argument that the right to own property in other human beings was one of the fundamental rights recognized by the Declaration of Independence and hence protected by the Constitution. Where the Declaration of Independence—and the Declarations of Rights in Massachusetts, New Hampshire, Pennsylvania, and Virginia—spoke of the inalienable rights with which all men were endowed, the Arkansas Declaration of Rights in 1836 and the Florida Declaration of Rights in 1839 limited the claim of inalienable rights to the same class of people that were under the equality umbrella, namely, those forming the social compact. Thus was the inalienable right to property interpreted in a way that allowed some—those who had formed the social compact—to make claims to ownership of property in other human beings without creating a conflict with those other individuals' own inalienable right to liberty. And in this misapplication of the Declaration's principles, the only legitimate purpose of government was to protect that property interest in human chattels, and the South was able to make the argument that it could alter or abolish its connection to the existing government, by secession, because that government, in pursing policies designed to vindicate the inalienable rights of all men, was failing to protect the new inalienable rights as defined by the South.

Following the Civil War, each of the southern states that had seceded from the Union adopted new constitutions. Perhaps not surprisingly, most of the new southern constitutions had provisions prohibiting slavery, but in addition the equality provision in several of these constitutions was amended to more closely track the language of the Declaration of Independence. In Article I of its 1865 constitution, for example, Alabama reiterated its statement of equality but deleted the reference to "freemen." The Arkansas Constitution of 1864 similarly replaced "all freemen" with "all men" in its statement of equality. And Missouri began its 1865 constitution by declaring: "That we hold it to be self-evident that all men are endowed by their Creator with certain inalienable rights, among which are life, liberty, the enjoyment of the fruits of their own labor, and the pursuit of happiness."

Perhaps because the Reconstruction republicans did not think the changes went far enough—several state constitutions, for example, continued to claim that only "freemen, when they form a social compact, have equal rights," and others continued to avoid any reference to equality or dropped their preexisting circumscribed reference to equality—a new round of constitutions was enacted in most of the South between 1867 and 1868. In these, the equality and unalienable rights language of the Declaration of Independence was prominently featured. The Alabama, Louisiana, and North Carolina constitutions of 1867 and

1868, for example, tracked the equality and inalienable rights language of the Declaration of Independence virtually word for word, and Florida and South Carolina adopted language similar to that of the Declaration. The Arkansas Constitution of 1868 recognized that the "equality of all persons before the law is recognized and shall ever remain inviolate," and Georgia's new constitution in 1868 tracked the Equal Protection language of the Fourteenth Amendment. As with the earlier constitutions adopted by many of the northern states, these provisions were included in declarations of rights that also contained many of the same judicially enforceable rights found in the U.S. Constitution's Bill of Rights. The principles of the Declaration, now codified in these states, thus should be viewed as judicially enforceable to the same extent as the rest of the provisions in those states' declarations of rights.

The Declaration of Independence recognizes that the people have a right to alter or abolish their government not whenever it suits them but whenever the government becomes destructive of the ends for which it was established, namely, the protection of inalienable rights. Several of the northern states adopted alter or abolish provisions in their own constitutions that tracked both aspects of this principle. The Maryland Constitution of 1776, for example, provided: "whenever the ends of government are perverted, and public liberty manifestly endangered, and all other means of redress are ineffectual, the people may, and of right ought, to reform the old or establish a new government." Similarly, Massachusetts provided in the preamble to its 1780 constitution that "whenever these great objects [of government] are not obtained, the people have

a right to alter the government." And the Ohio Constitution of 1802, the first formed under the Northwest Ordinance, provided in Article VIII: "to effect [the] ends [of protecting the people's rights and liberties and securing their independence, the people] have at all times a complete power to alter, reform, or abolish their government, whenever they may deem it necessary."

This principle was altered in several of the southern state antebellum constitutions, which recognized a right in the people to alter their government whenever they thought it expedient, not just when it ceased to protect inalienable rights. The Mississippi and Alabama constitutions of 1817 and 1819, for example, held that the people "have at all times an inalienable and indefeasible right to alter, reform, or abolish their form of government, in such manner as they may think expedient." The Missouri Constitution of 1820 similarly provided, in Article XIII, "that the people of this State have the inherent, sole, and exclusive right of regulating the internal government and police thereof, and of altering and abolishing their constitution and form of government whenever it may be necessary to their safety and happiness."

This change in formulation, though subtle, was extremely significant, for it enabled the South to claim a right to secede from the Union that existed wholly apart from the purpose for which, in the Declaration's formulation, the right existed. Thus, in its 1860 Declaration of Secession, South Carolina claimed that the Declaration of Independence recognized the right of the people to abolish their government whenever it became "destructive of the ends for which it was established." However, South Carolina avoided any mention of the Declaration's description of just what those ends were. In the South Carolina formulation, any ends would do; in the Declaration's formulation, only legitimate ends, grounded in human nature and hence unalienable, would support a claim of revolutionary right.

The southern formulation—a fallacy that had been put forward primarily by John C. Calhoun—was repudiated in several of the postwar constitutions. Missouri in 1865 recognized that the right to alter or abolish government "should be exercised in pursuance of law and consistently with the Constitution of the United States." The constitutions of Alabama, Arkansas, Florida, Mississippi, and Missouri all contained a provision expressly acknowledging that there was no right to secede from the Union. This, too, was more in line with the alter or abolish statement of principle contained in the Declaration of Independence—as long as the Union, now rid of the unfortunate compromises with slavery, was back in the business of protecting the unalienable and equal rights of all its citizens. The South's claim of a right to secede failed because its claim was not grounded on moral truth, which alone can serve as the basis for a claim of right. The South's claim of right would have been illegitimate even if the South had prevailed on the battlefield, for it was impossible for the South, having denied the self-evident truths of the Declaration, ever to make the appeal to nature and nature's God that Thomas Jefferson made in the Declaration.

## Conclusion

The nation had paid a dear price to vindicate the principles of the Declaration, and it was not about to let that victory slip away. The prin-

ciples of the Declaration were codified—and thus rendered enforceable—in the Reconstruction-era constitutions of the old confederate states. The Declaration was made even more binding on new states admitted thereafter. Nevada and Nebraska were admitted to statehood during the war years. In the Enabling Acts for each (March 21, 1864, and April 19, 1864, respectively), Congress required that the new states' constitutions, "when formed, shall be republican, and not repugnant to the Constitution of the United States and the principles of the Declaration of Independence." The requirement was repeated in the Enabling Acts for Colorado (March 3, 1875); Montana, North Dakota, South Dakota, and Washington (February 22, 1889); Utah (July 16, 1894); and Arizona, New Mexico, and Oklahoma (June 16, 1906). In these eleven states, the Declaration of Independence thus has the explicit force of positive law. In most of the others, the principles of the Declaration have the same force of law as other provisions in those states' Declaration of Rights. And finally, it might legitimately be said that all fifty states are bound by the principles of the Declaration, as encompassed by the Republican Guaranty Clause of the Constitution. Every state admitted since the Civil War under an Enabling Act binding it to the principles of the Declaration of Independence was also admitted on an equal footing with the original states. In a fitting bit of irony, that can only be true if the original states are likewise bound by the principles of the Declaration of Independence. The Madisonian presumption, which prevented such a conclusion in 1787, was decisively rebutted in the aftermath of Appomattox. The Constitution finally became, to paraphrase Abraham Lincoln, the shining picture of silver that it was intended to be, adorning and preserving the apple of gold, those fitly spoken principles of the Declaration of Independence.

## Notes

1. The Declaration of Independence uses the language of "all men," not "all human beings," but here the word *man* is used generically and not as a gender-specific reference. For an extended discussion of this point, see Thomas G. West, *Vindicating the Founders: Race, Sex, Class, and Justice in the Origins of America* (Lanham, Md.: Rowman and Littlefield, 1997).

2. Alexander Stephens, "Cornerstone Speech," March 21, 1861, in *Alexander H. Stephens in Public and Private with Letters and Speeches* (Philadelphia: National Publishing, 1866), 721–722. See also Harry V. Jaffa, *A New Birth of Freedom: Abraham Lincoln and the Coming of the Civil War* (Lanham, Md.: Roman and Littlefield, 2000), 222–223. Stephens's reference to modern science probably refers to Darwin's *Origin of the Species,* which had been published in 1859. Jefferson himself toyed with the idea of the inequality of the races three-quarters of a century earlier: "I advance it therefore as a suspicion only, that the blacks, whether originally a distinct race, or made distinct by time and circumstance, are inferior to the whites in the endowments both of body and mind." Thomas Jefferson, *Notes on the State of Virginia,* Query XIV, in Thomas Jefferson, *Writings,* ed. Merrill D. Peterson (New York: Library of America, 1984), 256, 270. But for Jefferson, any inequality in physical or intellectual attributes that might exist between the races was only "a powerful obstacle" to emancipation, not a ground for denying that both races were equally human, and therefore endowed with the same inalienable rights.

3. Of the remaining original states, Connecticut did not adopt a new constitution until 1818 and Rhode Island did not adopt a new constitution until 1842.

4. Vermont was not admitted to the Union until 1791, when a lingering dispute between Massachusetts, New Hampshire, and New York about whether Vermont was a separate territory or instead part of one of those states was finally resolved. Nevertheless, it operated as an independent state in the interim, adopting its own constitutions in 1777 and 1786, and another in 1793 after it was admitted to the Union.

5. Congress imposed the same terms on each of the other states that were admitted to the Union from the Northwest Territory: Indiana in 1816, Illinois in 1818, Michigan in 1837, and Wisconsin in 1848.

6. The Constitution's fugitive slave clause, Article IV, Section 2, Clause 3, is not textually limited to the original states, but the greater power to exclude slaves from new states altogether would render such a protection unnecessary.

7. Congress, perhaps recognizing that the protection of slavery was contrary to republican principles, did not mention the protection of slavery but chose to codify that protection only by referring obliquely to the North Carolina cession document.

8. Congress could not bring itself to mention the word *slavery* but extended the protections mandated by the Georgia and South Carolina cessions only with an oblique reference.

9. Kentucky was even clearer when it adopted a new constitution seven years later, providing, "That all free men, when they form a social compact, are equal." Kentucky Constitution of 1799, Article I, Section 1.

10. Both constitutions also recognized the right of the people to alter or abolish their government, not when it becomes destructive of the inalienable rights that it was established to protect, but whenever the people think it "expedient."

11. This point is made explicitly during debate over the Oregon Constitution of 1857. Oregon adopted language that paralleled the language first adopted a half century earlier by Kentucky, and opponents argued that the language "ignores all natural, unalienable rights inherited by man from his great Father. It acknowledges no rights outside of conventional compacts. The great fact enunciated by our forefathers,

that 'all men enjoyed the unalienable right to life, liberty and the pursuit of happiness,' and that 'governments are instituted among men to secure these rights,' is purposely lost sight of by this Constitution." "The Constitution," editorial, *Oregon Argus,* October 10, 1857, A1, quoted in Claudia Burton and Andrew Grade, "A Legislative History of the Oregon Constitution of 1857—Part I (Articles I & II)," Williamette Law Review 37 (summer 2001): 469, 490.

12. The lines of argument began even earlier, when Congress first sought to establish a provisional government for the new area. As David Currie has thoroughly detailed in his book *The Constitution in Congress: The Jeffersonians, 1801–1829* (Chicago: University of Chicago Press, 2001), 99–114, northern Federalists appealed to the Republican Guaranty Clause and to the spirit of the Constitution in opposing the plan for temporary government in the territory, which essentially combined legislative, executive, and judicial power into the hands of a single governor appointed by and serving under the direction of the president. Id. at 112 n.189 (citing 13 *Annals of Congress* 1056 (Rep. Elliott); Everett S. Brown, ed., *William Plumer's Memorandum of Proceedings in the United States Senate, 1803–1807* (Macmillan, 1923), 136). Ironically, it was the southern Democrats who argued that Congress had plenary power over the territories, a position that they would soon repudiate when Congress set its plenary power sights on slavery.

13. A similar concern led to an important difference between the Mississippi admission in 1817 and the Alabama admission in 1819. In the former, certain conditions regarding federal tax exemptions and free navigation were imposed as a condition on statehood; in the latter, the same conditions were imposed as a condition on grants of land. As David Currie noted, "The great Missouri debate had already begun, and Southern Congressmen had seen the dangers that inhered in broad authority to impose conditions on the admission of new states." *The Constitution in Congress,* 232.

14. 33 *Annals of Congress,* 308. Representative Poindexter was mistaken. The Ohio Constitu-

tion of 1802, Article VIII, Section 2, provided: "There shall be neither slavery nor involuntary servitude in this State, otherwise than for the punishment of crimes, whereof the party shall have been duly convicted; nor shall any male person, arrived at the age of twenty-one years, nor female person, arrived at the age of eighteen years, be held to serve any person as a servant, under the pretence of indenture or otherwise, unless such person shall enter into such indenture while in a state of perfect freedom, and on condition of a *bona-fide* consideration, received, or to be received, for their service, except as before excepted. Nor shall any indenture of any negro or mulatto, hereafter made and executed out of the State, or, if made in the State, where the term of service exceeds one year, be of the least validity, except those given in the case of apprenticeships."

## Bibliography

Articles of Agreement and Cession, between the United States and Georgia, Article I, Clause 5 (April 24, 1802). Public Lands Documents, 7th Cong., 1st sess., 125, 126.

Becker, Carl. *The Declaration of Independence: A Study in the History of Political Ideas.* New York: Harcourt Brace, 1922.

Currie, David P. *The Constitution in Congress: The Jeffersonians, 1801–1829.* Chicago: University of Chicago Press, 2001.

Jefferson, Thomas. *Notes on the State of Virginia.* In *Thomas Jefferson, Writings.* Ed. Merrill D. Peterson. New York: Library of America, 1984.

Lincoln, Abraham. "Fragment on the Constitution and the Union." In *The Collected Works of Abraham Lincoln.* Vol. 4. Ed. Roy P. Basler. New Brunswick: Rutgers University Press, 1953, 168–169.

Madison, James. "Vices of the Political System of the United States." In *The Papers of James Madison.* Vol. 9. Ed. William T. Hutchinson. Chicago: University of Chicago Press, 1962–1977, 350–351.

Northwest Ordinance. "An Act for the Government of the Territory of the United States Northwest of the River Ohio" (July 13, 1787), 1 Stat. 51 n.a.

Stephens, Alexander. "Cornerstone Speech," March 21, 1861. In *Alexander H. Stephens in Public and Private with Letters and Speeches*. Philadelphia: National Publishing, 1866.

Thorpe, Francis Newton, ed. *The Federal and State Constitutions, Colonial Charters, and Other Or-ganic Laws of the States, Territories, and Colonies Now or Heretofore Forming the United States of America*. 7 vols. Washington, D.C.: William S. Hein, 1993.

Virginia Act of Cession (December 20, 1783). In 2 Thorpe 955–956.

# The Declaration of Independence, Congress, and Presidents of the United States

### CHARLES A. KROMKOWSKI

With surprisingly few exceptions, students of the Declaration of Independence, the U.S. Congress, and the presidency have failed to recognize or to appreciate the enduring yet dynamic relationship between the nation's founding document and these two national institutions. This oversight, in part, reflects the incomplete and still contested integration of the Declaration of Independence into American political and social thought. The oversight also reflects the limitations of conventional scholarly perspectives that narrowly recognize and assess the Declaration as a singular historical event or as a reference point for interpreting and illuminating the Constitution and American public law.

The dearth of scholarship on the relationship between the Declaration and the legislative and executive branches of the national government is especially ironic. The Declaration of Independence was the most important legislative product of the Second Continental Congress, which commissioned the document, appointed its drafting committee, debated and revised its content, and ultimately endorsed the final version. The Continental Congress also was the first institution to use the Declaration for a public purpose, ordering the publication, dissemination, and public reading of the revo-

lutionary pronouncement to rally American and international support for the delegates' prior but private decision to dissolve the American colonies' political bonds with Great Britain. The Declaration bears early executive associations as well. John Hancock, president of the Continental Congress, sent the Declaration to various political and military leaders, including General George Washington, then the commander of the Continental Army. Upon receiving his copy, Washington ordered the reading of the Declaration of Independence to his troops to demonstrate that "the peace and safety of this Country depends (under God) solely on the success of our arms."

The irony of the prevailing yet narrow reading of the Declaration of Independence runs beyond its original legislative and executive associations. For subsequent members of Congress and presidents have continued and extended these associations—repeatedly engaging, debating, and using the Declaration in various public ways and for a variety of public purposes.

Several obstacles obstruct and consequently qualify the scope of this inquiry into the influences and public uses of the Declaration of Independence. The first is the massive number of times presidents and, especially, members of Congress have referred to the Declaration since 1776. The prevalence of these references and their intended public uses reflect deeply upon American political culture and its political vocabulary. However, many references and uses of the Declaration can be excluded from this analysis without apparent loss because most lack a sufficient substantive depth or political consequence to warrant more detailed consideration. George W. Bush's 2001 inaugural address, for example, includes the following ceremonial reference to the document: "After the Declaration of Independence was signed, Virginia statesman John Page wrote to Thomas Jefferson: 'We know the race is not to the swift nor the battle to the strong.' " Other inaugural addresses and innumerable speeches by members of Congress employ the Declaration in similarly fleeting ways and, therefore, can be omitted from further analysis.

The present structure of the historical record of Congress and individual presidents is another obstacle that requires some qualification. Although every history inevitably suffers the limitations of incomplete and occasionally inaccessible evidentiary sources, the subject and breadth of this inquiry make these limitations particularly apparent. Only a fraction of the more than two-hundred-year history of public debates in Congress is captured by the *Congressional Record* and its predecessors—and even then, the record is selective and incomplete. In addition, the official and private papers of members of Congress are not typically preserved, published, or widely available when archived. Presidential papers, by contrast, are voluminous, better preserved, and comparatively more accessible. Yet under the

best conditions, they typically are not electronically accessible or searchable, and they, too, remain highly selective representations of an individual's public actions and private motivations.

More problematic for this inquiry, the interpretation of presidential papers remains more an art than a science, as students of the presidency have developed few standardized methods that apply easily across time or individual. This methodological deficiency seems inconsequential for individual biographical studies, yet its effects may be significant. Historian David Thelen, for example, associated the reformist impulses of President Rutherford B. Hayes with "the heritage of the antebellum moral reformers" and concluded that "for the rest of his life [Hayes] never shed the earlier reformer's faith that the Bible and the Declaration of Independence held all the truths reformers need to know. They remained his only two inspirations." The portrait of Hayes clearly captures elements of his personality and historical era, but other biographical commentaries and the five-volume *Diary and Letters of Rutherford Birchard Hayes*—the first published diary of a president—offer relatively little textual evidence of the influence of the Declaration during Hayes's presidency (1877–1881). Similar interpretative problems plague the analysis of other presidential papers. For example, the indices of the thirty-volume *Documentary History of the Truman Presidency* and the twenty-one-volume *Papers of Dwight D. Eisenhower* include few and primarily incidental references to the Declaration of Independence. It would be incorrect, however, to infer that neither president used or was affected by the Declaration.

Given these qualifications, this analysis employs two complementary approaches to illuminate different elements of the substantive relationship between the Declaration of Independence and the individuals who have served in Congress and the presidency. The first approach identifies several general principles of the Declaration that are prominently (although inconsistently) reflected throughout the historical development of both national institutions. Revealed is how members of Congress and presidents have participated within—and, therefore, have been influenced by—a political context and tradition whose framework and principles were first articulated in the Declaration of Independence. With the general contours of the Declaration's relationship to these two institutions exposed, the second approach focuses upon the historical particulars that more directly define the content and development of this relationship. It provides for an examination of the specific ways in which individual members of Congress and presidents have employed and used the Declaration of Independence from 1776 through the bicentennial in 1976.

## General Principles

Although many conditions and individuals contributed directly to the formation and subsequent development of Congress and the presidency, several ideas articulated in the Declaration have been consistent and, more important, prior sources of influence upon these institutions. The first (and perhaps most obscure) idea and influences are derived from the ways in which the Declaration characterizes the world and human nature. The metaphysi-

cal premises underlying the Declaration's characterizations are uncomplicated and yet, for some, politically uncomfortable or analytically unfamiliar ways of acknowledging and ordering two critical relationships. These premises identify dependent relationships between the attributes of the world and of human nature and their prior and singular, shared cause. The first relationship is between the world (signified by the Declaration as "Nature") and God (identified in the possessive as "Nature's God"). The second relationship is between a set of human qualities and their divine creative origin. The Declaration identifies these human qualities as being "created equal"; as "endowed" with a set of individual "Rights" that include "Life," "Liberty," and "the pursuit of Happiness"; as "the Right of the people to alter ...[,] abolish ... , and to institute ... Government"; and as "the right of Representation in the Legislature." The Declaration identifies the ultimate divine source of these "unalienable" human endowments and rights as the "Creator." The authors of the Declaration further confirm their recognition of a divine grounding of the world and of the identified set of human attributes with monotheistic and religious references to the "Supreme Judge of the world," their "sacred Honor," and their "firm reliance on the Protection of Divine Providence."

The full consequences of the Declaration's descriptions of the world and of human nature are easily missed if they are perceived only as rhetorical devices or through their familiar, public reflections in Congress's traditional opening prayer rituals or a president's common invocations for God's blessings upon the nation. The additional and more substantive consequence of the Declaration's metaphysical expressions is that they create and sustain an extra-legal, philosophical logic and language that members of Congress, presidents, and others inside and outside of government have turned toward to make sense of, legitimize, critique, or reframe the practices and intentions of American governmental actors and institutions.

The Declaration's second general and long-term influence upon Congress and the presidency is related to its original and still remarkable commitment to—especially, for the eighteenth century—a form of government open to and dependent upon the public. The Second Continental Congress commissioned and published the Declaration as a public appeal to the American people and the world. This action was a testament to Congress's awareness of its dependency upon external sources for support and legitimization. The Declaration, moreover, submitted its self-evident "truths" and "Facts" for consideration by a "candid world" and "the opinions of mankind"—another recognition of the necessity and benefits of both political communication and rational public discourse. The authors of the Declaration also issued a public indictment against a British king who repeatedly called "together legislative bodies at places unusual, uncomfortable, and distant from the depository of their Public Records." The authors thereby committed themselves to a novel, more transparent form of government that openly could value and aspire to standardized governmental processes, political accessibility, and the provision of public information.

The Declaration's third enduring influence upon Congress and the presidency is its definition of the content and boundaries of governmental legitimacy. According to the Declara-

tion, governments are instituted to secure the human rights "of Life, Liberty and the pursuit of Happiness." Governments remain legitimate only as long as they receive "the consent of the governed," pursue "the public good," maintain "the Administration of Justice," and protect the people from "dangers of invasion from without, and convulsions within." The Declaration extends its definition of governmental legitimacy to include a justification that recognizes "the Right of the People to alter or to abolish" their government "and to institute new Government" whenever "any form" of government "becomes destructive of" its proper ends. These ideals have been the common, unexamined expectations of many members of Congress, presidents, and the American people up to the present day. However, they represent noteworthy breaks from mainstream eighteenth-century political thought and the context of American colonial experiences under British rule, which privileged the ideas, institutions, and practices of imperialism, colonialism, monarchical will, and parliamentary sovereignty.

The Declaration's endorsement of the right and expectation of constitutional change represents a fourth enduring influence upon Congress and the presidency. This original endorsement initiated a constitutional tradition within which many members of Congress and presidents have subsequently participated—a tradition that permits and encourages conceptions and pursuits of legal, political, and social alternatives to the status quo. Congress's creation of the Articles of Confederation (see Chapter 5), its acceptance of the 1787 Constitutional Convention, its repeated use of Article V amendment procedures, Abraham Lincoln's

Emancipation Proclamation, and twentieth-century New Deal programs and civil rights reforms are a few of the many social and political advances made possible by a larger political and cultural context initially legitimized and subsequently sustained by an adherence to the principles defined in the Declaration of Independence.

The Declaration's fifth general influence is reflected in the structure of the American constitutional order, particularly the ways in which legislative and executive authority have been defined and constituted. The details and consequences of these influences are integral parts of both the Articles of Confederation and the Constitution. The Declaration both announced the creation of the "United States of America"—the first use of the term—and simultaneously confirmed that the former colonies were "Independent States." The Declaration therefore was the first affirmation of the dual national and federal nature of the United States. The Declaration's explicit commitments to the "right of Representation" and "the consent of the governed" confirmed the necessity of establishing and maintaining an elected and representative national legislature, a political practice that has changed but remains unbroken since 1776. In a similar way, the Declaration's extended list of grievances against King George III initiated a long-cherished American suspicion that consistently has required formal and practical limitations upon the authority and capacities of the national executive and its administrative agents.

The final general influence of the Declaration of Independence upon Congress and U.S. presidents is reflected in its support and promotion of a democratic political culture. The Declaration sought consent for not only the

authority of the Continental Congress to speak "in the Name, and by Authority of the good People of these Colonies" but also more active forms of commitment and participation from its domestic audiences, which indiscriminately extended to all who shared the desire to participate in the birth of a new nation. In many localities, the first public reading of the Declaration of Independence prompted public celebrations, which likely were forerunners of Fourth of July celebrations in which the American people, members of Congress, presidents, and others have publicly commemorated the Declaration's anniversary. The Declaration and its annual celebrations also furthered the development of an activist democratic political culture once social groups and individuals (including political candidates) recognized the derivative rhetorical and political opportunities associated with these public events. Since at least 1800, the Declaration and the Fourth of July have been prominent parts of American civic discourses and political campaigns. They also have marked the beginning of many political careers, including U.S. representative and senator Daniel Webster, Adams/Anti-Jackson/Whig-Mass., whose early public speaking reputation began and grew with every Fourth of July speech he delivered.

## Historical Uses of the Declaration of Independence

In addition to the general influences of the Declaration of Independence upon Congress and the American presidency, the Declaration's relationship to both institutions can be assessed in terms of the specific substantive ways in which individual presidents and members of

Congress have used the Declaration since 1776.

### 1776–1819

Given the demands and disruptions of the American Revolution, the Declaration of Independence does not appear to have affected members of Congress in extraordinary ways during the earliest years of the nation. In 1780 Congress formally recognized the Declaration as one of the nation's most important constitutional documents, ordering its publication with the Articles of Confederation and the first state constitutions. Members of Congress recognized the anniversary of the Declaration, but with few legislative sessions extending into July, many were free to participate in Fourth of July celebrations in their local communities. As early as 1782, James Madison, D–R–Va., and other nonsigning members of Congress also apparently believed that they, too, were personally and solemnly bound by the Declaration "to maintain" its "Claim of Independence . . . at the risqué of [their] lives and fortunes."

Outside of Congress, the Declaration of Independence was revered both in private and in public celebrations throughout the Revolutionary years as the original public statement of the American cause. Its substantive content, however, was not widely contested or used to justify much beyond efforts to secure American independence from Great Britain. Little evidence exists that delegates to the 1787 Constitutional Convention consulted the Declaration when debating, composing, or ratifying the new Constitution. Too much, however, can be made of these early silences in the historical record, for much of the Constitution embodies the principles of consent, limited government, and constitutional change articulated originally in the Declaration (see Chapter 6).

By the 1790s, Fourth of July celebrations had become public, ritualized, principally local expressions of independence and American nationalism. To some, the popularity of these celebrations exposed a fuller understanding of the constitutional significance of the Declaration. As one Philadelphia newspaper writer argued in 1792, the Declaration of Independence was "not to be celebrated, merely as affecting the separation of one country from the jurisdiction of another, but as being the result of a rational discussion and definition of the rights of man, and the end of civil government." Antislavery advocates also recognized the value of marrying Fourth of July celebrations with their Declaration-supported arguments against slavery. "Throughout the 1790s and early 1800s," historian David Waldstreicher reports, Independence Day celebrations were used by these advocates "to damn slavery or to toast its end" and "were integral to making the case that slavery was a national problem that contradicted the nation's founding ideals."

Presidents and members of Congress were slower and more cautious in their early uses of the Declaration. An exception occurred when the First Congress debated an impost bill in 1789. Rep. Josiah Parker, Va., proposed adding a ten-dollar duty on slave imports, declaring his sincere belief that slavery was "contrary to the Revolution['s] principles, and ought not to be permitted." Parker admitted "it degrading the human species to annex" the character of a material good "to them; but he would rather do this than continue the actual evil of importing slaves a moment longer."

Furthermore, Parker continued, members of Congress ought to

do all that lay in their power to restore to human nature its inherent privileges and, if possible wipe off the stigma under which America labored. The inconsistency in our principles, with which we are justly charged, should be done away, that we may show, by our actions, the pure beneficence of the doctrine we hold out to the world in our Declaration of Independence.

Parker's proposal initiated a brief but spirited exchange in the U.S. House, which included discussion of House amendment rules, Congress's constitutional authority, the nature of human slaves, the evilness of the slave trade, the equity of taxing white slavery, the costs and future of slavery, and the will of the majority. In the end, at the urging of others including his Virginia colleague James Madison, Parker agreed to withdraw his original motion.

More commonly, early members of Congress and presidents occasionally found it useful to recall or echo parts of the Declaration in their public discussions and writings. In *Letters of Helvidius* (1793), for example, Madison rebutted Alexander Hamilton's expansive view of executive authority but also repeated the Declaration's familiar idea "that every Nation has a right to abolish an old government and establish a new one." This idea, Madison authoritatively noted, "was recorded in every public archive, written in every American heart, and sealed with the blood of a host of American martyrs." It also constituted "the only lawful tenure by which the United States hold their existence as a nation." In his 1796 farewell address, President George Washington offered a similar rendition of the Declaration's right of constitutional change, stating: "The

basis of our political systems is the right of the people to make and alter their constitutions of government."

Toward the end of the 1790s, opponents of President John Adams discovered additional political uses of the Declaration, employing it effectively in their efforts to build a national opposition party against Adams and the Federalists. Republicans transformed Fourth of July celebrations into explicitly partisan affairs that promoted and exploited Thomas Jefferson's dual reputation as the Declaration's author and the leader of their new political party. Without their consent and with little recourse, Federalists were recast as Tories in the new political drama as the Jeffersonian Republicans took advantage of the Declaration's original and socially enduring anti-British sentiments. Jefferson's victory over Adams in the 1800 presidential election altered the American political landscape as well as the symbolic value and political possibilities associated with the Declaration. For these first Republicans, Jefferson's inauguration on March 4, 1801, represented "a national revolution, a second Declaration of Independence, and in its aftermath," David Waldstreicher contends, "[i]t was described and celebrated in exactly that way, as another Fourth of July." Republican orators presented themselves as the rightful heirs to the Revolution, reading the Declaration in public and listing "the tyrannies of the Federal reign in the king-accusing syntax of the Declaration of Independence." Caught in opposition to the Declaration and, after 1801, with an unpalatable interpretation of the Constitution, Federalists were silenced by the new symbolic and conceptual consensus, never again regaining control of either Congress or the presidency.

Two additional uses of the Declaration of Independence before 1820 deserve mentioning. In 1811 Rep. John C. Calhoun, D–R–S.C., one of the war hawks who emerged in the U.S. House, explained his militant stand against Great Britain in language and a rhetorical style reminiscent of the Declaration. Calhoun argued that "[w]ar, in this country, ought never to be resorted to but when it is clearly justifiable and necessary." Any alleged causes must be "most urgent and necessary . . . in the eye of the nation." According to Calhoun, "The extent, duration, and character of the injuries received; the failure of those peaceful means heretofore resorted to for the redress of our wrongs is my proof that it is necessary." He added, "[T]he evil still grows, and in each succeeding year swells in extent and pretension beyond the preceding." In his annual message to Congress the same year, President James Madison echoed the war hawks' bellicose tone in his recital of a long list of American grievances against Great Britain, after which Congress responded with a formal declaration of war.

A second noteworthy use of the Declaration occurred in the aftermath of the War of 1812, when Congress and the nation's interests returned principally to domestic affairs. In addition to agreeing to rebuild parts of Washington, D.C., destroyed by the British, Congress and President Madison in 1817 commissioned four large paintings by the noted American artist John Trumbull on U.S. history topics. The first and most famous of the commissioned works is "The Declaration of Independence in Congress, At the Independence Hall, Philadelphia, July 4th, 1776." By design, the four paintings were to hang in the new grand Rotunda of the U.S. Congress that was

to be built between the House and Senate chambers—a building project that delayed completion of the Trumbull commission until 1826. In 1818 Trumbull completed his life-size painting of the presentation of the Declaration and with President James Monroe's approval he displayed it to almost twenty-one thousand paying viewers in New York, Boston, Philadelphia, and Baltimore before Congress formally accepted the 12' by 18' canvas in 1819. In November 1826, under the watchful eye of members of Congress and President John Quincy Adams, Trumbull's four paintings finally received their prominent and permanent places in the Capitol Rotunda.[1]

### 1820–1876

Between 1820 and the 1876 centennial, the Declaration of Independence was understood and employed in new and increasingly divisive ways. Most Americans continued to associate the Declaration with nationalist celebrations of the American Revolution, but with time fewer perceived much if any value in reliving the original document's anti-British and monarchical hostilities. With the conclusion of the 1812 war, foreign threats and invasions also seemed to grow increasingly distant and improbable for all but the most anxious nationalists. A variety of individuals and social groups infused the Declaration, shorn from traditional uses and conceptual moorings, with new meanings and uses. Abolitionists continued to look to the Declaration and its explicit endorsements of the Creator, human equality, and freedom as the great constitutional touchstone that legitimized their social cause. As historian Eric Foner has shown, other reformist groups such as labor advocates, women's rights groups (see Chapter 11), the Temperance movement, and various religious organizations also turned to the document as justification for their visions of American society. Not surprisingly, many of these groups wove their social reform agendas into the discourses and activities associated with annual yet still localized Fourth of July celebrations.

Members of Congress and presidents also employed and reacted to the Declaration of Independence in new and unconventional ways. During the often contentious debates over the admission of the Territory of Missouri as a slave state in 1819, Rep. Timothy Fuller, D–R–Mass., argued that the Declaration's support of "the glorious truth, that 'all men are born free and equal' " was irreconcilable with not only the extension of slavery in Missouri but also the notion that slavery, more broadly, was irreconcilable with a republican form of government and the long-term interests of slaveholders and the nation. Fuller contended that "the whole civilized world are spectators of the scene" in Congress and that, if Missouri were admitted with slavery, "[d]espots and their minions may justly despise, while the wise and good of every nation must pity our infatuation, or execrate our hypocrisy." Fuller's progressive arguments against slavery, however, ought to be qualified by his apparent support for a form of second-class status for "freedmen and their descendents," whom he believed could be given "personal liberty" and protection "against oppression, but not necessarily" be permitted to participate in "political power." They therefore "would remain the industrious and happy laborers in the fields, not of their masters, but their protectors."

In subsequent debates over the status of Missouri, Rep. Joseph Hemphill, Jacksonian/Federalist-Pa., employed the Declaration with less discrimination than Fuller, arguing that neither the Declaration nor the Constitution limited citizenship based upon skin color. In rebuttal to arguments made by Rep. James Barbour, Anti-Democrat/States Rights-Va., who denied "the rights of citizenship to any free black or mulatto man," Hemphill responded, "[T]his class of people lived among us, not in the character of foreigners. . . . [And] this was their native country, and as dear to them as to us." With a rhetorical style reminiscent of the Declaration, Hemphill continued his appeal to Congress and the nation:

Thousands of them were free born, and they composed a part of the people in the several States. They were identified with the nation, and its wealth consisted, in part, of their labor. They had fought for their country, and were righteously included in the principles of the Declaration of Independence. This was their condition when the Constitution of the United States was framed, and that high instrument does not cast the least shade of doubt upon any of their rights or privileges; but on the contrary, I may challenge gentlemen to examine it, with all the ability they are capable of, and see if it contains a single expression that deprives them of any privileges that is bestowed on others.

They have a right to pursue their own happiness, in as high a degree as any other class of people. Their situation is similar to others, in relation to the acquirement of property, and the various pursuits of industry. They are entitled to the same rights of religion and protection, and are subjected to the same punishments. They are enumerated in the census. They can be taxed, and made liable to militia duty; they are denied none of the privileges contained in the bill of rights; and, although many of these advantages are allowed to a stranger, during his temporary residence, yet, in no one instance is a free native black man treated as a foreigner.

Slavery apologists in Congress aggressively countered these new egalitarian interpretations of the Declaration of Independence. As historian Philip F. Detweiler recounts, Sen. Nathaniel Macon, R-N.C., "warned his colleagues against broad arguments from the Declaration, maintaining that if the equality clause of the preamble were interpreted as antislavery spokesmen desired, universal emancipation would result." Like others in Congress, Macon further "maintained that the Declaration simply was not part of the Constitution" and, therefore, it ought not influence Congress's decision on the admission of Missouri. Other members attacked their nonslave state critics for their recent embrace of the Declaration. Senator Richard M. Johnson of Kentucky sarcastically asked his northern state colleagues: "If your humanity has conquered your prejudice, till you know no color, where are your magistrates, your governors, your representatives, of the black population? You proclaim them equal, but you are still their lawgivers." Still other members of Congress found it simpler to dismiss the Declaration of Independence as filled with "abstract aphorisms" and "theoretical principles," which "are not truths at all, if taken literally."

The political compromises finally worked out to admit Missouri as a slave state in 1820 effectively tempered the rhetoric and sectional divisions that had dominated Congress for more than a year, but they did little to resolve the differences exposed over the meaning of the Declaration of Independence. These differences emerged again and again during subsequent years as the great ideological and ultimately sectional interests struggled both mightily and subtly to reconcile their political positions with the ideas and language expressed in the Declaration. In his 1825 inaugural address, for example, President John Quincy Adams auspiciously trumpeted: "The year of jubilee since the first formation of our Union has just elapsed; that of the declaration of our independence is at hand." Adams's "jubilee" year reference, however, suggested more than an occasion for an especially festive celebration. Within the Christian tradition, jubilee years were called periodically as opportunities for deeper spiritual reflection, pilgrimage, and penitential acts. And as historian Andrew Burstein notes, the jubilee reference certainly would have been understood as an allusion to the Hebraic ideal of releasing enslaved and indebted persons from their bondage every fiftieth year.

The jubilee celebrations of the Declaration of Independence that occurred across the United States in 1826 were followed by news of the coincidental deaths of Thomas Jefferson and John Adams on July 4, 1826—the final remaining individuals who had signed the Declaration in 1776. The heightened symbolic import of the Declaration of Independence would have been difficult for the nation to miss. In case someone did, President John Quincy Adams declared: "In this most singular coincidence, the finger of Providence is plainly visible! It hallows the Declaration of Independence as the Word of God, and is the bow in the Heavens, that promises its principles shall be eternal, and their dissemination universal over the Earth."

John Quincy Adams's public uses of the Declaration of Independence did not end with the death of his father or his loss to Andrew Jackson in the 1828 presidential election. As a

U.S. representative for Massachusetts in the 1830s and 1840s, Adams became one of the most vocal and disruptive antislavery voices in Congress. Prevented by convention and U.S. House debate rules from broaching the topic of slavery directly, Adams agitated Congress until his death in 1848 by repeatedly presenting and reading abolitionist petitions and memorials in the House. Many of these petitions justified their cause with references to the Declaration of Independence. Reading from one petition sent from Boston, Adams demanded the House consider the petitioners' request to relocate the federal government from the District of Columbia to a northern location where the principles of the Declaration of Independence were "not treated as mere rhetorical flourish."

Other members of Congress followed in Adams's path with similar antislavery uses of the Declaration. Notably, Sen. Samuel P. Chase, R-Ohio, argued during the debates over the Kansas-Nebraska bill:

In 1776, the Declaration of Independence, drafted by Jefferson, announced no such low and narrow principles as seem to be in fashion now. That immortal document asserted no right of the strong to oppress the weak, of the majority to enslave the minority. It promulgated the sublime creed of human rights. It declared that ALL MEN are created equal, and endowed by the Creator with inalienable rights of life and liberty.

Congressional defenders of slavery repeatedly rejected abolitionist petitions and interpretations of the Declaration and, in 1842, pursued a formal (but failed) effort to censure John Quincy Adams in the House of Representatives. In response to Adams and to the growing sectional conflicts in Congress in the late 1840s and 1850s, these individuals also devised proslavery interpretations of the Dec-

laration of Independence. Several repeated arguments articulated decades earlier during debates over the admission of Missouri. Sen. Stephen A. Douglas, D-Ill., for example, contended that the principles of the Declaration applied only to the original British colonials and their descendents and never to free or enslaved African Americans or, by implication, Americans with other non-British ancestral backgrounds. Others such as Senator Calhoun pursued a different interpretative strategy by challenging the Declaration's assertion that "all men are created equal." Calhoun insisted that "[m]en are not created; there were but two created, one man and one women" and the latter "was inferior to the man" like infants are neither free nor equal but always "subject to their parents." Calhoun thus dismissed the Declaration's claim of liberty and equality as a "hypothetical truism" that was not true or necessary to secure independence. Moreover, in the minds and mouths of its advocates within and without Congress, the idea that "all men are born free and equal" had become both "dangerous" and "productive of so much evil" in both the United States and Europe. In 1854 Sen. John Pettit, D-Ind., extended Calhoun's dismissal when he declared the so-called self-evident truth of the Declaration of Independence a "self-evident lie," observing—as Aristotle had in his *Politics*—that he saw "one man born a slave and another a master."

Others contributed to a third proslavery interpretation of the Declaration of Independence, one that employed the document to describe the Constitution as a voluntary compact between independent, sovereign states. This contractual view of the United States was not a conceptual innovation of the antebellum era as its lineage can be traced back to the Articles of Confederation and to early national era debates over the nature of the American Union. By the 1850s, advocates of this view employed the Declaration to redefine both the powers of the national government and the nature of relations between the states under the U.S. Constitution. In his 1855 annual message to Congress, President Franklin Pierce pronounced this contractual interpretation of the Union "the constitutional theory of our Government." Before the voluntary formation of "a confederation of independent States," according to Pierce, each state "assumed the powers and rights of absolute self-government . . . wholly without interference from any other" state. "In the language of the Declaration of Independence," Pierce noted, "each State had 'full power to levy war, conclude peace, contract alliances, establish commerce, and to do all other acts and things which independent states may of right do.' " As a result, the states created "a Federal Republic of the free white men of the colonies, constituted, as they were, in distinct and reciprocally independent State governments." For Pierce, therefore, the Congress was only a "congress of sovereignties" in which "cooperative action" required a static "balance of power" secured by "the separate reserved rights of the States and their equal representation in the Senate." Moreover, according to this president, "each [state] solemnly bound itself to all the others neither to undertake nor permit any encroachment upon or intermeddling with another's reserved rights."

As the secession crisis began to unfold in late 1860, President James Buchanan extended this contractual interpretation of the Constitution.

Buchanan blamed the crisis on "the long-continued and intemperate interference of the Northern people with the question of slavery in the Southern States," and he proposed that the natural recourse "against the tyranny and oppression of the Federal Government" was "the right of resistance." Without legal precedent or warrant from the Constitution, Buchanan argued this right "exists independently of all constitutions, and has been exercised at all periods of the world's history." He continued, "[I]t is embodied in strong and express language in our own Declaration of Independence."

The election of Abraham Lincoln in 1860 was a signal event in the development of the presidency as well as in the use and influence of the Declaration of Independence (see Chapter 3). In his first inaugural address in March 1861, President Lincoln dismissed the interpretations of the Declaration and the Constitution advanced by secessionists and his two presidential predecessors. In response to their compact theory of the Union, Lincoln inquired "if the United States be not a government proper, but an association of States in the nature of contract merely, can it, as a contract, be peacefully unmade by less than all the parties who made it? One party to a contract may violate it—break it, so to speak; but does it not require all to lawfully rescind it?" Lincoln further argued: "The Union is much older than the Constitution. It was formed, in fact by the Articles of Association in 1774. It was matured and continued by the Declaration of Independence in 1776," the Articles of Confederation in 1777, and the Constitution in 1787. As a result, "It follows from these views that no State upon its own mere motion can lawfully get out of the Union." For Lincoln, therefore, "acts of violence . . . against the authority of the United States, are insurrectionary or revolutionary" attempts to overthrow the national government, which he openly recognized as a "revolutionary right" retained by the people along with their "constitutional right" to amend the Constitution through its Article V procedures.

Lincoln's careful distinctions and conclusions deserve fuller attention because they reflect not only on the influence of the Declaration upon him but also his resolve during the secession crisis and his understanding of the Union and Constitution throughout the Civil War. In his 1861 inaugural address, Lincoln successfully turned the contractual exchange logic of the compact interpretation against its advocates simply by asking if "any right, plainly written in the Constitution, has been denied?" "Think, if you can," he challenged his listening and reading audiences, "of a single instance in which a plainly written provision of the Constitution has ever been denied." Without any demonstrated violation, Lincoln portrayed the secessionists and those who advocated breaking the original compact as revolutionaries—that is, individuals acting outside of the law. This distinction was important and became more so for rallying Unionists after Fort Sumter as Lincoln made clear in the first official message he sent to Congress on July 4, 1861. In this message, Lincoln pointed out that the secessionists unlawfully had broken the explicit terms of the Constitution, and they were attempting to accomplish this without just compensation. As Lincoln put it:

The nation purchased, with money, the countries out of which several of these States were formed. Is it just that they shall go off without leave, and without refunding? The nation paid large sums . . . to relieve Florida of the aboriginal tribes. Is it that she shall now be off without consent, or without making any return? The nation is now in debt for money applied to the benefit of these so-called seceding States, in common with the rest. Is it just, either that creditors shall go unpaid, or the remaining States pay the whole? . . . Again, if one State may secede, so may another; and when all shall have seceded, none is left to pay the debts. Is this quite just to creditors? Did we notify them of this sage view of ours, when we borrowed their money? If we now recognize this doctrine, by allowing the seceders to go in peace, it is difficult to see what we can do, if others choose to go, or to exhort terms upon which they will promise to remain.

Lincoln's 1861 inaugural address is significant for a second but more easily overlooked reason. Lincoln argued that the Union began with the Articles of Association in 1774 and not in 1776 with the Declaration of Independence. This dating scheme aided Lincoln's argument about the supremacy of the Union over the individual states, although it also dislodged the Declaration from a privileged constitutional or symbolic association with the Union's origins. For Lincoln, however, the relevance and value of the Declaration of Independence for the Union were exposed in the separation of the document's accidental historical associations from its more important substantive content. Unlike many of his presidential predecessors or members of Congress, President Lincoln did not invoke the Declaration as a mere authority or rhetorical prop to bolster an argument. And he did not value it because for many it still functioned as a symbolic proxy for the revered origins and "fathers" of the American Revolution. Instead, as Harry V. Jaffa notes, the transcendent qualities that Lincoln extracted from the Declaration of Independence, entwined with his understanding of the Union and the U.S. Constitution, and made the focal points of his presidency were the guide of his thinking and public speaking throughout the 1850s and the principal motivation for his run for the presidency in 1860. In a revealing pre-inaugural speech Lincoln gave at Independence Hall in Philadelphia, the president-elect boldly declared (to a cheering audience) that he "never had a feeling politically that did not spring from the sentiments embodied in the Declaration of Independence."

What were the transcendent qualities expressed in the Declaration of Independence that so inspired the last decade of Lincoln's public life? Lincoln's public speeches and private writings—especially between 1854 and his 1861 inaugural address—offer an extensive and accessible resource for answering this most important question, and for this reason alone these works deserve to be revisited and studied as often as *The Federalist Papers*. Among these works, one of the earliest and most important was an extended public speech Lincoln gave in 1854 in Peoria, Illinois, where he appeared in a debate with Senator Douglas. In the U.S. Senate, Douglas had been the principal author of the Kansas-Nebraska Act and the architect of Congress's repeal of the 1820 Missouri Compromise. In his Peoria speech, Lincoln expressed his moral opposition to "the monstrous injustice" of human slavery in terms of his "ancient faith" in the principle that "all men are created equal." This principle extended and was bound to a second one also expressed in the Declaration: "that no man is good enough to govern another man, without that other's consent," which Lincoln called (as Thomas Jefferson did before him) "the sheet

anchor of American republicanism." Yet for Lincoln the Declaration of Independence supported not simply the familiar idea that "the just powers of government are derived from the consent of the governed" but also a more activist and universalistic imperative: "Allow ALL the governed an equal voice in the government, and that, and that only is self-government." Any extension of slavery thus was morally unjustifiable and a constitutional abandonment of the Declaration's redemptive vision of humanity and its capacity for self-government. In a 1857 speech, Lincoln contended that the founding fathers well knew this vision did not accurately describe existing conditions, but they nevertheless expressed it "so that enforcement of it might follow as fast as circumstances should permit." They intended it to be "a stumbling block to those who" subsequently "might seek to turn a free people into the hateful paths of despotism." In his 1854 Peoria speech, Lincoln eloquently expressed his commitment to this vision:

Little by little, but steadily as man's march to the grave, we have been giving up the OLD for the NEW faith. Near eighty years ago we began by declaring that all men are created equal; but now from that beginning we have run down to the other declaration, that for SOME men to enslave OTHERS is a "sacred right of self-government." These principles can not stand together. They are as opposite as God and mammon; and whoever holds to the one, must despise the other. When Pettit, in connection with his support of the Nebraska bill, called the Declaration of Independence "a self-evident lie" he only did what consistency and candor require all other Nebraska men to do. Of the forty odd Nebraska Senators who sat present and heard him, no one rebuked him. Nor am I apprized that any Nebraska newspaper, or any Nebraska orator, in the whole nation, has ever yet rebuked him. . . . Let no one be deceived. The spirit of seventy-six and the spirit of Nebraska, are utter antagonisms; and the former is being rapidly displaced by the latter.

. . . Our republican robe is soiled, and trailed in the dust. Let us repurify it. Let us turn and wash it white, in the spirit, if not the blood, of the Revolution. Let us turn slavery from its claims of "moral right," back upon its existing legal rights, and its arguments of "necessity." Let us return it to the position our fathers gave it; and there let it rest in peace. Let us readopt the Declaration of Independence, and with it, the practices, and policy which harmonize with it. Let north and south—let all Americans—let all lovers of liberty everywhere—join in the great work. If we do this, we shall not only have saved the Union; but we shall have saved it, as to make, and keep it, forever worthy of saving. We shall have so saved it, that the succeeding millions of free happy people, the world over, shall rise up, and call us blessed, to the latest generation.

Toward the end of his long journey to Washington, D.C., President-elect Lincoln offered another important, pre-inaugural expression of his understanding of the Declaration and its significance. In his brief Independence Hall speech in Philadelphia, he publicly committed himself to these words:

I have often inquired of myself, what great principle or idea it was that kept this Confederacy so long together. It was not the mere matter of the separation of the colonies from the mother land; but something in that Declaration giving liberty, not alone to the people of this country, but hope to the world for all future time. (Great applause.) It was that which gave promise that in due time the weights should be lifted from the shoulders of all men, and that all should have an equal chance. (Cheers.) This is the sentiment embodied in that Declaration of Independence. Now, my friends, can this country be saved upon that basis? If it can, I will consider myself one of the happiest men in the world if I can help to save it. If it can't be saved upon that principle, it will be truly awful. But, if this country cannot be saved without giving up that principle—I was about to say I would

rather be assassinated on this spot than to surrender it.

Others shared or would come to grasp Lincoln's understanding and vision of the Declaration of Independence. Yet as the 1856 caning of Sen. Charles Sumner, R-Mass., the American Civil War, Lincoln's assassination, and the protracted efforts and failures of Congress's Reconstruction programs ably testify, the practical means and methods adopted to further the establishment of this vision—as circumstances would permit—proved inadequate for the intended task, too difficult and costly to implement, and too unpopular to sustain. Ironically, the centennial celebrations of independence and the principles of the Declaration in 1876 preceded the negotiated abandonment of federal supervision of Reconstruction after the next presidential election.

However partial the successes, Congress's initial determination and actions to reconstruct the Union after the Civil War manifested the practical influences and possibilities of the Declaration of Independence. Many of these efforts were conceived and led by Sumner in the Senate. In 1865, for example, he rejected Lincoln's plan to recognize the once rebellious but now subdued State of Louisiana, privately asserting, "We shall insist upon the Declaration of Independence as the foundation of the new State governments; and the argument will be presented, not merely on the grounds of Human Rights, but of self-interest." Congress agreed with Sumner, refusing to readmit any of the secessionist states until their state constitutions conformed to the Declaration's principles and only after they ratified the additional amendments Congress subsequently proposed to the Constitution. Since the Civil War, Congress has required every new state admitted into the Union to adhere to the principles of the Declaration of Independence in their state constitutions (see Chapter 7).

Sumner's unfailing attachment to the Declaration, "the great touchstone" of his efforts to "bring the Constitution into avowed harmony with the Declaration of Independence," compelled or influenced other significant although often vigorously contested legal and constitutional changes. One of these changes was the 1868 Expatriation Act, which Sumner shepherded through the Senate Committee on Foreign Relations. In this act, Congress extended the Declaration's rights to naturalized American immigrants, declaring voluntary expatriation "a natural and inherent right of all people, indispensable to the enjoyment of the rights of life, liberty, and the pursuit of happiness." Other changes bearing Sumner's commitment include, at least in part, the Thirteenth, Fourteenth, and Fifteenth Amendments, the 1866 and 1875 Civil Rights Acts, the Enforcement Acts, and his theory of constitutional interpretation by which "the Constitution can never be interpreted in any way inconsistent with the Declaration."

## 1877–1926

The failure of Senator Sumner and others to make the Declaration of Independence a "living letter instead of a promise" did not diminish the document's social or political importance in later years, yet it did leave open the possibility for new applications of the Declaration between 1877 and 1926. National immigration policy was one area in which members of Congress vigorously battled over the meaning and relevance of Declaration of Inde-

pendence. The original Declaration had indicted King George for restricting American population growth by "obstructing the Laws for Naturalization of Foreigners; refusing to pass others to encourage their Migrations hither, and raising the Conditions of new Appropriations of Lands." Consistent with these principles, Congress and the states actively encouraged population growth, foreign immigration and naturalization, and affordable westward lands for settlement for much of the nineteenth century. As a member of Congress explained to his Tennessee constituents in 1814:

The declaration of our independence, in terms peculiar to the bold and just conceptions of its author, has established the principle upon a basis that ought not—that cannot be shaken. . . .

In the pursuit of this happiness, man has no bounds but the limits of the world. He may pursue it in whatsoever region, or in whatsoever direction or course his hope, his judgment, or his caprice, may direct him.

By the mid-1870s attitudes toward unfettered immigration had shifted, especially with regard to Chinese immigrants. In 1882 Congress and President Chester A. Arthur responded by enacting three major immigration laws. One of these laws, the Chinese Exclusion Act, barred Chinese laborers for ten years. "Congressional debates over Chinese exclusion," political scientist Rogers Smith observes, reveal "that exclusionist congressmen redefined or even decried the nation's liberal traditions in favor of grim but popular" arguments based upon "evolutionary theories as well as economic and republican concerns." Opponents of these exclusionary acts contended that the restrictions undermined republican and Christian principles, in addition to the rights to life, liberty, and the pursuit of happiness identified in the Declaration of Independence. With either deep sarcasm or historical ignorance, Sen. George F. Hoar, R-Mass., suggested the "doctrine that free institutions are a monopoly of the favored races" was a proposition "of quite recent origin." As Smith further notes, Hoar "pointed out that many had condemned blacks as racially unfit for citizenship and that experience had proven otherwise." Hoar therefore suggested "the Chinese would assimilate adequately if they were freed from discriminatory state laws that now enchained them in menial trades and ghetto existences." Open-immigration opponents defended their positions with more restrictive interpretations of the Declaration of Independence. Several members of Congress contended the Declaration did not guarantee "the rights of entry" into the United States, while others resurrected older racialist interpretations that its principles applied only to white males. Other members pursued similarly worn dismissals of the Declaration by characterizing it as "sentimentalist," "speculative and Utopian." Rep. Aylett H. Buckner, D-Mo., also stepped forward, as others had before the Civil War, to proclaim the Declaration's principle that "all men are created equal" was "absolutely false."

Congressional and presidential views of the Declaration of Independence also influenced the development of other national policies. In April 1898 the United States declared war against Spain on the grounds that the people of Cuba "are and of right ought to be free and independent." After the war, however, members of Congress contested the meaning of the Declaration as they debated the future of the nation's recently acquired island territories, which included Hawaii by annexation in 1896 and Puerto Rico, Guam, the Philippines, and Cuba from Spain in the recent conquest. To many, such as Rep. William D. Vincent, Populist-Kan., the stakes of this contest were high. Vincent contended that if the United States adopted a "high-handed scheme of coercion" over these peoples, "we will violate every principle of self-government and repudiate every tradition we have cherished from the beginning of the nation's history." Sen. George G. Vest, D-Mo., similarly reminded his colleagues that any thought of "govern[ing] millions, without their consent, as mere chattels" contradicted the principles of the Declaration. Vest and others, therefore, debated the merits and means of granting statehood and full citizenship rights for the inhabitants of these territories and the practicalities of permitting them to become independent.

Other members of Congress felt compelled to propose different interpretations of the Declaration of Independence to justify the extension of American authority over these individuals and territories. Although the Declaration made explicit endorsement of colonial status difficult, Rogers Smith further observes that congressional imperialists expressed no reservations when they contended that the Declaration applied only to individuals "capable of self-government." Different national policies on these citizenship and territorial issues ultimately were devised by Congress and various presidents. Cuba and the Philippines became independent in 1902 and 1946, respectively; the residents of Puerto Rico and Guam received U.S. citizenship and unincorporated but self-governing territorial status in 1917 and 1949, respectively; and Hawaii became the fiftieth state in 1959.

Presidents also used and were influenced by the Declaration of Independence in other ways. Two presidents, in particular, deserve attention for their interpretations and uses of the Declaration. Like Lincoln and Sumner, President Woodrow Wilson repeatedly articulated his belief that declarations of rights needed to be translated "into definite action." Like the Progressives of his time, Wilson also believed that the Declaration "is of no consequence to us unless we can translate its general terms into examples of the present day and substitute them in some vital way for the examples it itself gives." Domestically, Wilson proposed that his "new declaration of independence" was a fight against the tyranny of "political machines" and "selfish business" interests that exploited "the people by legal and political means." Wilson proposed extending the application of the Declaration's natural rights beyond America's borders. Wilson said:

My dream is that as the years go on and the world knows more and more of America, it will also drink at the fountains of youth and renewal; that it will turn to America for those moral inspirations that lie at the basis of all freedom; that no country will ever fear America unless it feels that it is engaged in some enterprise which is inconsistent with the rights of humanity; that America will come into the full light of the day when all shall know that she puts human rights above all other rights and that her flag is not only of America, but of humanity.

What other great people has devoted itself to that exalted ideal? To what other nation can all eyes look for an instant sympathy that thrills the whole body politic when men anywhere are fighting for their rights? I do now know that there will ever be a declaration of grievances and of independence for mankind, but I believe that if any such document ever is drawn up, it will be drawn in the spirit of the American Declaration of Independence.

America has lifted high the light which will shine unto all generations and will guide the feet of mankind to the goal of justice, liberty and peace.

Calvin Coolidge was another president who demonstrated a novel appreciation and understanding of the Declaration of Independence. Coolidge's view of the Declaration was as expansive as Wilson's, although his focus was directed inward to the individual, whose rights, according to Coolidge, "were so clearly asserted in" and whose "wrongs" so clearly were guarded against by the Declaration. "Through it all," Coolidge contended, "runs the recognition of the dignity and worth of the individual, because of his possession of those qualities which are revealed to us by religion. It is this conception alone which warrants the assertion of the universal right of freedom. America has been the working out of the modern effort to provide a system of government and society which would give to the individual that freedom which his nature requires." "The end sought" by these Declaration-inspired efforts "has been to create a nation wherein the individual might rise to the full stature of manhood and womanhood."

Coolidge's understanding of the Declaration also differed from Wilson's in a second noteworthy way. Whereas Wilson sought to lead the nation to engage and to remake the world in his image of the Declaration's principles, Coolidge's use of the Declaration counseled transformations of a more personal nature, directed as he once said "to satisfy the longing of the soul." Like Lincoln and other presidents before him, Coolidge also attributed the nation's economic successes to the Declaration's principles. Yet for Coolidge, adherence to these principles required a fuller awareness and recognition of their spiritual foundations. "Equality, liberty, popular sovereignty, the rights of man," he declared, "are not elements which we can see and touch. They are ideals. They have their source and roots in the religious convictions. They belong to the unseen world. Unless," therefore, "the faith of the American people in these religious convictions is to endure, the principles of our Declaration will perish. We can not continue to enjoy the result if we neglect and abandon the cause." Thus despite the economic prosperity that marked his presidential tenure (1923–1929), Coolidge cautioned:

We live in an age of science and of abounding accumulation of material things. These did not create our Declaration. Our Declaration created them. The things of the spirit come first. Unless we cling to that, all our material prosperity, overwhelming though it may appear, will turn to a barren sceptre in our grasp. If we are to maintain the great heritage which has been bequeathed to us, we must be like minded as the father who created it. We must not sink into a pagan materialism. We must cultivate the reverence which they had for the things that are holy. We must follow the spiritual and moral leadership which they showed. We must keep replenished, that they may glow with a more compelling flame, the altar fires before which they worshipped.

### 1927–1976

The uses and influences of the Declaration of Independence upon Congress and the presidency from 1927 to 1976 are more familiar and accessible, and they have been identified and ably studied by a number of scholars. These uses and influences, however, are no less significant or expansive in their conceptual innovations or constitutional consequences than those identified in previous eras. Two presi-

dential uses deserve explicit recognition, although both had advocates and opponents in Congress. The first took its initial form shortly before the 1932 presidential election. In a speech before the Commonwealth Club in San Francisco, Franklin D. Roosevelt articulated his vision of a new, more energetic national government. As presidential scholar Sidney M. Milkis observes, Roosevelt argued that the function of the national government was "to assist in the development of an economic declaration of rights, an economic constitutional order." In this new order, "a resurgent executive would play the principal part in identifying new problems and searching for methods by which those problem might be solved."

The substantive breadth of Roosevelt's speech comes to light against the backdrop of prior uses of the Declaration. Whereas Parker, Hemphill, Adams, Chase, Lincoln, Sumner, and others had envisioned extending the rights identified in the Declaration to Americans without regard to skin color, and Lincoln, Vest, Wilson, and others envisioned these rights, in Lincoln's words, as a "hope to the world" for "all lovers of liberty everywhere," Roosevelt reinterpreted the original list of rights in the Declaration to include a new set of economic rights, placing the responsibilities for the fulfillment of these rights upon the national government. Thus, as Milkis notes, "the most significant aspect of the departure from" the conventional understanding of "natural rights to programmatic liberalism was the association of constitutional rights with the extension, rather than the restriction, of the programmatic commitments of the national government." Roosevelt's four-term tenure as president is filled with additional elaborations of this interpretation of the Declaration of Independence. One of the clearest statements is his 1944 State of the Union speech, when Roosevelt asserted that "it is our duty now to begin to lay the plans and determine the strategy for the winning of a lasting peace and the establishment of an American standard of living higher than ever before known." Roosevelt continued:

This Republic had its beginning, and grew to its present strength, under the protection of certain inalienable political rights—among them the right of free speech, free press, free worship, trial by jury, freedom from unreasonable searches and seizures. They were our rights to life and liberty.

As our Nation has grown in size and stature, however—as our industrial economy expanded— these political rights proved inadequate to assure us equality in the pursuit of happiness. . . . In our day these economic truths have become accepted as self-evident. We have accepted, so to speak, a second Bill of Rights under which a new basis of security and prosperity can be established for all— regardless of station, race, or creed.

Among these are: The right to a useful and remunerative job in the industries or shops or farms or mines of the Nation; The right to earn enough to provide adequate food and clothing and recreation; The right of every farmer to raise and sell his products at a return which will give him and his family a decent living; The right of every businessman, large and small, to trade in an atmosphere of freedom from unfair competition and domination by monopolies at home or abroad; The right of every family to a decent home; The right to adequate medical care and the opportunity to achieve and enjoy good health; The right to adequate protection from the economic fears of old age, sickness, accident, and unemployment; The right to a good education.

All of these rights spell security. And after this war [World War II] is won we must be prepared to move forward, in the implementation of these rights, to new goals of human happiness and well-being.

The second noteworthy use of the Declaration of Independence contributed to the na-

tional advancement of civil rights reforms in the second half of the twentieth century. One original source of this particular use of the Declaration can be traced back to President Harry S. Truman. As presidential scholar Garth E. Pauley observes, Truman addressed the issue of civil rights on numerous occasions in his first two years as president. He also appointed the 1946 Committee on Civil Rights, which subsequently issued its historic report *To Secure These Rights*. It, however, was Truman's 1947 Lincoln Memorial speech to the National Association for the Advancement of Colored People (NAACP) that signaled a critical turning point in his presidency and ultimately the nation's and the national government's commitment to civil rights reforms. Truman began this speech by noting "the long history of our country's efforts to guarantee freedom and equality to all our citizens." Truman marked this history from the earliest, "inspiring charters of human rights—the Declaration of Independence, the Constitution, the Bill of Rights and the Emancipation Proclamation" to the recent work by American "representatives, and those of other liberty-loving countries on the United Nations Commission on Human Rights" who were "preparing an International Bill of Rights."

Given "recent events," which included the heightened threat of communism, Truman noted the pressing importance of ensuring the enjoyment of civil rights by every American. Like Roosevelt before him, Truman advocated a more active role for the national government in achieving this result. Truman's concern, however, extended beyond economic rights and conventional conceptions of civil rights that emphasized "only the need of protection against the possibility of tyranny by the Government." Truman maintained that "[w]e must keep moving forward, with new concepts of civil rights to safeguard our heritage" and that "the Federal Government" must become "a friendly, vigilant defender of the rights and equalities of all Americans" so that each individual would "be guaranteed equality of opportunity" and freedom from "discrimination because of ancestry, or religion, or race, or color." For Truman, this new understanding of and commitment to civil rights also meant that

[w]e must not tolerate such limitations on the freedom of any of our people and on their enjoyment of the basic rights which every citizen in a truly democratic society must possess. Every man should have the right to a decent home, the right to an education, the right to adequate medical care, the right to a worthwhile job, the right to an equal share in the making of public decisions through the ballot, and the right to a fair trial in a fair court.

Truman defended his new vision of civil rights in subsequent statements, speeches, and executive actions. One of the fullest and most concise statements was his February 2, 1948, civil rights message to Congress. In this message, Truman not only invoked the Declaration as the inspiration for this new vision, but he also specified a set of national policy priorities that, with the similarly inspired assistance of members of Congress and Presidents John F. Kennedy and Lyndon B. Johnson in the 1960s, initiated a critique and reframing of the law and administration of civil rights in the United States. In this message, Truman argued:

The founders of the United States proclaimed to the world the American belief that all men are created equal, and that governments are instituted to secure the inalienable rights with which all men

are endowed. In the Declaration of Independence and the Constitution of the United States, they eloquently expressed the aspirations of . . . mankind for equality and freedom. . . .

We believe that all men are created equal and that they have the right to equal justice under law. We believe that all men have the right to freedom of thought and of expression and the right to worship as they please. We believe that all men are entitled to equal opportunities for jobs, for homes, for good health and for education. We believe that all men should have a voice in their government and that government should protect, not usurp, the rights of the people. These are the basic civil rights, which are the source and the support of our democracy. . . .

The Federal Government has a clear duty to see that Constitutional guarantees of individual liberties and of equal protection under the laws are not denied or abridged anywhere in our Union. That duty is shared by all three branches of the Government, but it can be fulfilled only if the Congress enacts modern, comprehensive civil rights laws, adequate to the needs of the day, and demonstrating our continuing faith in the free way of life. I recommend, therefore, that the Congress enact legislation at this session directed toward the following specific objectives: 1. Establishing a permanent Commission on Civil Rights, a Joint Congressional Committee on Civil Rights, and a Civil Rights Division in the Department of Justice. 2. Strengthening existing civil rights statutes. 3. Providing Federal protection against lynching. 4. Protecting more adequately the right to vote. 5. Establishing a Fair Employment Practice Commission to prevent unfair discrimination in employment. 6. Prohibiting discrimination in interstate transportation facilities. 7. Providing home-rule and suffrage in Presidential elections for the residents of the District of Columbia. 8. Providing Statehood for Hawaii and Alaska and a greater measure of self-government for our island possessions. 9. Equalizing the opportunities for residents of the United States to become naturalized citizens. 10. Settling the evacuation claims of Japanese-Americans.

Enactment of Truman's civil rights vision, one inspired by and explained in terms of the

Declaration of Independence, became the political subtext and legislative agenda that dominated both Congress and the presidency from the late 1950s into the 1960s. For the early part of these years, however, legislative reforms were regularly sidetracked by external events and by individuals in both institutions who did not share or could not publicly support this new understanding of the purpose and responsibilities of government. The resulting dissonance over the meaning of the Declaration exposed the incompatibility of numerous social and political practices in the United States and, ironically, irreconcilable divisions within the Democratic Party, which had dominated Congress with few exceptions since the 1932 elections. In the end, the congressional heirs of Truman's vision succeeded in enacting the 1964 Civil Rights Act, which President Lyndon Johnson signed into law on July 2, 1964—the anniversary of the Continental Congress's 1776 vote for independence. Congress and President Johnson also enacted the 1965 Voting Rights Act, the 1965 Immigration Reform Act, and the 1968 Civil Rights Act before other international and domestic issues—including the Vietnam War, the assassinations of Martin Luther King Jr. and Robert F. Kennedy, the Watergate scandal in the early 1970s, and the widely inclusive and national bicentennial celebration in 1976—redirected the nation's attention and activities as well as the focus of the Declaration's influence.[2]

## Conclusion

As they did when dealing with many momentous issues that defined America's past, members of Congress and presidents did not hesitate to turn to the Declaration of Independence to construct, to articulate, and to debate their positions in the early 1960s on the civil rights issues brought to the surface by Truman and others in 1947 and 1948. Again, as in previous eras and debates, the Declaration was an inspiration, although it was understood and employed in different ways and for starkly different ends. Again, as in the past, these disparate discourses often were suggested by, repeated, and, occasionally, extended ideas articulated earlier by other presidents and members of Congress. The serious, nationally televised, and ultimately consequential speeches by President John Kennedy on June 11, 1963, and President Lyndon Johnson on March 15, 1965, echo many of the better angels responsible for and to the broad discourse anchored around the Declaration of Independence. In particular, Kennedy's highly regarded June 11 ("Moral Crisis") speech calls to mind not only Adams, Lincoln, Sumner, and Coolidge, but also a September 22, 1880, speech by President Rutherford Hayes, which appropriately asks: "What is to be the future of this beautiful land?"

## Notes

1. In addition to the John Trumbull painting, Congress has adorned the Capitol with numerous commemorations of the Declaration of Independence and its original signers. For example, in the Old House Chamber, an elaborate reproduction of the Declaration is depicted with the thirteen original state seals. In the Rotunda, a bronze commemorative plaque was erected in 1932 and the frieze, which encircles the room, contains a scene by Filippo Castaggini of the Declaration's reading.
2. On July 4, 1966, President Lyndon B. Johnson signed a congressional joint resolution authorizing the creation of the American Revolution Bicentennial Commission (ARBC) to prepare for

the event in 1976. Johnson delayed announcement of his action until July 8, 1966—the anniversary of the ringing of the Liberty Bell. Much of the subsequent success of the bicentennial celebration, however, ought to be attributed to ARBC's successor, the American Revolution Bicentennial Administration (ARBA). In 1974 the Ninety-third Congress created and funded ARBA to coordinate, facilitate, and aid in the "scheduling of events, activities and projects of local, State, National and international significance sponsored by both governmental and nongovernmental entities in commemoration of the American Revolution Bicentennial."

## Bibliography

*Annals of Congress: The Debates and Proceedings in the Congress of the United States.* Washington, D.C.: Gales and Seaton, 1834–1856.

American Revolution Bicentennial Administration. *The Bicentennial of the United States of America: A Final Report to the People.* 5 vols. Washington, D.C.: U.S. Governmental Printing Office, 1977.

Basler, Roy P., ed. *Collected Works of Abraham Lincoln.* New Brunswick: Rutgers University Press, 1953.

Burstein, Andrew. *America's Jubilee.* New York: Knopf, 2001.

_____. *Sentimental Democracy: The Evolution of America's Romantic Self-Image,* New York: Hill and Wang, 1999.

Chandler, Alfred D., Jr., and others, eds. *Papers of Dwight D. Eisenhower.* 21 vols. Baltimore: Johns Hopkins University Press, 1970.

Chase, Philander D., ed. *Papers of George Washington: Revolutionary War Series.* Vol. 5: *June–August 1776.* Charlottesville: University Press of Virginia, 1993.

*The Congressional Globe: United States Congress.* Washington, D.C.: Blair and Rives, 1834–1873.

*Congressional Record: Proceedings and Debates of the United States Congress.* Washington, D.C.: U.S. Government Printing Office, 1874–2001.

Coolidge, Calvin. "Education: The Cornerstone of Self-Government" (July 4, 1924) and "The Inspiration of the Declaration" (July 5, 1926). In *Foundations of the Republic: Speeches and Ad-*

*dresses by Calvin Coolidge.* New York: Scribner's, 1926.

Cunningham, Noble, ed. *Circular Letters of Congressmen to Their Constituents 1789–1829.* Chapel Hill: University of North Carolina Press, 1978.

Detweiler, Philip F. "Congressional Debate on Slavery and the Declaration of Independence, 1819–1821." *American Historical Review* 63 (1958): 598–616.

_____. "The Changing Reputation of the Declaration of Independence: The First Fifty Years." *William and Mary Quarterly* 3d Ser. 19 (1962): 557–574.

Fields, Wayne. *Union of Words: A History of Presidential Eloquence.* New York: Free Press, 1996.

Foner, Philip S., ed., *We, The Other People: Alternative Declarations of Independence by Labor Groups, Farmers, Woman's Rights Advocates, Socialists, and Blacks, 1829–1975.* Urbana: University of Illinois Press, 1976.

Ford, Worthington C., and others, eds. *Journal of the Continental Congress.* Washington, D.C.: U.S. Governmental Printing Office, 1904–1937.

Hunt, Gaillard, ed. *Writings of James Madison.* Vol. 6: *1780–1802.* New York: Putnam, 1906.

Hutchinson, William T., ed. *Papers of James Madison.* 17 vols. Charlottesville: University Press of Virginia, 1962–1991.

Jaffe, Irma B. *John Trumbull: Patriot-Artist of the American Revolution.* Boston: Little, Brown, 1975.

Merrill, Dennis, ed. *Documentary History of the Truman Presidency.* 30 vols. Bethesda, Md.: University Publications of America, 1995–2001.

Milkis, Sidney M. "Franklin D. Roosevelt, Progressivism, and the Limits of Popular Leadership." In *Speaking to the People: The Rhetorical Presidency in Historical Perspective.* Ed. Richard J. Ellis. Amherst: University of Massachusetts Press, 1998, 182–210.

Miller, William Lee. *Arguing about Slavery: John Quincy Adams and the Great Battle in the United States Congress.* New York: Knopf, 1996.

Palmer, Beverly W., ed. *Selected Letters of Charles Sumner.* Boston: Northeastern University Press, 1990.

Pauley, Garth E. *The Modern Presidency and Civil Rights: Rhetoric on Race from Roosevelt to Nixon.* College Station: Texas A&M University Press, 2001.

Peterson, Merrill D. *The Jefferson Image in the American Mind.* New York: Oxford University Press, 1962.

Remini, Robert V. *Daniel Webster: The Man and His Time.* New York: W. W. Norton, 1997.

Smith, Rogers. *Civic Ideals: Conflicting Visions of Citizenship in U.S. History.* New Haven: Yale University Press, 1997.

Thelen, David P. "Rutherford B. Hayes and the Reform Tradition in the Gilded Age." *American Quarterly* 22 (1970): 150–165.

Tourtellot, Arthur B., ed. *Woodrow Wilson: Selections for Today.* New York: Duell, Sloan, and Pearce, 1945.

Waldstreicher, David. *In the Midst of Perpetual Fetes: The Making of American Nationalism, 1776–1820.* Chapel Hill: University of North Carolina Press, 1997.

Williams, Charles Richard, ed. *The Diary and Letters of Rutherford B. Hayes, Nineteenth President of the United States.* 5 vols. Columbus: Ohio State Archeological and Historical Society, 1922–1926.

Wilson, Woodrow. *The New Freedom: A Call for the Emancipation of the Generous Energies of a People.* New York: Doubleday, 1913.

# The Declaration of Independence in the Supreme Court

MARK DAVID HALL

Throughout its history, the U.S. Supreme Court, or, more precisely, particular Supreme Court justices, have referred to the Declaration of Independence in written opinions. By the end of the 2000 term, justices had explicitly invoked the Declaration in 184 opinions (106 majority, 54 dissenting, and 24 concurring or other type of opinion).[1]

The Declaration has been appealed to throughout American history to gain support for a variety of causes. It is often treated as a statement of principles upon which the United States was founded—and by which it can be judged. In a similar manner, parties appearing before the Supreme Court have invoked the Declaration as a source of rights that are not clearly enumerated in the U.S. Constitution and its amendments, or as a means of interpreting parts of the Constitution. Scholars and academic lawyers often applaud these efforts.

Whatever theoretical or rhetorical merit appealing to the Declaration holds, justices have rarely attempted to base their decisions solely upon the Declaration. Even though the Declaration is the first document in the *United States Code*, where it is classified by Congress as one of "The Organic Laws of the United States of America," justices of the Supreme Court have generally agreed with the position expressed by Justice Antonin Scalia in *Troxel v. Granville* (2000) that even if a judge believes a right is "among the 'unalienable Rights' with which the Declaration of Independence proclaims 'all Men . . . are endowed by their Creator,' " the Declaration "is not a prescription conferring powers upon the courts." In other words, justices may not base decisions on the Declaration, even if they believe that doing so would result in a morally correct decision.

Justices have referred to the Declaration in their opinions for two identifiable, and occasionally interrelated, reasons. First, they have considered the document to formally mark the independence of the United States of America. Second, they have appealed to it as a document that can cast light upon the founders' views or the principles underlying the Constitution. Some have gone so far as to argue that provisions of the Constitution were written to protect the rights proclaimed in the Declaration, but even these justices have always grounded their decisions on specific provisions of the Constitution.

In addition to these substantive reasons for invoking the Declaration, justices have made approximately twenty inconsequential references to the document in their opinions. For instance, in *McDaniel v. Paty* (1978), Chief Justice Warren Burger mentioned in passing that John Witherspoon was the only clergyman to sign the Declaration. Similarly, in *Board of Education of Central School District No. 1 v. Allen* (1968), Justice William O. Douglas, as an example of the sort of "sectarianism" that can "creep" into parochial schoolbooks, referred to a history text that made a point of noting that one of the signers of the Declaration of Independence was Catholic. That the author of the textbook thought it useful to note how many Catholics signed the Declaration, or that Burger felt it necessary to point out that Witherspoon signed the Declaration, suggests something about the importance of the document, but the references are of little significance beyond that.[2]

Study of the approximately 160 opinions that make substantive references to the Declaration of Independence serves several purposes. First, it helps to show how Americans have viewed the Declaration throughout the nation's history. Supreme Court justices are clearly not representative Americans, but they are at least partially products of American culture, and they write their opinions for relatively widespread consumption. Examining these opinions in their historical contexts sheds light on how the document was understood and used at different points in American history.

Second, given the number of activists, lawyers, and scholars who have argued that justices should use the Declaration to help interpret the Constitution, it is useful to consider how the Court has employed the document. When justices appeal to the Declaration, do they do so in a historically accurate manner?

Do justices simply appeal to the Declaration to write their own policy preferences into law? Do the justices who appeal to the Declaration more often than others share a common jurisprudence or ideology?

## Formal Marker of Independence

On July 2, 1776, the Continental Congress approved Richard Henry Lee's resolution that "these United Colonies are, and of right ought to be, free and independent States." John Adams suggested that the day should be "celebrated by succeeding generations as the great Anniversary Festival" marking American independence. Yet, beginning in 1777, Americans have celebrated on July 4, the anniversary of Congress's vote to approve the Declaration. Generations of authors and historians have pointed out that Americans are celebrating on the wrong date. But if Americans are mistaken, so is the Supreme Court.

Justices have used the Declaration approximately sixty times to mark American independence. They have never considered using Congress's July 2, 1776, vote to do so. In the first seventy years of the Court's existence, justices were forced to adjudicate a number of cases that turned on when America became an independent country. The specific issues in many of these cases may seem trivial (they often involved relatively small debts or inheritances, minor disagreements about state boundaries, and so on), but the reasoning employed by justices sheds light on important questions concerning international law, popular sovereignty, and the nature of the federal union.

Chief Justice John Jay, in his seriatim opinion in *Chisholm v. Georgia* (1793), was the first justice to use the Declaration to mark independence. More significant, though, is Justice Samuel Chase's opinion in *Ware v. Hylton* (1796). *Ware* involved a debt owed to a British subject that had been nullified by an act of the Virginia Assembly in October 1777. Chase and three other justices ruled that the 1783 Treaty of Paris, which required repayment of British creditors, nullified the state law. The case's primary significance is that it helped establish the supremacy of the national government in international affairs. However, in his opinion Chase touched on many significant issues relating to America's declaration of independence.

Chase recognized that some individual colonies had declared independence before July 4, 1776 (he noted that Virginia had done so in June of that year). He also acknowledged that as a matter of international law, areas not under the control of Great Britain could be considered to have de facto independence. Nonetheless, he concluded:

I have ever considered it as the established doctrine of the United States, that their independence originated from, and commenced with, the declaration of Congress, on the 4th of July, 1776; and that no other period can be fixed on for its commencement; and that all laws made by the legislatures of the several states, after the declaration of independence, were the laws of sovereign and independent governments.

Chase concluded that Article VI of the Constitution applied retroactively, so that a national treaty takes precedence over state laws. Justice James Wilson's seriatim opinion in *Ware* offered an additional reason for why the state law was void. He contended that "[w]hen the United States declared their independence, they were bound to receive the law of nations, in its modern state of purity and refinement. By

every nation, whatever is its form of government, the confiscation of debts has long been considered disreputable." Hence Wilson articulated the doctrine later accepted by diplomats such as John Quincy Adams that the Declaration marked the moment America became bound by international law.[3]

Since *Ware*, the Court has repeatedly relied upon the Declaration to mark America's independence. Many citizenship cases, for example, have turned on whether a person was born before or after July 4, 1776. As a rule, the Court has held that individuals born in America after the Declaration are American citizens, while individuals born before the Declaration could elect through their words or actions to become American citizens or remain British citizens (for example, *Inglis v. Trustees of Sailor's Snug Harbor* (1830), *Dawson's Lessee v. Godfrey* (1808), and *McIlvaine v. Coxe's Lessee* (1805)). British courts rejected this position, holding that Americans ceased to be British subjects with the 1783 Treaty of Paris.

In addition to citizenship, the justices have held that the Declaration is definitive for determining state boundaries. They have repeatedly maintained that state boundaries became fixed by Congress's July 4 declaration (for example, *State of New Jersey v. State of Delaware* (1934)). Similarly, in *Luther v. Borden* (1849), a case involving two governing bodies claiming to be the legitimate state government of Rhode Island, Chief Justice Roger Taney, for the Court, argued that the state government in existence at the time of the Declaration is the legitimate one and that Congress and the president must decide the legitimacy of changes to state constitutions made after July 4, 1776.

As cases and controversies involving actions and people from the Revolutionary era ceased to come before the Court, justices began primarily to use the Declaration to mark independence when discussing legal history. America's break with Great Britain has important implications for the relevance of British statutory and common law in America, so it is often mentioned by justices with an interest in the history of law. Most notable in this regard is Justice Horace Gray, who wrote twenty-four opinions that referred to the Declaration in the course of discussing the history of various legal doctrines (for example, *In re Sawyer* (1888), *Mackin v. U.S.* (1886), and *Smith v. Whitney* (1886)).

## Declaration as Framework for Interpreting the Constitution

Activists, attorneys, and academics have often urged Supreme Court justices to interpret the Constitution in light of the Declaration of Independence. While justices have hesitated to treat the Declaration as a source of justiciable rights, many have agreed with Justice David Brewer in *Gulf, Colorado & Santa Fe Railway v. Ellis* (1897) that "it is always safe to read the letter of the Constitution in the spirit of the Declaration of Independence." Accordingly, they have often looked to the document to shed light on the fundamental principles underlying the American system of government or specific provisions of the Constitution.

### Constitutional Principles

Because justices usually consider specific provisions of the Constitution when deciding cases, they seldom reflect on its overall charac-

ter. On occasion, however, they have made sweeping assertions about the connection between the Declaration and the Constitution. For example, Justice Harold Burton, in his majority opinion in *Bute v. People of the State of Illinois* (1948), argued that "[t]he Constitution was conceived in large part in the spirit of the Declaration of Independence which declared that to secure such 'unalienable Rights' as those of 'Life, Liberty and the pursuit of Happiness' . . . Governments are instituted among Men, deriving their just powers from the consent of the governed."

In a similar manner, Chief Justice Earl Warren, dissenting in *Perez v. Brownell* (1958), asked:

What is this government [of the United States], whose power is here being asserted? And what is the source of that power? The answers are the foundation of our Republic. To secure the inalienable rights of the individual, "Governments are instituted among Men, deriving their just powers from the consent of the governed." I do not believe the passage of time has lessened the truth of this proposition. It is basic to our form of government.

Like Burton and Warren, many justices have referred to the Declaration as an authoritative statement of abstract principles underlying the Constitution. Slightly more specific instances of this include Justice Felix Frankfurter appealing to the document to support his argument that America has a government of laws, not men (*United States v. United Mine Workers of America* (1947)), William O. Douglas citing it to advance his claim that the people are sovereign and that the national government is one of limited powers (*Schlesinger v. Reservists Committee to Stop the War* (1974)), and Justice John Catron invoking to it to support his claim that the founders desired widespread immigration (*Smith v. Turner* (1849)).

Justices have quoted the stirring principles found near the beginning of the document's second paragraph more than any other passage in the Declaration. Illustrative of this is Justice Arthur Goldberg's claim in *Bell v. State of Maryland* (1964) that "[t]he Declaration of Independence states the American creed: 'We hold these truths to be self-evident, that all men are created equal, that they are endowed by their Creator with certain unalienable Rights, that among these are Life, Liberty and the pursuit of Happiness.' " Many justices have clearly believed that the primary purpose of the Constitution is to protect the principles proclaimed in the Declaration.

*Federalism*

One of the most important debates in America's history has been whether its constitutional system is based on the sovereignty of the American people, the American states, or some combination of the two. In an attempt to resolve this issue, politicians, scholars, and justices have turned to the Declaration of Independence. However, the Declaration, like the Constitution, offers evidence for all of the above positions. For instance, the first sentence of the first paragraph in the Declaration suggests that Americans are rebelling as "one people." However, the first sentence of the last paragraph contains the claim that "these united colonies are, and of right ought to be, free and independent states."

The Court's first important case involving federalism was *Chisholm v. Georgia* (1793). At issue was a lawsuit in federal court against the state of Georgia by a citizen of another state. Georgia, appealing to the doctrine of sovereign

immunity, refused to respond to the suit. Five of the six justices then on the Court concluded that Georgia could be sued under Article III of the Constitution. The case is interesting not only for its specific holding, but also because several justices took the opportunity to reflect on the nature of American federalism. Two justices, James Wilson and John Jay, provided particularly powerful, highly controversial, seriatim opinions supporting national sovereignty. Notably, Chief Justice Jay, in the course of "determining the sense in which Georgia is a sovereign state," turned to the Declaration of Independence. He contended that when the Declaration was written, the American people were "already united for general purposes." Legally, the document caused sovereignty to pass from the Crown of Great Britain to the people of America. Following this logic, he concluded that the Constitution was created by the sovereign American people—it was not, in other words, a compact between states. State constitutions, and the governments they created, are grounded in the people of each state. It therefore makes no sense for a state government to claim sovereign immunity against suits clearly allowed by Article III of the Constitution.

The Court's holding in *Chisholm* was widely criticized and was overturned almost immediately by the Eleventh Amendment. Yet Jay's arguments about the nature of the federal union have remained an important part of American political and legal discourse. For example, in *Alden v. Maine* (1999), dissenting justices relied on the majority seriatim opinions in *Chisholm* to support their position.

A related view of the transfer of sovereignty brought about by the Declaration is found in Justice George Sutherland's majority opinion in *United States v. Curtiss-Wright Export Corporation* (1936). He contended that in

the Declaration of Independence, "the Representatives of the United States of America" declared the United (not the several) Colonies to be free and independent states, and as such to have "full Power to levy War, conclude Peace, contract Alliances, establish Commerce and to do all other Acts and Things which Independent States may of right do." As a result of the separation from Great Britain by the colonies, acting as a unit, the powers of external sovereignty passed from the Crown not to the colonies severally, but to the colonies in their collective and corporate capacity as the United States of America.

Sutherland did not emphasize the sovereignty of the American people, but he clearly believed that representatives of the united colonies created the Declaration and that the document transferred the powers of external sovereignty from the Crown to a union of the states, not thirteen sovereign entities.

Contrary to Jay and Sutherland, justices such as Henry Baldwin have argued that the effect of the Declaration was to pass sovereignty from the Crown to thirteen sovereign states. In his majority opinion in *Rhode Island v. Massachusetts* (1838), Baldwin contended that "[i]n the declaration of independence, the states assumed their equal station among the powers of the earth." He went on to note that the "states, being independent, reserved to themselves the power of settling their own boundaries," until they gave that power to the Continental Congress in 1781. He applied the logic of this argument to the U.S. Constitution in his concurring opinion in *Proprietors of Charles River Bridge v. Proprietors of Warren Bridge* (1837), when he noted that the "federal government itself is but a corporation, created by the grant or charter of the separate states."

Most justices who have believed that the Declaration created thirteen sovereign states have supported the view that the Constitution is a compact between states, not a creation of the American people. This connection between the Declaration and the Constitution was clearly expressed by Chief Justice Taney, in his majority opinion in *Kentucky v. Dennison* (1860). He wrote that, by the time the Articles of Confederation were written, the "colonies had then, by the Declaration of Independence, become separate and independent sovereignties." He pursued the logic of this claim to conclude that when the states created the Constitution, they made sure to protect their sovereignty. A popular corollary to this view is that if sovereign states created the Union, states can unmake it through secession. Unfortunately, eleven southern states exercised this option within a year of Taney's opinion.[4]

Taney's view of the Declaration and the Union was largely defeated by 1865, albeit on the battlefield and not in a courtroom or classroom. It is possible to find echoes of his approach in later cases, but never again has a justice claimed that the Declaration resulted in thirteen independent, sovereign states (for example, *Bute v. People of the State of Illinois* (1948) and *South Carolina v. Katzenbach* (1966)).

### Legislative, Executive, and Judicial Branches

The Supreme Court plays an important role in the system of checks and balances devised by the framers of the Constitution. In determining the proper respective roles of the legislative, executive, and judicial branches, justices have occasionally referred to the Declaration to help illuminate the framers' views. Justices have seldom appealed to the Declaration with respect to Congress per se, except in regard to political equality in national elections. This is likely because the Declaration is focused on the abuses of the Crown, not Parliament.

However, justices have invoked the Declaration to protest the excessive use of executive power on a number of occasions. For example, Justice Robert Jackson, in *Youngstown Sheet & Tube Company v. Sawyer* (1952), noted that "[t]he example of such unlimited executive power that must have most impressed the forefathers was the prerogative exercised by George III, and the description of its evils in the Declaration of Independence, leads me to doubt that they were creating their new Executive in his image." Accordingly, he concurred with the majority's opinion that President Harry S. Truman's seizure of steel mills was unconstitutional, even though Truman claimed that his action was necessary for the nation's security.

The decision in *Youngstown* notwithstanding, the last half of the twentieth century saw a tremendous increase in the power of the chief executive. Although the Supreme Court did not always challenge these increases, justices kept Jackson's admonition in mind, as is evidenced by Justice William Rehnquist's quoting him in his majority opinion in *Dames & Moore v. Regan* (1981). Likewise, in a separation of powers case that did not focus on executive power per se, Justice John Paul Stevens noted in his majority opinion in *Metropolitan Washington Airports Authority v. Citizens for Abatement of Aircraft Noise, Inc.* (1991) that "[t]he abuses by the monarch recounted in the Declaration of Independence provide dramatic evidence of the threat to liberty posed by a too powerful executive."

As one might expect, justices are especially protective of the judicial branch and have often appealed to the Declaration when opposing perceived encroachments on its independence. A good example of this is Sutherland's majority opinion in *O'Donoghue v. United States* (1933). The case involved an attempt by Congress to diminish the salary of judges in the District of Columbia. The Court determined that the judges in question were subject to the protections of Article III of the Constitution. Sutherland then noted that

[t]he anxiety of the framers of the Constitution to preserve the independence especially of the judicial department is manifested by the provision now under review, forbidding the diminution of the compensation of the judges of courts exercising the judicial power of the United States. This requirement was foreshadowed, and its vital character attested, by the Declaration of Independence, which, among the injuries and usurpations recited against the King of Great Britain, declared that he had "made judges dependent on his will alone, for the tenure of their offices, and the amount and payment of their salaries."

In a similar, but unsuccessful argument, Justice Pierce Butler appealed to the same passage in *O'Malley v. Woodrough* (1939). He contended that federal judges should not have to pay federal income taxes because income taxes diminish judicial compensation, which the Constitution prohibits (see also *United States v. Hatter* (2001), *Northern Pipeline Construction Company v. Marathon Pipe Line Company* (1982), and *United States v. Will* (1980)).

The Court has jealously guarded the independence of federal courts—or, to be more specific, Article III courts. Justices have been less protective of Article I courts (for example, military courts). For instance, in *Weiss v. United*

*States* (1994), Scalia concurred with the majority in allowing Congress to appoint military judges without fixed terms, even though he noted that the Declaration expressed concern that the king had "made Judges dependent on his Will alone, for the tenure of their offices." Likewise, Thurgood Marshall, in his dissenting opinion in *Soloria v. United States* (1987), invoked the Declaration to support his argument that the founders feared "broad military authority in courts-martial." Yet, because Congress clearly has the ability to constitute these courts on its own terms, justices have hesitated to challenge their structures or practices.

### The Bill of Rights

If the Constitution was written, at least in part, to protect the rights to "Life, Liberty, and the pursuit of Happiness" proclaimed by the Declaration, it is reasonable to ask why these rights were not specifically guaranteed in the body of the Constitution. The Anti-Federalists were critical of the absence of these guarantees, and their concern clearly contributed to the adoption of the Bill of Rights. But should justices interpret the rights guaranteed in the Bill of Rights in light of the Declaration? Justice Brewer certainly thought so. In his majority opinion in *Monongahela Navigation Company v. United States* (1893), he contended that

[t]he first 10 amendments to the constitution, adopted as they were soon after the adoption of the constitution, are in the nature of a bill of rights, and were adopted in order to quiet the apprehension of many that without some such declaration of rights the government would assume, and might be held to possess, the power to trespass upon those rights of persons and property which by the Declaration of Independence were affirmed to be unalienable rights.

Brewer went on in his opinion to declare unconstitutional the federal government's attempt to seize a lock and dam without paying "just compensation" as required by the Fifth Amendment.

Brewer's opinion contains a rare example in which a justice has invoked the Declaration to shed light on the Fifth Amendment's protection of private property. Far more common is for justices to appeal to the Declaration with respect to the First Amendment. For example, in the libel case *Curtis Publishing Company v. Butts* (1967), Justice John Marshall Harlan, in his majority opinion, wrote that the "dissemination of the individual's opinions on matters of public interest is for us, in the historic words of the Declaration of Independence, an 'unalienable right' that 'governments are instituted among men to secure.'" Although this reference to the Declaration did not contribute directly to the Court's result (which upheld a libel award against the *Saturday Evening Post*), Harlan articulated well the view of many justices that a major purpose of the Bill of Rights was to protect the liberties proclaimed in the Declaration.

One of the most interesting cases involving the Declaration and the First Amendment has at its center the Declaration itself. In 1954 George Anastaplo was denied admission to the Illinois bar because he refused to answer questions put to him by the bar's Committee on Character and Fitness. Anastaplo, a World War II veteran who had graduated from the University of Chicago Law School, had nothing in his past that would have aroused the bar's attention. However, in the process of answering routine questions in his application, he wrote that one of the basic principles underlying the Constitution is that government is constituted so as to secure certain inalienable rights, those rights to Life, Liberty and Pursuit of Happiness (and elements of these rights are explicitly set forth in such parts of the Constitution as the Bill of Rights). And, of course, whenever the particular government in power becomes destructive of these ends, it is the right of the people to alter or to abolish it and thereupon to establish a new government (*In re Anastapolo* (1961)).

Anastaplo's paraphrasing of the Declaration, with its support for the right of revolution, was a cause for concern among members of the bar's committee. Consequently, the committee questioned him intensely about his political and religious affiliations (primarily to determine if he was, or had ever been, a Communist). Anastaplo, appealing to the Declaration and the First Amendment, refused to answer these questions.

Anastaplo was ultimately denied admission to the Illinois bar, and, when he appealed his case to the Supreme Court, he lost there as well. Justice Harlan's majority opinion, which scrupulously avoided mentioning the Declaration, asserted that the bar did not improperly exclude Anastaplo because of his refusal to answer certain questions. Justice Hugo Black's dissenting opinion, however, emphasized that it was Anastaplo's adherence to the Declaration's principle that unjust governments may be overthrown, and to his belief that the First Amendment protects his liberty to refuse to answer questions about his political and religious affiliations, that caused him to be denied admission to the bar.[5]

Along with freedom of speech, freedom of religion is among the most important of all rights. The author of the Declaration also wrote a metaphor that has come for many to define one of the religion clauses—the Estab-

lishment Clause. In 1802 Thomas Jefferson, in his famous letter to the Danbury Baptist Association, contended that the Establishment Clause built "a wall of separation between the Church and the State." Although only referred to once by the Supreme Court between 1802 and 1947, since *Everson v. Board of Education* (1947) the metaphor has been routinely cited by advocates of the "strict separation" between church and state. Proponents of a more "accommodationist" relationship between church and state have been more inclined to cite another document Jefferson drafted—the Declaration of Independence (although some of the language accommodationists find most attractive was inserted into Jefferson's draft by Congress).

The first time a justice cited the Declaration in a case involving religion, the litigation revolved around an interpretation of a congressional law, not the First Amendment. In 1892 the Court decided a case, *Holy Trinity Church v. United States,* involving a minister from Great Britain who was brought to America to pastor a church. The immigration law at the time explicitly forbade bringing "foreigners" to America to "perform labor or service," but it made exceptions for "professional actors, artists, lecturers, singers, and domestic servants." Ministers were not excepted. Accordingly, the United States sought to fine the rector of the Holy Trinity Church for violating the statute.

Justice Brewer, in his opinion for a unanimous Court, held that Congress had not intended to prevent the immigration of ministers, even though the statute did not make an exception for them. Brewer looked carefully at the context and content of the legislation, and he concluded that its primary purpose was to prevent the importation of unskilled laborers. Although he could have rested his argument at this point, he proceeded to assert that "no purpose of action against religion can be imputed to any legislation, state or national, because this is a religious people. This is historically true." As evidence, he appealed to a variety of public documents, such as the fundamental orders of Connecticut and William Penn's charter. He also noted that

the declaration of independence recognizes the presence of the Divine in human affairs in these words: "We hold these truths to be self-evident, that all men are created equal, that they are endowed by their Creator with certain unalienable Rights, that among these are Life, Liberty, and the pursuit of Happiness." "We, therefore, the Representatives of the united States of America, in General Congress, Assembled, appealing to the Supreme Judge of the world for the rectitude of our intentions, do, in the Name and by Authority of the good People of these Colonies, solemnly publish and declare," etc.; "And for the support of this Declaration, with a firm reliance on the Protection of Divine Providence, we mutually pledge to each other our Lives, our Fortunes, and our sacred Honor."

After considering the Declaration, Brewer proceeded to examine state constitutions and the federal Constitution (including the First Amendment religion clauses). He concluded that "[t]here is no dissonance in these declarations. There is a universal language pervading them all, having one meaning. They affirm and reaffirm that this is a religious nation. These are not individual sayings, declarations of private persons. They are organic utterances. They speak the voice of the entire people."

Brewer's opinion is a good example of how the Declaration has been used to show that America is a religious nation and that the founders did not seek to separate church and state (other than to prevent the establishment of a national church). It is also important for his defense of why the Declaration should be given more weight in constitutional interpretation than the "individual sayings" of the founders or their "declarations of private purposes." Simply put, he believed that documents created by representatives acting in their official capacities, especially "organic" documents such as the Declaration, better reflect the national purpose than private sentiments (including private comments of individuals involved in making the organic documents, such as James Madison's famous "Detached Memoranda").

Throughout the twentieth century, justices have followed Brewer's strategy of citing the Declaration as evidence that the founders did not desire a high wall of separation between the church and the state. For example, in *Engel v. Vitale* (1962), the decision that declared state-sponsored prayer in public schools unconstitutional, Justice Potter Stewart invoked the Declaration in his dissent. Like Brewer, he argued that the founders did not intend to create a "wall of separation" between church and state. As evidence, he quoted a number of instances where founders, presidents, and members of Congress had issued calls for prayers and provided publicly funded chaplains to lead them. He concluded his argument by appealing to the origins of the nation.

What each has done has been to recognize and to follow the deeply entrenched and highly cherished spiritual traditions of our Nation—traditions which come down to us from those who almost two hundred years ago avowed their "firm Reliance on the Protection of divine Providence" when they proclaimed the freedom and independence of this brave new world.

And, in case anyone missed the reference to the Declaration of Independence, he included a footnote citing the document and quoting its concluding line.

Black's majority opinion in *Engle* did not attempt to refute Stewart's arguments in any detail, but he did respond to his brethren's invocation of the Declaration. In a footnote, he stated that nothing in the majority opinion "is inconsistent with the fact that school children and others are officially encouraged to express love for our country by reciting historical documents such as the Declaration of Independence which contain references to the Deity."

Moving from the First Amendment to Amendments IV through VIII, justices clearly have often appealed to the Declaration to demonstrate the importance the founders placed upon due process protections in legal proceedings. Notably, they have often quoted specific accusations against the king of England to demonstrate that the founders were concerned about a particular issue. The best general statement of the connection between the Declaration and the Constitution in this regard is found in Justice Black's dissenting opinion in *Green v. United States* (1958).

I cannot help but believe that this arbitrary power to punish by summary process, as now used, is utterly irreconcilable with first principles underlying our Constitution and the system of government it created—principles which were uppermost in the minds of the generation that adopted the Constitution. Above all that generation deeply feared and bitterly abhorred the existence of arbitrary, unchecked power in the hands of any government official, particularly when it came to punishing alleged offenses against the state. A great concern for protecting individual liberty from even the possibility of irresponsible official action was one of the momentous forces which led to the Bill of Rights. And the Fifth, Sixth, Seventh and Eighth Amendments were directly and purposefully designed to confine the power of courts and judges, especially with regard to the procedures used for the trial of crimes. As manifested by the Declaration of Independence, the denial of trial by jury and its subversion by various contrivances was one of the principal complaints against the English Crown.

Black's opinion is worth quoting at length because he appeals to the "first principles underlying our Constitution," which he clearly considers to be articulated well by the Declaration. Moreover, he argues specifically for a connection between these principles and the due process protections of Amendments IV–VIII, especially the protections offered by jury trials.

A particularly good, early instance of a justice appealing to the Declaration of Independence in support of the right to trial by jury is the first Justice John Marshall Harlan's dissent in *Maxwell v. Dow* (1900). The majority opinion upheld the conviction of Charles Maxwell by a state jury of fewer than twelve members. Dissenting, Harlan reflected on the importance of juries in American history and noted that "the value of that institution was recognized by the patriotic men of the revolutionary period when in the Declaration of Independence they complained that the King of Great Britain had deprived the people of the colonies in many cases of the benefits of trial by jury."

Many justices have adopted this argument and referred to the Declaration in cases upholding or extending the right to trial by jury. For example, Justice Black cited the Declaration when upholding the right of a civilian defendant, who murdered a member of the armed forces, to have a civilian trial by jury (*Reid v. Covert* (1957)). Similarly, Justice Ruth

Bader Ginsburg cited the Declaration's complaint of the king "transporting us beyond Seas to be tried for pretended offenses" when requiring a trial by jury in a local venue (*United States v. Cabrales* (1998)).[6]

When interpreting the Bill of Rights, justices have often cited the Declaration to shed light on particular provisions. They often have appealed to the bill of particulars to show that the founders thought a specific action was problematic, and a number of them have invoked the majestic principles of the Declaration, which they claim the Constitution was adopted to protect. Even including the Bill of Rights, however, the Constitution fell far short of protecting one of the most important rights articulated in the Declaration: the right to be treated equally.

### The Fourteenth Amendment

To many people, the worst example of hypocrisy in American history is that the man who wrote—and many of the men who signed—the document that proclaimed, "We hold these truths to be self-evident, that all men are created equal," owned slaves. A number of responses have been offered to this criticism, including Abraham Lincoln's argument that the authors of the Declaration "meant simply to declare the right, so that the enforcement of it might follow as fast as circumstances should permit." Whatever the truth of this claim, it is indisputable that proponents of equality have often used the Declaration to support their causes.

In one case, however, the justices appealed to the Declaration to support inequality. *Dred Scott v. Sandford* (1856) is often described as the worst decision ever made by the Supreme Court. It involved a slave, Scott, who had resided with his owner in the free territory of Wisconsin and the free state of Illinois. Upon being returned to Missouri he sued for his freedom, arguing that his residency in a free territory and a free state made him a free man. Chief Justice Taney, in a sweeping opinion for a divided Court, held that "negroes" were not citizens of the United States, that they could not sue in federal courts, and that the Missouri Compromise of 1820 was unconstitutional.

Central to Taney's argument that "negroes" could not be citizens of the United States was his view that they were not considered part of the "political community formed and brought into existence by the Constitution of the United States." To substantiate this point, he returned to America's separation from Great Britain and concluded that

the legislation and histories of the times, and the language used in the Declaration of Independence, show, that neither the class of persons who had been imported as slaves, nor their descendants, whether they had become free or not, were then acknowledged as a part of the people, nor intended to be included in the general words used in that memorable instrument.

Taney conceded that some of the words in the Declaration "seem to embrace the whole human family," and he even quoted the memorable phrase "We hold these truths to be self-evident: that all men are created equal." However, he concluded that the framers of the document could not have meant to include "negroes," because, if they did, the actions of many of those who signed the Declaration would have been "flagrantly inconsistent" with these principles.

Chief Justice Taney's opinion in *Dred Scott* has been widely criticized, but the arguments he advanced in the opinion have been nevertheless widely adopted by those who endeavor to show that America's founding was permeated with racism. For example, Thurgood Marshall, the first African American appointed to the Supreme Court, in his separate opinion in *Regents of University of California v. Bakke* (1978) argued that the colonists proclaimed "as 'self-evident' that 'all men are created equal' and are endowed 'with certain unalienable rights,' including those to 'Life, Liberty, and the pursuit of Happiness.' The self-evident truths and the unalienable rights were intended, however, to apply only to white men." He went on to contend that the "implicit protection of slavery embodied in the Declaration of Independence was made explicit in the Constitution." Hence, one does not have to be a racist or an advocate of slavery to accept Taney's arguments, but that does not necessarily make them good arguments.

Two justices dissented from the majority opinion in *Dred Scott*. Notably, Benjamin Curtis provided a powerful response to Taney's selective use of history and his arguments about the Declaration. With respect to the former, Curtis demonstrated that in many states free "negroes" were considered citizens and could vote. With respect to the Declaration, he contended, in an argument that would later be made with great effect by Abraham Lincoln, that the authors of the Declaration meant to proclaim "universal abstract truths" when they wrote that "all men are created equal." The political realities of the time, however, did not allow them to abolish slavery. (See Chapter 3.)

Justices have been far more likely to follow Curtis in using the Declaration to promote equality than to follow Taney to frustrate it. In particular, they have often appealed to the Declaration in cases involving the Fourteenth Amendment. In doing so, they follow the lead of Justice Stephen Field, who, in his dissenting opinion in the *Slaughterhouse Cases* (1872), said that the Fourteenth Amendment "was intended to give practical effect to the declaration of 1776 of inalienable rights, rights which are the gift of the Creator, which the law does not confer, but only recognizes." Field was more interested in economic rights than political or civil rights, but the general sentiment he expressed has been shared by many of his fellow justices.

With respect to race, the connection between the Declaration and the Fourteenth Amendment is best illustrated by Justice Goldberg's concurring opinion in *Bell v. State of Maryland* (1964).

The Declaration of Independence states the American creed: "We hold these truths to be self-evident, that all men are created equal, that they are endowed by their Creator with certain unalienable Rights, that among these are Life, Liberty and the pursuit of Happiness." This ideal was not fully achieved with the adoption of our Constitution because of the hard and tragic reality of Negro slavery. The Constitution of the new Nation, while heralding liberty, in effect declared all men to be free and equal—except black men who were to be neither free nor equal. This inconsistency reflected a fundamental departure from the American creed, a departure which it took a tragic civil war to set right. With the adoption, however, of the Thirteenth, Fourteenth, and Fifteenth Amendments to the Constitution, freedom and equality were guaranteed expressly to all regardless "of race, color, or previous condition of servitude."

Throughout the 1950s and the 1960s the Supreme Court interpreted the Fourteenth Amendment along the lines suggested by Goldberg to declare unconstitutional a large number of laws discriminating against racial minorities. In the 1970s, however, the Court began to face vexing affirmative action cases, where government policies arguably discriminated in favor of racial minorities. Justices who believed these policies violated the Fourteenth Amendment appealed to the Declaration to defend their opinions. For instance, in his dissenting opinion in *Fullilove v. Klutznick* (1980), Justice Stewart argued that "[t]he Fourteenth Amendment was adopted to ensure that every person must be treated equally by each State regardless of the color of his skin. The Amendment promised to carry to its necessary conclusion a fundamental principle upon which this Nation had been founded—that the law would honor no preference based on lineage." To support this claim, he wrote in a footnote that "[t]he words Thomas Jefferson wrote in 1776 in the Declaration of Independence . . . contained the seeds of a far broader principle: 'We hold these truths to be self-evident: that all men are created equal.' "[7]

In addition to racial equality, justices have often appealed to the Declaration in conjunction with the Fourteenth Amendment to promote political equality. For example, Justice Douglas, in an opinion in *Gray v. Sanders* (1963) striking down a primary election system that gave greater weight to rural voters than urban voters, argued that "[t]he conception of political equality from the Declaration of Independence, to Lincoln's Gettysburg Address, to the Fifteenth, Seventeenth, and Nineteenth Amendments can mean only one thing—one person, one vote." Douglas's appeal was later quoted by Chief Justice Warren, in his famous majority opinion in *Reynolds v.*

*Sims* (1964), which applied the principle of "one person, one vote" to the apportionment of seats for state legislative districts. Similarly, Douglas's appeal to the Declaration has been quoted in decisions such as *Chisom v. Roemer* (1991), which struck down an electoral system because it was found to discriminate against racial minorities.

In addition to equality, justices serving on the Court between 1872 and 1936 often connected the Declaration and the Fourteenth Amendment in opinions purporting to protect the economic liberty of citizens (some of these cases arguably protect a form of equality—equality of opportunity). This connection was made in the first important case involving the Fourteenth Amendment to reach the Supreme Court, the *Slaughterhouse Cases* (1872). These cases involved a Louisiana law requiring anyone wanting to butcher animals in the New Orleans area to use the facilities of the privately owned Crescent City Live-Stock Landing and Slaughtering Company. The company was thereby given a profitable monopoly. Several butchers challenged the monopoly as a violation of their rights under the Privileges or Immunities Clause of the recently ratified Fourteenth Amendment. Justice Samuel Miller's majority opinion rejected this claim, arguing that the clause only prevented states from abridging the rights of national citizenship (for example, access to federal courts). He concluded that it was never intended to interfere with a state health regulation.

Four justices dissented from Miller's opinion. Most notably, Justice Field contended that the Fourteenth "amendment was intended to give practical effect to the declaration of 1776 of inalienable rights, rights which are the gift of the Creator, which the law does not confer, but only recognizes." Specifically, the Privileges or Immunities Clause protects the rights of citizens to "life, liberty and the pursuit of happiness," which are "the equivalent to the rights of life, liberty, and property" and are "fundamental rights." The right to labor is one of these fundamental rights, and it cannot be denied without due process of law, which Field found to be lacking in this case.

The Court had a chance to revisit the *Slaughterhouse Cases* in 1884, when it ruled in *Butchers' Union v. Crescent City Slaughterhouse Company* on the constitutionality of Louisiana's repeal of the monopoly it gave the company. The repeal was upheld, and Justices Joseph Bradley and Field wrote concurring opinions primarily to point out that the monopoly had been unconstitutional in the first place. Bradley's dissent is notable, however, because it contains his much-quoted claim that

[t]he right to follow any of the common occupations of life is an inalienable right, it was formulated as such under the phrase "pursuit of happiness" in the declaration of independence, which commenced with the fundamental proposition that "all men are created equal; that they are endowed by their Creator with certain inalienable rights; that among these are life, liberty, and the pursuit of happiness." This right is a large ingredient in the civil liberty of the citizen. To deny it to all but a few favored individuals, by investing the latter with a monopoly, is to invade one of the fundamental privileges of the citizen, contrary not only to common right, but, as I think, to the express words of the constitution.

Bradley went on to argue that this right is protected by three different clauses of the Fourteenth Amendment: the Privileges or Immunities Clause, the Due Process Clause, and the Equal Protection Clause.

When it became clear that the Court had little interest in resurrecting the Privileges or Immunities Clause (which was made virtually irrelevant by the 1872 *Slaughterhouse Cases*, but which has apparently witnessed a rebirth in the 1999 case *Saenz v. Roe*), justices interested in protecting economic liberty began to rely on the Due Process Clause of the Fourteenth Amendment. Again, Justice Field led the way, using the Declaration to shed light on the amendment. For example, in *Powell v. Commonwealth of Pennsylvania* (1888), the majority upheld a Pennsylvania law prohibiting the sale of oleomargarine. Field dissented, arguing that

[t]he right to pursue one's happiness is placed by the declaration of independence among the inalienable rights of man, with which all men are endowed, not by the grace of emperors or kings, or by force of legislative or constitutional enactments, but by their Creator; and to secure them, not to grant them, governments are instituted among men. The right to procure healthy and nutritious food, by which life may be preserved and enjoyed, and to manufacture it, is among these inalienable rights, which, in my judgment, no state can give, and no state can take away, except in punishment for crime. It is involved in the right to pursue one's happiness.

As such, Field would have struck down the law as a violation of the Due Process Clause of the Fourteenth Amendment.

Field dissented alone in *Powell*, but nine years later the Court finally adopted his and Bradley's arguments when they used the Due Process Clause of the Fourteenth Amendment to strike down a state economic regulation (*Allgeyer v. State of Louisiana* (1897)). Justice Rufus Peckham, in his majority opinion, quoted Bradley's claim that "the right to follow any of the common occupations of life is an inalienable right. It was formulated as such under the phrase 'pursuit of happiness' in the Declaration of Independence."

Between 1897 and 1937 the Court declared unconstitutional almost two hundred state and federal economic regulations. The Declaration was referred to in about a dozen of these cases. After 1937 the Court began to subject economic legislation to far less scrutiny than it had during the four previous decades. Since that date, justices have written only two opinions connecting economic liberty to the Declaration, and in both instances the opinions were dissents and were quoting previous cases. Most recently, Justice Marshall, dissenting from the majority opinion in *Massachusetts Board of Retirement v. Murgia* (1976), which upheld the constitutionality of a statute requiring police officers to retire at the age of fifty, quoted Justice Bradley's opinion that " 'the right of the individual . . . to engage in any of the common occupations of life . . . is an inalienable right; it was formulated as such under the phrase 'pursuit of happiness' in the declaration of independence.' "[8]

## Conclusion

Justices have appealed to the Declaration of Independence throughout the history of the Court. Their use of the document has been proportionately distributed between majority, concurring, and dissenting opinions, as illustrated in Table 9-1.

The Court decided far fewer cases in the early nineteenth century than it did in the late twentieth century, and justices in the latter period were far more likely to issue concurring and dissenting opinions than were their predecessors. Taking this into account, it becomes

apparent that the justices' use of the Declaration has remained relatively consistent over time. The major exceptions to this are the decades between 1880 and 1900, but a large percentage of the increase during this time is attributable to Justice Gray, who cited the Declaration twenty-four times to mark American independence while discussing legal history.

The Declaration has been cited in opinions written by more than one-half of the justices who have served on the Supreme Court, and

**Table 9-1.** The Declaration in the Supreme Court by Decade and Type of Opinion

| Decade | Cases | Majority | Con-curring | Dis-senting |
|---|---|---|---|---|
| 1790–1799 | 3 | 4 | | |
| 1800–1809 | 3 | 3 | | |
| 1810–1819 | 0 | | | |
| 1820–1829 | 2 | 2 | | |
| 1830–1839 | 5 | 3 | 2 | 2 |
| 1840–1849 | 4 | 2 | 1 | 3 |
| 1850–1859 | 7 | 6 | 1 | 2 |
| 1860–1869 | 2 | 2 | | |
| 1870–1879 | 6 | 4 | | 3 |
| 1880–1889 | 13 | 8 | 2 | 1 |
| 1890–1899 | 21 | 18 | 1 | 3 |
| 1900–1909 | 7 | 5 | 1 | 2 |
| 1910–1919 | 1 | | | 1 |
| 1920–1929 | 1 | 1 | | |
| 1930–1939 | 8 | 5 | | 3 |
| 1940–1949 | 6 | 5 | 2 | |
| 1950–1959 | 10 | 4 | 4 | 4 |
| 1960–1969 | 18 | 9 | 3 | 10 |
| 1970–1979 | 17 | 7 | 4 | 10 |
| 1980–1989 | 8 | 5 | | 5 |
| 1990–1999 | 17 | 9 | 3 | 5 |
| 2000–2001 | 2 | 1 | | 1 |

*Source:* Compiled by author.
*Note:* Some decades have more opinions than cases because different opinions in the same case refer to the Declaration of Independence. Seriatim opinions in the majority are counted as majority opinions. Opinions concurring in part and dissenting in part are counted as concurring opinions.

virtually all of the others have joined in opinions that have referred to the document. Only five justices have written more than five opinions citing the Declaration: Horace Gray (twenty-four), William O. Douglas (eleven), Hugo Black (eleven), Antonin Scalia (eight), and John Paul Stevens (eight). Of these men, Gray often cited the Declaration in majority opinions; Douglas, in dissenting opinions; and Black, Scalia, and Stevens, in a mixture of majority, concurring, and dissenting opinions. It is difficult to discern any pattern as to how most justices have used the Declaration (that is, they refer to it in a proportionate number of majority, concurring, and dissenting opinions).

Similarly, justices who cite the Declaration are no more likely to be advocates of judicial activism than they are to be advocates of judicial self-restraint. For instance, Douglas is considered to be one of the most activist judges, whereas Black is famous for his strict adherence to the text of the Constitution. While the contrast is not as extreme, many scholars would put Stevens and Scalia on different sides of the activist-restraint scale. The same holds true for justices who cite the Declaration less frequently.

Although no clear patterns of activism or restraint emerge among justices who cite the Declaration, individual study of each justice would show that some judges are more likely to use the Declaration in a particular way than others. Justice Douglas, for instance, used it to support arguments for unenumerated rights (often in dissenting opinions), whereas Justice Black was more likely to use it to shed light on the text of the Constitution. The point, however, is that the Declaration is not simply used by activists and ignored by advocates of judicial restraint, or vice versa.

Have justices appealed to the Declaration in a manner that is faithful to the text and context of the document, or have they appealed to it in an ahistorical manner? This is a difficult question to answer, because a variety of scholarly opinions surrounds the meaning, nature, and effect of the Declaration. Notably, scholars disagree vehemently over the relationship between the Declaration and the Constitution. Nevertheless, the justices' use of the Declaration has generally fallen within the boundaries of mainstream scholarship, and no instances can be cited in which they have used the Declaration in a patently misleading manner.

A separate but related question is why, given the large number of lawyers, activists, and scholars who have insisted that the Constitution was written to protect the principles of the Declaration—and the number of justices who have apparently agreed with this position—has the document not been cited in more cases? The answer to this question likely lies in the nature of the judicial process. If justices are attempting to break new constitutional ground, they will attempt to rely as much as possible on the Constitution and precedents so that they will not be accused of going beyond the bounds of the Constitution. However, once they succeed in breaking new ground, they can rely on their groundbreaking decisions as precedents and hence have no need to appeal to the Declaration.

Justices have not appealed to the Declaration as many times as some lawyers, activists, and scholars would like, but they have appealed to it a number of times—and often in important cases. They have used it to mark American independence and to shed light on the Constitution. However, they have resisted the call of some to treat it as a source of justiciable rights. Whether America would be better off if they had depends upon one's view of the place of the Declaration in America's constitutional system and the ability of justices to correctly discern and apply the great principles of the Declaration.

## Notes

1. These numbers are based on Westlaw searches for the phrase "Declaration of Independence," abbreviations such as "Decl. of Indp.," and commonly quoted phrases from the document such as "We hold these truths to be self-evident." In addition, I discovered a few opinions that rely on ideas similar to those in the Declaration or that loosely paraphrase words from the document. I do not include these opinions in my analysis because it is not evident that their authors are appealing to the Declaration. For an example of such a case, see *Marbury v. Madison* (1803).

2. Justices also mention several times that Thomas Jefferson was particularly proud of having written the Declaration (for example, see *Rosenberger v. Rector and Visitors of University of Virginia* (1995)).

3. John Quincy Adams, in a speech quoted by Felix Frankfurter in his concurring opinion in *Reid v. Covert* (1957), wrote that "[t]he Declaration of Independence recognized the European law of nations, as practiced among Christian nations, to be that by which they considered themselves bound, and of which they claimed the rights."

4. Secession is a possible, but not the only, corollary of the compact theory of the federal union. Justice Henry Baldwin, for instance, argued in *Charles River Bridge* that although the Union is a creation of states, each "state has made an irrevocable restriction on its own once plenary sovereignty, which it cannot loosen, without the concurrence of such a number of states, as are competent to amend the constitution." He went on to cite the Declaration to support his argument that charters and contracts were highly valued among the founders.

5. Anastaplo went on to become a highly regarded professor. He has been one of the most important academic advocates for the idea that the Constitution should be interpreted in light of the Declaration of Independence.

6. Justices have been less inclined to cite the Declaration with respect to other due process issues. One exception is *Berger v. State of New York* (1967). Justice Tom Clark's majority opinion cites the Declaration's complaint against general warrants in the course of striking down a New York statute that made it too easy (in the Court's opinion) for police officers to obtain search warrants.

7. See also Stevens's dissent in *Fullilove*, and Clarence Thomas's concurring opinion in *Adarand Constructors, Inc. v. Peña*.

8. In an interesting but isolated opinion, Justice Stevens argued that interpreting the Fourteenth Amendment in light of the Declaration should lead the Court to allow individuals (or guardians acting on their behalf) to refuse life-sustaining medical procedures (*Cruzan by Cruzan v. Director, Missouri Department of Health* (1990)).

## Bibliography

Anastaplo, George. *The Constitution of 1787: A Commentary*. Baltimore: Johns Hopkins University Press, 1989.

Becker, Carl. *The Declaration of Independence: A Study in the History of Ideas*. New York: Vintage Books, 1942.

Cosgrove, Charles. "The Declaration of Independence in Constitutional Interpretation: A Selective History and Analysis." *University of Richmond Law Review* 32 (January 1998): 107–164.

Diamond, Martin. "The Declaration and the Constitution: Liberty, Democracy, and the Founders." *Public Interest* 41 (fall 1975): 39–55.

Garet, Ronald R. "Creation and Commitment: Lincoln, Thomas, and the Declaration of Independence." *Southern California Law Review* 65 (March 1992): 1477–1496.

Gerber, Scott Douglas. *To Secure These Rights: The Declaration of Independence and Constitutional Interpretation*. New York: New York University Press, 1995.

Himmelfarb, Dan. "The Constitutional Relevance of the Second Sentence of the Declaration of

Independence." *Yale Law Journal* 100 (October 1990): 169–187.

Mahoney, Dennis J. "The Declaration of Independence as a Constitutional Document." In *The Framing and Ratification of the Constitution.* Ed. Leonard Levy and Dennis Mahoney. New York: Macmillan, 1987.

Reinstein, Robert J. "Completing the Constitution: The Declaration of Independence, Bill of Rights and Fourteenth Amendment." *Temple Law Review* (summer 1993): 361–418.

Thomas, Clarence. "Toward a 'Plain Reading' of the Constitution—The Declaration of Independence in Constitutional Interpretation." *Howard Law Journal* 30 (1987): 983–985.

Torzilli, Paolo. "Reconciling the Sanctity of Human Life, the Declaration of Independence, and the Constitution." *Catholic Lawyer* (fall 2000): 197–226.

Tushnet, Mark. *Taking the Constitution Away from the Courts.* Princeton: Princeton University Press, 1999.

# 10
# Frederick Douglass, Martin Luther King Jr., and Malcolm X Interpret the Declaration of Independence

## Keith D. Miller

According to David Howard-Pitney, author of *The Afro-American Jeremiad,* three elements underlie African American speeches of protest (or jeremiads): past Promise, current Failure, and eventual Fulfillment. Orators such as Frederick Douglass attacked slavery by making three essential claims. First, they argued that the founders built America on the promise of democracy and justice. Second, they maintained that slavery exemplified the current, gross failure of that promise. Third, they held that the Bible and the Declaration of Independence articulate the promise and guarantee its eventual fulfillment. By appealing to scriptural and patriotic authorities, speakers invoked and reinforced what is often called American civil religion. In the twentieth century, civil rights advocate the Rev. Dr. Martin Luther King Jr. and other African American leaders used similar means to advance the call of equal rights as promised in the Declaration of Independence. Nation of Islam (NOI) follower Malcolm X, however, employed a method that challenged Promise/Failure/Fulfillment.

## Frederick Douglass

Born a slave in Maryland in 1818, Frederick Douglass eventually escaped to the North, where he became a Christian preacher and then a magnetic antislavery orator. He regularly structured his orations according to Promise/Failure/Fulfillment. Interpreting the Declaration as a promise, he often paraphrased or quoted it, especially the passage "all men are created equal," which he used to hammer slavery. According to his argument, whites were hypocritical when they stated that their nation was founded on equality while they practiced slavery. Despite this hypocrisy, Douglass insisted, the Declaration was "a true doctrine," and its promise was genuine. Eventually, he declared, the nation would implement equality. Because slavery violated God's goodness, he further contended, it could not ultimately prevail.

Douglass and others who opposed slavery were engaged in ideological warfare with white slaveowners. At that time most white people strongly believed that people from Africa were unalterably inferior. Many Southern whites said that they believed their slaves were happy. Some whites claimed to have scientific proof of whites' genetic superiority. For example, popular writer Josiah Nott argued that people from Africa were barely superior to apes. As authority for their convictions, white supremacists cited not only science, but also the Bible. Slavery, they claimed,

**161**

reflected biblical principles. Southern members of the U.S. Senate and House of Representatives were also convinced that the U.S. Constitution sanctioned slavery forever. With some initial success, they struggled to prevent Northern members of Congress from even introducing antislavery petitions into congressional debate.

In 1852, delivering "What to the Slave Is the Fourth of July?," his most celebrated speech, Douglass issued a blistering assault on slavery. He contended that bondage was evil, in part, because it conflicted with the principles of God and the nation. The Bible and the Declaration, he argued, contained the promise that slavery would eventually disappear. Quoting a poem by William Lloyd Garrison, he concluded that, once slavery died, all Americans would live in harmony and a lovely utopia would unfold throughout the nation.

Douglass was wrong.

Once the Civil War ended and bondage was abolished, the white majority did not embrace equality. Nor did whites live harmoniously with African Americans. Instead, for the most part, Reconstruction collapsed. Northern whites refused to treat African Americans as equals. In the South, former slaveowners continued white supremacy, in part by stuffing ballot boxes. They also exploited their ex-slaves by forcing them into sharecropping. Some white men formed the Ku Klux Klan, a group that terrorized African Americans. Disdaining jury trials, Klansmen and other lawless, white vigilantes lynched African Americans at will and without legal consequence.

Douglass responded to this grim situation by updating the Promise/Failure/Fulfillment structure of his jeremiads. Instead of denouncing slavery, as he had before, he labeled share-

cropping a disguised form of slavery. Emulating Ida B. Wells, a younger woman who crusaded against lynching, he also railed at murder-by-rope and other crimes of Southern white terrorists. He continued to cite the Declaration and its promise of equality and kept reiterating that the promise would eventually be realized. He often gave bittersweet speeches at annual ceremonies held to commemorate the end of slavery.

## Reconstruction through the Progressive Era

During and after Reconstruction, other prominent African American leaders—including Wells, Robert Elliott, Francis Grimke, William Crogman, and Archibald Carey—delivered jeremiads similar to those of Douglass. Like Douglass, they based their hopes on the Declaration, the Emancipation Proclamation, and the Bible. They further appealed to the Constitution, citing the Thirteenth, Fourteenth, and Fifteenth Amendments, which Congress passed in the aftermath of the Civil War.

In 1874, for example, Robert Elliott, an African American member of Congress, eloquently pleaded for Congress to pass a civil rights bill that would outlaw racial segregation in restaurants, hotels, and passenger trains. Elliott hailed the Emancipation Proclamation and the Thirteenth, Fourteenth, and Fifteenth Amendments as efforts to implement the promise of the Declaration. He also quoted the Bible.

In 1905 Francis Grimke, an eminent minister, employed the Declaration as a plumb line to gauge the stupendous failures of Reconstruction. He mentioned the "right to life, liberty, and the pursuit of happiness" and the precept that "all men are born free and equal," then decried racism in the South as being so horrific that "the life of a Negro isn't worth as much as that of a dog." In 1919 he supplied a comparable appeal as he quoted the Declaration while exposing "this horrid record of lynching."

Condemning lynching in 1893, Ida B. Wells also quoted the Declaration in a jeremiad that employed the structure of Promise/Failure/Fulfillment and ended with an idealistic vision of racial harmony. In 1952 Archibald Carey, one of Martin Luther King Jr.'s friends and models, argued similarly as he cited the Declaration approvingly, assailed racism, and finished with a vision as optimistic as Wells's.

A relatively small number of African Americans disagreed with the jeremiad and its structure of Promise/Failure/Fulfillment. These speakers and writers—notably Martin Delany, Henry McNeal Turner, and Marcus Garvey—wanted listeners to separate from their white oppressors. A bishop in the African Methodist Episcopal Church, Turner visited Liberia and urged American blacks to emigrate to Africa. In an attempt to challenge white supremacy and promote racial pride, he once proclaimed, "God is a Negro." During the 1910s and early 1920s Garvey, who also embraced Christianity, staged popular parades in Harlem for the purpose of instilling racial pride. Like Turner, the charismatic Garvey advocated emigration to Africa and, for a brief period, gained a large following in Harlem.

W. E. B. Du Bois, the first African American to graduate with a Ph.D. from Harvard University, helped found the National Association for the Advancement of Colored People (NAACP). He proved indefatigable as a soci-ologist, historian, journalist, literary figure, and agitator for African American rights. Booker T. Washington earned fame and Du Bois's wrath by currying favor with whites while refusing to seek the right to vote. But Du Bois, the radical, and Washington, the moderate, both sought to assimilate with whites. Douglass, Elliott, Grimke, Wells, Du Bois, and Washington gained many more followers than did Delany, Turner, and Garvey.

## Martin Luther King Jr.

In 1929 Martin Luther King Jr. was born to a middle-class African American family in Atlanta, Georgia. His father, who was active in civic affairs, served as minister of Ebenezer Baptist Church; his mother played the organ for the choir. In 1944, at age fifteen, King won an oratory contest by offering a precise example of an African American jeremiad. In this youthful speech, King cited the Bible and the Declaration as touchstones that condemned racism.

Before finishing his doctorate at Boston University, King assumed the ministry of Dexter Avenue Baptist Church in Montgomery, Alabama. There, in December 1955, Rosa Parks was arrested for refusing to surrender her bus seat to a white man. JoAnn Robinson and the Women's Political Council immediately organized a boycott of all city buses. The eloquent King was soon chosen as leader of the protest, which catapulted him into the national spotlight. After thousands of African Americans in Montgomery shunned buses for one year, the U.S. Supreme Court validated their cause by outlawing racial discrimination on buses.

For the rest of his life, King hopscotched the nation, delivering hundreds, if not thousands, of speeches and sermons. In virtually all of them, he attacked American segregation. Often invoking the Bible, the Declaration of Independence, and the Constitution, he assaulted the intertwining "triple evils" of poverty, racism, and war.

In 1963 King and Fred Shuttlesworth led highly publicized racial protests in Birmingham, Alabama. The fire and police departments of Birmingham used powerful hoses and attack dogs on King's nonviolent demonstrators, including young children. Soon afterward, King joined A. Philip Randolph and other important leaders in orchestrating the March on Washington. For this event, approximately 200,000 people assembled to hear speakers endorse President John F. Kennedy's civil rights legislation. King capped the event by delivering "I Have a Dream," one of the most esteemed American speeches of the twentieth century.

Many of King's speeches reflect long-established patterns of African American political oratory, specifically a bittersweet expression of protest that began before the Civil War and that continues to this day. Orators normally play to listeners' long-held convictions, then ask audiences to extend those convictions to an issue in question. During the nineteenth century, for example, antislavery speakers often expressed their faith in the principles of the Bible and the Declaration of Independence. Most people in Victorian America accepted those two authorities. Opponents of slavery urged their audiences to reject bondage as a violation of the Bible and the Declaration. Because all men were created equal, abolitionists reasoned, slavery must be wrong. Similarly, they held that, if loving your neighbor is a godly principle, slavery must be evil.

During the 1950s and 1960s King gained fame by offering superlative, traditional African American jeremiads. They included his first address during the Montgomery bus boycott. There he condemned racial exploitation and invoked God and the Supreme Court, which, he insisted, guaranteed the eventual triumph of justice.

Several of King's mentors traveled to India to speak with Mahatma Gandhi, who led India in its triumphant nonviolent campaign to overthrow British rule. Spurred by his mentors' interest in Gandhi, King implemented and popularized Gandhi's political philosophy and tactics. According to Gandhian theory, those who suffer should, if necessary, violate unjust laws openly and publicly. Gandhi and King maintained that volunteering for jail can dramatize injustice and hasten the arrival of justice. The drama can be especially effective if lawbreakers are so numerous that they overflow the jail cells. In that case, they strain the legal system; authorities do not know what to do with them. Such lawbreaking—or civil disobedience—attempts to persuade. But masses of lawbreakers also exert huge political pressure on authorities. Television can evoke sympathy for a protest if viewers witness police brutality against nonviolent, hymn-singing demonstrators. This process occurred often during the civil rights movement, notably during King's Birmingham campaign of 1963.

A few months after the crucible of Birmingham, King climbed the steps of the Lincoln Memorial to deliver "I Have a Dream." It is a classic African American jeremiad that follows the structure of Promise/Failure/Fulfillment. He began by praising the Emancipation Proclamation. Immediately reversing himself, he explained that, despite the promise of Lincoln's edict, African Americans were still not free. He depicted a nightmare of racial injustice. Then he proclaimed, "I have a dream that one day this nation will rise up and live out the true meaning of its creed: 'We hold these truths to be self-evident, that all men are created equal.' " This statement repeats Douglass's frequent appeals to the Declaration and hope for the fulfillment of its promise, despite the failures of the moment.

King began the conclusion of "I Have a Dream" by quoting the lyrics of "America" ("My country 'tis of thee"). Then, following the pattern of Douglass in 1852, Wells in 1893, and Carey in 1952, King unfolded a utopian vision of the magnificent harmony that would come about once racism disappears. Like Wells and Carey at the conclusion of their speeches, King generated his image of harmony by comparing future Americans with members of a choir smoothly blending their voices. King borrowed this ending directly from Carey.

A sharecropper with little formal education, Fannie Lou Hamer emerged as a commanding figure in the racial struggle in Mississippi, where King did not play a prominent role. In 1964, speaking at the Democratic National Convention, Hamer eloquently demanded equality. Her speech followed the classic structure of Promise/Failure/Fulfillment and incorporated phrases from "The Star-Spangled Banner."

In 1965 King's Southern Christian Leadership Conference and the Student Nonviolent Coordinating Committee picked Selma, Alabama, as a site to agitate for voting rights. On a day known as Bloody Sunday, horse-riding state troopers used tear gas and nightsticks to assault nonviolent African American protestors led by Hosea Williams and John Lewis, a future member of Congress. Televised images of this barbaric police behavior upon well-dressed, unoffending people galvanized even greater national support for civil rights. Many members of Congress thundered their anger at the state troopers and at George Wallace, the governor of Alabama.

Marshaling supporters from around the nation, King and Lewis led them on a fifty-mile trek from Selma to Montgomery, the state capital. There they demanded the right to vote. Using the hypnotic cadences of the black folk pulpit, King recited a litany of racial horrors. But he sounded even more optimistic than he did during the Montgomery bus boycott or in "I Have a Dream." He concluded his emotional address by quoting idealistic lyrics from "The Battle Hymn of the Republic." Through this anthem, both patriotic and religious, he appealed once more to American civil religion. His argument of Promise/Failure/Fulfillment again animated his listeners.

In the hands of popular African American orators, Promise/Failure/Fulfillment offered an Argument by Trajectory. Frederick Douglass implied that the nation glimpsed the principle of equality in 1776, that it moved toward equality when slavery ended, and that it would grant full equality to all its citizens eventually. Imbued with a similar faith, a host of subsequent orators argued similarly. At the Montgomery bus boycott, in "I Have a Dream," and at the end of the march from Selma to Montgomery, King supplied a parallel argument. From 1955 through 1965 he reiterated the view that the nation would continue moving from a slaveholding society to an egalitarian one.

African American agitators depicted promise and fulfillment in part to motivate listeners.

Merely railing at horrors would likely not prompt anyone to overthrow slavery or any other huge injustice. Only people with prodigious hope will hurl themselves at gargantuan evils. If speakers only sketch terrifying visions, their listeners could lapse into despair and helplessness. They could simply withdraw to their homes and nurture their families. But, by envisioning that social movements could usher in utopia, orators could inspire listeners to initiate profound moral crusades.

## Malcolm X

Malcolm X viewed interracial utopia as impossible. As James Cone, the founder of black theology, explains, Malcolm X's differences with King stemmed largely from their contrasting boyhoods.

Born in Omaha, Nebraska, in 1925, Malcolm Little grew up near Lansing, Michigan, where he suffered greatly from racism and from the poverty of the Great Depression. At times he and his siblings had almost nothing to eat. Unlike King's successful, nurturing parents, Earl Little, a follower of Marcus Garvey, died suddenly, while his children were still young. Little's widow, Louise Little, struggled to raise her children alone while trying to cope with meddlesome welfare workers. She was institutionalized in a mental hospital. After growing up in foster homes, Malcolm Little migrated to Boston and New York. There he reveled in a youthful counterculture of zoot suits, acrobatic jazz dancing, draft dodging, marijuana peddling, and gangsterism.

Imprisoned for theft, Malcolm Little began to reassess his identity. He corresponded with Elijah Muhammad, head of the Nation of Islam (NOI), an unorthodox form of the Muslim religion. As Malcolm Little enthusiastically converted to the NOI, he changed his name to Malcolm X. The "X" substituted for the African name that his ancestors lost when whites forced them into slavery.

Instead of appealing to his listeners' Christian faith, Malcolm X urged his audiences to abandon it. Through dozens of speeches in New York City, Chicago, Detroit, Boston, Los Angeles, and elsewhere, he persuaded thousands to join the NOI. Like his mentor Elijah Muhammad, he rejected racial integration and preached Black Nationalism. The NOI not only advocated racial separatism, but it also implemented its doctrine. Its members operated their own temples, stores, restaurants, bakeries, schools, and a newspaper with a sizable readership.

When most whites learned about the NOI, they were shocked by Malcolm X's calls for separation and his refusal to endorse nonviolence. Many had difficulty believing that a sane person could reject white America. But Malcolm X drew vigorous applause when debating leading exponents of nonviolence, including Bayard Rustin and James Farmer. Malcolm X disparaged King and the entire nonviolent effort in the South. His indictment of white America proved so eloquent that white hosts of television and radio shows clamored to put him on the air. He also spoke at numerous, largely white universities.

Malcolm X repeatedly alluded to the African American jeremiad. Like many before him, he sometimes discussed the promise of the Declaration and of Christianity as he constantly castigated the failure of racism. But he exploded the hope for fulfillment. He encapsulated his logic in highly original, provocative aphorisms.

You didn't come here on the *Mayflower.*
You came here on a slave ship.

We didn't land on Plymouth Rock . . .
Plymouth Rock landed on *us*!

I'm not a Democrat,
I'm not a Republican,
And I don't even consider myself an American.

You're nothing but Africans.
Nothing but Africans.

He repeatedly characterized himself and his listeners as "ex-slaves" and contended that, for them, the United States constituted a "prison."

This entire appeal challenged Promise/Failure/Fulfillment by exploiting a huge, obvious problem. Fully one hundred years after emancipation, equality was nowhere in sight. Instead, white supremacy still ruled. During the 1950s and 1960s racial discrimination clouded African American lives. Most Southern blacks were consistently denied the right to vote, the right to a good education, the right to use public libraries, the right to eat in restaurants, and many other rights and opportunities. In the South, whites could still murder African Americans without fear of being convicted by an all-white jury. Southern white men who raped African American women would rarely be indicted. In the North, Midwest, and West, as well as the South, huge numbers of African Americans suffered from poverty and deprivation.

Despite their severe mistreatment of African Americans, whites routinely boasted that America was a Christian nation and the leader of the "free world." On every Fourth of July, whites celebrated the American Revolution and expressed their reverence for America.

They regarded their nation as the apotheosis of freedom and justice.

Responding to the anthem of the civil rights movement, "We Shall Overcome," Malcolm X asked simply, "How in the world can a Negro talk about the Declaration of Independence when he is still singing 'We Shall Overcome'?" By raising this question, Malcolm X claimed that, for almost two hundred years, the phrase "all men are created equal" meant nothing. The real principle of America, he insisted, was white supremacy.

Instead of identifying himself with American civil religion, Malcolm X assaulted such identification. Instead of telling blacks to celebrate Thanksgiving, he urged them to disdain the Pilgrims. As he sharply criticized King, he was rejecting the work—and even the goal—of the dominant African American leadership over many generations. He implied that Douglass and a long cavalcade of African American notables had built their main argument on an unjustified faith in whites.

Unlike King, Malcolm X considered racial equality to be a foreign concept for whites. He failed to discern the principle of racial equality lurking within the Declaration—or within the Emancipation Proclamation or the Constitution. For him, the core American principle of white supremacy was never seriously challenged during the American Revolution, the Civil War, or Reconstruction. He implied that African Americans were projecting the concept of equality onto slaveholders, such as Thomas Jefferson. Jefferson, the main author of the Declaration, owned slaves throughout his entire adult life.

In short, Malcolm X charged that eminent black leaders were trying to sell a new, alien tenet of equality by mislabeling it as a great American tradition. These leaders, he maintained, were trying to beautify an extremely ugly situation. They refused, he insisted, to recognize the emptiness of whites' promise. And they refused, he contended, to recognize the impossibility of a color-blind, utopian America, which they kept saying was imminent.

Malcolm X implied that, for prominent African American orators, the argument from Promise/Failure/Fulfillment had become merely a habit. He implied that, instead of examining their main argument, speakers had routinized it by appealing to a set of identifications that they uncritically accepted.

In Malcolm X's argument, not only were the slaves of 1776 exempt from the clause "all men are created equal," but all other Americans were as well. For Malcolm X, the rattling of the slaves' chains spoke much louder than the pretty words written by Jefferson and other slaveowners. For him, while the Declaration appeared to institute equality, the slaves' loss of freedom nullified Jefferson's famous phrase. In this argument, even the white landowners who signed the Declaration were not free.

Malcolm X further challenged the jeremiad when he claimed that the Declaration had nothing to do with nonviolence. Instead, he insisted, the Declaration was a Declaration of War. Through it, Jefferson and the other patriots of 1776 announced their desire to overthrow British rule. Refusing to tolerate "taxation without representation," they took up arms to defeat the British army. African Americans, Malcolm X noted, paid taxes in 1964, but huge numbers could not vote and were not represented in Congress. Why, he asked, should they tolerate taxation without representation?

He held that they needed independence just as the whites of 1776 needed it. And why, he inquired, did whites think violence was justified in 1776 but not in 1964? Slavery and segregation, he maintained, were far more terrifying than anything experienced by wealthy white landowners in 1776.

Here Malcolm X replaced the Argument by Trajectory with a very different interpretation of the Declaration of Independence. To him, the Declaration did not offer a promise that would gradually be realized. Instead it provided a model for violent upheaval by colonized people against their colonizers. And, he insisted, whites in 1964 were still colonizing African Americans.

One can view all or parts of the Declaration as statements of timeless truths. But Malcolm X interpreted the Declaration in its situatedness. For him, it was an act of defiance and rebellion—an act of war; an act spawning violence, which was sanitized by celebrants on the Fourth of July; an act that legitimized violence in 1776 and that was subsequently alleged to legitimize nonviolence; an act that should be viewed as a precedent for armed struggle.

## Comparing King and Malcolm X

Many people have viewed King and Malcolm X as opposites. King was a Christian minister. Malcolm X evangelized for Elijah Muhammad's NOI. King preached and practiced nonviolence. Malcolm X doubted that approach would prove fruitful for African Americans. King accepted money from white donors, consulted white advisers, and conferred with Presidents Kennedy and Lyndon B. Johnson. For most of his career, Malcolm X disdained white allies. He agitated on the margins of established American politics.

In one respect, King and Malcolm X shared common ground. To them both, the Declaration raised the issue of racial equality, not gender equality. Their position was in sharp contrast to that of Frederick Douglass, for example, who had advocated women's right to vote and the principle of women's equality.

Scholars have noted that the rivalry between Malcolm X and King enabled them to work synergistically. Malcolm X made King seem much more moderate than King would otherwise have appeared. When President Kennedy asked nonviolent leaders to stop organizing the March on Washington, A. Philip Randolph mollified the president. Randolph claimed that blacks needed a disciplined outlet for their anger. He implied that peaceful demonstrations were not the only means of pursuing civil rights. This comment referred to the powerful leadership of Malcolm X. By posing an alternative to mainline civil rights organizations, Malcolm X and the NOI made those groups appear much less threatening. Even though they sought significant social change, many undecided whites learned to sympathize with their nonviolent appeals.

King also aided Malcolm X. The enormous scope of the civil rights movement in the South affirmed the unity of African Americans. The Southern struggle prodded them to reassess their racial identity and to affirm their solidarity. Northern blacks welcomed Malcolm X's call for racial pride in part because they were heartened to see a stiff challenge to white supremacy in Alabama and Mississippi.

Further, as James Cone explains, in some important ways, late in their lives, King and Malcolm X were moving closer together. After completing a pilgrimage to Mecca, the Muslim holy city, Malcolm X publicly broke with Elijah Muhammad and embraced a more orthodox version of Islam. He stopped labeling all white people "devils," affirming instead that Islam welcomed people of every color. Establishing ties with important leaders in the Middle East and Africa, he reemphasized the need for a worldwide struggle against colonialism. In his autobiography, he combined these themes and urged blacks to form their own businesses and to control the money in their own communities.

Not long after Malcolm X's assassination in 1965, King became more radical. He championed the cause of impoverished Americans of every color. Mobilizing a Poor People's Campaign designed to converge on Washington, D.C., he was preparing to lead activists to occupy government offices and demand an end to poverty. Interrupting that effort, he ventured to Memphis, Tennessee, in April 1968 to assist striking garbage workers. In his speech, "I've Been to the Mountaintop," he instructed them and their supporters to pool their money and run their own banks and businesses. He also reemphasized African American ties to worldwide movements against colonial rule.

In his 1967 book *Where Do We Go from Here?*, King acknowledged a big problem with his own argument of Promise/Failure/Fulfillment. While he had offered "radiant promises of progress" in his earlier speeches, those promises, he observed, had not been realized. Instead, he explained, his disappointed listeners witnessed an unresponsive government, destructive riots, and an unjustified war in Vietnam. His "dream," he noted, had become "a frustrating nightmare."

Recent scholars emphasize that, late in his life, King invoked American civil religion less and less. He adopted the stance of a biblical prophet whose authority stemmed from God, not a political document. For example, in "I've Been to the Mountaintop," he referred to the Bill of Rights and briefly recalled Abraham Lincoln. But he repeatedly invoked scripture. Like Moses at the end of his life, King declared, he hiked a mountain and gazed at the Promised Land, which God would not allow him to enter. But King promised that, despite his own inability to reach the Promised Land, "we as a people" would eventually arrive at that sacred place.

King was assassinated the day after he delivered "I've Been to the Mountaintop."

One can view King's shift from American civil religion to biblical prophecy as an outgrowth of his own reflections. One can also view his shift as a thoughtful response to the ultimate weakness of the Argument by Trajectory, a weakness that Malcolm X noticed long before King did.

For many younger African Americans—and King—appeals of Promise/Failure/Fulfillment eventually seemed more and more like casuistic stretching. And for them, the stretching had finally overextended itself. While antislavery crusaders never sneered at Douglass's Argument by Trajectory, demoralized young people booed King in 1967. Their reaction may have prodded him to turn more to the Bible.

While most of Malcolm X's discussions of violence were somewhat indirect and politic, King criticized Malcolm X for refusing to endorse nonviolence. This refusal continued through Malcolm X's entire public career, even after he returned from Mecca and broke with Elijah Muhammad and the NOI. King made the obvious point that whites badly outnumbered African Americans. An armed black insurgency, he insisted, would inevitably culminate in a bloodbath. Blacks, he argued, would die by the thousands and their uprising would fail. Cone observed that the King-Malcolm X disagreement about nonviolence was unresolvable.

One can believe Malcolm X's statements, including his refusal to embrace nonviolence. Malcolm X appeared to insist that he always meant exactly what he said. He captivated many listeners in part because he seemed unusually direct and honest. He seemed never to varnish his words.

But Malcolm X's life evidenced ambiguity. King observed that African American leaders who discussed armed rebellion chose not to lead a revolt themselves. After Malcolm X stepped out of prison into the NOI, he apparently never committed violence. He lambasted King and others for not retaliating when police dogs attacked children. But Malcolm X never attacked police dogs himself. In 1962, when Los Angeles police murdered an NOI member outside an NOI temple, he flew immediately to the scene. But neither he nor anyone else in the NOI exacted revenge against the Los Angeles Police Department. After this incident, he confided to a close friend: "We spout our militant revolutionary rhetoric and we preach Armageddon . . . but when our own brothers are brutalized or killed, we do nothing." This statement revealed his recognition of his own inconsistency. Despite his blazing language, he practiced nonviolence.

Perhaps Malcolm X's most important goal was, in his words, to "awaken" African Americans whom he regarded as "brainwashed" or "dead." He explained the problem as follows.

[We] hated our African characteristics.
We hated our heads,
We hated the shape of our nose . . .
We hated the color of our skin,
Hated the blood of Africa that was in our veins . . .
And we hated ourselves.
By saying
You didn't come here on the *Mayflower*.
You came here on a slave ship

We didn't land on Plymouth Rock . . .
Plymouth Rock landed on *us*!

He proposed what Kenneth Burke calls a "perspective by incongruity," which, in Burke's words, shatters "the sense of what properly goes with what." White Americans associated the *Mayflower* and Plymouth Rock with freedom and the beginning of a great, new nation. For African Americans, identifying with the *Mayflower* and Plymouth Rock meant sharing whites' reverence for all things European. But, for Malcolm X, the entire European arrival spelled terrifying crimes and pitiless exploitation. For that reason, he developed a perspective by incongruity that would attack blacks' identification with white patriotic symbols, such as the *Mayflower* and Plymouth Rock.

Perspective by incongruity may have been Malcolm X's chief means of reviving those whom he considered "brainwashed." Some, he held, were not only sick, but also "dead" from overidentification with Plymouth Rock, the Declaration, and Euro-American culture. To Malcolm X, this overidentification produced self-hatred among many, who wished for lighter skin.

Malcolm X prodded ordinary people to nurture self-respect by refusing to imitate whites on Thanksgiving or the Fourth of July. His rhetoric helped inspire young activists to begin the Black Power Movement and the Black Panther Party. His orations also encouraged young poets and dramatists to rewrite American literature as they proclaimed their racial pride on street corners throughout Harlem and in other cities. New presses in Detroit and Chicago issued their vibrant works. By generating the Black Arts Movement, these authors helped develop audiences for such later, world-renowned authors as August Wilson, Alice Walker, and Toni Morrison—all of whom write almost exclusively about African American life. The self-respect of young people who responded to Malcolm X did not spring from the Argument by Trajectory and its promise of utopia. Their self-respect sprang from their own racial and cultural pride.

King and Malcolm X confronted frozen white sensibilities and whites' repeated and consistent failure to implement the promise of the Declaration. And they both faced masses of African Americans tempted to despair because racial equality seemed forever distant.

King, Hamer, and their cohorts translated Gandhi's Hindu precepts into a Judeo-Christian idiom that Americans could understand. Civil rights agitators were the first grassroots activists to manipulate television for political ends. Their productions were gut-wrenching. In them, Southern sheriffs routinely emerged as villains, and African Americans emerged as peaceable, freedom-loving hymn singers. The well-choreographed melodramas pressured whites to confront the principles of the Declaration, the Emancipation Proclamation, and the Thirteenth, Fourteenth, and Fifteenth Amendments to the Constitution.

Malcolm X undertook a different, equally difficult task. He sought to alter a body of identifications that exceedingly gifted orators had cemented for over a hundred years. He shattered patriotic piety developed through long-standing identification with white America. Exalting the NOI, he challenged a highly churched African American community to reassess its habitual loyalties. He did so again when, after returning from the Middle East, he evangelized for a more orthodox Islam. Defamiliarizing the *Mayflower,* Plymouth Rock, and the Declaration, he rejected the old, essentially unaltered Argument by Trajectory. Further, he challenged King's claim that the Declaration authorized Gandhian nonviolence, insisting instead that it authorized a violent revolution against England.

In "I Have a Dream," King deemed the Declaration "a promissory note" that had come back "marked insufficient funds." Following the form of Promise/Failure/Fulfillment, he heralded America's great "vaults of opportunity," vaults that would eventually redeem the promissory note. He and Hamer urged Americans to integrate and thereby fulfill the old American promise. Like Douglass and their other predecessors, he and Hamer taught African Americans that they need not despair or remain docile. Nor would they always remain subordinate to whites.

## Conclusion

Through the Argument by Trajectory, Douglass and other abolitionists prodded America to dismantle slavery. The Argument by Trajectory also yielded major political victories during the 1950s and 1960s, most notably the demise of legalized racism. Despite these triumphs, by the end of his life, King appeared, like Malcolm X, to recognize the eventual

weakness of the African American jeremiad. Like Malcolm X, he seemed to view it as a form of casuistic stretching that was badly overextended. Unlike Douglass and unlike his own mentors, King maneuvered through and around the Declaration, eventually curtailing his appeals to American civil religion and shifting toward biblical prophecy.

Malcolm X's perspective by incongruity disturbed familiar identifications in African American life, especially a long-established, widespread attachment to American civil religion. His refusal to revere Christian America prodded blacks to achieve a decidedly greater measure of self-definition.

By re-imagining the Pilgrims and the Declaration, Malcolm X did not seek to integrate outcasts into the American mainstream. Instead, he helped create a people.

## Bibliography

Andrews, William, ed. *The Oxford Frederick Douglass Reader.* New York: Oxford University Press, 1996.

Breitman, George, ed. *Malcolm X Speaks.* New York: Grove, 1965.

Burke, Kenneth. *Attitudes toward History.* Berkeley: University of California Press, 1959.

Carson, Clayborne, and others, eds. *The Papers of Martin Luther King Jr.* Berkeley: University of California Press, 1982.

Cone, James. *Martin and Malcolm and America.* Maryknoll, N.Y.: Orbis, 1991.

Grimke, Francis J. "The Negro and His Citizenship." In *The Works of Francis J. Grimke.* Vol. I: *Addresses Mainly Personal and Racial.* Ed. Carter Woodson. Washington, D.C.: Associated Publishers, 1942.

————. "The Race Problem as It Respects Colored People and the Christian Church, in the Light of the Developments of the Last Year." In *The Works of Francis J. Grimke.* Vol. I: *Addresses Mainly Personal and Racial.* Ed. Carter Woodson Washington, D.C.: Associated Publishers, 1942.

Howard-Pitney, David. *The Afro-American Jeremiad: Appeals for Justice in America*. Philadelphia: Temple University Press, 1990.

Karim, Benjamin, with Peter Skutches and David Gallen. *Remembering Malcolm*. New York: Carroll and Graf, 1992.

King, Martin Luther, Jr. *Where Do We Go From Here: Chaos or Community?* New York: Harper, 1967.

X, Malcolm. *Malcolm X on Afro-American History*. New York: Pathfinder, 1970.

_____. *Two Speeches by Malcolm X*. New York: Pathfinder, 1965.

X, Malcolm, and Alex Haley. *The Autobiography of Malcolm X*. New York: Ballantine, 1965.

Washington, James, ed. *Testament of Hope: The Essential Writings of Martin Luther King Jr*. New York: Harper, 1986.

# 11 Women, Equality, and the Declaration of Independence

BONNIE L. FORD

The Declaration of Independence proclaims that "all men are created equal." For more than 225 years, women have sought to be a part of the Declaration's conception of equality—insisting that "men" includes "women"; that women possess natural rights to life, liberty, and the pursuit of happiness; and that they are entitled to give their consent to be governed through their exercise of the vote. Women have turned to the Declaration repeatedly for inspiration and for justification of their demands. However, the subordinate position women have historically occupied in American society and the paternalistic beliefs about women's nature have made it difficult for them to convince their male counterparts of the legitimacy of their claims.

## Women's Traditional Sphere

At the time the Declaration of Independence was written, women's roles were constrained by law and custom. With rare exceptions, the boundaries of most women's lives were drawn around the household. Care of home and children consumed women's lives, leaving little time for leisure. Moreover, women were prohibited from serving on juries, from voting, from holding public office, and from most other civic responsibilities. If married, their husbands represented them to the larger world. It was not even clear that women were citizens. Citizenship at the time brought with it the ability to come to the armed defense of the body politic, but women were not permitted to join the armed forces.

African American women in slavery were not confined to the domestic hearth, but rather to the households, farms, and plantations of their masters. Work was assigned by gender, and it included heavy agricultural labor. Not only could African American women own no property, but they also were considered to be property—as were their children. Like African American men, they could not testify in court.

In addition to the limited sphere they occupied in the eighteenth century, women—white and black—faced strong prejudice. Women were considered ignorant, irrational, weak, and easily swayed—especially by their husbands, who wielded virtually unlimited authority over them.

John Adams, one of the leading figures of America's founding period, described the private sphere to which custom had relegated women in a letter to fellow Massachusetts political leader James Sullivan in May 1776. His ruminations concerned the extent to which suffrage should be afforded to women, men who owned no property, and children. Adams wrote that women should not be granted the right to vote "because their delicacy renders them unfit for practice and experience in the great businesses of life, and the hardy enterprises of war. . . . [B]esides, their attention is so much engaged with the necessary nurture of their children that nature had made them fittest for domestic cares." Although these may not have been Adams's personal sentiments—his wife, Abigail, was a woman of strong opinions—they were plainly the sentiments of most men of the time.

The common law of England, to which the colonies were bound, further limited women's role in society. According to Sir William Blackstone's *Commentaries on the Laws of England* (1765), a wife's legal identity merged with that of her husband at marriage, when her own legal existence ceased. The French term *femme couvert*, or a woman under the cover of her husband, aptly described the condition. The husband controlled all property in marriage; a married woman could not own property, make a contract, sue or be sued, keep her own earnings, or write a will. Moreover, under the laws of most of the colonies, men could physically chastise their wives, and divorce was severely limited.

Abigail Adams was reacting to these limitations when she applied Revolutionary ideology to this state of the law. On March 31, 1776, just a few months before the Declaration was written, she wrote to her husband, John:

I long to hear that you have declared an independency—and by the way in the new Code of Laws which I suppose it will be necessary for you to make, I desire you would Remember the Ladies, and be more generous and favorable to them than your ancestors. Do not put such unlimited power into the hands of the Husbands. Remember all Men would be tyrants if they could. If particular care and attention is not paid to the Ladies, we are determined to foment a Rebellion, and will not hold ourselves bound by any Laws in which we have no voice, or Representation.

Abigail Adams's plea to her husband well illustrates the extent to which Revolutionary ideology had permeated contemporary thought. During the colonial period, 1765 to 1776, women had been drawn into the public sphere by colonial resistance, which demanded their action. When boycotts were placed on British goods, women most likely were the consumers of those goods and therefore had to understand the reason for doing without them. Women showed their solidarity with the Revolutionaries by organizing spinning bees, where thread was spun for weaving into cloth. This was considered a patriotic act, and women were imbued with Revolutionary philosophy to participate with conviction in these sorts of activities.

Adams's letters to her husband appeared to have as their object a change in the laws of marriage, but in trying to convince him of this she claimed a right to have a voice in lawmaking in general—and a right to rebel against tyrannous rule. Although John Adams's April 14, 1776, reply dismissed his wife's demands, his message presaged the Revolutionary War's effect on women's consciousness and on the ideas of all subordinate classes. Not only did he foretell the long-term effect of the Revolution, but he also posited the argument that women enjoyed enormous power in the private realm to dominate their husbands' thinking. He humorously describes women's power over men, a common argument raised against women's rights:

We have been told that our Struggle has loosened the bands of Government everywhere. That Children and Apprentices were disobedient—that schools and colleges were grown turbulent—that Indians slighted their Guardians, and Negroes grew insolent to their Masters. But your Letter was the first Intimation that another Tribe more numerous and powerful than all the rest were grown discontented. . . .

Depend upon it, We know better than to repeal our Masculine systems. Although they are in full Force, you know they are little more than Theory. We dare not exert our Power in its full Latitude. We are obliged to go fair, and softly, and in Practice you know We are the subjects. We have only the Name of Masters, and rather than give up this, which would completely subject Us to the Despotism of the Petticoat, I hope General Washington, and all our Heroes would fight.

## The Impact of the Declaration on Women's Thought

When Thomas Jefferson penned the second paragraph of the Declaration of Independence, he wrote only of "men." However, his words have proved to be a manifesto for human rights. He wrote:

We hold these truths to be self-evident, that all men are created equal, that they are endowed by their Creator with certain unalienable rights, that among these are life, liberty, and the pursuit of happiness. That to secure these rights, governments are instituted among men, deriving their just powers from the consent of the governed.

Both the Declaration's text (see Chapter 1) and the Enlightenment thinking that informed it (see Chapter 2) gradually transformed

women's consciousness. All of the elements of this timeless paragraph—equality among all by virtue of their humanity; inalienable rights, including life, liberty, and the pursuit of happiness; government formed by the consent of the people—have shone like beacons in the night for more than two centuries.

Although they would not markedly change the role of women in the years immediately following the American Revolution, certain trends were put in motion by Revolutionary ideology. According to historian Mary Beth Norton, more women were choosing their spouses free of parental restraint, the birth rate in the last two decades of the eighteenth century began to decline, and more divorces were sought as women began to challenge the tyranny of marriage. Historian Linda Kerber cites an anonymous poet, calling herself "Republic," who wrote in *Massachusetts* magazine in 1794:

No ties shall perplex me, no fetters shall bind,
That innocent freedom that dwells in my mind.
At liberty's spring such draughts I've imbibed,
That I hate all the doctrines by wedlock prescrib'd.

"Republic" asked why women consented to their prescribed status. Philosophers of women's rights were asking the same question. For example, Mary Wollstonecraft, an eighteenth-century English feminist and the author of the influential *Vindication of the Rights of Women* (1792), sought to bridge the gap between Enlightenment ideas and the reality of women's place in Western culture. Wollstonecraft endeavored to show that women should enjoy the same natural rights as men. She also argued that women, instead of pursuing their own happiness, had been given a false consciousness that made them affect a demeanor that was designed to please men. According to Wollstonecraft, women

spend many of the first years of their lives in acquiring a smattering of accomplishments; meanwhile strength of body and mind are sacrificed to libertine notions of beauty, to the desire of establishing themselves,—the only way women can rise in the world,—by marriage. And this desire making mere animals of them, when they marry they act as such children may be expected to act:—they dress; they paint, . . . . Can they be expected to govern a family with judgment, or take care of the poor babes whom they bring into the world?

Judith Sargent Murray, an important American feminist of the post–Revolutionary period, believed that women should have the right to determine the shape of their own lives. To have the power to do so, Murray insisted, they needed to be educated so that they could choose to marry or not and, most important, so they would be capable of supporting themselves whether single or widowed. Murray wrote in 1798: "The *idea of the incapability* of women, is, we conceive, in this *enlightened age,* totally *inadmissible;* and we have concluded, that establishing the *expediency* of admitting them to share the blessings of equality, will remove every obstacle to their advancement."

Twentieth-century historians have seen "republican motherhood" as the steppingstone to education that then would lead to further progress for women. Republican motherhood was premised on the idea that virtue, a prime character trait, must be nurtured in the men of the republic. Who better to instill virtue than the mothers of the republic's next generation? The founding of secondary schools, such as the Troy Seminary (New York) in 1821, characterized the post–Revolutionary period and, by the 1830s, produced a generation of women who were more self-confident than their predecessors. Emma Willard, founder of the Troy Seminary, offered a rigorous course of study to young women. Elizabeth Cady Stanton attended the school in 1831, where she studied algebra, Greek, logic, botany, geometry, and modern history, as well as the more traditional subjects of female seminarians, such as piano.

## Antislavery Influences on Women's Quest for Equality

For African American women, the Declaration of Independence signaled that they should pursue their freedom. Women used the gradual emancipation acts in the North to their advantage. In 1824 in New York, for example, Sojourner Truth sued for the return of her son, who had been illegally sold to an out-of-state resident. Frustration and delay marked the case, but her child was eventually returned to her. Truth was one of the first African American women to win a lawsuit.

During the 1830s, many women in the North felt deeply about the plight of slaves and wished to publicly express their views. The issue kindled a firestorm of controversy. One of the first American women to speak publicly against slavery was Maria Stewart, a free black woman who believed that free African Americans should claim their full rights—including freedom of speech. In her last public speech she implicitly recalled the Declaration of Independence: "It was asserted that we were 'a ragged set crying for liberty.' I reply to it, the whites have so long and so loudly proclaimed the theme of equal rights and privileges, that our souls have caught the flame also, ragged as we are." Stewart also believed in the ability of education to lead to freedom and equality. Opposition on account of her gender eventually caused her to give up speaking in public, but she had broken new ground for women.

The antislavery movement was focused primarily in churches, and clerical authority often was challenged as a result. For example, Angelina and Sarah Grimke, daughters of South Carolina slaveholders, moved north and shared their experiences with congregations. Because they were members of the slaveholding class speaking out against slavery—a rare occurrence—their lectures were well attended. During their 1837 speaking tour, a pastoral letter was circulated by the Congregational ministerial association of Massachusetts condemning the sisters for speaking in public on the ground that it was against Biblical tradition for women to do so. This letter was to be read from the pulpit of every Congregational church in Massachusetts. In response, Sarah Grimke wrote *Letters on the Equality of the Sexes* (1838)—the first major feminist treatise published in the United States. It was primarily a religious argument, but she also echoed the inalienable rights theme of the Declaration of Independence when she wrote: "Whatsoever it is morally right for a man to do, it is morally right for a woman to do. . . . [S]he is clothed by her Maker with the same rights . . . and the same duties."

When the London Antislavery Convention of 1840 convened, Lucretia Mott, a Quaker minister from Philadelphia, met Elizabeth Cady Stanton, a newly married reformist from New York. Male abolitionists, who were championing the cause of equality and freedom for slaves, refused women the right to participate in the meeting. They were relegated to the balcony where they could merely observe. As a result, Mott and Stanton became determined to hold a women's rights convention in the United States.

## The Declaration of Sentiments and Resolutions

Eight years later, Stanton and Mott met again. This time, they planned an impromptu convention in Seneca Falls, New York. With only ten days to prepare, they, along with Martha Coffin Wright (Mott's sister) and Mary Ann McClintock, decided to use the Declaration of Independence as the focal point of the convention. They recast the first two paragraphs of the Declaration to better suit their purpose and completely rewrote the last two sections, renaming their document the Declaration of Sentiments. The first paragraph was a clever rephrasing that substituted "one portion of the family of man" for "one people," as stated in the Declaration of Independence—which better reflected the situation of women.

When in the course of human events, it becomes necessary for one portion of the family of man to assume among the people of the earth a position different from that which they have hitherto occupied, but one to which the laws of nature and of nature's god entitle them, a decent respect to the opinions of mankind requires that they should declare the causes that impel them to such a course.

This opening passage succinctly juxtaposed women's customary and limited sphere in society with the place to which the participants in the Seneca Falls Convention felt natural law entitled them. Only two words were added to the second paragraph, but they (indicated by italics, below) were important.

We hold these truths to be self-evident: that all men *and women* are created equal; that they are endowed by their Creator with certain inalienable rights, that among these are life, liberty and the pursuit of happiness; that to secure these rights governments are instituted among men, deriving their just powers from the consent of the governed.

The Declaration of Sentiments, like the Declaration of Independence, included a list of grievances. It specified the ways in which men had established tyranny over women. The founding fathers had listed eighteen grievances against the king in the Declaration of Independence, and the framers of the Declaration of Sentiments wanted no fewer in their document. After all, these women believed their grievances against men were far greater than the colonists' grievances against the king had been. The first nine grievances described laws that discriminated against women, while the second nine addressed less formal practices that kept women in a subordinate position. According to the charges, men had repeatedly tyrannized women by "compelling her to submit to laws, in the formation of which she had no voice." In addition, "[h]e has monopolized nearly all the profitable employments, and from those she is permitted to follow, she receives but a scanty remuneration" and "[h]e has denied her the facilities for obtaining a thorough education—all colleges being closed against her." Finally, "he has endeavored, in every way that he could, to destroy her confidence in her own powers, to lessen her self-respect, and to make her willing to lead a dependent and abject life."

In the final paragraph of the Declaration of Sentiments, the women declared their intention to gain "all the rights and privileges which belonged rightfully to them as citizens of the United States." They then announced their methods for achieving equality—employing agents, petitioning the government, circulating tracts, enlisting the pulpit, calling conventions—all tactics they had learned by participating in other reform movements, particularly the antislavery movement.

The Declaration of Sentiments was adopted unanimously by the convention. In addition, twelve resolutions were presented for discussion and approval. The introductory paragraph to the resolutions invoked natural law as the major justification.

Whereas, the great precept of nature is conceded to be that "man shall pursue his own true and substantial happiness." Blackstone in his Commentaries remarks, that this law of Nature being coeval with mankind, and dictated by God himself, is of course superior in obligation to any other. It is binding over all the globe, in all countries and at all times; no human laws are of any validity, and all their authority, mediately and immediately, form this original,

Therefore,

*Resolved*. That such laws as conflict, in any way, with the true and substantial happiness of woman, are contrary to the great precept of nature and of no validity, for this is "superior in obligation to any other."

*Resolved*. That all laws which prevent woman from occupying such a station in society as her conscience shall dictate, or which place her in a position inferior to that of man, are contrary to the great precept of nature, and therefore of no force or authority.

*Resolved*. That woman is man's equal—was intended to be so by the Creator, and the highest good of the race demands that she should be recognized as such.

*Resolved*. That it is the duty of the women of this country to secure to themselves their sacred right to the elective franchise.

All of the resolutions, with the exception of the suffrage resolution, passed unanimously. The debate over suffrage was intense. Even Stanton's husband threatened to leave town if she included the resolution. She did include it, and he did leave town.

During the debate over the right to vote, Stanton made the argument to which she would revert many times over the years: "drunkards, idiots, horseracing rumselling rowdies, ignorant foreigners, and silly boys" could vote, while educated women were barred from the franchise. "The right is ours. Have it we must. Use it we will." The measure passed, but some participants believed that this resolution would subject them to ridicule. Newspaper articles and editorials derided the convention. But in the end, the Declaration of Sentiments and the accompanying resolutions became the bedrock of American feminism. The main feature of these two documents was their constant reference to the natural rights doctrine expressed so eloquently by Thomas Jefferson in the Declaration of Independence.

## The Women's Movement in the 1850s

In the 1850s feminists petitioned legislatures, deployed agents to organize, and circulated tracts. They also conducted a series of women's rights conventions. Meetings were held in Indiana, Massachusetts, New York, Ohio, and Pennsylvania. At all of these conventions women demanded the right to vote—suffrage was never again questioned after Seneca Falls— and the vote became the mechanism through which feminists hoped to secure other substantive rights. The conventions were the embryonic basis of the women's rights movement,

which would emerge after the Civil War. Because no existing organization was devoted to women's causes, convention organizers turned to antislavery societies to gain adherents. The Declaration of Independence was repeatedly invoked for inspiration and justification.

In 1850 and 1851 national conventions were held in Worcester, Massachusetts. Behind the scenes of the 1850 convention a controversy developed over the extent to which men were responsible for the wrongs against women. The convention's organizer, Paulina Wright Davis, had a definite opinion on this matter. In her opening address, she stated:

The first principles of human rights have now for a long time been abstractly held and believed, and both in Europe and America whole communities have put them into practical operation. . . . Equality before the law, and the right of the governed to choose their governors, are established maxims of reformed political science; but in the countries most advanced, these doctrines and their actual benefits are yet enjoyed exclusively by the sex that in the battle-field and the public forum has wrenched them from the old time tyrannies. They are yet denied to woman, because she has not yet so asserted or won them for herself; for political justice pivots itself upon the barbarous principle that "Who would be free, themselves must strike the blow."

Davis clearly placed some of the blame on women themselves whom, she believed, needed to stand up and fight for their rights.

Another of the speakers, Abby Pine, took on the daunting task of trying to square women's differences with their natural rights. She stated: "[I]n contending for this co-equality of woman's with man's rights, it is not necessary to argue, either that the sexes are by nature equally and indiscriminately adapted to the same positions and duties, or they are absolutely equal in physical and intellectual ability; but only that they are absolutely equal in their rights to life, liberty, and the pursuit of happiness."

At the second national convention in Worcester, held the following year, Ernestine Potowski Rose described the Declaration of Independence as "a declaration borne, like the vision of hope, on wings of light to the remotest parts of the earth, an omen of freedom to the oppressed and down-trodden children of man—when even here, in the very face of this eternal truth, woman, the mockingly so-called 'better half' of man, has yet to plead for her rights, nay, for her life."

The following resolution, which was passed at the 1851 convention, demanded that the Declaration of Independence be interpreted to include women.

[W]e charge that man with gross dishonesty or ignorance, who shall contend that "men" in the memorable document from which we quote does not stand for the human race; that "life, liberty, and the pursuit of happiness," are the "inalienable rights" of half only of the human species; and that by "the governed," whose consent is affirmed to be the only source of just power, is meant that half of mankind only who, in relation to the other, have hitherto assumed the character of governors.

Women could point to a number of tangible successes during the decade. Most Northern states, and some Southern states, had passed married women's property acts, which afforded married women the right to hold separate property (usually property acquired by gift or inheritance). In some states, women also were permitted to control their own earnings and to enjoy equal claim to the guardianship of their children. Further, many women had been admitted to professional schools, particularly medical schools, and they had begun professional careers after graduating. At the 1856 national convention, a resolution was passed that stated, "Resolved, that the main power of the woman's rights movement lies in this: that while always demanding for woman better education, better employment, and better laws, it has kept steadily in view the one cardinal demand for the right of suffrage: in a democracy, the symbol and guarantee of all other rights." However, the momentum generated by a decade of conventions was halted by the Civil War.

## The Civil War and Its Aftermath

Women from the antislavery and women's rights movements joined together in 1863 to form the Women's Loyal National League. Using their only political right—the right to petition in the First Amendment—members gathered 400,000 signatures to present to Congress urging a constitutional amendment to abolish slavery. Most women leaders, Susan B. Anthony and Elizabeth Cady Stanton in particular, saw the rights of women and slaves as intertwined. After all, had not women been ardent abolitionists? Consequently, a resolution was placed before the league, which stated, "There never can be a true peace in the republic until the civil and political rights of all citizens of African descent and all women are practically established." When the Thirteenth Amendment was ratified in 1865, abolitionists were thrilled. Theodore Tilton, an abolitionist newspaper editor, wrote to Anthony, "Three cheers for God."

In 1866 an Equal Rights Association was formed with the purpose of ensuring that women and African Americans were guaranteed their rights in the aftermath of the war. Unfortunately, the other two post–Civil War amendments—the Fourteenth and Fifteenth Amendments—presented the association with a quandary.

The Fourteenth Amendment defined citizens as persons who were born or naturalized in the United States. Though the amendment did not guarantee African Americans the right to vote, it encouraged it by penalizing Southern states if they did not enfranchise African American males. The amendment used the word *male* for the first time in the Constitution—and it did so in conjunction with the word *vote*. Consequently, it seemed clear that Congress did not intend to include women in the franchise.

Ultimately, Congress decided to grant the vote to the freedmen. The Republican-controlled Congress was motivated partly by the freedmen's military service during the war, partly by a desire to protect the freedmen against prejudice and white enmity, and partly by the hope of gaining Republican votes in the South. The result was the Fifteenth Amendment, which specified that the right to vote could not be denied on the basis of "race, color or previous condition of servitude." Unfortunately for feminists, gender was conspicuously omitted from the equation.

The Fifteenth Amendment was problematic for the Equal Rights Association. Should the association abandon the demand for women's suffrage to secure immediate rights for the freedmen? The question fractured the alliance. One faction, headed by Stanton and Anthony, insisted that while the door to constitutional equality was open, women should be allowed to walk through it. Another faction, headed by

Lucy Stone, believed it was "the Negro's hour." The bitterness of the divide was profound, and it would last more than two decades.

Each faction formed its own suffrage association. Stanton and Anthony led the National Woman Suffrage Association; Stone, the American Woman Suffrage Association. The national association called for a constitutional amendment that guaranteed women the right to vote. The American association advocated working state by state to secure the franchise. In her first address to the national association, Stanton urged suffrage for women—calling forth the Declaration of Independence, which, she said

Our fathers used when battling Old King George and the British Parliament for their rights to representation, and a voice in the laws by which they were governed. There are no new arguments to be made on human rights, our work today is to apply to ourselves those familiar to all, to teach that woman is not an anomalous being, outside all laws and constitutions, but one whose rights are to be established by the same process of reason as that by which he demands his own.

Stanton also pointed to several bills then before Congress that would have afforded women the right to vote. She demanded: "This fundamental principle of our government—the equality of all the citizens of the Republic—should be incorporated into the Federal Constitution there to remain forever."

## A New Interpretation of the Civil War Amendments

Despite the strong opposition of Stanton and Anthony, the Fourteenth and Fifteenth Amendments were ratified in 1868 and 1870, respectively. Many women initially viewed the amendments as disastrous to their quest for equal rights. However, an alternative interpretation soon emerged. At the grassroots level, some women began to insist that they were included in the Fourteenth Amendment's guarantee of the "privileges or immunities" of citizenship—and that the right to vote was among these privileges of citizenship. By 1872 hundreds of women were flocking to the polls all over the country.

In 1872 Susan B. Anthony was arrested and tried for voting illegally. At trial, she offered one of the most forceful arguments for women's suffrage ever presented. After being found guilty, the judge asked whether she had anything to say. She answered:

I have many things to say; for in your ordered verdict of guilty, you have trampled underfoot every vital principle of our government. My natural rights, my civil rights and my political rights, my judicial rights—are all alike ignored. Robbed of the fundamental privilege of citizenship, I am degraded from the status of a citizen to that of a subject; and not only myself individually, but all of my sex, are, by your honor's verdict, doomed to political subjection under this, so-called, form of government. . . . Your denial of my citizen's right to vote is the denial of my right of consent as one of the governed, the denial of my right of representation as one of the taxed, the denial of my right to a trial by a jury of my peers as an offender against law, therefore, the denial of my sacred rights to life, liberty, property, and—

The judge cut her off and fined her $100 (which she never paid). Another woman voter, Virginia Minor, appealed her own conviction on the same charges all the way to the Supreme Court of the United States. She was unsuccessful, however. In *Minor v. Happersett* (1875), the nation's highest court ruled that the right to vote was not coextensive with citizenship, thereby ending women's efforts to acquire the vote through the courts.

## The Centennial of the Declaration of Independence

Having failed to secure the vote through the courts, women next tried to capitalize on the centennial celebration of the Declaration of Independence. On July 3, 1876, in Philadelphia—the birthplace of the Declaration—a women's group requested permission to submit a declaration of rights at the celebration to be held the next day. The celebration's president refused to permit it, stating, "Tomorrow we celebrate what we have done the last hundred years, not what we have failed to do."

Undeterred, the women took direct action. Five of them, including the tenacious Anthony, managed to secure press credentials, which allowed them to be seated at the ceremony. After the Declaration of Independence was read to the crowd, the women stood up from their seats and proceeded to the speaker's platform, where they presented for the record the Declaration of the Rights of the Women of the United States.

The Declaration of the Rights of the Women of the United States differed from the Declaration of Sentiments in major ways. The former was more narrowly focused on political and legal rights. It also evidenced a more sophisticated political philosophy and more highly developed constitutional arguments. The document was presented in the form of articles of impeachment against men, and it referenced unlawful bills of attainder, violations of the writ of habeas corpus, the absence of women on juries, taxation without representation, unequal general laws, the lack of representation in government, the denial of universal suffrage, and a biased judiciary.

The Declaration of the Rights of the Women of the United States opened by reaffirming the ideals of the Declaration of Independence.

Our faith is firm and unwavering in the broad principles of human rights proclaimed in 1776, not only as abstract truths, but as the cornerstones of a republic. Yet we cannot forget, even in this glad hour, that while all men of every race, and clime, and condition, have been invested with the full rights of citizenship under our hospitable flag, all women still suffer the degradation of disfranchisement.

The history of our country the past hundred years has been a series of assumptions and usurpations of power over woman, in direct opposition to the principles of just government, acknowledged by the United States at its foundation.

The reference in the Declaration of the Rights of the Women of the United States to the enfranchisement of all men illustrated how much circumstances had changed. All males—white and African American—were now enfranchised, although they had not been as recently as 1848. Women's position vis-à-vis men had worsened, because they were the only remaining group stigmatized by exclusion from the suffrage. To reinforce this point, the women returned in the conclusion of the document to the ideals of the Declaration of Independence.

It was the boast of the founders of the republic, that the rights for which they contended were the rights of human nature. If these rights are ignored in the case of one-half of the people, the nation is surely preparing for its downfall. . . .

And so, at the close of a hundred years, as the hour-hand of the great clock that marks the centuries points to 1876, we declare our faith in the principles of self-government; our full equality with man in natural rights; that woman was made first for her own happiness, with the absolute right to herself—to all the opportunities and advantages life affords for her complete development; and we deny that dogma of the centuries, incorporated in the codes of all nations—that woman was made for man—her best interests, in all cases, to be sacrificed to his will. We ask of our rulers, at this hour, no special privileges, no special legislation. We ask justice, we ask equality, we ask that all the civil and political rights that belong to citizens of the United States, be guaranteed to us and our daughters forever.

## The Struggle Continues

The women's suffrage movement lost its momentum from the 1870s through the 1890s. Leaders such as Elizabeth Cady Stanton, Susan B. Anthony, and Lucy Stone were aging, and though younger women such as Carrie Chapman Catt and Anna Howard Shaw were joining the movement, they had not yet developed their full leadership potential. Some areas of progress could be found, particularly in the West, where the new states of Colorado, Idaho, Utah, and Wyoming had afforded women the right to vote through their state constitutions. Though the number of states was small, the breakthrough was significant.

In 1890 the two competing suffrage organizations, the National Woman Suffrage Association and the American Woman Suffrage Association, reached a truce. They combined to form the National American Woman Suffrage Association (NAWSA). In addition, in 1899 Frances Willard, the leader of the Women's Christian Temperance Union, took up the cause of women's suffrage. Willard believed that if women were allowed to vote, government could better respond to women's problems, particularly by the prohibition of alcohol.

Intemperate alcohol use was blamed for spousal abuse and abandonment of families. This brought a new set of arguments into the mix, namely, that women's frailty and victimization meant that they desperately needed the vote to protect the home. Social feminists such as Jane Addams argued for the franchise on the basis of social housekeeping: To keep the house clean, women needed to keep the streets clean, thrusting them out of the household and into the public where decisions were made about municipal services.

The argument that women were morally superior to men gained supporters. Some women argued that educated white women would be able to outvote ignorant male immigrants and black men, appealing to the prejudices of audiences both north and south. Women secured the vote in seven more states between 1910 and 1914.

Carrie Chapman Catt and Anna Howard Shaw, like many leaders of the women's rights movement had done before them, called upon the Declaration of Independence to advance their cause. In 1917, for example, Catt addressed a meeting of the NAWSA as follows.

Woman suffrage became an assured fact when the Declaration of Independence was written. It matters not at all whether Thomas Jefferson and his compatriots thought of women when they wrote that immortal document. They conceived and voiced a principle greater than any man. "A power not of themselves which makes for righteousness" gave them the vision and they proclaimed truisms as immutable as the multiplication table, as changeless as time. The Hon. Champ Clark announced that he had been a woman suffragist ever since he "got the hang of the Declaration of Independence." So it must be with every other American. The amazing thing is that it has required so long a time for a people, most of whom know how to read, "to get the hang of it."

Catt went on to say that "[t]he maxims of the Declaration were once called 'fundamental principles of government.' They are now called 'American principles' or even 'Americanisms.' They have become the slogans of every movement toward political liberty the world around."

Catt's powerful speech undoubtedly influenced Congress, which was then considering a constitutional amendment that would have guaranteed women the right to vote in all federal and state elections. On January 10, 1918, the U.S. House of Representatives approved the amendment, albeit by the narrowest of margins. A year and a half later, the Senate followed suit. Finally, on August 26, 1920, the required three-fourths of the states ratified the Nineteenth Amendment. One hundred and forty-four years after the Declaration of Independence was written, women were given the right to vote. The Nineteenth Amendment, however, gave women more than the right to vote. It put them in the political arena, and it revolutionized their role in civil society.

## Equality under Law

Three years after the Nineteenth Amendment was ratified, the National Woman's Party (NWP), which had been the most radical of the groups that had fought for women's suffrage, called for another amendment—an Equal Rights Amendment (ERA). The proposed amendment stated: "Men and women shall have equal rights throughout the United States and every place subject to its jurisdiction. Congress shall have power to enforce this article by appropriate legislation."

The proposed amendment seemed radical at the time, given that it was designed to immediately rid the United States of all gender-based discriminatory laws. And although its proponents seldom invoked the language of the Declaration of Independence, the amendment was clearly a logical extension of the Declaration's core concept: "all men are created equal." This said, the proposed amendment had a number of practical problems, one of which was that during the Progressive Era (1900–1917) hundreds of statutes were enacted to address the plight of female workers. If the amendment was ratified, it was believed that these statutes likely would be unconstitutional.

This period in U.S. history saw reformers passing laws protecting all workers. One of their earliest victories was the passage of a law in New York limiting the number of hours bakers—both male and female—could work to ten per day or sixty per week. The law was eventually struck down by the U.S. Supreme Court in the notable case of *Lochner v. New York* (1905). In a 5 to 4 decision, the Court held that the "freedom of contract" guaranteed by the Fourteenth Amendment included the right to purchase and sell labor. Therefore, any statute interfering with this right would be invalid "unless there are circumstances which exclude that right."

The reformers were not deterred. Emphasizing the frailty of women and their role as mothers, Progressives secured passage of a law in Oregon that limited the number of hours women could work in factories and laundries to ten per day. The Supreme Court in *Muller v. Oregon* (1908) unanimously upheld the law. In what would be viewed as a highly paternalistic opinion, the Court reasoned that women were the "weaker sex" who were in need of protection from the harsh realities of industrializa-

tion. Once the precedent had been established for the validity of protective labor legislation, hundreds of similar state labor laws were enacted. Eventually it was commonplace for legislation to restrict women's ability to work at night, establish a minimum wage for women, and require rest breaks at work.

The female reformers who lobbied for these laws, later termed "social feminists" by historians, emphasized, as the Supreme Court had done in *Muller,* women's physical makeup and childbearing capacity. For example, Florence Kelley, the executive secretary of the National Consumers League, argued that all men and women were not created equally.

Sex is a biological fact. The political rights of citizens are not properly dependent upon sex, but social and domestic relations and industrial activities are. All modern-minded people desire that women should have full political equality and the opportunity in business and the professions. No enlightened person desires that they should be excluded from jury duty or denied the equal guardianship of children, or that unjust inheritance laws or discriminations against wives should be perpetuated.

The inescapable facts are, however, that men do not bear children, are freed from the burdens of maternity, and are not susceptible, in the same measures as women, to poisons now increasingly characteristic of certain industries, and to the universal poison of fatigue. These are differences so far reaching, so fundamental, that it is grotesque to ignore them. . . . The inherent differences are permanent. Women will always need many laws different from those needed by men.

The ERA threatened this body of protective labor legislation, and social feminists and women workers and their unions fought against the National Woman's Party's attempts to enact it. Fortunately for the opponents of the ERA, they had an ally in Eleanor Roosevelt, wife of President Franklin D. Roosevelt. Consequently, social feminists dominated the ranks of women who held government positions in President Roosevelt's New Deal administration in the 1930s, effectively sidelining the ERA for a decade.

In the 1940s Congress took up the ERA because of the substantial contributions many women had made to the war effort. After World War II the NWP managed to attract the support of the National Federation of Business and Professional Women. In 1947 Alma Lutz, the spokesperson for the NWP, drew upon the Declaration of Independence when urging passage of the ERA. Lutz said: "Human rights and fundamental freedoms are above physical structure and biological function. . . . They belong to every human being, and need no safeguards before they are offered to women." The ERA was unable to garner the necessary public support and political momentum crucial for its passage.

During the post–World War II years, unprecedented numbers of women attended college, entered the workforce, and stopped having children at an earlier age. Many were prepared for professional careers by their education, though most educated women were working as teachers, nurses, or secretaries. After the advent of the birth control pill in 1960, women began delaying childbearing to still later ages. And as more women entered the workforce, they came face-to-face with discrimination. Educated women who stayed home also were showing signs of dissatisfaction, which Betty Friedan documented in *The Feminine Mystique* (1963).

John F. Kennedy, who was elected president in 1960, raised women's expectations when he appointed a Presidential Commission on the Status of Women (PCSW). The president established the commission in 1961 at the behest of Esther Peterson, the head of the Women's Bureau in the Department of Labor and a key figure in Kennedy's election. Peterson wanted to dispense with the ERA. She agreed with the contention that the ERA threatened protective labor legislation. The PCSW, chaired by Eleanor Roosevelt until her death in 1962, issued a wide-ranging critique of the role of women in America. The commission's strategy was to rid the nation of laws that discriminated against women by litigating them one at a time via the equal protection guarantees of the Fifth and Fourteenth Amendments. This strategy, they believed, would leave the protective legislation in place. A challenge, however, arose from an unexpected source.

President Lyndon B. Johnson was one of the greatest champions of civil rights ever to occupy the White House. Widely recognized as the most important domestic policy accomplishment of his administration, the Civil Rights Act of 1964 outlawed discrimination in housing, education, and employment. The employment provisions of the act—Title VII—forbade discrimination based on both race and sex. Momentum for a civil rights bill had been so strong that the provisions outlawing sex discrimination in employment were passed without much discussion of how they would impact the protective labor laws for which prior generations of women had so forcefully fought. Unfortunately, when women sought redress under the act their claims were largely ignored by an Equal Employment Opportunity Commission (EEOC)—the federal agency established in 1965 and charged with enforcing the statute—that believed its limited time and resources were better spent addressing racial discrimination.

The National Organization for Women (NOW) was founded in 1966 to persuade the government in general and the EEOC in particular to pay sufficient attention to employment discrimination against women. NOW also called for equal treatment under law in all areas of American life. It was not long before NOW reenergized the ERA and made it a mainstream issue.

Some of the more radical women's groups had a dramatically different agenda, however. A few called for the overthrow of the American system of government; others advocated and created separate institutions for women, such as rape crisis centers and feminist health clinics. NOW and related groups such as the Women's Equity Action League were more in tune with the promise of the Declaration of Independence. In 1969, for example, they convinced President Richard M. Nixon to appoint a Task Force on Women's Rights and Responsibilities. This task force published the first official statement of government support for the ERA.

The ERA, like the right to vote before it, became a rallying point for the women's rights movement. Congress passed the following version of the amendment in 1972.

Section 1. Equality of rights under the law shall not be denied or abridged by the United States or by any State on account of sex.

Section 2. The Congress shall have the power to enforce, by appropriate legislation, the provisions of this article.

Section 3. This amendment shall take effect two years after the date of ratification.

Congress required that the ERA be ratified by the requisite three-fourths of the states within seven years of passage if it was to take effect. A number of states immediately approved the amendment. However, by the mid-1970s an antifeminist movement opposed to the amendment sprang up under the leadership of Phyllis Schlafly, a conservative lawyer. Like the social feminists before them, the opponents of the ERA emphasized the biological and social differences between women and men. They insisted that equality under the law might mean that wives would be forced to leave their homes and enter the workforce to support husbands. Separate restrooms for women and men likely would be declared illegal, and women would be drafted into the armed forces. The same religious arguments used against the Grimke sisters in 1837 were recounted. The assertion was that God had given men and husbands authority over women and wives. Debate centered not on the natural rights principles of the Declaration of Independence, but on the fear of unpredictable consequences of legal equality.

Meanwhile, the seven-year deadline for ratification forced feminists to lobby Congress for additional time. In February 1978 NOW circulated a memorandum declaring a "state of emergency." The memorandum drew upon the Declaration of Independence when it stated: "[I]f we who believe most passionately that all women and men are created equal are not willing to fight when the last chance to realize that dream in our lifetime is in dire peril, *who will*?"

Feminists did manage to convince Congress to extend the ratification period, but it was all for naught. The ERA failed to win ratification by the requisite number of states—a consequence of the increasingly conservative mood of the country. According to Susan Faludi, author of *Backlash: The Undeclared War against American Women,* "Ultimately, the people who defeated the ERA were not ordinary women but a handful of very powerful men in three key state legislatures. These were men who opposed the ERA not because it would hurt women's protections but because it challenged their own belief that, as one of the . . . legislators put it, 'a woman should serve her husband.' "

Although feminists were unable to get the Declaration's promise of equality written into the Constitution, they did acquire substantive legal equality with men. They achieved this by confronting in piecemeal fashion the laws they deemed discriminatory. At the state level, feminists were successful in having equality written into thousands of state laws where sexual differentiation existed. For instance, when California ratified the ERA, its legislature formed a Joint Committee on Legal Equality to evaluate its laws to bring them into conformity with the ERA. Similarly, at the federal level, Congress enacted a number of laws that provided greater equality for women, most notably what has become known as Title IX, which prohibits sex discrimination in any federally funded educational program.

Courts also have been more willing in recent decades to protect women's rights via the Equal Protection Clause of the Fourteenth Amendment and the Due Process Clause of the Fifth Amendment. For example, in *Reed v. Reed* (1971) the U.S. Supreme Court struck down an Idaho law that had given preference to men over women as executors of estates. Similarly, in *Frontiero v. Richardson* (1973) the Court ruled that it was unconstitutional to draw distinctions between men and women under state dependent pay laws. This said, the nation's highest court has never invoked the "strict scrutiny" test it employs in racial discrimination cases to questions of gender discrimination. Instead, a gender-based classification will survive constitutional scrutiny if the classification is "substantially" related to an "important" government interest. In practical terms, this so-called intermediate scrutiny means that the Court can choose the gender discrimination it will allow.

## Conclusion

From 1776 to the dawn of the twenty-first century, the principles of the Declaration of Independence have moved generations of women to demand equality. However, women's biology and the traditional roles they have occupied in society often have impeded their quest. The Declaration was used to challenge the common law rules of domestic relations, the refusal to allow women to vote, and the discriminatory treatment that women have received in law and custom throughout the course of American history. In response, the common law has been extensively reformed, the franchise has been secured, but complete equality still eludes women. The barriers have been high and progress has been slow, but the last thirty years have been a time of rapid advancement for women. Much work remains to be done before women enjoy true equality, but the Declaration of Independence will continue to light the way.

## Bibliography

Bernhard, Virginia, and Elizabeth Fox-Genovese. *The Birth of American Feminism: The Seneca*

*Falls Woman's Convention of 1848.* St. James, N.Y.: Brandywine Press, 1995.

Campbell, Karlyn Kohrs. *Man Cannot Speak for Her: Key Texts of the Early Feminists.* New York: Greenwood Press, 1989.

Hartmann, Susan, M. *From Margin to Mainstream: American Women and Politics since 1960.* New York: Knopf, 1989.

Kerber, Linda K. *No Constitutional Right to Be Ladies.* New York: Hill and Wang, 1998.

———. *Women of the Republic: Intellect and Ideology in Revolutionary America.* Chapel Hill: University of North Carolina Press, 1980.

Marilley, Suzanne M. *Woman Suffrage and the Origins of Liberal Feminism in the United States, 1820–1920.* Cambridge: Harvard University Press, 1996.

McClymer, John F. *This High and Holy Moment: The First National Woman's Rights Convention, Worcester, 1850.* New York: Harcourt Brace, 1999.

Sklar, Kathryn Kish. *Women's Rights Emerges within the Antislavery Movement, 1830–1870.* Boston: Bedford/St. Martin's Press, 2000.

Wagner, Sally Roesch. *The Declaration of Rights of Women: 1876.* Aberdeen, S.D.: Aberdeen Chapter of NOW, 1975.

# 12 Reception of the Declaration of Independence

### DAVID THELEN

On September 12, 1821, Thomas Jefferson sat at his desk at Monticello composing a letter to his former partisan rival and revolutionary comrade John Adams. The times were dark. Europe's autocratic leaders were consolidating their counterattacks to smother revolutionary challenges that had swept across the North Atlantic world in the late eighteenth century. "I will not believe our labors are lost," a hopeful Jefferson wrote Adams, who had served with him on the committee that drafted the Declaration of Independence. "The flames kindled on the 4th of July, 1776 have spread over too much of the globe to be extinguished by the feeble engines of despotism; on the contrary they will consume these engines and all who work them."

Jefferson was right. The American Declaration of Independence has inspired people over the globe and the centuries in their quests for liberty, equality, and independence. Residents of Amsterdam declared their immediate identification with the American revolt, which triggered memories of the Dutch declaration of independence from the Spanish Crown in 1581 and the creation of a Dutch Republic. Revolutionaries have not only followed the American example of writing formal declarations to jus-

tify their courses of action, but they have also often drawn on words in the American document. In revolting against the Austrian Empire in 1789, Belgian rebels wrote separate declarations of independence in each province, and revolutionaries in Flanders appropriated words from the American Declaration. In writing a declaration to proclaim Vietnam's independence from French colonialism, Ho Chi Minh in l945 opened his document by lifting two sentences directly from what he termed Jefferson's "immortal" declaration.

The larger story of the reception of the Declaration, however, is not that Jefferson charted a course for others to follow toward freedom, but that the Declaration provided language that individuals grappled creatively and critically with as they charted their own struggles. The story of that reception begins with individual creativity, centers in different local struggles for freedom, and includes ongoing debate across time and space about how to turn vague yearnings and abstract claims for freedom into practice. Ideas, writings, people, and institutions flowed across national, cultural, and linguistic barriers, creating a transnational, transcultural arena from which individuals derived experience, adapted ideas, and chose language to advance their claims out of intensely local political conflicts and debates. As these individuals considered the Declaration's relevance to their struggles, they had to sort among the three different things its authors were trying to do: justify a revolution against legal authority; establish a people and a nation; and state civic objectives for that nation-state and define rights that citizens should possess, enjoy, and use to measure the behavior of states, including the United States.

Interest in the words of the Declaration was inseparable from interest in the nation it created. The Declaration of Independence was, as Carl Becker observed long ago, "an event, or at least the chief symbol of an event of surpassing historical importance, as well as a literary document which set forth in classic form a particular philosophy of politics. Fact and document, stubborn fact married to uncompromising theory; . . . an inspiration or a scandal to half the world, but in any case impossible to be ignored, with difficulty to be accepted or rejected the one without the other." The Declaration often circulated outside the United States, both in English and translation, in collections with other American founding documents.

## Eighteenth-Century North Atlantic Origins

The world that nurtured the Declaration of Independence was at once more intensely local and more richly transnational and transcultural than it would become in the nineteenth and twentieth centuries. Before Gen. George Washington could distribute copies of the Declaration for his commanders to read to their troops in New York, the document had been translated and was circulating in German—in the *Pennsylvanischer Staatsbote*—among immigrants who discussed the meaning of American independence. It took over a month for the first copies to reach Georgia, not much longer than it took to reach London, and from there for newspapers to publish it in English and for the first French translation (dated August 30, 1776) to circulate around Europe in that continent's lingua franca. On August 20, 1776, Counsellor V. G. Lizakevich reported contents of the Declaration from the Russian embassy in London to the College of Foreign Affairs and through it to Catherine the Great in St. Petersburg. But in the document that circulated so quickly across geographic and cultural borders, the signers proclaimed not the right to become a single nation, but the right to become thirteen "Free and Independent States." This action reflected a world in which local provinces clung to their own traditions, laws, religions, languages, and accents and jealously guarded their local prerogatives against centralizing powers.

The Declaration traveled so quickly, and engaged so many, because it was both a product of and a contributor to the broader movement of ideas its champions called the Enlightenment. Placing faith in reason and humanity, advocating natural rights by which people could shape their own destinies and pursue their own happiness, and exalting the sovereignty of citizens over that of monarchs, Europeans had formulated principles they would associate with a cosmopolitan "republic of letters" well before Americans declared the first modern republic in 1776. Some said they were merely recovering and restating principles that reached back to classical antiquity. To debate and sharpen these ideas people created new arenas in the eighteenth century for making and disseminating ideas—academies of science, salons, coffeehouses, taverns, Masonic lodges, pamphlets, newspapers—where they hoped to create a new authority in history, something they called "public opinion," that could mobilize ideas to challenge established authorities. The emergence of what scholars have called this new "public sphere," and with it the challenge of testing and applying Enlightenment ideas, burst across cultural boundaries in the eighteenth-century North Atlantic world. Voltaire wrote in 1734 that William Penn had "brought to the world that golden age of which men talk so much and which probably has never existed anywhere except in Pennsylvania." Leaders of the French Enlightenment, as Durand Echeverria has traced, immediately recognized Benjamin Franklin as a perfect embodiment of the Enlightenment, initiating him into the Masonic Lodge of the Nine Sisters and the Academy of Sciences.

The North Atlantic world of the late eighteenth century developed its cosmopolitan character as much from the circulation of people as ideas. Many people fulfilled Enlightenment dreams of escaping oppression and pursuing happiness by leaving the familiar behind and exploring possibilities in new lands. Believing that America offered relief from British oppression, thirty-seven thousand passengers sailed from Ireland to America on 152 ships between 1769 and 1774 alone. Travelers came as merchants, farmers, soldiers, intellectuals, and even as revolutionaries, and in the process they reproduced in America many European cultures and debates. From England came Thomas Paine whose *Common Sense*

focused the demands for a declaration of independence from Britain. From France came first Marquis de Lafayette and then eight thousand French troops who contributed mightily to the British defeat. The American struggle against Britain became a magnet for those seeking to fulfill the Enlightenment. And the American Congress recognized the cosmopolitan nature of their struggle by dispatching Benjamin Franklin to Paris and John Adams to The Hague to recruit supporters for the revolution.

Europeans recognized in the meetings and pamphlets in which Americans expressed their growing frustration with Britain familiar ideas of the Enlightenment. Jefferson later claimed that he intended the Declaration of Independence not to aim "at originality of principle or sentiment," but instead "to place before mankind the common sense of the subject, in terms so plain and firm as to command their assent, and to justify ourselves in the independent stand we are compelled to take." Upon first reading it in August 1776 in London, envoy Wilhelm Roemer dispatched his government in Wuerttemberg that the Declaration contained "some well-known general principles," as Horst Dippel reported. Matthias Christian Sprengel, writing from Goettingen, claimed that many of the grievances were copied from "the rhetorical flourishes of [Paine's] *Common Sense*." R. R. Palmer observed more than forty years ago that "all these ideas were perfectly familiar in Europe, and that is why the American Revolution was of such interest to Europeans."

This circulation of ideas of popular sovereignty ran up against regimes with borders, armies, institutions, and traditions, and against rulers who sought to harness or restrain the movement of people and ideas. Some powerful monarchs—Louis XIV, Frederick the Great—patronized Enlightenment thinkers and sought to govern by their principles. Ancient military rivalries and patriotic mobilizations among European powers—notably English and French, but also Austrian, Dutch, Portuguese, Russian, and Spanish—played out on colonial battlefields over trade, territory, immigration, and defense. Eighteenth-century struggles among European powers and between colonial peripheries in the Western Hemisphere and European metropolitan centers were part of a larger transition from commercial to industrial capitalism, of the emergence of colonial and creole elites to challenge the right of metropolitan elites to rule them, and of a cultural quest for natural spoken languages in which to express newfound natural rights and law. Monarchical French and Spanish regimes made military alliances with the revolutionary and republican Americans against monarchical Great Britain. As Britain became the enemy, French officials eased censorship constraints against permitting the Declaration of Independence, which after all called for popular sovereignty, to circulate in France. Frederick the Great reflected how national interest came first as he tried to keep his subjects from emigrating from Prussia and mocked German princes who provided mercenary troops to help the British army quash the American rebels. In a pattern that has persisted since 1776, revolutionaries told Benjamin Franklin that they were struggling first to change France or Ireland, but if their revolutions failed they planned to migrate to America.

Americans began their struggle not as part of a wider movement for universal rights, but as attempts to change policies in London. They stood in a long line of English reformers reaching back to the Magna Carta, the English Civil War, and the Glorious Revolution, who championed the rights of Englishmen against privileged rulers. In the 1760s and 1770s that line extended across the empire from the tens of thousands of electors from around London who petitioned for "Wilkes and Liberty" to the Liberty Boys in Dublin and the Sons of Liberty in New York, Boston, New Haven, and New Jersey. From the perspective of British history, the American Revolution was one episode in the movement for republican government, or at least for a more representative British Parliament. From the perspective of the "rights of Englishmen," it was a member of the British Parliament, Edmund Burke, who argued that the British government "drove them [the Americans] into the declaration of independence, *not* as a *matter of choice*, but *necessity*." Burke, addressing Americans, said that "you are upholding our common [English] liberty."

The Declaration of Independence became the act that turned what had begun as a colonial struggle for the rights of Englishmen into a struggle for the rights of man. It climaxed what Europeans were coming to see as the most creative and unique contribution of Americans to the Enlightenment vision of popular sovereignty. The stunning achievement of the Americans was to show how to transform abstract ideas into practice, to provide a model for how citizens might constitute themselves as a government and provide popular legitimacy to a regime dedicated to the protection of inalienable natural rights. Back in the 1760s Benjamin Franklin had tried to persuade French thinkers that the American colonies were struggling to put Enlightenment ideas into practice.

When he returned to Paris a few months after copies of the Declaration had reached that city, he discovered that "all Europe is on our side of the question." The Russian ambassador to France was so overwhelmed by the reception for Franklin that he wrote the Court at St. Petersburg: "Franklin arrived in Paris yesterday. The public is so taken with him that they no longer talk about anything else except the reasons for his arrival here." The marquis de Condorcet concluded that Americans had put the Enlightenment into practice: "It is not enough that the rights of man be written in the books of philosophers and inscribed in the hearts of virtuous men; the weak and ignorant must be able to read them in the example of a great nation. America has given us this example." "All Ireland is *America mad,*" observed Horace Walpole: "So is all the Continent." For British radicals, G. D. H. Cole and Raymond Postgate wrote, the Declaration showed how to put into practice a complete theory of popular control over government. The *Freeman's Journal* exhorted its Irish readers to collapse the theory of John Locke into the practice of the Americans.

By establishing themselves a constitutional Congress and declaring independence, the Americans almost enacted the Enlightenment theory of the social contract. Out of what looked to some Europeans like a wilderness, perhaps even a metaphorical state of nature, Americans came together and created a Congress that claimed to derive its sovereignty from the people. On a more practical level, as John Adams wrote his wife, Abigail, the most practical consequence of the Declaration was stated in the resolution of independence that Congress passed on July 2: "that these United Colonies are, and of right ought to be, free and independent States, and as such they have, and of right ought to have, full power to make war, conclude peace, establish commerce and to do all other acts and things which other States may rightfully do." Thomas Paine, among many others, insisted that the real need for declaring independence from Britain was to permit the colonies to negotiate military alliances with other nations—particularly France, which was withholding aid because it feared the colonies might be coaxed back into the British Empire. And to give independence practical effect Congress dispatched its most recognizably Enlightenment figure, Benjamin Franklin, to France to try to arrange a military alliance. Edmund Burke opposed the Declaration because he thought that liberty was a cultural and historical construction, not a human and universal one, that could not survive independently from its English roots. "That very liberty, which you so justly prize above all things," Burke wrote British colonists in America after learning of the Declaration, "originated here: and it may be very doubtful whether, without being constantly fed from the original fountain, it can be at all perpetuated or preserved in its native purity and perfection." Whether seen from Britain or the Continent, it was in the act of declaring independence and of constituting "one people" with a government to represent their unalienable rights that Europeans saw the incredibly original American contribution.

## "One People"

Even as readers reported that the Declaration conveyed familiar sentiments, they stumbled over particular words and phrases and in that stumbling helped reveal that the secret to the Declaration's longevity may rest, as Moses Coit Tyler and Carl Becker observed nearly a century ago, on the ambiguity and criticism it has generated. As translators struggle to find words to convey their understandings of the text to readers unfamiliar with its original language, the range and limitations of its applicability as well as the original Declaration itself appear in stranger and clearer light. New meanings and possibilities are made visible by the different ways that cultures and languages describe the world, make sense of their experiences, and understand what it takes to be free and independent. And what struck its original readers so forcefully is reinforced: The hard, creative part lies in putting abstract principles into practice.

For readers who believed that the Declaration's most stunning contribution was to put the principle of popular sovereignty into practice, the problems of translation began with the very first clause: "When in the Course of human events, it becomes necessary for one people to dissolve the political bands which have connected them with another." What did Jefferson mean that the Declaration was creating "one people"? What made the colonists "one people," when did they become "one people," and, for that matter, what made the British "another" people? Because its authors were trying to ground the legitimacy of the new government in its capacity to represent "one people" better than the existing regime, it mattered how they understood what constituted peoplehood. That is, it mattered from what shared basis they claimed rights and particularly the right to "alter or to abolish" their existing government and create a new one.

To understand "one people," the German American translator for the *Pennsylvanischer Staatsbote* in the summer of 1776 wavered between *Volk* (meaning people with a deeply shared cultural past) and *Einwohner* (meaning simply the inhabitants of a common place). Over the years Polish translators likewise have had trouble with the word "people," reports Jerzy Kutnik. In the most recent translation (1992), translators chose *narod* (nation) as the best Polish synonym for "people" instead of *lud* (which more closely approximates "people"). The Communist translators had preferred *lud* because it connotes "those people who are not nobles, not high in rank, position," the part of the nation that more nearly resembled the proletariat. And the alternative *narod* had been the rallying cry of middle- and upper-class Poles in the nineteenth century as they sought to persuade lower classes to assert Polish national identity against Russian, German, and Austro-Hungarian governments that had divided Poland between them and left no independent state. The concept of "nation" was important to the upper classes, which saw it as their responsibility to teach the uneducated masses (the *lud*) the importance of *narod*. To a Japanese champion of the Meiji enlightenment in the 1860s, Jefferson's vision of "the people" made best sense as a bond of blood or marriage. Fukuzawa Yukichi translated "one people" as a "kin group of people" who were declaring independence from "the government of another [British] nation." In his 1969 translation into Hebrew, Yohushua Arieli easily picked the word *'am,* but he added a footnote to explain that "people" to Americans implies "members of society," while *'am* to Hebrew speakers has a more collective sense to encompass nation, community, populace, tribe, or crowd. In trying to decipher what Jefferson meant by "one people," Germans had to pick between place of residence and shared cultural pasts; Poles weighed implications of class, ideology, and nationalism; Japanese tried to untangle family relationships from nations; and Hebrew translators chose among many collective connotations.

For French speakers, the question of who "the people" were, where they came from, how they formulated and claimed rights, when they brought nationality into existence, and how they participated in government were matters of great urgency as they sought to define a course for their own revolution. The Declaration of Independence provided a useful tool with which to work. In their study of those uses, Elise Marienstras and Naomi Wulf analyzed nine different translations into French between 1776 and 1789. Faced with Jefferson's varied uses of "the people," French translators had to specify whether the Declaration referred to citizens in their political capacity or as inhabitants of a geographic place. "The people" could mean, Marienstras and Wulf point out, either a specific people, responding to external causes and events, or a general, universal expression of what Rousseau had called the "general will." And in the political language of late eighteenth-century France, "the people" became part of the debate over what part of the French population was being discussed, given that in 1789 the third estate (bourgeois and plebeian sectors) endowed itself with the national power of government formerly held by the king and shared with nobility and clergy. Each of these ambiguities in the original English had to be clarified before French readers

could use the Declaration. As Marienstras and Wulf observe, Jefferson's shifting and evolving use of "the people" in the original Declaration becomes clearer when French translators addressed their task. Over time, "the people" in the Declaration moved from being victims, subject to "suffer" grievances from Britain, to being actors who take hold of their own sovereignty. Furthermore, their voice ranged between universalist claims to natural rights and a specific catalog of grievances suffered by particular people. Finally, from Jefferson's decision to ground his final pronouncement of the right to be free and independent states "by Authority of the good People of these Colonies," Marienstras and Wulf wonder whether the Declaration assumed that the "one people" already existed prior to July 4, 1776, as this clause implies, or whether the "one people" were brought into being by the Declaration itself. A Chinese translator in 1901, for example, chose a term that retranslated as "the people of our country," thereby implying that "one people" existed prior to the Declaration.

To French readers struggling with how to overcome their own oppression, "the people" of the Western Hemisphere faced such fundamentally different circumstances that it was hard to know how to apply their conclusions. "Please ponder the enormous difference existing between a new [naissant] people recently born to the universe, a colonial people breaking away from a distant government, and an ancient people" like the French, declared a member of the National Assembly, Trophime Gerard comte de Lally-Tollendal. French readers envisioned the American people as "new men" enjoying their "primitive sovereignty . . . in the bosom of nature," as a delegate to that assembly, Pierre-Victor Malouet, declared. Another delegate wondered what a new nation could teach an old nation in need of regeneration.

Many other European, notably British, readers believed that American conceptions of "the people" grew from the presumed new, primitive, innocent, and naive uniqueness of their history. Reading the colonists' grievances, George III could see only youthful American rebels and a wise English parent: "With firmness and perseverance America will be brought to submission: . . . Old England . . . yet will be able to make her rebellious children rue the hour they cast off obedience." In calling for a declaration of independence Thomas Paine passionately challenged British use of the phrase "*parent* or *mother country*" to attempt to discredit American revolutionaries as unappreciative children. But even Paine believed that people grew in maturity, declaring that Americans had now become old enough to exercise liberty. And Edmund Burke, a leading parliamentary champion of the American cause, counseled the colonists against declaring independence because they lacked maturity in the exercise of liberty: "We apprehend that you are not now, nor for ages likely to be, capable of" self-government without the steadying, experienced hand of the English constitution. Even as he warmly embraced the Declaration of Independence, a German philosopher, Isaak Iselin, repeated this familiar regret: "In this declaration we miss the respect that children owe to their parents and people owe to their kings, even after they have freed themselves of the latter's authority." Contrasting their situation as an "antique" people with existing laws and traditions, many delegates to the French National Assembly in 1789 agreed with pastor Jean-Paul

Rabaut de Saint-Etienne that American revolutionaries were different because they had broken "the ties with a distant mother country; they were a new people who destroyed everything in order to rebuild everything anew." By the act of throwing off established authority and constituting themselves an independent people, Americans seemed to others (and perhaps themselves) to be fashioning themselves as the youthful future, the place where Old World constraints on new ideas could be cast aside. "The youth of America is their oldest tradition," summed up Oscar Wilde.

The problems raised in translating "one people" gripped translators as they struggled to decide the larger challenge of emphasizing the universality or the particularity of the document and its authors. Translators could make the Declaration more familiar by emphasizing its universal appeals or make it intimate by, for example, Russifying or Japanizing it, giving it resonating eloquence in their readers' languages even when those words and allusions were not in the original. Frank Li reported that a Chinese translator imported words from *The Analects of Confucius* into his rendering of the Declaration into Chinese. Or translators could make the text seem strange and distant by emphasizing the uniqueness of the grievances or of Philadelphia, 1776, or the British Empire.

Fuzukawa Yukichi made the first Japanese translation of the Declaration in 1866 into a best-seller as he crafted it into a document that would inspire Meiji readers to throw off the established hierarchies of Tokugawa Japan. He revealed his dream most vividly in his choice of words to translate Jefferson's statement that people would revolt only when they faced extreme provocation: "Prudence, indeed, will dictate that governments long established should not be changed for light and transient causes; and accordingly all experience hath shown that mankind are more disposed to suffer, while evils are sufferable, than to right themselves by abolishing the forms to which they are accustomed." But Fuzukawa, as Tadashi Aruga has retranslated his words back into English, turned these words to a different conclusion in Japanese: "To a timid conservative mind, it may seem that a government established long ago cannot be changed easily or lightly." Only "timid" or "conservative" people would fail to appreciate that the proper and normal course was for people to resist oppression. He tried to draw the American document close to his Japanese agenda.

At the opposite extreme stands the translator Friedrich Schoenemann, who in 1942 sought to draw Nazi lessons from the American Revolution for German readers. Historian Willi Paul Adams shows that, in contrast to many other German translators, Schoenemann fluently recreated the message and words of the original Declaration. However, he dramatically distanced the American from the German experience by insisting that the Declaration and American Revolution were the unique *Schicksalsgang,* the course of fate, of Americans. It grew from the unique "*Blut und Boden*" (blood and soil) that nurtured the unique "American mind." The fate of Germans was to be carried along by the force of their own history toward opposition to the "western" and "foreign" doctrines of human agency and popular sovereignty expressed in the Declaration of Independence. While Fukuzawa drew the American experience near, perhaps too near, Schoenemann pushed the Declaration far away

from his German readers, arguing that fate and force shaped the course of history, one fate for each nation, and individuals would be carried along, powerless, to their destinies.

The claim that ideals of self-government were somehow created by the "race" or "character" of particular peoples and their histories extended far wider than the Nazis. The particular "character" or "genius" of Americans or English people, what some called the Anglo-American "race," was to love liberty, many insisted. In arguing against issuing the Declaration of Independence, Edmund Burke warned the colonists against English ministers who tried "to poison your minds against the origins of your race," which was to struggle for liberty. By rejecting the grievances of American colonists the English ministers were "enemies to their own blood on the American continent."

French translations in the eighteenth century and a Chinese one in 1901 turned the original text's universalist appeal to humanity into the historical record of a distant and particular nation. They did this by changing its voice from the first person plural ("we" and "us," the oppressed and the actors who often were conflated by Jefferson with "the people" who were revolting), to the third person plural ("the Americans," as in the Chinese translation, "[t]he privations suffered by the Americans are extreme"). The use of *Americaine* in translations, Marienstras and Wulf conclude, "introduces a distance between the French reader and the translated text and renders the Declaration of Independence more foreign to the French public." In the aftermath of World War II, the Japanese struggled to modify the new constitution that the Occupation government sought to impose on them by building from the ideas and language of the Declaration of Independence. They changed the word to describe "people" from *jinmin,* a term that included people broadly and derived from the nineteenth-century people's rights movement, to the word *kokumin,* which best translated to the more nationalist-sounding "national people."

As translators grappled with the meaning of Jefferson's phrase "one people," new meanings and questions emerged. Jefferson was writing a justification for people to overturn existing authority, but he was also either constituting a people and a nation or giving voice to an existing people (if not nation).

### "Unalienable Rights"

The claim that people possess and may assert "unalienable rights" puzzled many readers who wondered where rights came from, who defined them and how, what made them "unalienable" and from whom or what, whether they belonged to individuals or collectives, and whether they were lost privileges from the past or new powers to be acquired. They began by understanding "unalienable" rights as "eternal," "rights they cannot pass on," and rights "you cannot buy or sell or give up" in German translations, "inviolable" in Polish, "unremovable" in Japanese, "unseizable" in Chinese, and "so much the essence of a human being that no power on earth has the right to regulate or legislate them" in Spanish.

Readers stumbled first over the question of what rights were and where they came from. Many French revolutionaries wanted to ground rights not in nature, which they associated with a primitive, even biological state, or in the assertion of traditional privileges, but in the

workings of what Marienstras and Wulf call "a man-made and radically new civil society." Unlike in the British colonies, French revolutionaries believed that the ancien régime had to be more or less completely overturned and the power of the king somehow ended. They thought that new rights needed to replace traditional governing principles as means to imagine and bring into being the new society. Given that they were struggling to bring rights into being, not asserting them as a premise for political independence, French revolutionaries were eager to spell them out. In the 1789 Declaration of the Rights of Man and the Citizen, the "natural, unalienable and sacred rights" were "liberty, security, property, and resistance to oppression." By 1793 the "natural and imprescribable rights" included "equality" and "resistance to oppression" was dropped. French revolutionaries read the Declaration of Independence and its list of grievances mainly as a means to reclaim traditional rights and privileges that the British government had undermined.

The decade-long debates and civil warfare in Mexico that culminated in the Act of Independence of September 28, 1821, combined American and French visions of rights while asserting a unique "creole patriotism," as Josefina Zoraida Vázquez observed. The act proclaimed that Mexico was "restored to all its recognized and sacred rights" lost in the Spanish conquest: "The Mexican nation, which for three hundred years has neither had its own will nor free use of its voice, today leaves the oppression in which it has lived." But beyond an assumption of self-government, the act named neither the "recognized rights" it sought to recover nor the rights it hoped to live by. Instead, it declared, "the Mexican nation is free to constitute itself through its representatives, in any way convenient to its happiness."

While readers in other lands certainly recognized acting to resist oppression, they did not associate resistance to oppression with claims to rights. For Sun Yat-sen and early twentieth-century Chinese revolutionaries, the American Declaration simply did not correspond to the "common sense" of Chinese experience, writes Frank Li, which was not to claim liberties or rights but simply to replace one oppressive ruler with a new monarch and centralized state. The Nazi translator Friedrich Schoenemann easily dismissed any mention of rights: "A state is not the result of a contract, and there are no inborn rights," Willi Paul Adams quotes him as saying.

For many readers the hardest and strangest justification was the Declaration's assertion that unalienable rights derived from "the Laws of Nature and of Nature's God." Four of the eighteenth-century French translations were so puzzled by this claim that they did not include it in their translations. After strictly separating church from state in 1904, French political discourse relegated discussion of God from public arena to private life. Italian translators in the nineteenth and twentieth centuries introduced phrases that interpret the laws of "Nature's God" as divine laws, reports Tiziano Bonazzi, replacing the theist-inspired American idea with one that reflects European natural law tradition in which God cannot be reduced to an architect of nature. The Japanese Meiji translator, Fukuzawa, transcended Western religious views of God by rendering the phrase "the nature of the reason of the physical world and that of the way of heaven."

From the Declaration's (and larger Enlightenment's) proclamation that "all men" were entitled to "unalienable rights," readers have grappled with whether rights were expressed and experienced by people in their individual capacity or as parts of a collective. The closely related question was whether rights were mainly political protections for individuals against an oppressive government or broadly social entitlements the nation or state owed to its members. Using the American document to help them name how they wanted to be similar and different, French revolutionaries since the eighteenth century have often emphasized a more positive, expansive, social view of rights as guarantees of social security—a feature of many twentieth-century social revolutions. Americans, meanwhile, stressed greater protection for individual civil liberties against the state. Some students of the French Revolution insisted that the Declaration of the Rights of Man and the Citizen in 1789 pushed their rejection of the American formulation of rights still further by rejecting the Lockean idea of a civil compact and the Rousseaean idea of a social compact in which rights and government originate in individual grants of authority.

By creating their own framing of "unalienable rights," French revolutionaries soon forced Americans to rethink their original purposes. Could the Declaration of Independence be read to support a French understanding of revolution and rights? Issuance of the French Declaration of the Rights of Man and the Citizen was followed by years of struggle over what that document would mean in practice, culminating in the execution of Louis XVI and the Terror of 1794. During this same time period, the United States adopted a new federal

Constitution and George Washington was elected the first president. Many of Washington's Federalist colleagues were appalled by what the French were doing with their revolution. They worried that the proclamations that "all men are created equal" and had the right to "alter or to abolish" governments seemed too, well, French, as historian Pauline Maier has observed. Jefferson and other builders of the new Republican Party challenged the Federalists with their own interpretation of founding principles, making the Declaration of Independence an important source of the party's defining traditions. They sympathized with some of the more social and democratic tendencies of the French Revolution even as they marshaled the American Declaration's defense of individual liberties to resist Federalist attempts to suppress their party. Explorations of the meaning of equality, liberty, republicanism, and revolution circled back and forth across the North Atlantic world of the 1790s. The French debate framed not only partisan debate in the United States but also a slave uprising and revolution that ultimately brought independence to the second republic in the Western Hemisphere, Haiti.

The Declaration of Independence's proclamation of rights has been the standard for change twice in modern Japan, as Tadashi Aruga has argued. When Gen. Douglas MacArthur insisted that the defeated Japanese frame their postwar constitution around American models, some Japanese recalled Meiji debates in the late nineteenth century that had held up the Declaration as the model for a future Japanese polity. American occupiers and Japanese participants reconciled individual with social conceptions of rights by declaring:

The people's "right to life, liberty and the pursuit of happiness within the limits of the general welfare shall be the supreme consideration of all law and all governmental action." They inserted social security clauses not only from the French Declaration of 1789, but also from the Soviet Constitution of 1918 and particularly the German Weimar Constitution of 1919, which went the furthest to extend the idea of human rights to include social and economic rights. A major participant in drafting the new constitution, the Marxist-oriented constitutional historian Suzuki Yasuzo, argued that twentieth-century democracies had to be social democracies—that in the New Deal the United States had shown how the original Declaration could be made a base for building social democracy. Chapter 2 of the constitution quoted Franklin D. Roosevelt; it proclaimed the right to be "free from fear and want."

Israel's Declaration of Independence of 1948, reports Ilan Troen, uses rights in ethnic and national terms to describe how the new state could fulfill Jewish national purposes and collective goals instead of individual liberties. Each of the seven uses of the word *right* in Israel's declaration refers to this national context. It proclaims, for example, "the right of the Jewish people and national renewal in its own land" and "the power of our natural and historical right," among other things, to a state of their own in Palestine.

The struggle over whether rights were individual or collective—over what rights were— came most plainly into view as readers struggled with Jefferson's use of "the pursuit of Happiness" as one of his three enumerated "unalienable Rights." Eighteenth-century French translators debated between *bonheur* (happiness) and *bien-être* (well-being) and then between envisioning its quest as a *recherche* (pursuit) and a *désir* (desire). French translators thus agonized, as Marienstras and Wulf argue, over whether Jefferson intended a global and diffuse right to pursue happiness or a more subjective and intimate right to an easier, more felicitous life. According to Willi Paul Adams, the same choice faced the first German translator on the European continent, Isaak Iselin, as he rendered the pursuit as a desire (perhaps because he was working from a French translation) and happiness as *Wohlstand* (a combination of welfare and prosperity akin to the French *bien-être*). Unable to understand Jefferson's "pursuit of Happiness," the Meiji advocate Fukuzawa picked up some of the French sense by translating it as *kofuku*, "the wish to enjoy happiness."

In choosing to replace John Locke's "property" with "the pursuit of Happiness," Jefferson made a choice that has drawn much comment from his day to ours. The dean of Russian Americanists of the past generation, Nikolai N. Bolkhovitinov, reporting that he "lived in a country where the citizens were deprived of property," concluded on the basis of his Russian experience that Locke had been correct and that the right to property was the basis for independence. French revolutionaries agreed with that conclusion by including property as an inalienable right in both 1789 and 1793 declarations. Several state constitutions during the American Revolution had preceded the French in naming property among unalienable rights. As he tried to understand Jefferson's decision, Bolkhovitinov finally accepted Jefferson's own explanation for excluding property from natural rights: "No individual has, of natural right, a separate property in an acre of land, for instance. . . . Stable ownership is the gift of social law, and is given late in the progress of society." The fascination of Soviet scholars with Jefferson's choice reflected the larger ideological difference between championing rights as means to social welfare or as means to individual fulfillment. In both Soviet and East German commentaries the Declaration was dismissed as bourgeois, narrow, and individualistic, and happiness was conceived as something people experience collectively.

For still other readers the "pursuit of Happiness" seemed incomprehensible for religious reasons. In a materialistic world the pursuit of happiness is achievable, as Eugene Eoyang points out, but in Chinese and Japanese cultures, especially for Buddhists, the pursuit of happiness may be both futile and a human vanity. In Spanish Catholic teaching, reports Joaquim Oltra, this world is only a "valley of tears" through which people pass on their way to the next, and it is only in the next world that happiness is attainable.

## Proclamation versus Practice

From 1776 to the present the toughest challenge of all has been how to reconcile the Declaration's words with everyday practice. Through the Declaration the United States came into being as the first modern nation-state grounded in ideals. The Declaration announced the principles by which the new regime intended to live. To ground nationality in ideals was such a remarkable and strange departure that people ever since—particularly critics of those ideals or of the whole idea that values should influence a nation's actions—

have struggled to understand American ideals by looking at American practices and to understand American practices by looking at how they squared with the Declaration's ideals.

Some observers, particularly foreigners interested principally in the American nation-state's behavior and influence on others, have presented the gap as a fundamental American hypocrisy that undermines American moral authority to speak and act. Other foreigners have tried to blunt the challenge of ideals either by prohibiting the Declaration's circulation within their borders or by translating its language in ways that make its ideas inaccessible. Americans have certainly expressed their own variations on these approaches—as, for example, by protesting American foreign policies that seemed to undermine American ideals—but they have developed a wider repertoire of approaches for reconciling the gap between proclamation and practice. They have contested the intentions of the original authors and the accuracy of those authors' assertions. They have debated whether and how the original document might or might not provide a meaningful vehicle for moving into the future. And they have even rewritten the original words to incorporate what they wished the original authors had said.

German translators have illustrated the difficulties many foreigners have had in reconciling the American theory and practice of liberty. In his magisterial exploration of late eighteenth-century German responses to the American Revolution, Horst Dippel concluded that members of German middle classes exclaimed admiration for the abstract ideal of liberty but failed to recognize the relevance of that ideal for the kind of political liberty

Americans were putting into practice. While the Declaration created a nation-state out of ideals of popular sovereignty, German debate separated the ideal of nation building from that of government by consent, Willi Paul Adams shows. Expecting a gulf between theory and practice, some Germans maintained that the problem was less with the ideals than with their hypocritical application. A Weimar era monarchist, Emil Kimpen, wrote in his 1923 history: "The honorable signers forgot that there were half a million Negro slaves among the colonists, and many whites whom need forced to live in so-called voluntary servitude. They, too, would have had a natural right to freedom. The enthusiasm for human rights [expressed in the Declaration] meant nothing but resounding phrases to deceive the naive." The charge of hypocrisy echoed through an East German history in the l980s: "The document proclaims as basic human rights 'life, liberty and the pursuit of happiness'—rights which the modern USA opposes all over the world and this paradoxically in the name of 'human rights.' . . . Here it must be pointed out that only enfranchised citizens were meant, i.e. women, blacks, Indians, etc. were excluded. . . . The Declaration of Independence . . . proclaimed and underlined the right of a people to revolution, a right which the imperialist bourgeoisie of the USA everywhere and especially in its own country tramples underfoot." The charge of hypocrisy reconciled puzzling gaps between ideals and practices.

Another way of making it harder for readers to explore the Declaration's relevance to their experience was to block people from engaging those ideals in the first place. By simple censorship Russian authorities prevented the

Declaration from circulating freely in their country until Alexander II's reforms in the 1860s. And even when Russian translators tried to make the Declaration's ideas available to readers, those ideas were so unfamiliar that translators rendered them as vague (and harmless) abstractions, a rendering that blunted the challenge of the Declaration to existing practice. The most difficult moment for Russian translators, Marina A. Vlasova reports, was to figure out what Jefferson had meant by the phrase "to throw off such Government, and to provide Guards for their future security." Facing the difficulty of imagining that government could guarantee people's security, they retreated into an abstract plural term in 1863, 1897, 1991, and 1993 translations. In 1901 a translator chose a term she retranslates as "principles and forms of the new government which will guarantee the security and welfare of the state."

People in other parts of the world had trouble not only translating the Declaration into their own experience, but also making sense of how the United States understood and applied its principles. Louis Kossuth, the leader of Hungary's revolt against the Hapsburg empire in 1848, called the Declaration "that noblest, happiest page of mankind's history." But in the 1840s, as in the 1950s, the United States did not come to the aid of Hungarian revolutionaries as France had aided Americans in the 1770s. Even more puzzling was that U.S. interventions often seemed to try to block or at least shape the course of other peoples' revolutions. These interventions to suppress popular sovereignty reminded critics of the role Great Britain had played, a role that had provoked Americans to declare independence.

William James invoked the Declaration of Independence as his inspiration when he called on the United States not to interfere in other peoples' movements for self-government, to let them shape their own fates: "We are now openly engaged in crushing out the sacredest thing in this great human world—the attempt of a people long enslaved to attain to the possession of itself, to organize its laws and government, to be free to follow its internal destinies according to its own ideals." Believing that the Declaration had proclaimed the right of people to chart their own courses, James said the best hope for halting American suppression of self-determination was for "the [Declaration's] older American beliefs and sentiments coming to their rights again."

But the people who faced the most urgent challenge and greatest difficulty in translating the Declaration's values into practice were the Americans themselves. From 1776 to the present the most persistent challenge has been how to apply the phrase "all men are created equal" to blacks, Indians, women, and others whom Americans have denied equal access to democratic promise and institutions. Even as he participated on the committee drafting the Declaration, John Adams heard from his wife, Abigail: "If particular care and attention are not paid to the ladies we are determined to foment a rebellion and will not hold ourselves bound to obey any laws in which we have no voice or representation." The difficulty of squaring the Declaration's words with practice began in the drafting of the Declaration. Congress directed Jefferson to remove a lengthy paragraph in which he had written that the "piratical" and "execrable" slave trade was a "cruel war against human nature itself, violating its most sacred rights of life and liberty." Jefferson himself embodied the paradox by holding slaves, at least one as a lover, while writing these words; trying unsuccessfully to insert into the Virginia Constitution of 1776 the provision "no person hereafter coming into the state would be held in slavery"; and mostly famously steering "all men are created equal" into the final Declaration.

Before the ink was dry on the Declaration many Americans struggled with how to apply the Declaration's words to the practice of chattel slavery. The wealthy South Carolinian Henry Laurens, a former slave trader and later president of the Continental Congress, declared that the Declaration's principles applied to blacks as well as whites. Within weeks after the Declaration was published, he wrote that he was ready to free his slaves despite "the laws and customs of my country, my own and the avarice of my countrymen." Many other southerners were equally troubled that slavery contradicted the ideal of equality, but they resolved it by striking out in the opposite direction from Laurens. Six southern states wrote constitutions, Carl Becker documented, that resolved the contradiction by adding a four-letter modifier to Jefferson's key word: "All *free*men . . . are equal," they declared. Northern states concluded, by contrast, that the Declaration left them no choice about slavery. They set in motion a variety of legal processes that culminated in the abolition of slavery within their borders. Vermont abolished it outright, the first political unit in the world to set the example that French revolutionaries such as Robespierre would argue was inherent in the logic of revolutionary equality and that France would follow in 1794 when it abolished

slavery throughout its empire (only to have Napoleon restore it after the revolutionary enthusiasm had subsided).

The failure of the American Revolution to abolish slavery while setting in motion ideas of liberty and equality created the greatest challenge to increasingly nation-centered nineteenth- and twentieth-century readers who, as Carl Becker observed, saw the Declaration less as a justification for revolution and more as a statement of the founding ideals for a nation. The struggle over how to apply the Declaration's words ultimately ended in bloody civil war. Americans agonized over what the Declaration meant in practice. To the strongly antislavery New Yorker John Jay, an author of *The Federalist Papers*, the failure of the Revolution to end slavery turned the Declaration of Independence from a statement of fact in the present into a statement of a commitment for the nation to fulfill in the future, Jay's biographer Richard B. Morris argued. When the federal government required northerners to assist slaveholders by returning runaway slaves to their owners while doing nothing to abolish slavery, abolitionists framed the Declaration as the statement of a promise that the Constitution had betrayed in practice. By 1847 William Lloyd Garrison and Wendell Phillips called on "every citizen . . . to devote himself to the destruction of the Union and the Constitution, which have already shipwrecked the experiment of civil liberty." They hoped that "out of the wreck" would come a state more faithful to "the principles of the Declaration of Independence, whose promises made us once the admiration of the world."

As abolition gained support in the North as a fulfillment of the Declaration's ideals, critics grew increasingly defensive. At first the "false and dangerous" notion that all men were created equal "lay dormant," wrote John C. Calhoun, "but in the process of time it began to germinate and produce its poisonous fruits." In response, critics developed their own interpretations of the signers' intentions and words, as Harry V. Jaffa and Pauline Maier have sketched. From John C. Calhoun of South Carolina to John Pettit of Indiana to Stephen Douglas of Illinois, they dismissed the idea that "all men are created equal" as a "self-evident lie." Because people were clearly unequal in fact, the Declaration's "self-evident truths must be the veriest abstractions, totally unapplicable to a practical world," as Rufus Choate put it, nothing but "glittering and sounding generalities." Many critics developed the answer that Douglas gave Abraham Lincoln in a debate: The signers had in view only "white men, men of European descent, and had no reference either to the negro, the savage Indians, the Feejee, the Malay, or any other inferior and degraded race, when they spoke of the equality of men." The signers would have sided with Douglas against Lincoln: "I do not question Mr. Lincoln's conscientious belief that the negro was made his equal, and hence is his brother, but for my own part I do not regard the negro as my equal, and positively deny that he is my brother or any kin to me whatever." If the founders had intended slaves to be equals of whites, wrote Chief Justice Roger B. Taney, they would have abolished slavery in 1776. Instead, what the founders meant by equality, southerners from Calhoun to Jefferson Davis insisted, was the equality of the thirteen original states. Calhoun argued that by creating thirteen "free and independent states" Congress had made each state as independent of

each other state as it was of Great Britain. And the proof was that Congress had rejected New Hampshire's proposal to create one "free and independent State" instead of thirteen. Each state was the key arena for popular sovereignty, each free to interpret the Declaration as it liked. And as secessionists and Confederates came to compare their new nation to the Revolution of 1776, as Emory Thomas has argued, they came to blend the rights of Englishmen into the southern way of life, the oppressions of the British king and parliament into the black Republican president Abraham Lincoln and the Yankee Congress. And, after all, the original Declaration had proclaimed the right of people to create new governments when existing ones no longer represented them.

The Union army's victory and Abraham Lincoln's reframing of the founding ideals seemed to settle this debate over the Declaration's meaning. In the Gettysburg Address, Lincoln insisted that the Civil War would settle the issues of whether a government dedicated to the proposition that all men are created equal, a government of, by, and for the people, would survive. Out of the Civil War Lincoln developed most fully the formulation that has largely prevailed ever since of how to reconcile the Declaration's words with American practice (see Chapter 3). Arguing that Douglas's claim that some races were "inferior or degraded" left the Declaration a "mere wreck," a "mangled ruin," Lincoln insisted that the Declaration's authors wanted "simply to declare the *right* so that the *enforcement* of it might follow as fast as the circumstances should permit. They meant to set up a standard maxim for free men which should be familiar to all, and revered by all; constantly looked to, and constantly labored for, and even though never perfectly attained, constantly approximated and thereby constantly spreading and deepening its influence, and augmenting the happiness and value of life to all people of all colors everywhere." Lincoln believed that Jefferson's greatness had been to have "the coolness, forecast, and capacity to introduce into a merely revolutionary document, an abstract truth, applicable to all men and all times, and so to embalm it there, that to-day, and in all coming days, it shall be a rebuke and a stumbling-block to the very harbingers of re-appearing tyranny and oppression." On July 4, 1861, he told Congress that the main significance of a Confederate victory would be "to overthrow the principle that all men were created equal."

In his "I Have a Dream" speech of August 28, 1963, the Rev. Dr. Martin Luther King Jr. gave fresh expression to Lincoln's formulation that the Declaration "was always a declaration of intent rather than reality." From the steps of the Lincoln Memorial, a hundred years after Lincoln had spoken at Gettysburg, King proclaimed that the huge rally before him—which he hoped "will go down in history as the greatest demonstration for freedom in the history of our nation"—had "come to our nation's capital to cash a check." By the "magnificent words" of the Declaration the "architects of our republic" "were signing a promissory note to which every American was to fall heir. This note was the promise that all men, yes, black men as well as white men, would be guaranteed the unalienable rights of life, liberty, and the pursuit of happiness.... And so we've come to cash this check, a check that will give us upon demand the riches of freedom and the security of justice."

While Lincoln and King reconciled ideals with practice by proclaiming America's mission to try to practice what it preached, other Americans continued to reread the Declaration's words for clues about whether some silence or lie in the original words made it difficult to transform those words into reality. Some found the original words so remote that they denied that the Declaration was relevant to their lives. As Keith D. Miller says (see Chapter 10), many African Americans refused to celebrate July 4th because, as ex-slave and abolitionist Frederick Douglass told a Rochester, New York, audience on July 5, 1852: "I am not included within the pale of this glorious anniversary! . . . This Fourth of July is *yours,* not mine. You may rejoice, but I must mourn." In the same spirit the *National Labor Tribune* questioned whether workers would have anything to celebrate at the centennial on July 4, 1876: "Capital has now the same control over us that the aristocracy of England had at the time of the Revolution." The first revolution was so irrelevant to an industrial world that, in the words of the Chicago *Workingmen's Advocate,* "another revolution [is] as essential today as that inaugurated in 1776." As Bonnie L. Ford suggests (see Chapter 11), Susan B. Anthony and the National Woman Suffrage Association found an ambivalent way to mark the Declaration's 1876 centennial: Women would stage demonstrations in their communities and declare themselves "free and independent," no longer bound to obey American law.

A more common resolution was to seize the Declaration, make it their own, and if necessary rewrite it to make explicit how it could extend to people who felt marginalized or excluded. By the 1820s and 1830s, Philip S.

Foner has shown, workers began to rewrite the Declaration to envision restoring rights employers "have robbed us of." In December 1829, George Henry Evans published "The Working Men's Declaration of Independence" in the *Working Men's Advocate,* which he edited. " 'When, in the course of human events, it becomes necessary' for one class of a community to assert their natural and unalienable rights in opposition to other classes of their fellow men, 'and to assume among' them a political 'station of equality to which the laws of nature and of nature's God,' as well as the principles of their political compact, 'entitle them,' " it began and proceeded to list grievances and call for united working-class political action against employers and politicians. As revolution against established authorities swept across Europe in the 1840s, many Americans rewrote the Declaration, most memorably, as Bonnie Ford suggests, at the women's rights convention in July 1848 at Seneca Falls, New York. Elizabeth Cady Stanton turned the Declaration of Independence into a Declaration of Sentiments and Resolutions. "When, in the course of human events, it becomes necessary for one portion of the family of man to assume among the people of the earth a position different from that which they have hitherto occupied, but one to which the laws of nature and nature's God entitle them," it began. "All men and women are created equal," this document insisted, but "the history of mankind is a history of repeated injuries and usurpations on the part of man toward woman, having in direct object the establishment of an absolute tyranny over her." It then listed grievances and adopted resolutions that could produce true equality in public and private spheres. Foner

reprinted twenty-four "alternative" declarations of independence by groups that had filled the chasm between the Declaration's sentiments and American practice by rewriting the Declaration to comprehend their quests.

Many turned to the Declaration for inspiration and confidence as they tried to imagine new constitutional practices that would extend government from the privileged to those it excluded. The largest mass movement in nineteenth-century America, the farmers' alliance movements of the South and West, chose July 4, 1892, at Omaha to declare their independence from the existing two-party system and to create a new party, a People's Party, to lead them to a future. "We believe that the power of government—in other words, of the people," they asserted in a breathtaking social formulation, "should be expanded . . . as rapidly and as far as the good sense of an intelligent people and the teachings of experience shall justify, to the end that oppression, injustice, and poverty shall eventually cease in the land." And in his call to remake government so that people could rule directly without intervening representative institutions, progressive J. Allen Smith in *The Spirit of American Government* (1907) contended that he was simply reenacting the revolutionary struggle. The quarrel with England provided an opportunity for the "forces which had been silently and unconsciously working toward democracy" to find expression in the Declaration of Independence and its call to introduce new forms of government that better represented people. The monied interests and aristocracy had thwarted the democratic thrust of the Declaration by enacting a Constitution designed to check popular democracy. Direct democracy, he insisted, could restore the movement toward popular democracy that was expressed in the Declaration. The Declaration of Independence had thus found its spot in American culture: to buttress struggles to produce a more democratic future or, as historian Joyce Appleby has put it, to add to the Constitution's fundamental law a vision of inalienable rights.

## Conclusion

"The Declaration of Independence was always a hard nut for official Russia to crack, under both the tsarist and Soviet regimes," Nikolai N. Bolkhovitinov concluded from his survey of Russian engagements with the document over two centuries. Official Russians believed that the United States was too republican for the czars and too capitalist and imperialist for the Soviets, and yet there was something appealing about the Declaration of Independence that transcended how their regimes understood America. The same conclusion could encapsulate American engagements with the Declaration. Americans, too, have embraced the Declaration, perhaps because they have viewed it as the standard for understanding and measuring practice. And so the greatness of the Declaration of Independence is that it cuts through both theory and practice, generating criticism as it challenges people everywhere to explore how to reconcile theory with practice, how to fulfill the Enlightenment dream that people should be free to pursue their own happiness in a world in which established regimes have tried to corral them. Through the difficulties Americans and others have had translating the Declaration into words and deeds, questions remain about what the founding fathers intended, what those ideals mean, and what is

to be made from their ambiguous legacy. People all over the world, Americans and others, have developed a rich history of trying to make the Declaration a living statement they can use on their own terms. Through their eyes "all men are created equal" can be seen afresh, as Fukuzawa Yukichi rendered it: "Heaven did not create a person above another person, nor a person below another person."

## Bibliography

Adams, Willi Paul. *The First American Constitutions: Republican Ideology and the Making of the State Constitutions in the Revolutionary Era.* Trans. Rita Kimber and Robert Kimber. Lanham, Md.: Rowman and Littlefield, 2001.

_____. "German Translations of the Declaration of Independence." *Journal of American History* 85 (March 1999): 1325–1349.

Aldridge, A. Owen. *Thomas Paine's American Ideology.* Newark: University of Delaware Press, 1984.

Appleby, Joyce. "The American Heritage: The Heirs and the Disinherited." *Journal of American History* 74 (December 1987): 798–813.

_____. "Recovering America's Historic Diversity: Beyond Exceptionalism." *Journal of American History* 79 (September 1992): 419–431.

Aruga, Tadashi. "The Declaration of Independence in Japan: Translation and Transplantation, 1854–1997." *Journal of American History* 85 (March 1999): 1409–1431.

Ascoli, Peter. "American Propaganda in the French Language Press during the American Revolution." In *La Révolution Américaine et L'Europe.* Ed. Claude Fohlen and Jacques Godechot. Paris: Colloques Internationaux No. 577, Centre National de la Recherche Scientifique, 1979.

Becker, Carl L. *The Declaration of Independence: A Study in the History of Political Ideas.* New York: Vintage Books, 1942.

Beisner, Robert L. *Twelve against Empire: The Anti-Imperialists, 1898–1900.* New York: McGraw-Hill, 1968.

Bolkhovitinov, Nikolai N. "The Declaration of Independence: A View from Russia." *Journal of American History* 85 (March 1999): 1389–1398.

_____. *Russia and the American Revolution.* Trans. and ed. C. Jay Smith. Tallahasee: Diplomatic Press, 1976.

Bonazzi, Tiziano. *"Tradurre/Tradire:* The Declaration of Independence in the Italian Context." *Journal of American History* 85 (March 1999): 1350–1361.

Burke, Edmund. *On the American Revolution: Selected Speeches and Letters.* Ed. Elliott Robert Barkan. New York: Harper Torchbooks, 1966.

Calhoun, Craig, ed. *Habermas and the Public Sphere.* Cambridge: MIT Press, 1992.

Chinard, Gilbert. "Notes on the American Origins of the Déclaration des Droits de l'Homme et du Citoyen." *Proceedings of the American Philosophical Society* 98:6 (1954): 383–396.

Cole, G. D. H., and Raymond Postgate. *The Common People, 1746–1946.* London: University Paperback, 1961.

Dippel, Horst. *Germany and the American Revolution, 1770–1800.* Trans. Bernard A. Uhlendorf. Chapel Hill: University of North Carolina Press, 1977.

Donoughue, Bernard. *British Politics and the American Revolution: The Path to War, 1773–1775.* London: Macmillan, 1964.

Echeverria, Durand. *Mirage in the West: A History of the French Image of American Society to 1815.* Princeton: Princeton University Press, 1957.

Eoyang, Eugene. "Life, Liberty and the Pursuit of Linguistic Parity: Multilingual Perspectives on the Declaration of Independence." *Journal of American History* 85 (March 1999): 1449–1454.

Fliegelman, Jay. *Declaring Independence: Jefferson, Natural Language, and the Culture of Performance.* Stanford: Stanford University Press, 1993.

Fohlen, Claude. "The Impact of the American Revolution on France." In *The Impact of the American Revolution Abroad.* Ed. Library of Congress. Washington, D.C.: Library of Congress, Symposia on the American Revolution, 1976, 21–38.

Foner, Philip S., ed. *We, the Other People: Alternative Declarations of Independence by Labor Groups, Farmers, Woman's Rights Advocates, Socialists, and Blacks, 1829–1975.* Urbana: University of Illinois Press, 1976.

Hamnett, Brian. "Process and Pattern: A Reexamination of the Ibero-American Independence Movements, 1808–1826." *Journal of Latin American Studies* 29 (May 1997): 279–328.

Jaffa, Harry V. *A New Birth of Freedom: Abraham Lincoln and the Coming of the Civil War.* Lanham, Md.: Rowman and Littlefield, 2000.

King, Martin Luther, Jr. *A Testament of Hope: The Essential Writings and Speeches of Martin Luther King Jr.* Ed. James M. Washington. New York: HarperCollins, 1991.

Kraus, Michael. "America and the Irish Revolutionary Movement in the Eighteenth Century." In *The Era of the American Revolution.* Ed. Richard B. Morris. New York: Columbia University Press, 1939, 332–348.

Kutnik, Jerzy. "The Declaration of Independence in Poland." *Journal of American History* 85 (March 1999): 1385–1388.

Lemay, Edna Hindie. "Lafitau, Démeunier and the Rejection of the American Model at the French National Assembly, 1789–1791." In *Images of America in Revolutionary France.* Ed. Michele R. Morris. Washington, D.C.: Georgetown University Press, 1990, 171–184.

Li, Frank. "East Is East and West Is West: Did the Twain Ever Meet? The Declaration of Independence in China." *Journal of American History* 85 (March 1999): 1432–1448.

Logan, John A. *The Great Conspiracy: Its Origins and History.* New York: A. R. Hart, 1886.

Maier, Pauline. *American Scripture: Making the Declaration of Independence.* New York: Knopf, 1997.

Marienstras, Elise, and Naomi Wulf. "French Translations and Reception of the Declaration of Independence." *Journal of American History* 85 (March 1999): 1299–1324.

McDowell, R. B. *Irish Public Opinion, 1750–1800.* London: Faber and Faber, 1944.

Morris, Richard B. *The Emerging Nations and the American Revolution.* New York: Harper and Row, 1970.

O'Connell, Maurice R. *Irish Politics and Social Conflict in the Age of the American Revolution.* Philadelphia: University of Pennsylvania Press, 1965.

Oltra, Joaquim. "Jefferson's Declaration of Independence in the Spanish Political Tradition." *Journal of American History* 85 (March 1999): 1370–1379.

Palmer, R. R. *The Age of the Democratic Revolution: A Political History of Europe and America,*

*1760–1800.* 2 vols. Princeton: Princeton University Press, 1964.

Plumb, J. H. "The Impact of the American Revolution on Great Britain." In *The Impact of the American Revolution Abroad.* Ed. Library of Congress. Washington, D.C.: Library of Congress, Symposia on the American Revolution, 1976, 65–80.

_____. "Political Man." In *Man Versus Society in Eighteenth-Century Britain.* Ed. James L. Clifford. Cambridge: Cambridge University Press, 1968, 1–21.

Rahv, Philip, ed. *Discovery of Europe: The Story of American Experience in the Old World.* Garden City, N.J.: Anchor Books, 1960.

Schulte Nordholt, Jan Willem. *The Dutch Republic and American Independence,* trans. Herbert H. Rowen. Chapel Hill: University of North Carolina Press, 1982.

_____. "The Impact of the American Revolution on the Dutch Republic." In *The Impact of the American Revolution Abroad.* Ed. Library of Congress. Washington, D.C.: Library of Congress, Symposia on the American Revolution, 1976, 41–64.

Smith, J. Allen. *The Spirit of American Government.* Cambridge: Harvard University Press, 1965.

Stourzh, Gerald. "The Declaration of Rights: Popular Sovereignty and the Supremacy of the Constitution: Divergences between the American and French Revolutions." In *La Révolution Américaine et L'Europe.* Ed. Claude Fohlen and Jacques Godechot. Paris: Colloques Internationaux, No. 577, Centre National de la Recherche Scientifique, 1979, 347–367.

Thelen, David, ed. *The Constitution and American Life.* Ithaca: Cornell University Press, 1988.

_____. "Individual Creativity and the Filters of Language and Culture: Interpreting the Declaration of Independence by Translation." *Journal of American History* 85 (March 1999): 1289–1298.

Thomas, Emory M. *The Confederacy as a Revolutionary Experience.* Englewood Cliffs, N.J.: Prentice-Hall, 1971.

Troen, S. Ilan. "The Hebrew Translation of the Declaration of Independence." *Journal of American History* 85 (March 1999): 1380–1384.

Vazquez, Josefina Zoraida. "The Mexican Declaration of Independence." *Journal of American History* 85 (March 1999): 1362–1369.

Vlasova, Marina A. "The American Declaration of Independence in Russian: The History of Translation and the Translation of History." *Journal of American History* 85 (March 1999): 1399–1408.

Wakelyn, Jon L. *Southern Pamphlets on Secession: November 1860–April 1861.* Chapel Hill: University of North Carolina Press, 1996.

# Documents

*(keyed to relevant chapter)*

# 1.1    John Adams's Copy of the Declaration of Independence

*John Adams (1735–1826), a member of the congressional committee appointed to draft a Declaration of Independence, made a copy of Thomas Jefferson's draft before it was circulated to other members of the committee. Adams's copy is the earliest surviving unedited complete copy of the Declaration. It serves as a vital benchmark in analyzing the drafting of the document. The final version of the Declaration precedes Chapter 1.*

A Declaration by the Representatives of the United States of America in general Congress assembled

When in the Course of human Events it becomes necessary for a People to advance from that Subordination, in which they have hitherto remained and to assume among the Powers of the Earth, the equal and independent Station to which the Laws of Nature and of Nature's God entitle them, a decent Respect to the opinions of Mankind requires that they should declare the Causes, which impell them to the Change.

We hold these Truths to be self evident; that all Men are created equal and independant; that from that equal Creation they derive Rights inherent and unalienable; among which are the Preservation of Life, and Liberty, and the Pursuit of Happiness; that to secure these Ends, Governments are instituted among Men, deriving their just Powers from the Consent of the governed; that whenever, any form of Government, shall become destructive of these Ends, it is the Right of the People to alter, or to abolish it, and to institute new Government, laying its Foundation on such Principles, and organizing its Powers in such Form, as to them shall Seem most likely to effect their Safety and Happiness. Prudence indeed will dictate that Governments long established should not be changed for light and transient Causes; and accordingly all Experience hath shown, that Mankind are more disposed to Suffer, while Evils are Sufferable, than to right themselves, by abolishing the Forms to which they are accustomed. But when a long Train of Abuses and Usurpations, begun at a distinguish'd Period, and pursuing invariably, the Same Object, evinces a Design

to reduce them under absolute Power, it is their Right, it is their Duty, to throw off Such Government, and to provide new Guards for their future Security. Such has been the patient Sufferance of these Colonies; and such is now the Necessity, which constrains them to expunge their former Systems of Government. The History of his present Majesty, is a History of unremitting Injuries and Usurpations, among which no one Fact stands Single or Solitary to contradict the Uniform Tenor of the rest, all of which have in direct object, the Establishment of an absolute Tyranny over these States. To prove this, let Facts be Submitted to a candid World, for the Truth of which We pledge a Faith, as yet unsullied by Falsehood.

He has refused his Assent to Laws, the most wholesome and necessary for the public Good.

He has forbidden his Governors to pass Laws of immediate and pressing Importance, unless suspended in their operations, till his Assent should be obtained; and when so suspended he has neglected utterly to attend to them.

He has refused to pass other Laws for the Accommodation of large Districts of People, unless those People would relinquish the Right of Representation in the Legislature, a Right inestimable to them, and formidable to Tyrants only.

He has dissolved Representative Houses, repeatedly, and continuously, for opposing with manly Firmness his Invasions on the Rights of the People.

He has refused, for a long Space of Time after such Dissolutions, to cause others to be elected, whereby the legislative Powers, incapable of annihilation, have returned to the People at large for their Exercise, the State remaining in the mean Time, exposed to all the Dangers of Invasion, from without, and Convulsions within.

He has endeavoured to prevent the Population of these States; for that purpose obstructing the Laws for naturalization of foreigners; refusing to pass others to encourage their Migrations hither; and raising the Conditions of new Appropriations of Lands.

He has suffered the Administration of Justice totally to cease in some of these Colonies, refusing his Assent to Laws for establishing Judiciary Powers.

He has made our Judges dependent on his Will alone, for the Tenure of their offices, and amount of their Salaries:

He has erected a Multitude of new offices by a Self-assumed Power, and sent hither swarms of officers to harrass our People and eat out their Substance.

He has kept among us, in Times of Peace, Standing Armies and Ships of War.

He has affected to render the military, independent of, and Superiour to, the Civil Power.

He has combined with others to subject us to a Jurisdiction foreign to our Constitution and unacknowledged by our Laws; giving his Assent to their pretended Acts of Legislation; for quartering large Bodies of armed Troops among us; for protecting them by a Mock Tryal from Punishment for any Murders they should commit on the Inhabitants of these States; for cutting off our Trade with all Parts of the World; for imposing Taxes on us without our Consent; for depriving Us of the Benefits of Trial by Jury; for transporting us beyond Seas to be tried for pretended offenses; for taking away our Charters, and altering fundamentally the Forms of our Government; for suspending our own Legislatures and declaring themselves invested with Power to legislate for us in all Cases Whatsoever.

He has abdicated Government here, withdrawing his Governors, and declaring us, out of his Allegiance and Protection.

He has plundered our Seas, ravaged our Coasts, burnt our Towns, and destroyed the Lives of our People.

He is at this Time transporting large Armies of foreign Mercenaries to compleat the Works of death, Desolation, and Tyranny, already begun with Circumstances of Cruelty and Perfidy unworthy the Head of a civilized Nation.

He has endeavoured to bring on the Inhabitants of our Frontiers, the merciless Indian Savages, whose known Rule of Warfare is an undistinguished Destruction of all Ages, Sexes, and Conditions of existence.

He has incited treasonable Insurrections our Fellow Citizens, with the Allurement of Forfeiture and Confiscation of our Property.

He has waged cruel War against human Nature itself, violating its most sacred Rights of Life and Liberty in the Persons of a distant People who never offended him, captivating and carrying them into Slavery in another Hemisphere, or to incur miserable Death, in their Transportation thither. This piratical Warfare, the opprobrium of infidel Powers, is the Warfare of the Christian King of Great Britain.

He has prostituted his Negative for Suppressing every legislative Attempt to prohibit or to restrain an execrable Commerce, determined to keep open a Markett where Men Should be bought and sold. And that this assemblage of Horrors might want no Fact of distinguished Die.

He is now exciting those very People to rise in Arms among us, and to purchase their Liberty of which he has deprived them, by murdering the People upon whom he also obtruded them: thus paying off, former Crimes committed against the Liberties of one People, with Crimes which he urges them to commit against the Lives of another.

In every Stage of these oppressions we have petitioned for redress, in the most humble Terms; our repeated Petitions have been answered by repeated Injury. A Prince, whose Character is thus marked by every Act which may define a Tyrant, is unfit to be the Ruler of a People who mean to be free. future Ages will Scarce believe, that the Hardiness of one Man, adventured, within the Short Compass of twelve years only, on so many Acts of Tyranny, without a Mask, over a People, fostered and fixed in the Principles of Liberty.

Nor have we been wanting in Attentions to our British Brethren. We have warned them from Time to Time of attempts of their Legislature to extend a Jurisdiction over these our States. We have reminded them of the Circumstances of our Emigration and Settlement here, no one of which could warrant So Strange a Pretension. That these were effected at the expense of our own Blood and Treasure, unassisted by the Wealth or the Strength of Great Britain: that in constituting indeed, our Several Forms of Government, We have adopted one common King, thereby laying a Foundation for Perpetual League and Amity with them; but that Submission to their Parliament, was no Part of our Constitution, nor ever in Idea, if History may be credited; and we appealed to their Native Justice and Magnanimity, as well as to the Ties of our common Kindred to disavow these usurpations, which were likely to interrupt our Correspondence and Connection. They too have been deaf to the Voice of Justice and of Consanguinity, and when occasions have been given them by the regular Course of their Laws of removing from their Councils, the Disturbers of our Harmony, they have by their free Election, re-established them in Power. At this very Time too, they are permitting their Chief Magistrate to send over not only soldiers of our common Blood, but Scotch and foreign Mercenaries, to invade and deluge us in Blood. These Facts

have given the last Stab to agonizing affection and manly Spirit bids us to renounce forever these unfeeling Brethren. We must endeavour to forget our former Love for them, and to hold them, as we hold the rest of Mankind, enemies in War, in Peace Friends. We might have been a free and a great People together but a Communication of Grandeur and of Freedom it seems is below their Dignity. Be it so, since they have it: The Road to Happiness and to Glory is open to us too; We will climb it, apart from them, and acquiesce in the Necessity which denounces our eternal Separation.

We therefore the representatives of the United States of America in General Congress assembled, do, in the Name, and by the Authority of the good People of these States, reject and renounce all Allegiance and Subjection to the Kings of Great Britain, and all others, who may hereafter claim by, through, or under them; We utterly dissolve and break off, all political Connection which may have heretofore Subsisted between us and the People or Parliament of Great Britain, and finally We do assert and declare these Colonies to be free and independant States, and that as free and independant States they shall hereafter have Power to levy War, conclude Peace, contract Alliances, establish Commerce, and to do all other Acts and Things which independent States may of Right do. And for the Support of this Declaration, we mutually pledge to each other our Lives, our Fortunes, and our Sacred Honour.

---

## 1.2    The Declaration of Independence as Revised by the Continental Congress

*Thomas Jefferson (1743–1826) prepared the following revised copy of the Declaration of Independence to show friends, such as James Madison (1751–1836). Jefferson indicated changes to the document made after it was presented to Congress on June 28, 1776. Words written in the margin by Jefferson are in { } brackets and placed where Jefferson had marked the text with a caret. The parts deleted by Congress are underlined. Jefferson also placed [ ] brackets around many of the deletions.*

A Declaration by the representatives of the United States of America, in [General] Congress assembled

When in the course of human events it becomes necessary for one people to dissolve the political bands which have connected them with another, & to assume among the powers of the earth the separate & equal station to which the laws of nature & of nature's god entitle them, a decent respect to the opinions of mankind requires that they should declare the causes which impel them to the separation.

We hold these truths to be self evident: that all men are created equal; that they are endowed by their creator with {certain} <u>inherent &</u> inalienable rights; that among these are life, liberty & the pursuit of happiness: that to secure these rights, governments are instituted among men, deriving their just powers from the consent of the governed; that whenever any form of government becomes destructive of these ends, it is the right of the people to alter or to abolish it, & to institute new government, laying it's foundation on such principles, & organising it's powers in such form, as to them shall seem most likely to effect their safety & happiness. prudence indeed will dictate that governments long established should not be changed for light & transient causes; and accordingly all experience hath shewn that mankind are more disposed to suffer while evils are sufferable than to right themselves by abolishing the forms to which they are accustomed. but when a long train of abuses & usurpations [<u>begun at a distinguished period and</u>] pursuing invariably the same object, evinces a design to reduce them under absolute despotism, it is their right, it is their duty to throw off such government, & to provide new guards for their future security. such has been the patient sufferance of these colonies, & such is now the necessity which constrains them to {alter} [<u>expunge</u>] their former systems of government: the history of the present king of Great Britain is a history of {repeated} [<u>unremitting</u>] injuries & usurpations, [<u>among which appears no solitary fact to contradict the uniform tenor of the rest but all have</u>] {all having} in direct object the establishment of an absolute tyranny over these states. to prove this let facts be submitted to a candid world [<u>for the truth of which we pledge a faith yet unsullied by falsehood.</u>]

he has refused his assent to laws the most wholsome & necessary for the public good.

he has forbidden his governors to pass laws of immediate & pressing importance, unless suspended in their operation till his assent should be obtained; & when so suspended, he has utterly neglected to attend to them.

he has refused to pass other laws for the accommodation of large districts of people, unless those people would relinquish the right of representation in the legislature, a right inestimable to them, & formidable to tyrants only.

he has called together legislative bodies at places unusual, uncomfortable, & distant from the depository of their public records, for the sole purpose of fatiguing them into compliance with his measures.

he has dissolved representative houses repeatedly [<u>& continually</u>] for opposing with manly firmness his invasions on the rights of the people.

he has refused for a long time after such dissolutions to cause others to be elected, whereby the legislative powers, incapable to annihilation, have returned to the people at large for their exercise, the state remaining in the mean time exposed to all the dangers of invasion from without & convulsions within.

he has endeavored to prevent the population of these states; for that purpose obstructing the laws for naturalization of foreigners, refusing to pass others to encourage their migrations hither, & raising the conditions of new appropriations of lands.

he has {obstructed} [<u>suffered</u>] the administration of justice [<u>totally to cease in some of these states</u>] {by} refusing his assent to laws for establishing judiciary powers.

he has made [<u>our</u>] judges dependant on his will alone, for the tenure of their offices, & the amount & paiment of their salaries.

he has erected a multitude of new offices [<u>by a self assumed power</u>] and sent hither swarms of new officers to harrass our people and eat out their substance.

he has kept among us in times of peace standing armies [<u>& ships of war</u>] without the consent of our legislatures.

he has affected to render the military independant of, & superior to the civil power.

he has combined with others to subject us to a jurisdiction foreign to our constitutions & unacknoleged by our laws, giving his assent to their acts of pretended legislation for quartering large bodies of armed troops among us; for protecting them by a mock trial from punishment for any murders which they should commit on the inhabitants of these states; for cutting off our trade with all parts of the world; for imposing taxes on us without our consent; for depriving us {in many cases} of the benefits of trial by jury; for transporting us beyond seas to be tried for pretended offences; for abolishing the free system of English laws in a neighboring province, establishing therein an arbitrary government, and enlarging it's boundaries, so as to render it at once an example and fit instrument for introducing the same absolute rule into these {colonies} [states]; for taking away our charters, abolishing our most valuable laws, and altering fundamentally the forms of our governments; for suspending our own legislatures, & declaring themselves invested with power to legislate for us in all cases whatsoever.

he has abdicated government here {by declaring us out of his protection & waging war against us} [withdrawing his governors, & declaring us out of his allegiance & protection.]

he has plundered our seas, ravaged our coasts, burnt our towns, & destroyed the lives of our people.

he is at this time transporting large armies of foreign mercenaries to compleat the works of death, desolation & tyranny already begun with circumstances of cruelty and perfidy {scarcely paralleled in the most barbarous ages, & totally} unworthy the head of a civilized nation.

he has constrained our fellow citizens taken captive on the high seas to bear arms against their country, to become the executioners of their friends & brethren, or to fall themselves by their hands.

he has {excited domestic insurrections amongst us, & has} endeavored to bring on the inhabitants of our frontiers the merciless Indian savages, whose known rule of warfare is an undistinguished destruction of all ages, sexes, & conditions [of existence.]

[he has incited treasonable insurrections of our fellow-citizens, with the allurements of forfeiture & confiscation of our property.

he has waged cruel war against human nature itself, violating it's most sacred rights of life & liberty in the persons of a distant people who never offended him, captivating & carrying them into slavery in another hemisphere or to incur miserable death in their transportation thither. this piratical warfare, the opprobrium of *infidel* powers, is the warfare of the *Christian* king of Great Britain. determined to keep open a market where *Men* should be bought & sold, he has prostituted his negative for suppressing every legislative attempt to prohibit or to restrain this execrable commerce. and that this assemblage of horrors might want no fact of distinguished die, he is now exciting those very people to rise in arms among us, and to purchase that liberty of which he has deprived them, by murdering the people on whom he also obtruded them: thus paying off former crimes committed against the *Liberties* of one people, with crimes which he urges them to commit against the *lives* of another.]

In every stage of these oppressions we have petitioned for redress in the most humble terms: our repeated petitions have been answered only by repeated injuries. a prince whose character is thus marked by every act which may define a tyrant is unfit to be the ruler of a {free} people [who mean to be free. future ages will scarcely believe that the hardiness of one man adventured, within the short compass of twelve years only, to lay a foundation so broad & so undisguised for tyranny over a people fostered & fixed in principles of freedom.]

Nor have we been wanting in attentions to our British brethren. we have warned them from time to time of attempts by their legislature to extend {an unwarrantable} [a] jurisdiction over {us} [these our states.] we have reminded them of the circumstances of our emigration & settlement here, [no one of which could warrant so strange a pretention: that these were effected at the expence of our own blood & treasure, unassisted by the wealth or the strength of Great Britain: that in constituting indeed our several forms of gov-ernment, we had adopted one common king, thereby laying a foundation for perpetual league & amity with them: but that submission to their parliament was no part of our constitution, nor ever in idea, if history may be credited: and,] we {have} appealed to their native justice and mag-nanimity {and we have conjured them by} [as well as to] the ties of our common kindred to disavow these usurpations which {would inevitably} [were likely to] interrupt our connection and corre-spondence. they too have been deaf to the voice of justice & of consanguinity, [and when occa-sions have been given them, by the regular course of their laws, of removing from their councils the disturbers of our harmony, they have, by their free election, re-established them in power. at this very time too they are permitting their chief mag-istrate to send over not only soldiers of our com-mon blood, but Scotch & foreign mercenaries to invade & destroy us. these facts have given the last stab to agonizing affection, and manly spirit bids us to renounce for ever these unfeeling brethren. we must endeavor to forget our former love for them, and to hold them as we hold the rest of mankind enemies in war, in peace friends. we might have been a free & a great people to-gether; but a communication of grandeur & of freedom it seems is below their dignity. be it so, since they will it. the road to happiness & to glory is open to us too. we will treat it apart from

them, and] {we must therefore} acquiesce in the necessity which denounces our [eternal] separa-tion {and hold them as we hold the rest of mankind enemies in war, in peace friends}.

We therefore the representatives of the United States of America in General Congress assembled {appealing to the supreme judge of the world for the rectitude of our intentions} do in the name, & by the authority of the good people of these [states reject & renounce all allegiance & subjec-tion to the kings of Great Britain & all others who may hereafter claim by, through or under them: we utterly dissolve all political connection which may heretofore have subsisted between us & the people or parliament of Great Britain: & finally we do assert & declare these colonies to be free & independant states,] {colonies, solemnly publish & declare that these United colonies are & of right ought to be free & independant states: that they are absolved from all allegiance to the British crown, and that all political connection between them & the state of Great Britain is, & ought to be, totally dissolved;} and that as free & independant states, they have full power to levy war, conclude peace, contract alliances, establish commerce, & to do all other acts & things which independant states may of right do. and for the support of this declaration {with a firm reliance on the protection of divine providence} we mu-tually pledge our lives, our fortunes & our sacred honor.

---

*1.3*  **Thomas Jefferson's *A Summary View of the Rights of British America*, 1774**

*Thomas Jefferson intended his* A Summary View of the Rights of British America *to serve as instruc-tions to the Virginia delegates to the First Continental Congress. Here Jefferson asserts that America has always been free and independent, condemns British support for the slave trade, and provides a long list of abuses by the King and parliament. All of these concepts were refined and found voice in his draft of the Declaration of Independence.*

Resolved, that it be an instruction to the said deputies, when assembled in general congress with the deputies from the other states of British

America, to propose to the said congress that an humble and dutiful address be presented to his majesty, begging leave to lay before him, as chief magistrate of the British empire, the united complaints of his majesty's subjects in America; complaints which are excited by many unwarrantable encroachments and usurpations, attempted to be made by the legislature of one part of the empire, upon those rights which God and the laws have given equally and independently to all. To represent to his majesty that these his states have often individually made humble application to his imperial throne to obtain, through its intervention, some redress of their injured rights, to none of which was ever even an answer condescended; humbly to hope that this their joint address, penned in the language of truth, and divested of those expressions of servility which would persuade his majesty that we are asking favours, and not rights, shall obtain from his majesty a more respectful acceptance. And this his majesty will think we have reason to expect when he reflects that he is no more than the chief officer of the people, appointed by the laws, and circumscribed with definite powers, to assist in working the great machine of government, erected for their use, and consequently subject to their superintendance. And in order that these our rights, as well as the invasions of them, may be laid more fully before his majesty, to take a view of them from the origin and first settlement of these countries.

To remind him that our ancestors, before their emigration to America, were the free inhabitants of the British dominions in Europe, and possessed a right which nature has given to all men, of departing from the country in which chance, not choice, has placed them, of going in quest of new habitations, and of there establishing new societies, under such laws and regulations as to them shall seem most likely to promote public happiness. That their Saxon ancestors had, under this universal law, in like manner left their native wilds and woods in the north of Europe, had possessed themselves of the island of Britain, then less charged with inhabitants, and had established there that system of laws which has so long been the glory and protection of that country. Nor was ever any claim of superiority or dependence asserted over them by that mother country from

which they had migrated; and were such a claim made, it is believed that his majesty's subjects in Great Britain have too firm a feeling of the rights derived to them from their ancestors, to bow down the sovereignty of their state before such visionary pretensions. And it is thought that no circumstance has occurred to distinguish materially the British from the Saxon emigration. America was conquered, and her settlements made, and firmly established, at the expence of individuals, and not of the British public. Their own blood was spilt in acquiring lands for their settlement, their own fortunes expended in making that settlement effectual; for themselves they fought, for themselves they conquered, and for themselves alone they have right to hold. Not a shilling was ever issued from the public treasures of his majesty, or his ancestors, for their assistance, till of very late times, after the colonies had become established on a firm and permanent footing. That then, indeed, having become valuable to Great Britain for her commercial purposes, his parliament was pleased to lend them assistance against an enemy, who would fain have drawn to herself the benefits of their commerce, to the great aggrandizement of herself, and danger of Great Britain. Such assistance, and in such circumstances, they had often before given to Portugal, and other allied states, with whom they carry on a commercial intercourse; yet these states never supposed, that by calling in her aid, they thereby submitted themselves to her sovereignty. Had such terms been proposed, they would have rejected them with disdain, and trusted for better to the moderation of their enemies, or to a vigorous exertion of their own force. We do not, however, mean to under-rate those aids, which to us were doubtless valuable, on whatever principles granted; but we would shew that they cannot give a title to that authority which the British parliament would arrogate over us, and that they may amply be repaid by our giving to the inhabitants of Great Britain such exclusive privileges in trade as may be advantageous to them, and at the same time not too restrictive to ourselves. That settlements having been thus effected in the wilds of

America, the emigrants thought proper to adopt that system of laws under which they had hitherto lived in the mother country, and to continue their union with her by submitting themselves to the same common sovereign, who was thereby made the central link connecting the several parts of the empire thus newly multiplied.

But that not long were they permitted, however far they thought themselves removed from the hand of oppression, to hold undisturbed the rights thus acquired, at the hazard of their lives, and loss of their fortunes. A family of princes was then on the British throne, whose treasonable crimes against their people brought on them afterwards the exertion of those sacred and sovereign rights of punishment reserved in the hands of the people for cases of extreme necessity, and judged by the constitution unsafe to be delegated to any other judicature. While every day brought forth some new and unjustifiable exertion of power over their subjects on that side of the water, it was not to be expected that those here, much less able at that time to oppose the designs of despotism, should be exempted from injury.

Accordingly that country, which had been acquired by the lives, the labours, and the fortunes, of individual adventurers, was by these princes, at several times, parted out and distributed among the favourites and followers of their fortunes, and, by an assumed right of the crown alone, were erected into distinct and independent governments; a measure which it is believed his majesty's prudence and understanding would prevent him from imitating at this day, as no exercise of such a power, of dividing and dismembering a country, has ever occurred in his majesty's realm of England, though now of very antient standing; nor could it be justified or acquiesced under there, or in any other part of his majesty's empire.

That the exercise of a free trade with all parts of the world, possessed by the American colonists, as of natural right, and which no law of their own had taken away or abridged, was next the object of unjust encroachment. . . .

That these exercises of usurped power have not been confined to instances alone, in which themselves were interested, but they have also intermeddled with the regulation of the internal affairs of the colonies. The act of the 9th of Anne for establishing a post office in America seems to have had little connection with British convenience, except that of accommodating his majesty's ministers and favourites with the sale of a lucrative and easy office.

That thus have we hastened through the reigns which preceded his majesty's, during which the violations of our right were less alarming, because repeated at more distant intervals than that rapid and bold succession of injuries which is likely to distinguish the present from all other periods of American story. Scarcely have our minds been able to emerge from the astonishment into which one stroke of parliamentary thunder has involved us, before another more heavy, and more alarming, is fallen on us. Single acts of tyranny may be ascribed to the accidental opinion of a day; but a series of oppressions, begun at a distinguished period, and pursued unalterably through every change of ministers, too plainly prove a deliberate and systematical plan of reducing us to slavery. . . .

That these are the acts of power, assumed by a body of men, foreign to our constitutions, and unacknowledged by our laws, against which we do, on behalf of the inhabitants of British America, enter this our solemn and determined protest; and we do earnestly entreat his majesty, as yet the only mediatory power between the several states of the British empire, to recommend to his parliament of Great Britain the total revocation of these acts, which, however nugatory they be, may yet prove the cause of further discontents and jealousies among us.

That we next proceed to consider the conduct of his majesty, as holding the executive powers of the laws of these states, and mark out his deviations from the line of duty: By the constitution of Great Britain, as well as of the several American states, his majesty possesses the power of refusing to pass into a law any bill which has already passed the other two branches of legislature. His majesty, however, and his ancestors, conscious of the impropriety of opposing their single opinion to the united wisdom of two houses of parliament, while their proceedings were unbiassed by interested principles, for several ages past have modestly declined the exercise of this power in that part of his empire called Great Britain. But by change of circumstances, other principles than those of justice simply have obtained an influence on their determinations; the addition of new states to the British empire has produced an addition of new, and sometimes opposite interests. It is now, therefore, the great office of his majesty, to resume the exercise of his negative power, and to prevent the passage of laws by any one legislature of the empire, which might bear injuriously on the rights and interests of another. Yet this will not excuse the wanton exercise of this power which we have seen his majesty practise on the laws of the American legislatures. For the most trifling reasons, and sometimes for no conceivable reason at all, his majesty has rejected laws of the most salutary tendency. The abolition of domestic slavery is the great object of desire in those colonies, where it was unhappily introduced in their infant state. But previous to the enfranchisement of the slaves we have, it is necessary to exclude all further importations from Africa; yet our repeated attempts to effect this by prohibitions, and by imposing duties which might amount to a prohibition, have been hitherto defeated by his majesty's negative: Thus preferring the immediate advantages of a few African corsairs to the lasting interests of the American states, and to the rights of human nature, deeply wounded by this infamous practice. Nay, the single interposition of an interested individual against a law was scarcely ever known to fail of success, though in the opposite scale were placed the interests of a whole country. That this is so shameful an abuse of a power trusted with his majesty for other purposes, as if not reformed, would call for some legal restrictions.

With equal inattention to the necessities of his people here has his majesty permitted our laws to lie neglected in England for years, neither confirming them by his assent, nor annulling them by his negative; so that such of them as have no suspending clause we hold on the most precarious of all tenures, his majesty's will, and such of them as suspend themselves till his majesty's assent be obtained, we have feared, might be called into existence at some future and distant period, when time, and change of circumstances, shall have rendered them destructive to his people here. And to render this grievance still more oppressive, his majesty by his instructions has laid his governors under such restrictions that they can pass no law of any moment unless it have such suspending clause; so that, however immediate may be the call for legislative interposition, the law cannot be executed till it has twice crossed the atlantic, by which time the evil may have spent its whole force.

But in what terms, reconcileable to majesty, and at the same time to truth, shall we speak of a late instruction to his majesty's governor of the colony of Virginia, by which he is forbidden to assent to any law for the division of a county, unless the new county will consent to have no representative in assembly? That colony has as yet fixed no boundary to the westward. Their western counties, therefore, are of indefinite extent; some of them are actually seated many hundred miles from their eastern limits. Is it possible, then, that his majesty can have bestowed a single thought on the situation of those people, who, in order to obtain justice for injuries, however great or small, must, by the laws of that colony, attend their county court, at such a distance, with all their witnesses, monthly, till their litigation be determined? Or does his majesty seriously wish, and publish it to the world, that his subjects should give up the glorious right of representation, with all the benefits derived from that, and submit themselves the absolute slaves of his sovereign will? Or is it rather meant to confine the legislative body to their present numbers, that they may be the cheaper bargain whenever they shall become worth a purchase.

One of the articles of impeachment against Tresilian, and the other judges of Westminister Hall, in the reign of Richard the second, for which they suffered death, as traitors to their country, was, that they had advised the king that he might dissolve his parliament at any time; and succeeding kings have adopted the opinion of these unjust judges. . . . But how different their language and his practice here! To declare, as their duty required, the known rights of their country, to oppose the usurpations of every foreign judicature, to disregard the imperious mandates of a minister or governor, have been the avowed causes of dissolving houses of representatives in America. But if such powers be really vested in his majesty, can he suppose they are there placed to awe the members from such purposes as these? When the representative body have lost the confidence of their constituents, when they have notoriously made sale of their most valuable rights, when they have assumed to themselves powers which the people never put into their hands, then indeed their continuing in office becomes dangerous to the state, and calls for an exercise of the power of dissolution. Such being the causes for which the representative body should, and should not, be dissolved, will it not appear strange to an unbiassed observer, that that of Great Britain was not dissolved, while those of the colonies have repeatedly incurred that sentence?

But your majesty, or your governors, have carried this power beyond every limit known, or provided for, by the laws: After dissolving one house of representatives, they have refused to call another, so that, for a great length of time, the legislature provided by the laws has been out of existence. From the nature of things, every society must at all times possess within itself the sovereign powers of legislation. The feelings of human nature revolt against the supposition of a state so situated as that it may not in any emergency provide against dangers which perhaps threaten immediate ruin. While those bodies are in existence to whom the people have delegated the powers of legislation, they alone possess and may exercise those powers; but when they are dissolved by the lopping off one or more of their branches, the power reverts to the people, who may exercise it

to unlimited extent, either assembling together in person, sending deputies, or in any other way they may think proper. We forbear to trace consequences further; the dangers are conspicuous with which this practice is replete.

That we shall at this time also take notice of an error in the nature of our land holdings, which crept in at a very early period of our settlement. . . . Our ancestors, however, who migrated hither, were farmers, not lawyers. The fictitious principle that all lands belong originally to the king, they were early persuaded to believe real; and accordingly took grants of their own lands from the crown. And while the crown continued to grant for small sums, and on reasonable rents; there was no inducement to arrest the error, and lay it open to public view. But his majesty has lately taken on him to advance the terms of purchase, and of holding to the double of what they were; by which means the acquisition of lands being rendered difficult, the population of our country is likely to be checked. It is time, therefore, for us to lay this matter before his majesty, and to declare that he has no right to grant lands of himself. From the nature and purpose of civil institutions, all the lands within the limits which any particular society has circumscribed around itself are assumed by that society, and subject to their allotment only. This may be done by themselves, assembled collectively, or by their legislature, to whom they may have delegated sovereign authority; and if they are alloted in neither of these ways, each individual of the society may appropriate to himself such lands as he finds vacant, and occupancy will give him title.

That in order to enforce the arbitrary measures before complained of, his majesty has from time to time sent among us large bodies of armed forces, not made up of the people here, nor raised by the authority of our laws: . . .

To render these proceedings still more criminal against our laws, instead of subjecting the military to the civil powers, his majesty has expressly made the civil subordinate to the military. But can his majesty thus put down all law under his feet? Can he erect a power superior to that which erected himself? He has done it indeed by force; but let him remember that force cannot give right.

That these are our grievances which we have thus laid before his majesty, with that freedom of language and sentiment which becomes a free people claiming their rights, as derived from the laws of nature, and not as the gift of their chief magistrate: Let those flatter who fear; it is not an American art. To give praise which is not due might be well from the venal, but would ill beseem those who are asserting the rights of human nature. They know, and will therefore say, that kings are the servants, not the proprietors of the people. Open your breast, sire, to liberal and expanded thought. Let not the name of George the third be a blot in the page of history. You are surrounded by British counsellors, but remember that they are parties. You have no ministers for American affairs, because you have none taken from among us, nor amenable to the laws on which they are to give you advice. It behoves you, therefore, to think and to act for yourself and your people. The great principles of right and wrong are legible to every reader; to pursue them requires not the aid of many counsellors. The whole art of government consists in the art of being honest. Only aim to do your duty, and mankind will give you credit where you fail. No longer persevere in sacrificing the rights of one part of the empire to the inordinate desires of another; but deal out to all equal and impartial right. Let no act be passed by any one legislature which may infringe on the rights and liberties of another. This is the important post in which fortune has placed you, holding the balance of a great, if a well poised empire. This, sire, is the advice of your great American council, on the observance of which may perhaps depend your felicity and future fame, and the preservation of that harmony which alone can continue both to Great Britain and America the reciprocal advantages of their connection. It is neither our wish, nor our interest, to separate from her. We are willing, on our part, to sacrifice every thing which reason can ask to the restoration of that tranquillity for which all must wish. On their part, let them be ready to establish union and a generous plan. Let them name their terms, but let them be just. Accept of every commercial preference it is in our power to give for such things as we can raise for their use, or they make for ours. But let them not think to exclude us from going to other markets to dispose of those commodities which they cannot use, or to supply those wants which they cannot supply. Still less let it be proposed that our properties within our own territories shall be taxed or regulated by any power on earth but our own. The God who gave us life gave us liberty at the same time; the hand of force may destroy, but cannot disjoin them. This, sire, is our last, our determined resolution; and that you will be pleased to interpose with that efficacy which your earnest endeavours may ensure to procure redress of these our great grievances, to quiet the minds of your subjects in British America, against any apprehensions of future encroachment, to establish fraternal love and harmony through the whole empire, and that these may continue to the latest ages of time, is the fervent prayer of all British America!

*1.4*   ## The Virginia Declaration of Rights, Adopted June 12, 1776

*The Virginia Declaration of Rights, drafted by George Mason (1725–1792) and Thomas Ludwell Lee (1730–1778), was a key document in galvanizing the thoughts of Thomas Jefferson about independence and the rights of men. It is not mere coincidence that both documents asserted that all men are by nature equally free and cited life, liberty, and the pursuit of happiness as fundamental rights.*

A DECLARATION OF RIGHTS made by the representatives of the good people of Virginia, assembled in full and free convention which rights do pertain to them and their posterity, as the basis and foundation of government.

Section 1. That all men are by nature equally free and independent and have certain inherent rights, of which, when they enter into a state of society, they cannot, by any compact, deprive or divest their posterity; namely, the enjoyment of life and liberty, with the means of acquiring and possessing property, and pursuing and obtaining happiness and safety.

Section 2. That all power is vested in, and consequently derived from, the people; that magistrates are their trustees and servants and at all times amenable to them.

Section 3. That government is, or ought to be, instituted for the common benefit, protection, and security of the people, nation, or community; of all the various modes and forms of government, that is best which is capable of producing the greatest degree of happiness and safety and is most effectually secured against the danger of maladministration. And that, when any government shall be found inadequate or contrary to these purposes, a majority of the community has an indubitable, inalienable, and indefeasible right to reform, alter, or abolish it, in such manner as shall be judged most conducive to the public weal.

Section 4. That no man, or set of men, is entitled to exclusive or separate emoluments or privileges from the community, but in consideration of public services; which, nor being descendible, neither ought the offices of magistrate, legislator, or judge to be hereditary.

Section 5. That the legislative and executive powers of the state should be separate and distinct from the judiciary; and that the members of the two first may be restrained from oppression, by feeling and participating the burdens of the people, they should, at fixed periods, be reduced to a private station, return into that body from which they were originally taken, and the vacancies be supplied by frequent, certain, and regular elections, in which all, or any part, of the former members, to be again eligible, or ineligible, as the laws shall direct.

Section 6. That elections of members to serve as representatives of the people, in assembly ought to be free; and that all men, having sufficient evidence of permanent common interest with, and attachment to, the community, have the right of suffrage and cannot be taxed or deprived of their property for public uses without their own consent or that of their representatives so elected, nor bound by any law to which they have not, in like manner, assembled for the public good.

Section 7. That all power of suspending laws, or the execution of laws, by any authority, without consent of the representatives of the people, is injurious to their rights and ought not to be exercised.

Section 8. That in all capital or criminal prosecutions a man has a right to demand the cause and nature of his accusation, to be confronted with the accusers and witnesses, to call for evidence in his favor, and to a speedy trial by an impartial jury of twelve men of his vicinage, without whose unanimous consent he cannot be found guilty; nor can he be compelled to give evidence against himself; that no man be deprived of his liberty except by the law of the land or the judgment of his peers.

Section 9. That excessive bail ought not to be required, nor excessive fines imposed, nor cruel and unusual punishments inflicted.

Section 10. That general warrants, whereby an officer or messenger may be commanded to search suspected places without evidence of a fact committed, or to seize any person or persons not named, or whose offense is not particularly described and supported by evidence, are grievous and oppressive and ought not to be granted.

Section 11. That in controversies respecting property, and in suits between man and man, the ancient trial by jury is preferable to any other and ought to be held sacred.

Section 12. That the freedom of the press is one of the great bulwarks of liberty, and can never be restrained but by despotic governments.

Section 13. That a well-regulated militia, composed of the body of the people, trained to arms, is the proper, natural, and safe defense of a free state; that standing armies, in time of peace, should be avoided as dangerous to liberty; and

that in all cases the military should be under strict subordination to, and governed by, the civil power.

Section 14. That the people have a right to uniform government; and, therefore, that no government separate from or independent of the government of Virginia ought to be erected or established within the limits thereof.

Section 15. That no free government, or the blessings of liberty, can be preserved to any people but by a firm adherence to justice, moderation, temperance, frugality, and virtue and by frequent recurrence to fundamental principles.

Section 16. That religion, or the duty which we owe to our Creator, and the manner of discharging it, can be directed only by reason and conviction, not by force or violence; and therefore all men are equally entitled to the free exercise of religion, according to the dictates of conscience; and that it is the mutual duty of all to practise Christian forbearance, love, and charity toward each other.

---

## 1.5 Preamble to the Virginia Constitution, Adopted June 29, 1776

*Thomas Jefferson considered the writing of the Virginia Constitution one, if not the most, important object of the American Revolution. He wrote no less than three drafts of the constitution before beginning to draft the Declaration of Independence. His charges against the king, which are the backbone of the Declaration, were included as the preamble to the Virginia Constitution.*

WHEREAS *George* the third, king of *Great Britain* and *Ireland,* and elector of *Hanover,* heretofore intrusted with the exercise of the kingly office in this government, hath endeavoured to pervert the same into a detestable and insupportable tyranny,

By putting his negative on laws the most wholesome and necessary for the publick good:

By denying his governours permission to pass laws of immediate and pressing importance, unless suspended in their operation for his assent, and, when so suspended, neglecting to attend to them for many years:

By refusing to pass certain other laws, unless the persons to be benefitted by them would relinquish the inestimable right of representation in the legislature:

By dissolving legislative Assemblies repeatedly and continually, for opposing with manly firmness his invasions of the rights of the people:

When dissolved, by refusing to call others for a long space of time, thereby leaving the political system without any legislative head:

By endeavouring to prevent the population of our country, and, for that purpose, obstructing the laws for the naturalization of foreigners:

By keeping among us, in times of peace, standing armies and ships of war:

By affecting to render the military independent of, and superiour to, the civil power:

By combining with others to subject us to a foreign jurisdiction, giving his assent to their pretended acts of legislation:

For quartering large bodies of armed troops among us:

For cutting off our trade with all parts of the world:

For imposing taxes on us without our consent:

For depriving us of the benefits of trial by jury:

For transporting us beyond seas, to be tried for pretended offences:

For suspending our own legislatures, and declaring themselves invested with power to legislate for us in all cases whatsoever:

By plundering our seas, ravaging our coasts, burning our towns, and destroying the lives of our people:

By inciting insurrections of our fellow subjects, with the allurements of forfeiture and confiscation:

By prompting our negroes to rise in arms among us, those very negroes whom, by an inhuman use of his negative, he hath refused us permission to exclude by law:

By endeavouring to bring on the inhabitants of our frontiers the merciless Indian savages, whose known rule of warfare is an undistinguished destruction of all ages, sexes, and conditions of existence:

By transporting, at this time, a large army of foreign mercenaries, to complete the works of death, desolation, and tyranny, already begun with circumstances of cruelty and perfidy unworthy the head of a civilized nation:

By answering our repeated petitions for redress with a repetition of injuries:

And finally, by abandoning the helm of government, and declaring us out of his allegiance and protection.

By which several acts of misrule, the government of this country, as formerly exercised under the crown of *Great Britain,* IS TOTALLY DISSOLVED.

## 2.1 Verbal Parallels in the Declaration of Independence and *The Second Treatise of Government*

*John Locke (1632–1704) was the first political theorist to put the leading themes of liberalism into a coherent whole. The verbal parallels between his* Second Treatise of Government *and the* Declaration of Independence *illustrate the influence Locke's ideas had on the Declaration.*

### Human Nature

| Declaration of Independence | The Second Treatise of Government |
|---|---|
| "We hold these truths to be self-evident, that all men are created equal" | "Mankind . . . being all equal and independent" (Chapter 2, Section 6) |
| | "all men by nature are equal" (Chapter 4, Section 54) |
| | "Men being, as has been said, by Nature, all free, equal and independent" (Chapter 8, Section 95) |
| "that they are endowed by their Creator with certain unalienable rights" | "that equal Right that every man hath, to his Natural Freedom" (Chapter 6, Section 54) |
| "that among these are Life, Liberty, and the pursuit of Happiness" | "Man being born, as has been proved, with a Title to perfect Freedom, and an uncontrolled enjoyment of all the Rights and Privileges of the Law of Nature, equally with any other Man, or number of men in the world, hath by Nature a Power, not only to preserve his Property, that is, his Life, Liberty and Estate, against the Injuries and Attempts of other Men; but to judge of, and punish the breaches of that Law in others" (Chapter 7, Section 87) |
| | "Everyone as he is bound to preserve himself" (Chapter 2, Section 6) |
| | "Men, being once born, have a right to their preservation" (Chapter 5, Section 25) |

*(Continues)*

# 2.1    *(continued)*

## Government

| Declaration of Independence | The Second Treatise of Government |
|---|---|
| "to secure these rights, Governments are instituted among Men, deriving their just powers from the consent of the governed" | "Man . . . seeks . . . to joyn in society with others . . . to unite for the mutual Preservation of their Lives, Liberties and Estates" (Chapter 9, Section 123) |
| | "Civil Society is . . . agreeing with other Men to joyn and unite . . . in a secure Enjoyment of their Properties, and a Greater Security" (Chapter 8, Section 95) |
| "to provide new Guards for their future security" | "And thus that, which begins and actually constitutes any Political Society, is nothing but the consent . . . of a majority to unite and incorporate into such a society. And this is that, and that only, which did, or could give beginning to lawful Government in the World" (Chapter 8, Section 99) |
| | "The Liberty of Man, in society, is to be under no other Legislative Power, but that established, by consent" (Chapter 4, Section 22) |
| | "Political Power is that Power which every man having in the state of Nature, has given up into the hands of Society, and therein to the Governours. . . . That it shall be employed for their good, and the preservation of their Property . . . their Lives, Liberties, and Possessions . . . only from Compact and Agreement, and the mutual Consent of those who make up the Community" (Chapter 15, Section 171) |

*(Continues)*

## 2.1    *(continued)*

### Revolution

| Declaration of Independence | The Second Treatise of Government |
|---|---|
| "whenever any Form of Government becomes destructive of these ends, it is the Right of the People to alter or to abolish it, and to institute new Government" | "when the Government is dissolved, the People are at Liberty to provide for themselves, by erecting a new Legislative" (Chapter 19, Section 220) |
| "Prudence, indeed, will dictate that Governments long established should not be changed for light and transient causes" | "Revolutions happen not upon every little mismanagement in public affairs. Great mistakes in the ruling part, many wrong and inconvenient Laws, and all the slips of human frailty will be born by the people, without mutiny or murmur" (Chapter 19, Section 225) |
| "mankind are more disposed to suffer, while evils are sufferable, than to right themselves by abolishing the forms to which they are accustomed" | "the People, who are more disposed to suffer, than right themselves by Resistence" (Chapter 19, Section 230) |
| "But when a long train of abuses and usurpations, pursuing invariably the same Object evinces a design to reduce them under absolute Despotism" | "But if a long train of Abuses . . . all tending the same way, make the design visible to the People" (Chapter 19, Section 225) |
| "it is their right, it is their duty, to throw off such Government, and to provide new Guards for their future security" | " 'tis not to be wonder'd, that they should then rouze themselves, and endeavor to put the rule into such hands, which may secure them the ends for which Government was at first erected" (Chapter 19, Section 225) |

## 2.2 Aristotle's *The Politics*

*Aristotle (384–322 B.C.) was a leading ancient Greek philosopher. The following excerpts from his most influential book,* The Politics, *contain examples of several of the ideas that proponents of the Classical Republican interpretation of the Declaration of Independence find in America's founding document.*

### Nature and Origin of the State

Every state is a community of some kind, and every community is established with a view to some good; for mankind always act in order to obtain that which they think good. But, if all communities aim at some good, the state or political community, which is the highest of all, and which embraces all the rest, aims at good in a greater degree than any other, and at the highest good.

Some people think that the qualifications of a statesman, king, householder, and master are the same, and that they differ, not in kind, but only in the number of their subjects. For example, the ruler over a few is called a master; over more, the manager of a household; over a still larger number, a statesman or king, as if there were no difference between a great household and a small state. The distinction which is made between the king and the statesman is as follows: when the government is personal, the ruler is a king; when, according to the rules of the political science, the citizens rule and are ruled in turn, then he is called a statesman.

But all this is a mistake; for governments differ in kind, as will be evident to any one who considers the matter according to the method which has hitherto guided us. As in other departments of science, so in politics, the compound should always be resolved into the simple elements or least parts of the whole. We must therefore look at the elements of which the state is composed, in order that we may see in what the different kinds of rule differ from one another, and whether any scientific result can be attained about each one of them. . . .

### Citizenship

He who would inquire into the essence and attributes of various kinds of governments must first of all determine "What is a state?" At present this is a disputed question. Some say that the state has done a certain act; others, no, not the state, but the oligarchy or the tyrant. And the legislator or statesman is concerned entirely with the state; a constitution or government being an arrangement of the inhabitants of a state. But a state is composite, like any other whole made up of many parts;—these are the citizens, who compose it. It is evident, therefore, that we must begin by asking, "Who is the citizen," and what is the meaning of the term? For here again there may be a difference of opinion. He who is a citizen in a democracy will often not be a citizen in an oligarchy. Leaving out of consideration those who have been made citizens, or who have obtained the name of citizen in any other accidental manner, we may say, first, that a citizen is not a citizen because he lives in a certain place, for resident aliens and slaves share in the place; nor is he a citizen who has no legal right except that of suing and being sued; for this right may be enjoyed under the provisions of a treaty. Nay, resident aliens in many places do not possess even such rights completely, for they are obliged to have a patron, so that they do but imperfectly participate in citizenship, and we call them citizens only in a qualified sense, as we might apply the term to children who are too young to be on the register, or to old men who have been relieved from state duties. Of these we do not say quite simply that they are citizens, but add in the one case that they are not of age, and in the other, that they are past the age, or something of that sort; the precise expression is immaterial, for our meaning is clear. Similar difficulties to those which I have mentioned may be raised and answered about deprived citizens and about exiles. But the citizen whom we are seeking to define is a citizen in the strictest sense, against whom such exception can be taken, and his special characteristic is that he shares in the administration of justice, and in offices. Now of offices some are discontinuous, and the same persons are not allowed to hold them twice, or can only hold them after a fixed interval; others have no limit of time—for example, the office of dicast or ecclesiast. It may, indeed, be argued that these are not magistrates at all, and that their functions give them no share in the government. But surely it is ridiculous to say that those who have the supreme power do not govern. Let us not dwell further upon this, which is a purely verbal question; what we want is a common term including both dicast and ecclesiast. Let us, for the sake of distinction, call it "indefinite office," and we will assume that those who share in such office are citizens. This is the most comprehensive definition of a citizen, and best suits all those who are generally so called.

---

## 2.3   Cicero's *The Republic* and *The Laws*

*Marcus Tullius Cicero (106–43 B.C.) was a Roman orator, lawyer, politician, and philosopher. The following excerpts from two of his most influential works,* The Republic *and* The Laws, *contain examples of several of the ideas that proponents of the Classical Republican interpretation of the Declaration of Independence find in America's founding document, especially with regard to military virtue.*

[Without active patriotism we] . . . could [never] have delivered [our native land] from attack; nor could Gaius Duelius, Aulus Atilius, or Lucius Metellus have freed [Rome] from her fear of Carthage; nor could the two Scipios have extinguished with their blood the rising flames of the Second Punic War; nor, when it broke forth again with greater fury, could Quintus Maximus have reduced it to impotence or Marcus Marcelus have crushed it; nor could Pulius Africanus have torn it from the gates of this city and driven it within the enemy's walls. . . . I will content myself with asserting that Nature has implanted in the human race so great a need of virtue and so great a desire to defend the common safety that the strength thereof has conquered all the allurements of pleasure and ease.

. . . I could not hesitate to expose myself to the severest storms, and, I might almost say, even to thunderbolts, for the sake of the safety of my fellow-citizens, and to secure, at the cost of my own personal danger, a quiet life for all the rest.

For, in truth, our country has not given us birth and education without expecting to receive some sustenance, as it were, from us in return; nor has it been merely to serve our convenience that she has granted to our leisure a safe refuge and for our moments of repose a calm retreat; on the contrary, she has given us these advantages so that she may appropriate to her own use the greater and more important part of our courage, our talents, and our wisdom, leaving to us for our own private uses only so much as may be left after her needs have been satisfied.

. . . If [the State] leaves [the selection of its rulers] to chance, it will be as quickly overturned as a ship whose pilot should be chosen by lot from among the passengers. But if a free people chooses the men to whom it is to entrust its fortunes, and, since it desires its own safety, chooses the best men, then certainly the safety of the State depends upon the wisdom of its best men, especially since Nature has provided not only that those men who are superior in virtue and in spirit should rule the weaker, but also that the weaker should be willing to obey the stronger.

But they claim that this ideal form of State has been rejected on account of the false notions of men, who, through their ignorance of virtue—for just as virtue is possessed by only a few, so it can be distinguished and perceived by only a few—think that the best men are those who are rich, prosperous, or born of famous families. For when, on account of this mistaken notion of the common people, the state begins to be ruled by the riches, instead of the virtue, of a few men, these rulers tenaciously retain the title, though they do not possess the character of the "best." For riches, names, and power, when they lack wisdom and the knowledge of how to live and to rule over others, are full of dishonour and insolent pride, nor is there any more depraved type of State than that in which the richest are accounted the best.

## 2.4 John Calvin's *On Civil Government*

*John Calvin (1509–1564) was a leading thinker of the Protestant Reformation. The following excerpts from his most influential work,* On Civil Government, *contain examples of several of the ideas that proponents of the Christian interpretation of the Declaration of Independence find in America's founding document.*

Having already stated that man is the subject of two kinds of government, and having sufficiently discussed that which is situated in the soul, or the inner man, and relates to eternal life—we are, in this chapter, to say something of the other kind which relates to civil justice and the regulation of the external conduct. For, though the nature of this argument seems to have no connection with the spiritual doctrine of faith which I have undertaken to discuss, the sequel will show that I have sufficient reason for connecting them together, and, indeed, that necessity obliges me to it, especially since, on the one hand, infatuated and barbarous men madly endeavor to subvert this ordinance established by God, and, on the other hand, the flatterers of princes, extolling their power beyond all just bounds, hesitate not to oppose it to the authority of God himself. Unless both these errors be resisted, the purity of the faith will be destroyed. . . .

Yet this distinction does not lead us to consider the whole system of civil government as a polluted thing which has nothing to do with Christian men. Some fanatics who are pleased with nothing but liberty, or rather licentiousness without any restraint, do indeed boast and vociferate, that since we are dead with Christ to the elements of this world and, being translated into the kingdom of God, sit among the celestials, it is a degradation to us and far beneath our dignity to be occupied with those secular and impure cares which relate to things altogether uninteresting to a Christian man. Of what use, they ask, are laws without judgments and tribunals? But what have judgments to do with a Christian man? And if it be unlawful to kill, of what use are laws and judgments to us? But as we have just suggested that this kind of government is distinct from the spiritual and internal reign of Christ, so it ought to be known that they are in no respect at variance with each other. For that spiritual reign, even now upon earth, commences within us some preludes of the heavenly kingdom, and in this mortal and transitory life affords us some prelibations of immortal and incorruptible blessedness; but this civil government is designed, as long as we live in this world, to cherish and support the external worship of God, to preserve the pure doctrine of religion, to defend the constitution of the Church, to regulate our lives in a manner requisite for the society of men, to form our manners to civil justice, to promote our concord with each other, and to establish general peace and tranquility all of which I confess to be superfluous if the kingdom of God, as it now exists in us, extinguishes the present life. But if it is the will of God that while we are aspiring toward our true country, we be pilgrims on the earth, and if such aids are necessary to our pilgrimage, they who take them from man deprive him of his human nature. . . .

The Lord has not only testified that the function of magistrates has his approbation and acceptance, but has eminently commended it to us, by dignifying it with the most honorable titles. We will mention a few of them. When all who sustain the magistracy are called, "gods," it ought not to be considered as an appellation of trivial importance, for it implies that they have their command from God, that they are invested with his authority and are altogether his representatives, and act as his viceregents. This is not an invention of mine, but the interpretation of Christ, who says, "If he called them gods, unto whom the word of God came, and the Scripture cannot be broken." . . .

This consideration ought continually to occupy the magistrates themselves, since it is calculated to furnish them with a powerful stimulus by which they may be excited to their duty, and to afford them peculiar consolation by which the difficulties of their office, which certainly are many and arduous, may be alleviated. For what an ardent pursuit of integrity, prudence, clemency moderation, and innocence ought they to prescribe to themselves who are conscious of having been constituted ministers of the Divine justice! With what audacity will they pronounce an unjust sentence with that mouth which they know to be the destined organ of Divine truth? With what conscience will they subscribe to impious decrees with that hand which they know to be appointed to register the edicts of God? In short, if they remember that they are the viceregents of God, it behooves them to watch with all care, earnestness, and diligence, that in their administration they may exhibit to men an image, as it were, of the providence, care, goodness, benevolence, and justice of God. And they must constantly bear this in mind that if in all cases "he be cursed that doeth the word of the Lord deceitfully," a far heavier curse awaits those who act fraudulently in a righteous calling. . . .

And this admonition is entitled to have considerable weight with them; for if they fail in their duty, they not only injure men by criminally distressing them but even offend God by polluting his sacred judgments. On the other hand, it opens a source of peculiar consolation to them to reflect that they are not employed in profane things, or occupations unsuitable to a servant of God, but in a most sacred function, inasmuch as they execute a Divine commission.

---

## 3.1    Abraham Lincoln, Speech on the *Dred Scott* Decision, June 26, 1857

*Abraham Lincoln (1809–1865) delivered the following speech during his unsuccessful campaign to become a U.S. senator from Illinois. Stephen A. Douglas was elected to the seat, but Lincoln's speech criticizing the U.S. Supreme Court's decision in* Dred Scott v. Sandford *is probably the most famous speech about the Declaration of Independence delivered during the nineteenth century. Lincoln would later become the sixteenth president of the United States. He ranks as one of the greatest presidents in U.S. history because of his vital role in preserving the Union during the Civil War and beginning the process that led to the end of slavery.*

FELLOW CITIZENS:—I am here to-night, partly by the invitation of some of you, and partly by my own inclination. Two weeks ago Judge [Stephen A.] Douglas spoke here on the several subjects of

Kansas, the Dred Scott decision, and Utah. I listened to the speech at the time, and have read the report of it since. It was intended to controvert opinions which I think just, and to assail (politically, not personally,) those men who, in common with me, entertain those opinions. For this reason I wished then, and still wish, to make some answer to it, which I now take the opportunity of doing. . . .

And now as to the Dred Scott decision. That decision declares two propositions—first, that a negro cannot sue in the U.S. Courts; and secondly, that Congress cannot prohibit slavery in the Territories. It was made by a divided court—dividing differently on the different points. Judge Douglas does not discuss the merits of the decision; and, in that respect, I shall follow his example, believing I could no more improve on [Justice John] McLean and [Justice Benjamin R.] Curtis, than he could on [Chief Justice Roger B.] Taney.

He denounces all who question the correctness of that decision, as offering violent resistance to it. But who resists it? Who has, in spite of the decision, declared Dred Scott free, and resisted the authority of his master over him?

Judicial decisions have two uses—first, to absolutely determine the case decided, and secondly, to indicate to the public how other similar cases will be decided when they arise. For the latter use, they are called "precedents" and "authorities."

We believe, as much as Judge Douglas, (perhaps more) in obedience to, and respect for the judicial department of government. We think its decisions on Constitutional questions, when fully settled, should control, not only the particular cases decided, but the general policy of the country, subject to be disturbed only by amendments of the Constitution as provided in that instrument itself. More than this would be revolution. But we think the Dred Scott decision is erroneous. We know the court that made it, has often over-ruled its own decisions, and we shall do what we can to have it to over-rule this. We offer no *resistance* to it.

Judicial decisions are of greater or less authority as precedents, according to circumstances. That this should be so, accords both with com-

mon sense, and the customary understanding of the legal profession.

If this important decision had been made by the unanimous concurrence of the judges, and without any apparent partisan bias, and in accordance with legal public expectation, and with the steady practice of the departments throughout our history, and had been in no part, based on assumed historical facts which are not really true; or, if wanting in some of these, it had been before the court more than once, and had there been affirmed and re-affirmed through a course of years, it then might be, perhaps would be, factious, nay, even revolutionary, to not acquiesce in it as a precedent.

But when, as it is true we find it wanting in all these claims to the public confidence, it is not resistance, it is not factious, it is not even disrespectful, to treat it as not having yet quite established a settled doctrine for the country—But Judge Douglas considers this view awful. Hear him:

"The courts are the tribunals prescribed by the Constitution and created by the authority of the people to determine, expound and enforce the law. Hence, whoever resists the final decision of the highest judicial tribunal, aims a deadly blow to our whole Republican system of government—a blow, which if successful would place all our rights and liberties at the mercy of passion, anarchy and violence. I repeat, therefore, that if resistance to the decisions of the Supreme Court of the United States, in a matter like the points decided in the Dred Scott case, clearly within their jurisdiction as defined by the Constitution, shall be forced upon the country as a political issue, it will become a distinct and naked issue between the friends and the enemies of the Constitution—the friends and the enemies of the supremacy of the laws."

Why this same Supreme court once decided a national bank to be constitutional; but Gen. [Andrew] Jackson, as President of the United States, disregarded the decision, and vetoed a bill for a re-charter, partly on constitutional ground, declaring that each public functionary must support the Constitution, "as he understands it." . . .

I drop the quotations merely to remark that all there ever was, in the way of precedent up to the

Dred Scott decision, on the points therein decided, had been against that decision. . . .

Again and again have I heard Judge Douglas denounce that bank decision, and applaud Gen. Jackson for disregarding it. It would be interesting for him to look over his recent speech, and see how exactly his fierce philippics against us for resisting Supreme Court decisions, fall upon his own head. . . .

I have said, in substance, that the Dred Scott decision was, in part, based on assumed historical facts which were not really true; and I ought not to leave the subject without giving some reasons for saying this; I therefore give an instance or two, which I think fully sustain me. Chief Justice Taney, in delivering the opinion of the majority of the Court, insists at great length that negroes were no part of the people who made, or for whom was made, the Declaration of Independence, or the Constitution of the United States.

On the contrary, Judge Curtis, in his dissenting opinion, shows that in five of the then thirteen states, to wit, New Hampshire, Massachusetts, New York, New Jersey and North Carolina, free negroes were voters, and, in proportion to their numbers, had the same part in making the Constitution that the white people had. He shows this with so much particularity as to leave no doubt of its truth; and, as a sort of conclusion on that point, holds the following language:

"The Constitution was ordained and established by the people of the United States, through the action, in each State, of those persons who were qualified by its laws to act thereon in behalf of themselves and all other citizens of the State. In some of the States, as we have seen, colored persons were among those qualified by law to act on the subject. These colored persons were not only included in the body of 'the people of the United States,' by whom the Constitution was ordained and established; but in at least five of the States they had the power to act, and, doubtless, did act, by their suffrages, upon the question of its adoption."

Again, Chief Justice Taney says: "It is difficult, at this day to realize the state of public opinion in relation to that unfortunate race, which prevailed in the civilized and enlightened portions of the world at the time of the Declaration of Independence, and when the Constitution of the United States was framed and adopted." And again, after quoting from the Declaration, he says: "The general words above quoted would seem to include the whole human family, and if they were used in a similar instrument at this day, would be so understood."

In these the Chief Justice does not directly assert, but plainly assumes, as a fact, that the public estimate of the black man is more favorable *now* than it was in the days of the Revolution. This assumption is a mistake. In some trifling particulars, the condition of that race has been ameliorated; but, as a whole, in this country, the change between then and now is decidedly the other way; and their ultimate destiny has never appeared so hopeless as in the last three or four years. In two of the five States—New Jersey and North Carolina—that then gave the free negro the right of voting, the right has since been taken away; and in a third—New York—it has been greatly abridged; while it has not been extended, so far as I know, to a single additional State, though the number of the States has more than doubled. In those days, as I understand, masters could, at their own pleasure, emancipate their slaves; but since then, such legal restraints have been made upon emancipation, as to amount almost to prohibition. In those days, Legislatures held the unquestioned power to abolish slavery, in their respective States; but now it is becoming quite fashionable for State Constitutions to withhold that power from the Legislatures. In those days, by common consent, the spread of the black man's bondage to new countries was prohibited; but now, Congress decides that it will not continue the prohibition, and the Supreme Court decides that it *could* not if it would. In those days, our Declaration of Independence was held sacred by all, and thought to include all; but now, to aid in making the bondage of the negro universal and eternal, it is assailed, and sneered at, and construed, and hawked at, and torn, till, if its framers could rise from their graves, they could not at all recognize it. All the powers of earth seem rapidly combining against him. Mammon is after him; ambition follows, and philosophy follows, and the Theology of the day is fast joining the cry. They have him in his prison house; they have searched his person, and left no prying instrument with him. One after another they have closed the heavy iron doors upon him, and now they have him, as it were, bolted in with a lock of a hundred keys, which can never be unlocked without the concurrent of every key; the keys in the hands of a hundred different men, and they scattered to a hundred different and distant places; and they stand musing as to what invention, in all the dominions of mind and matter, can be produced to make the impossibility of his escape more complete than it is.

It is grossly incorrect to say or assume, that the public estimate of the negro is more favorable now than it was at the origin of the government. . . .

There is a natural disgust in the minds of nearly all white people, to the idea of an indiscriminate amalgamation of the white and black races; and Judge Douglas evidently is basing his chief hope, upon the chances of being able to appropriate the benefit of this disgust to himself. If he can, by much drumming and repeating, fasten the odium of that idea upon his adversaries, he thinks he can struggle through the storm. He therefore clings to this hope, as a drowning man to the last plank. He makes an occasion for lugging it in from the opposition to the Dred Scott decision. He finds the Republicans insisting that the Declaration of Independence includes ALL men, black as well as white; and forthwith he boldly denies that it includes negroes at all, and proceeds to argue gravely that all who contend it does, do so only because they want to vote, and eat, and sleep, and marry with negroes! He will have it that they cannot be consistent else. Now I protest against that counterfeit logic which concludes that, because I do not want a black woman for a *slave* I must necessarily want her for a *wife*. I need not have her for either, I can just leave her alone. In some respects she certainly is not my equal; but in her natural right to eat the bread she earns with her own hands without asking leave of any one else, she is my equal, and the equal of all others.

Chief Justice Taney, in his opinion in the Dred Scott case, admits that the language of the Declaration is broad enough to include the whole human family, but he and Judge Douglas argue that the authors of that instrument did not intend to include negroes, by the fact that they did not at once, actually place them on an equality with the whites. Now this grave argument comes to just nothing at all, by the other fact, that they did not at once, *or ever afterwards,* actually place all white people on an equality with one or another. And this is the staple argument of both the Chief Justice and the Senator, for doing this obvious violence to the plain unmistakable language of the Declaration. I think the authors of that notable instrument intended to include all men, but they did not intend to declare all men equal in all respects. They did not mean to say all were equal in color, size, intellect, moral developments, or social capacity. They defined with tolerable distinctness, in what respects they did consider all men created equal—equal in "certain inalienable rights, among which are life, liberty, and the pursuit of happiness." This they said, and this meant. They did not mean to assert the obvious untruth, that all were then actually enjoying that equality, nor yet, that they were about to confer it immediately upon them. In fact they had no power to confer such a boon. They meant simply to declare the *right,* so that the *enforcement* of it might follow as fast as circumstances should permit. They meant to set up a standard maxim for free society, which should be familiar to all, and revered by all; constantly looked to, constantly labored for, and even though never perfectly attained, constantly approximated, and thereby constantly spreading and deepening its influence, and augmenting the happiness and value of life to all people of all colors everywhere. The assertion that "all men are created equal" was of no practical use in effecting our separation from Great Britain; and it was placed in the Declaration, not for that, but for future use.

Its authors meant it to be, thank God, it is now proving itself, a stumbling block to those who in after times might seek to turn a free people back into the hateful paths of despotism. They knew the proneness of prosperity to breed tyrants, and they meant when such should re-appear in this fair land and commence their vocation they should find left for them at least one hard nut to crack.

I have now briefly expressed my view of the *meaning* and *objects* of that part of the Declaration of Independence which declares that "all men are created equal."

Now let us hear Judge Douglas' view of the same subject, as I find it in the printed report of his late speech. Here it is:

"No man can vindicate the character, motives and conduct of the signers of the Declaration of Independence, except upon the hypothesis that they referred to the white race alone, and not to the African, when they declared all men to have been created equal— that they were speaking of British subjects on this continent being equal to British subjects born and residing in Great Britain—that they were entitled to the same inalienable rights, and among them were enumerated life, liberty and the pursuit of happiness. The Declaration was adopted for the purpose of justifying the colonists in the eyes of the civilized world in withdrawing their allegiance from the British crown, and dissolving their connection with the mother country."

My good friends, read that carefully over some leisure hour, and ponder well upon it—see what a mere wreck—mangled ruin—it makes of our once glorious Declaration.

"They were speaking of British subjects on this continent being equal to British subjects born and residing in Great Britain!" Why, according to this, not only negroes but white people outside of Great Britain and America are not spoken of in that instrument. The English, Irish and Scotch, along with white Americans, were included to be sure, but the French, Germans and other white people of the world are all gone to pot along with the Judge's inferior races.

I had thought the Declaration promised something better than the condition of British subjects; but no, it only meant that we should be *equal* to them in their own oppressed and *unequal* condition. According to that, it gave no promise that having kicked off the King and Lords of Great Britain, we should not at once be saddled with a King and Lords of our own.

I had thought the Declaration contemplated the progressive improvement in the condition of all men everywhere; but no, it merely "was adopted for the purpose of justifying the colonists in the eyes of the civilized world in withdrawing their allegiance from the British crown, and dissolving their connection with the mother country." Why, that object having been effected some eighty years ago, the Declaration is of no practical use now—mere rubbish—old wadding left to rot on the battle-field after the victory is won.

I understand you are preparing to celebrate the "Fourth," to-morrow week. What for? The doings of that day had no reference to the present; and quite half of you are not even descendants of those who were referred to at that day. But I suppose you will celebrate; and will even go so far as to read the Declaration. Suppose after you read it once in the old fashioned way, you read it once more with Judge Douglas' version. It will then run thus: "We hold these truths to be self-evident that all British subjects who were on this continent eighty-one years ago, were created equal to all British subjects born and then residing in Great Britain."

And now I appeal to all—to Democrats as well as others,—are you really willing that the Declaration shall be thus frittered away?—thus left no more at most, than an interesting memorial of the dead past? thus shorn of its vitality, and practical value; and left without the *germ* or even the *suggestion* of the individual rights of man in it?

# 3.2    Abraham Lincoln, Fragment on the Constitution and the Union, January 1861

*The following excerpt illustrates that Abraham Lincoln remained committed to the ideals expressed in the Declaration of Independence after he was elected president of the United States.*

All this is not the result of accident. It has a philosophical cause. Without the *Constitution* and the *Union,* we could not have attained the result; but even these, are not the primary cause of our great prosperity. There is something back of these, entwining itself more closely about the human heart. That something is the principle of "Liberty to all"—the principle that clears the *path* for all—gives hope to all—and, by consequence, *enterprize,* and *industry* to all.

The *expression* of that principle, in our Declaration of Independence, was most happy, and fortunate. *Without* this, as well as with it, we could have declared our independence of Great Brittain; but without it, we could not, I think, have secured our free government, and consequent prosperity. No oppressed people will fight, and endure, as our fathers did, without the promise of something better, than a mere change of masters.

The assertion of that *principle,* at *that time,* was the word, *"fitly spoken"* which has proved an "apple of gold" to us. The Union, and the *Constitution,* are the *picture* of *silver,* subsequently framed around it. The picture was made, not to *conceal,* or *destroy* the apple; but to *adorn,* and *preserve* it. The *picture* was made for the apple—*not* the apple for the picture.

So let us act, that neither *picture,* or *apple* shall ever be blurred, or bruised or broken.

That we may so act, we must study, and understand the points of danger.

# 3.3    Abraham Lincoln, Speech at Independence Hall, Philadelphia, Pennsylvania, February 22, 1861

*The following excerpt likewise illustrates that Abraham Lincoln remained committed to the ideals expressed in the Declaration of Independence after he was elected president. No president has said more about the Declaration than Lincoln.*

I am filled with deep emotion at finding myself standing here in the place where were collected together the wisdom, the patriotism, the devotion to principle, from which sprang the institutions under which we live. You have kindly suggested to me that in my hands is the task of restoring peace to our distracted country. I can say in return, sir, that all the political sentiments I entertain have been drawn, so far as I have been able to draw them, from the sentiments which originated, and were given to the world from this hall in which we stand. I have never had a feeling politically that did not spring from the sentiments embodied in the Declaration of Independence. (Great cheering.) I have often pondered over the dangers which were incurred by the men who assembled here and adopted that Declaration of Independence—I have pondered over the toils that were endured by the officers and soldiers of the army, who achieved that Independence. (Applause.) I have often inquired of myself, what great principle or idea it was that kept this Confederacy so long together. It was not the mere matter of the separation of the colonies from the mother land; but something in that Declaration giving liberty, not alone to the people of this country, but hope to the world for all future time. (Great applause.) It was that which gave promise that in due time the weights should be lifted from the shoulders of all men, and that *all* should have an equal chance. (Cheers.) This is the sentiment embodied in that Declaration of Independence.

Now, my friends, can this country be saved upon that basis? If it can, I will consider myself one of the happiest men in the world if I can help to save it. If it can't be saved upon that principle, it will be truly awful. But, if this country cannot be saved without giving up that principle—I was about to say I would rather be assassinated on this spot than to surrender it. (Applause.)

---

## 4.1    Clarence Thomas, Notes on Original Intent

*The following notes were made public during Clarence Thomas's 1991 confirmation hearing to be an associate justice of the U.S. Supreme Court. They appear to have been prepared during Robert Bork's unsuccessful 1987 Supreme Court confirmation hearing. The notes provide an early glimpse into Thomas's views about the relationship between the Declaration of Independence and the Constitution.*

The young [Alexander] Hamilton defended American rights against a Tory by arguing "the fundamental source of all your errors, sophisms, and false reasonings is a total ignorance of the natural rights of mankind." This could apply to virtually any judge or dare I say any teacher of law today. . . . I would advocate . . . a true jurisprudence of original intent, one which understands the Constitution in light of the moral and political teachings of human equality in the Declaration. Here we find both moral backbone and the strongest defense of individual rights against collectivist schemes, whether by race or over the economy. Morality and political judgment are understood in objective terms, the Founders' notions of natural rights.

---

## 4.2    Clarence Thomas, 'The Modern Civil Rights Movement: Can a Regime of Individual Rights and the Rule of Law Survive,' April 18, 1988

*The following excerpt is taken from one of many speeches Clarence Thomas gave while he was chairman of the Equal Employment Opportunity Commission. It shows his individual rights approach to civil rights: an approach that traces to the Declaration of Independence.*

In both the judicial and the legislative branches we find growing acceptability in treating blacks as a separate group. This is not only to the long term disadvantage of black Americans, but it reflects as well on the health of our politics in general. The critical weakness in Congress is traceable to the decline of the notion of a common good or public interest above and beyond the desires of interest groups. . . .

The Voting Rights Act of 1965 certainly was crucial legislation. It has transformed the policies in the South. Unfortunately, many of the Court's decisions in the area of voting rights have presupposed that blacks, whites, Hispanics, and other ethnic groups will inevitably vote in blocs. Instead of looking at the right to vote as an individual right, the Court has regarded the right as protected when the individual's racial or ethnic group has sufficient clout.

## 4.3    Clarence Thomas, Confirmation Hearing, 1991

*The following is an excerpt of testimony taken from Clarence Thomas's 1991 confirmation hearing to be an associate justice of the U.S. Supreme Court. Thomas's individual rights approach to civil rights stirred controversy. He finds support for his approach in the Declaration of Independence.*

Senator [Arlen] Specter. . . . My question to you is: Don't you think, aside from the generalization of individualism, that there is some very important objective to be reached through the Voting Act to have a group with an adequate meaningful participation in the political process?

Judge [Clarence] Thomas. . . . My attitude was that if, indeed, there is proportional representa-

tion that that presupposes—I think that is the word I used in that speech—that presupposes that all minorities would vote alike or all minorities thought alike. And that is something that I have—those kinds of stereotypes are matters that I have felt in the past were and continue to feel are objectionable.

## 4.4    Clarence Thomas, Concurring Opinion in *Adarand Constructors, Inc. v. Peña* (1995)

*The following document is Justice Clarence Thomas's concurring opinion in* Adarand Constructors, Inc. v. Peña, *a major civil rights case. It is Thomas's most significant appeal to the Declaration of Independence to date as a member of the U.S. Supreme Court.*

I agree with the majority's conclusion that strict scrutiny applies to all government classifications based on race. I write separately, however, to express my disagreement with the premise underlying JUSTICE [JOHN PAUL] STEVENS' and JUSTICE [RUTH BADER] GINSBURG's dissents: that there is a racial paternalism exception to the principle of equal protection. I believe that there is a "moral [and] constitutional equivalence" . . . between laws designed to subjugate a race and those that distribute benefits on the basis of race in order to foster some current notion of equality. Government cannot make us equal; it can only recognize, respect, and protect us as equal before the law.

That these programs may have been motivated, in part, by good intentions cannot provide refuge from the principle that under our Constitution, the government may not make distinctions on the basis of race. As far as the Constitution is concerned, it is irrelevant whether a government's racial classifications are drawn by those who wish to oppress a race or by those who

have a sincere desire to help those thought to be disadvantaged. There can be no doubt that the paternalism that appears to lie at the heart of this program is at war with the principle of inherent equality that underlies and infuses our Constitution. See Declaration of Independence ("We hold these truths to be self-evident, that all men are created equal, that they are endowed by their Creator with certain unalienable Rights, that among these are Life, Liberty, and the pursuit of Happiness").

These programs not only raise grave constitutional questions, they also undermine the moral basis of the equal protection principle. Purchased at the price of immeasurable human suffering, the equal protection principle reflects our Nation's understanding that such classifications ultimately have a destructive impact on the individual and our society. Unquestionably, "[i]nvidious [racial] discrimination is an engine of oppression. . . ." It is also true that "[r]emedial" racial preferences may reflect "a desire to foster equality in society. . . ." But there can be no doubt that racial paternalism and its unintended consequences can be as poisonous and pernicious as any other form of discrimination. So-called "benign" discrimination teaches many that because of chronic and apparently immutable handicaps, minorities cannot compete with them without their patronizing indulgence. Inevitably, such programs engender attitudes of superiority or, alternatively, provoke resentment among those who believe that they have been wronged by the government's use of race. These programs stamp minorities with a badge of inferiority and may cause them to develop dependencies or to adopt an attitude that they are "entitled" to preferences. Indeed, JUSTICE STEVENS once recognized the real harms stemming from seemingly "benign" discrimination. . . .

In my mind, government-sponsored racial discrimination based on benign prejudice is just as noxious as discrimination inspired by malicious prejudice.[1] In each instance, it is racial discrimination, plain and simple.

---

1. It should be obvious that every racial classification helps, in a narrow sense, some races and hurts others. As to the races benefitted, the classification could surely be called "benign." Accordingly, whether a law relying upon racial taxonomy is "benign" or "malign" . . . either turns on "whose ox is gored" . . . or on distinctions found only in the eye of the beholder.

---

## 4.5  Clarence Thomas, 'The Virtue of Practical Wisdom,' February 9, 1999

*Justice Clarence Thomas's most important speech to date about the Declaration of Independence was delivered at the Claremont Institute's 1999 Lincoln Day Dinner honoring Professor Harry V. Jaffa, the leading political theorist of Abraham Lincoln and the Declaration.*

I had an opportunity recently to review a small portion of my confirmation hearings. That is not something that I do on a regular basis—I assure you. That is sort of like digging in old wounds. But one of the things that came through loud and clear was the need to protect our Constitution and the principles that underlie our Constitution. It is something that I certainly carry with me to my job and something that I preach to my law clerks.

That is, if the Constitution goes, this grand experiment is over. This is not a game of law review articles. It is not a game of "gotcha." It is not a game of cute phrases and glib remarks in important documents. It is the preservation of this grand experiment and it is a serious endeavor. If there is anything I could convey before I move into my prepared remarks, it would be just how important it is to preserve that document. . . .

We gather here tonight in memory of a great man, a great president whose noble words and selfless deeds enabled this great nation to fulfill its promises of equality and liberty for all—to itself, to all mankind and to the Creator. To borrow a passage from one of that great president's speeches, the world will little note nor long remember what we say here, but the world will never forget what he accomplished for the cause of freedom . . .

Oddly, the Great Emancipator, the man most known for bringing an end to slavery in this corner of the earth, was himself willing to compromise with that heinous institution, that stain on the principle of the nation's founding, in defense of the rule of law. Not just any rule of law, but a rule of law in a regime that was itself good, that was dedicated to the proposition that all men—all human beings—are created equal, that they are endowed with certain unalienable rights, including the rights to "life, liberty and the pursuit of happiness."

How is it that I, a descendant of slaves, could use the word "good" in describing a nation that condoned slavery? Does not the very existence of that peculiar institution give lie to the claim that this nation was founded on the principle of universal human equality? Or, at least, severely undermine the Founders' devotion to that principle? Our Founders, after all, did more than just suffer the existence of slavery. They codified it. They protected it. They inscribed it into the fundamental charter of our government: the Constitution of the United States.

Was the claim in the Declaration of Independence "that all men are created equal" *nothing*? Nothing but a self-evident lie? Were our Founders just hypocrites, cynics, willing to throw off the rule of British law for something as minor as a tax on tea, while trumpeting the virtues of the rule of American law, in defense of their own claim to property in other men—their slaves? How can [Abraham] Lincoln or I or anyone else dare to call such a nation "good"?

The answer depends on the alternatives that were available to the Founders. For if the Founders had no alternative but to compromise with slavery, we can hardly fault them for failing to accomplish the impossible. That is the first lesson that we must learn from Lincoln. Politics, at its root, is the art of the possible. To be sure, if the Founders had it within their power to abolish slavery and did not do so, then they were either cowards or hypocrites. If they compromised with slavery knowing that the compromise was unnecessary, or compromised with slavery to further some selfish end, then our Founding was truly flawed and not worthy of the respect and the continued allegiance of good men and women.

Did the Founders have it within their power to abolish slavery? By the time of the Constitutional Convention of 1787, nine of the thirteen original states—representing roughly 3/5 of the nation's population—had abolished slavery. The forces of freedom, thus, had a clear majority to prohibit slavery in the national charter itself. By the ordinary measure, therefore, it would appear that the Founders did have it in their power to pay more than lip service to the lofty principles that Jefferson had penned just a decade before.

When one delves a little deeper, however, one learns that the ordinary measure is not adequate to answer the question. As Tom West, a former student of Professor [Harry V.] Jaffa's, described in his book, *Vindicating the Founders,* "Had the North refused to compromise with slavery in 1787, the likely, indeed virtually certain, result would have been a failure to establish a national union of the United States."

One's first response might be, "So what? Who cares? Is not the existence of slavery a more serious matter than whether the thirteen original states joined together in a single union, instead of continuing to operate as thirteen separate states loosely joined for common defense purposes?"

That question brings me back to Lincoln's lesson for us, to an understanding of what Aristotle referred to as the "virtue of practical wisdom." For, in the Founders' political judgment, only a union of all the states—even one tarnished by a compromise with slavery—offered the prospect of putting slavery on the course of ultimate extinction.

Without the national union, a confederation of the slave-holding states would have been likely—a confederation based not on the self-evident truth of human equality, but on that awful maxim followed throughout most of human history that it was acceptable for one man to rule another without the other's consent and to live off the sweat of that man's brow.

The South had their slaves anyway. What did the constitutional compromise with slavery accomplish, other than to tarnish the whole nation, rather than merely the southern part? Certainly, from the point of view of the slaves, it did not matter whether they were the slaves in a southern confederacy, proclaiming that slavery was a "positive good," or whether they were slaves in a national union that purported to be based on the equality of all men. In any case, they were slaves. Would it not, thus, have been better for the North to break away clean, to establish a government in the North that was pure in its devotion to the principle of equality?

That answer, too, called for the exercise of political judgment. The North had to ask itself: "What would be the likely result of such an endeavor?" One likely consequence was that neither North nor South would survive—that, once divided, they would prove no match for the European powers that still had envious eyes on the New World—and that all, not just a part, of the continent would be enslaved.

Another possible consequence was that the South would flourish, expanding the hated institution of slavery beyond its borders into the as yet largely unsettled lands beyond the Appalachians, threatening the free states of the North every step of the way. Only through a national union could these principles be avoided and the principles of liberty and equality articulated in the Declaration of Independence given a fighting chance for full vindication.

In other words, the Founders made the political judgment that, given the circumstances at the time, the best defense of the Declaration's principles and, ironically, the most beneficial course for the slaves themselves was to compromise with slavery while, at the same time, establishing a union that, at its root, was devoted to the principle of human equality.

We can question whether they were right in that judgment. I happen to think that they were, without calling into question their devotion to the principles they articulated. For, if they were right about the likely consequences of failing to achieve a national union, then their compromise with slavery was the morally right thing to do.

But what of Lincoln? He also compromised with slavery, after all, rejecting the calls of the Abolitionists and contending, instead, that fugitive slave laws must be obeyed, a half century after the Constitution was enacted. Can a compromise with an evil so fundamentally at odds with the Founding principle of equality extend through not just one generation but two, and do so without calling into question the very character of the regime, even if the initial compromise with slavery was a necessary one?

Was not Lincoln's devotion to the rule of law in a regime that for nearly four score and seven years had not only failed to eradicate slavery,

but seemed bent on its expansion? Was not this in reality a defense of a regime that was not longer worthy of a defense? By so defending a bad regime, did Lincoln himself become a bad man?

As with our assessment of the Founders, our assessment of Lincoln must also look to the alternatives that were open to him and the nation at the time and to the prudent assessment of those alternatives. Lincoln, of course, was an opponent of slavery, but he waged a lifelong battle for the rule of law. He urged the Abolitionists time and again to comply with and enforce the law, even the fugitive slave laws.

Early in his career, in an address to the Young Men's Lyceum in Springfield, Illinois, he eloquently pressed the point:

Let every American, every lover of liberty, every well-wisher to his posterity swear by the blood of the Revolution never to violate in the least particular the laws of the country and never tolerate their violation by others. As the patriots of '76 did to support the Declaration of Independence, so to the support of the Constitution and laws let every American pledge his life, his property and his sacred honor. Let every man remember that to violate the law is to trample on the blood of his father and to tear down the charter of his own and his children's liberty. Let reverence for the law be breathed by every American mother to the lisping babe that prattles on her lap. Let it be taught in the schools and the seminaries and the colleges. Let it be written in the primers, spelling books and in the almanacs. Let it be preached from the pulpit, proclaimed in the legislative halls and enforced in the Courts of justice. And, in short, let it become the political religion of the nation. And let the old and the young, the rich and the poor, the grave and the gay of all sexes and tongues and colors and conditions sacrifice unceasingly upon its altars.

Lincoln made clear that his admonition applied with equal force to bad laws.

When I so pressingly urge a strict observance of all the laws, let me not be understood as saying that there are no bad laws, nor that grievances may not arise for the redress of which no legal provisions have been made. I mean to say no such thing, but I do mean to say that bad laws, if they exist, should be repealed as soon as possible. Still while they continue in force, for the sake of example, they shall be religiously observed.

Even on the eve of Civil War, in his First In-augural Address, Lincoln reiterated his belief that he had no authority over, and, hence, would not abolish, slavery in the existing states. "I have," said Lincoln, "no purpose, directly or indirectly, to interfere with the institution of slavery in states where it exists. I believe I have no right to do so. And I have no inclination to do so."

At first blush, Lincoln's devotion to the rule of law, when the law itself protected an institution as heinous as slavery, would seem not to merit our praise, but rather to deserve our collective con-demnation. Devotion to the law in pre-[Nelson] Mandela South Africa meant a defense of apar-theid. Support for the law in [Joseph] Stalin's Soviet Union gave strength to a regime bent on op-pressing, not just its own people, but peoples throughout the world. And adherence to the law in Nazi Germany meant participation in the Holo-caust. Thus, it cannot be the rule of law for the law's sake that merits our support, or Lincoln's.

What was it about Lincoln's support of the rule of law in a nation whose Constitution con-doned slavery that distinguishes it from these other examples? It is, again, political judgment—prudence. For Lincoln understood—rightly, in my view—that the old problem with slavery faced by the Founders had not been abated.

In fact, the problem had grown much worse, due in no small part to the Supreme Court's failure in the *Dred Scott* case to distinguish between the compromises of the Constitution and its prin-ciples, and to give effect to the principles whenever the letter of the compromise did not prevent it.

Lincoln understood that if the Constitutional compromises were not enforced, secession would be the probable result. In Lincoln's day, no less than in the Founding era, secession meant the es-tablishment of a regime on this continent, de-voted to the perpetuation of slavery, rather than merely one which suffered its existence. And it meant the likely expansion of slavery into new territory, beyond the Mississippi.

The rule of law, on the other hand, as preached by Lincoln, gave effect to the principles of the Constitution as far as possible—permitting

the federal government to outlaw slavery in the territories and vindicating the guarantee of a re-publican form of government in new states, as they were admitted to the union. While it did nothing to interfere with the institution of slavery in the existing states, it did confine it there, where Lincoln fully and reasonably expected it would wither and die.

For Lincoln, as for the Founders, the moral course, the prudent course, the course most likely to lead to the ultimate abolition of slavery was, in fact, not to join with the Abolitionists. Lin-coln's lesson for us, however, is even more pro-found: the realization that prudence is sometimes a compromise with principle, in order, ultimately, to vindicate that principle.

Chief Justice [Roger B.] Taney, too, compro-mised with slavery. In his infamous opinion for the Court in the *Dred Scott* case, he gave effect to the fugitive slave clause. But he did much more: he gave force to the compromise of 1787 in a way that severely and permanently crippled the prin-ciples of the Declaration itself. His compromise with slavery was, thus, a capitulation on the question of principle, not an exercise of prudence and ultimate furtherance of principle.

Chief Justice Taney's opinion was a crossing of the Rubicon for this Republic on the slavery question, and Lincoln well knew it. If that opin-ion stood, the expansion of slavery would not be prevented or could not be prevented—not in the territories, not in the newly-admitted states, not even in the existing free states—the very thing which for the Founders and for Lin-coln made the Constitution's pact with the slave forces palatable.

If the *Dred Scott* opinion stood, good men such as Lincoln could not continue to support the Constitution or the rule of law. In other words, they would have to become bad citizens and seek to overthrow the existing government, much like the Founders became bad subjects of the English Crown in 1776 and revolted—as it was their right and duty to do so—against what had be-come a bad government, destructive of their fun-damental rights, and instituting in its place a new form of government that seemed "most likely to effect their safety and happiness."

Justice Taney's opinion in *Dred Scott* brought about a "crisis of the house divided," which Lincoln so presciently described in his debates with Stephen Douglas . . .

But what has this to do with us? I began by urging that we learn from Lincoln . . . but learn what? Slavery is no longer with us. Yet, as we stand on the threshold of the 21st Century, many of our fellow citizens have forgotten—or rather, our modern world has rejected—"the laws of Nature and Nature's God," against which the institution of slavery was so self-evidently wrong and against which we must judge our own generation's assault on the unalienable rights to property, to liberty and to life.

. . . For Lincoln, knowing the wrongness of slavery was only half the battle—the easier half. The Abolitionists got that part right. Even the Southerners got that part right, at least until John C. Calhoun came home. Knowing how to bring about slavery's extinction in a manner that preserved freedom and the possibility of freedom, knowing how to distinguish prudent compromise from cowardly capitulation—that was the tougher piece.

In the present day, we have our own Abolitionists. There are those among us who believe that our nation has crossed a Rubicon in one fashion or another, from compromising on the moral and constitutional issues of our day to tolerating a federal government that, arguably, is little constrained by the limits of its constitutional charter.

Has the time come to join our present day Abolitionists? Or, should we, like Lincoln, pledge our support for the rule of law, having faith that in thus compromising with the nation's principles, we will be choosing the path that affords the greatest prospect for the cause of liberty? That, my friends, is the real question before us.

I urge you, Professor Jaffa, and others in this room, to be ever vigilant in reminding us—me and everyone else who has the privilege of serving our nation through public office—of the principles of our Founding and how they apply to the controversies of our time.

I challenge each of you to help us with the much more difficult task of charting the course that is most likely to vindicate the principles of the Declaration and to lead to the safety and happiness of this great and blessed people. Recognizing that sometimes the wise and prudent course is to compromise with our principles, and even to make alliance with those who have rejected or misunderstood them, help us to know the difference between a prudent compromise that advances the cause of liberty and a capitulation on principle that snuffs it out.

Do that, and 40 years from now, our children and our children's children will still be celebrating Harry Jaffa's life work and the liberty that was so preciously purchased with the lives, the fortunes and the sacred honor of the Founders in 1776 at our nation's birth, and resurrected in 1860 by Abraham Lincoln at its rebirth—its new birth of freedom. We must assume the mantle of the Great Commission from the hallowed grounds of Gettysburg:

It is for us the living, rather, to be dedicated here to the unfinished work which they who fought here have thus far so nobly advanced. It is rather for us to be here dedicated to the great task remaining before us—that from these honored dead we take increased devotion to that cause for which they gave the last full measure of devotion—that we here highly resolve that these dead shall not have died in vain—that this nation, under God, shall have a new birth of freedom—and that government of the people, by the people, for the people, shall not perish from the earth.

So let us raise a glass to our Founding Fathers; to Abraham Lincoln, The Great Emancipator; and to Harry Jaffa, who reminds us of their great achievements in the fight for freedom and enables us to pass on their great legacy to a new generation of Americans.

## 5.1  The Articles of Confederation, 1776–1777, 1781

*The Articles of Confederation and Perpetual Union was the first constitution of the United States. It was drafted in 1776–1777 by the same Continental Congress that adopted the Declaration of Independence and was ratified by the states in 1781. The following excerpt from the Articles reflects principles and a political temperament similar to that of the Declaration.*

Articles of Confederation and perpetual Union between the States of New Hampshire, Massachusetts-bay, Rhodeisland and Providence Plantations, Connecticut, New York, New Jersey, Pennsylvania, Delaware, Maryland, Virginia, North Carolina, South Carolina, and Georgia.

ARTICLE I. The stile of this confederacy shall be "The United States of America."

ARTICLE II. Each State retains its sovereignty, freedom, and independence, and every power, jurisdiction and right, which is not by this confederation expressly delegated to the United States in Congress assembled.

ARTICLE III. The said States hereby severally enter into a firm league of friendship with each other, for their common defence, the security of their liberties, and their mutual and general welfare, binding themselves to assist each other, against all force offered to, or attacks made upon them, or any of them, on account of religion, sovereignty, trade, or any other pretence whatever.

ARTICLE IV. The better to secure and perpetuate mutual friendship and intercourse among the people of the different States in this Union, the free inhabitants of each of these States, paupers, vagabonds, and fugitives from justice excepted, shall be entitled to all privileges and immunities of free citizens in the several States; and the people of each state shall have free ingress and regress to and from any other State, and shall enjoy therein all the privileges of trade and commerce, subject to the same duties, impositions and restrictions as the inhabitants thereof respectively, provided that such restrictions shall not extend so far as to prevent the removal of property imported into any State, to any other State of which the owner is an inhabitant; provided also

that no imposition, duties, or restriction shall be laid by any State, on the property of the United States, or either of them.

If any person guilty of, or charged with treason, felony, or other high misdemeanor in any State, shall flee from justice, and be found in any of the United States, he shall upon demand of the Governor or Executive power, of the State from which he fled, be delivered up and removed to the State having jurisdiction of his offence.

Full faith and credit shall be given in each of these States to the records, acts and judicial proceedings of the courts and magistrates of every other State.

ARTICLE V. For the more convenient management of the general interests of the United States, delegates shall be annually appointed in such manner as the legislature of each State shall direct, to meet in Congress on the first Monday in November, in every year, with a power reserved to each State, to recall its delegates, or any of them, at any time within the year, and to send others in their stead, for the remainder of the year.

No State shall be represented in Congress by less than two nor by more than seven members; and no person shall be capable of being a delegate for more than three years in any term of six years; nor shall any person, being a delegate, be capable of holding any office under the United States, for which he, or another for his benefit receives any salary, fees or emolument of any kind.

Each State shall maintain its own delegates in a meeting of the States and while they act as members of the committee of the States.

In determining questions in the United States, in Congress assembled, each State shall have one vote.

Freedom of speech and debate in Congress shall not be impeached or questioned in any court, or place out of Congress, and the members of Congress shall be protected in their persons from arrests and imprisonments, during the time of their going to and from, and attendance on Congress, except for treason, felony, or breach of the peace.

ARTICLE VI. No State, without the consent of the United States in Congress assembled, shall send any embassy to, or receive any embassy from, or enter into any conference, agreement, alliance, or treaty with any king, prince, or state; nor shall any person holding any office of profit or trust under the United States, or any of them, accept of any present, emolument, office, or title of any kind whatever from any king, prince or foreign state; nor shall the United States in Congress assembled, or any of them, grant any title of nobility.

ARTICLE VIII. All charges of war, and all other expenses that shall be incurred for the common defence or general welfare, and allowed by the United States in Congress assembled, shall be defrayed out of a common treasury, which shall be supplied by the several States, in proportion to the value of all land within each State, granted to or surveyed for any person, as such land and the buildings and improvements thereon shall be estimated according to such mode as the United States in Congress assembled, shall from time to time direct and appoint.

The taxes for paying that proportion shall be laid and levied by the authority and direction of the Legislatures of the several States within the time agreed upon by the United States in Congress assembled.

ARTICLE IX. The United States in Congress assembled, shall have the sole and exclusive right and power of determining on peace and war, except in the cases mentioned in the sixth article—of sending and receiving ambassadors—entering into treaties and alliances, provided that no treaty of commerce shall be made whereby the legislative power of the respective States shall be restrained from imposing such imposts and duties

on foreigners, as their own people are subjected to, or from prohibiting the exportation or importation of any species of goods or commodities whatsoever—of establishing rules for deciding in all cases, what captures on land or water shall be legal, and in what manner prizes taken by land or naval forces in the service of the United States shall be divided or appropriated—of granting letters of marque and reprisal in times of peace—appointing courts for the trial of piracies and felonies committed on the high seas and establishing courts for receiving and determining finally appeals in all cases of captures, provided that no member of Congress shall be appointed a judge of any of the said courts.

The United States in Congress assembled shall have authority to appoint a committee, to sit in the recess of Congress, to be denominated "a Committee of the States," and to consist of one delegate from each State; and to appoint such other committees and civil officers as may be necessary for managing the general affairs of the United States under their direction—to appoint one of their number to preside, provided that no person be allowed to serve in the office of president more than one year in any term of three years. . . .

The Congress of the United States shall have power to adjourn to any time within the year, and to any place within the United States, so that no period of adjournment be for a longer duration than the space of six months, and shall publish the journal of their proceedings monthly, except such parts thereof relating to treaties, alliances or military operations, as in their judgment require secrecy; and the yeas and nays of the delegates of each State on any question shall be entered on the journal, when it is desired by any delegate; and the delegates of a State, or any of them, at his or their request shall be furnished with a transcript of the said journal, except such parts as are above excepted, to lay before the Legislatures of the several States.

ARTICLE X. The committee of the States, or any nine of them, shall be authorized to execute, in the recess of Congress, such of the powers of

Congress as the United States in Congress assembled, by the consent of nine States, shall from time to time think expedient to vest them with; provided that no power be delegated to the said committee, for the exercise of which, by the articles of confederation, the voice of nine States in the Congress of the United States assembled is requisite. . . .

ARTICLE XIII. Every State shall abide by the determinations of the United States in Congress assembled, on all questions which by this confederation are submitted to them. And the articles of this confederation shall be inviolably observed by every State, and the Union shall be perpetual; nor shall any alteration at any time hereafter be made in any of them; unless such alteration be agreed to in a Congress of the United States, and be afterward confirmed by the Legislatures of every State.

And whereas it has pleased the Great Governor of the world to incline the hearts of the Legislatures we respectively represent in Congress, to approve of, and to authorize us to ratify the said articles of confederation and perpetual union. Know ye that we the undersigned delegates, by virtue of the power and authority to us given for that purpose, do by these presents, in the name and in behalf of our respective constituents, fully and entirely ratify and confirm each and every of the said articles of confederation and perpetual union, and all and singular the matters and things therein contained: and we do further solemnly plight and engage the faith of our respective constituents, that they shall abide by the determinations of the United States in Congress assembled, on all questions, which by the said confederation are submitted to them. And that the articles thereof shall be inviolably observed by the States we re[s]pectively represent, and that the Union shall be perpetual. In witness whereof we have hereunto set our hands in Congress.

## 5.2    J. Hector St. John De Crèvecoeur, 'What Is an American?,' 1782

*J. Hector St. John De Crèvecoeur (1735–1813) spent most of his life in his native France. However, he achieved distinction as an American writer with his* Letters from an American Farmer. *The most famous of these letters, "What Is an American?," addresses some of the most important American cultural questions of the confederation era, including a distinctive American identity and its unique association with nature.*

I wish I could be acquainted with the feelings and thoughts which must agitate the heart and present themselves to the mind of an enlightened Englishman when he first lands on this continent. He must greatly rejoice that he lived at a time to see this fair country discovered and settled; he must necessarily feel a share of national pride when he views the chain of settlements which embellishes these extended shores. When he says to himself, this is the work of my countrymen, who, when convulsed by factions, afflicted by a variety of miseries and wants, restless and impatient, took refuge here. They brought along with them their national genius, to which they principally owe what liberty they enjoy and what substance they possess. Here he sees the industry of his native country displayed in a new manner, and traces in their works the embryos of all the arts, sciences, and ingenuity which flourish in Europe. Here he beholds fair cities, substantial villages, extensive fields, an immense country filled with decent houses, good roads, orchards, meadows, and bridges, where a hundred years ago all was wild, woody, and uncultivated! What a train of pleasing ideas this fair spectacle must suggest; it is a prospect which must inspire a good citizen with the most heartfelt pleasure. The difficulty consists in the manner of viewing so extensive a scene. He is arrived on a new continent; a modern society offers itself to his contemplation, different from what he had hitherto seen. It is not composed, as in Europe, of great lords who possess everything, and of a herd of people who have nothing. Here are no aristocratical families, no courts, no kings, no bishops, no ecclesiastical dominion, no invisible power giving to a few a very visible one; no great manufacturers employing thousands, no great refinements of luxury. The rich and the poor are not so far removed from each other as they are in Europe. Some few towns excepted, we are all tillers of the earth, from Nova Scotia to West Florida. We are a people of cultivators, scattered over an immense territory, communicating with each other by means of good roads and navigable rivers, united by the silken bands of mild government, all respecting the laws without dreading their power, because they are equitable. We are all animated with the spirit of industry, which is unfettered and unrestrained, because each person works for himself. If he travels through our rural districts, he views not the hostile castle and the haughty mansion, contrasted with the clay-built hut and miserable cabin, where cattle and men help to keep each other warm, and dwell in meanness, smoke, and indigence. A pleasing uniformity of decent competence appears throughout our habitations. The meanest of our log-houses is a dry and comfortable habitation. . . .

The laws, the indulgent laws, protect them as they arrive, stamping on them the symbol of adoption; they receive ample rewards for their labors; these accumulated rewards procure them lands; those lands confer on them the title of freemen; and to that title every benefit is affixed which men can possibly require. This is the great operation daily performed by our laws. From whence proceed these laws? From our government. Whence that government? It is derived from the original genius and strong desire of the people, ratified and confirmed by the crown. This is the great chain which links us all, this is the picture which every province exhibits, Nova Scotia excepted. There the crown has done all; either there were no people who had genius, or it was not much attended to: the consequence is that the province is very thinly inhabited indeed; the power of the crown, in conjunction with the musketos, has prevented men from settling there. Yet some part of it flourished once, and it contained a mild, harmless set of people. But for the fault of a few leaders the whole were banished. The greatest political error the crown ever committed in America was to cut off men from a country which wanted nothing but men! . . .

The American is a new man, who acts upon new principles; he must, therefore, entertain new ideas and form new opinions. From involuntary idleness, servile dependence, penury, and useless labor he has passed to toils of a very different nature, rewarded by ample subsistence.—This is an American. . . .

Men are like plants; the goodness and flavor of the fruit proceed from the peculiar soil and exposition in which they grow. We are nothing but what we derive from the air we breathe, the climate we inhabit, the government we obey, the system of religion we profess, and the nature of our employment. Here you will find but few crimes; these have acquired as yet no root among us. I wish I were able to trace all my ideas. If my ignorance prevents me from describing them properly, I hope I shall be able to delineate a few of the outlines, which are all I propose. . . .

Exclusive of those general characteristics, each province has its own, founded on the government, climate, mode of husbandry, customs, and peculiarity of circumstances. Europeans submit insensibly to these great powers, and become in the course of a few generations not only Americans in general but either Pennsylvanians, Virginians, or provincials under some other name. Whoever traverses the continent must easily observe those strong differences, which will grow more evident in time. The inhabitants of Canada, Massachusetts, the middle provinces, the southern ones will be as different as their climates; their only points of unity will be those of religion and language. . . .

An European, when he first arrives, seems limited in his intentions as well as in his views; but he very suddenly alters his scale; 200 miles formerly appeared a very great distance; it is now but a trifle. He no sooner breathes our air than he forms schemes and embarks in designs he never would have thought of in his own country. There the plenitude of society confines many useful ideas, and often extinguishes the most laudable schemes which here ripen into maturity. Thus Europeans become Americans. . . .

After a foreigner from any part of Europe has arrived and become a citizen; let him devoutly listen to the voice of our great parent, which says to him, "Welcome to my shores, distressed European; bless the hour in which thou didst see my verdant fields, my fair navigable rivers, and my green mountains! If thou wilt work, I have bread for thee; if thou wilt be honest, sober, and industrious, I have greater rewards to confer on thee—

ease and independence. I will give thee fields to feed and clothe thee; a comfortable fireside to sit by, and tell thy children by what means thou hast prospered; and a decent bed to repose on. I shall endow thee, besides, with the immunities of a freeman. If thou wilt carefully educate thy children, teach them gratitude to God, and reverence to that government, that philanthropic government which has collected here so many men and made them happy. I will also provide for thy progeny, and to every good man this ought to be the most holy, the most Powerful, the most earnest wish he can possibly form, as well as the most consolatory prospect when he dies. Go thou, and work and till; thou shalt prosper, provided thou be just, grateful, and industrious."

## 5.3   'Centinel,' 'To the People of Pennsylvania,' 1787

*During the political battle over the ratification of the U.S. Constitution, a series of articles by "Centinel" began appearing in the Philadelphia Independent Gazette. Initially they were thought to have been written by George Bryan (1731–1791), a state supreme court judge who led the Anti-Federalist opposition to the Constitution in Pennsylvania. Historians now believe they were written by his son, Samuel Bryan (1759–1821). The second "Centinel" article, excerpted below, warns the people of Pennsylvania that the proposed Constitution threatens the very rights that the American regime, as formed by the Declaration of Independence and the Articles of Confederation, was founded to protect.*

Mr. [James] Wilson asks, "What controul can proceed from the federal government to shackle or destroy that *sacred palladium* of national freedom, the *liberty of the press?*" What!—Cannot Congress, when possessed of the immense authority proposed to be devolved, restrain the printers, and put them under regulation.—Recollect that the omnipotence of the federal legislature over the State establishments is recognized by a special article, viz.—"that this Constitution, and the laws of the United States which shall be made in pursuance thereof, and all treaties made, or which shall be made, under the authority of the United States, shall be the *supreme law* of the land; and the judges in every State shall be bound thereby, any thing in the *Constitutions* or laws of any State to the contrary

notwithstanding."—After such declaration, what security does the *Constitutions* of the severals State afford or the *liberty of the press and other invaluable personal rights,* not provided for by the new plan?—Does not this sweeping clause subject every thing to the controul of Congress?

In the plan of Confederation of 1778, now existing, it was thought proper by Article the 2d, to declare that "each State retains its sovereignty, freedom and independence[,] and every power, jurisdiction and right, which is not by this Confederation expressly delegated to the United States in Congress assembled." *Positive* grant was not *then* thought sufficiently descriptive and restraining upon Congress, and the omission of such a declaration *now,* when such great devolutions of power are proposed, manifests the design of reducing the several States to shadows. But Mr. Wilson tells you, that every right and power not specially granted to Congress is considered as withheld. How does this appear? Is this principle established by the proper authority? Has the Convention made such a stipulation? By no means. Quite the reverse; the *laws* of Congress are to be "the *supreme law* of the land, any thing in the *Constitutions* or laws of any State to the contrary notwithstanding;" and consequently, would be paramount to all State authorities. The lust of power is so universal, that a speculative unascertained rule of construction would be a *poor* security for the liberties of the people.

Such a body as the intended Congress, unless particularly inhibited and restrained, must grasp at omnipotence, and before long swallow up the Legislative, the Executive, and the Judicial powers of the several States. . . .

[I]t is evident, that the general government would necessarily annihilate the particular governments, and that the security of the personal rights of the people by the state constitutions is superseded and destroyed; hence results the necessity of such security being provided for by a bill of rights to be inserted in the new plan of federal government. What excuse can we then make for the omission of this grand palladium, this barrier between *liberty* and *oppression*. For universal experience demonstrates the necessity of the most express declarations and restrictions, to protect the rights and liberties of mankind, from the silent, powerful and ever active conspiracy of those who govern.

The new plan, it is true, does propose to secure the people of the benefit of personal liberty by the *habeas corpus;* and trial by jury for all crimes, except in case of impeachment: but there is no declaration, that all men have a natural and unalienable right to worship Almighty God, according to the dictates of their own consciences and understanding; and that no man ought, or of right can be compelled to attend any religious worship, or erect or support any place of worship, or maintain any ministry, contrary to, or against his own free will and consent; and that no

authority can or ought to be vested in, or assumed by any power whatever, that shall in any case interfere with, or in any manner controul, the right of conscience in the free exercise of religious worship: that the trial by jury in civil causes as well as criminal, and the modes prescribed by the common law for safety of life in criminal prosecutions shall be held sacred; that the requiring of excessive bail, imposing of excessive fines and cruel and unusual punishments be forbidden; that monopolies in trade or arts, other than to authors of books or inventors of useful arts, for a reasonable time, ought not to be suffered; that the right of the people to assemble peaceably for the purpose of consulting about public matters, and petitioning or remonstrating to the federal legislature ought not to be prevented; that *the liberty of the press be held sacred;* that the people have a right to hold themselves, their houses, papers and possessions free from search or seizure; and that therefore warrants without oaths or affirmations first made, affording a sufficient foundation for them, and whereby any officer or messenger may be commanded or required to search suspected places, or to seize any person or his property, not particularly described, are contrary to that right and ought not to be granted; and that standing armies in time of peace are dangerous to liberty, and ought not to be permitted but when absolutely necessary; all which is omitted to be done in the proposed government.

But Mr. *Wilson* says, the new plan does not arrogate perfection, for it provides a mode of alteration and correction, if found necessary. This is one among the numerous deceptions attempted on this occasion. True, there is a mode prescribed for this purpose. But it is barely possible that amendments may be made. The fascination of power must first cease, the nature of mankind undergo a revolution, that is not to be expected on this side of eternity. For to effect this (Art. 6.) it is provided, that if *two thirds* of both houses of the federal legislature shall propose them; or when two thirds of the several states by their legislatures, shall apply for them, the federal assembly shall call a convention for proposing amendments, which when ratified by three fourths of the state legislatures, or conventions, as Congress shall see best, shall controul and alter the proposed confederation. Does history abound with examples of a voluntary relinquishment of power, however injurious to the community? No; it would require a general and successful rising of the people to effect anything of this nature.—This provision therefore is mere sound.

The opposition to the new plan (says Mr. Wilson) proceeds from interested men, *viz.* the officers of the state governments. He had before denied that the proposed transfer of powers to Congress would annihilate the state governments. But he here lays aside the masque, and avows the fact. For, the truth of the charge against *them* must entirely rest on such consequence of the new plan. For if the state establishments are to remain unimpaired, why should officers peculiarly connected with them, be interested to oppose the adoption of the new plan? Except the collector of the impost, judge of the admiralty, and the collectors of excise (none of whom have been reckoned of the opposition) they would otherwise have nothing to apprehend.—But the charge is unworthy and may with more propriety be retorted on the expectants of office and emolument under the intended government.

The opposition is not so partial and interested as Mr. *Wilson* asserts. It consists of a respectable yeomanry throughout the union, of characters far removed above the reach of his unsupported assertions. It comprises many worthy members of the late convention, and a majority of the present Congress, for a motion made in that honorable body, for their *approbation* and *recommendation* of the new plan, was after two days animated discussion, prudently withdrawn by its advocates, and a simple *transmission* of the plan to the several states could only be obtained; yet this has been palmed upon the people as the approbation of Congress; and to strengthen the deception, the bells of the city of Philadelphia were rung for a whole day.

Are Mr. W—n, and many of his coadjutors in the late C—n, the disinterested patriots they would have us believe? Is their conduct any recommendation of their plan of government? View them the foremost and loudest on the floor of Congress, in our Assembly, at town meetings, in sounding its eulogiums:—View them preventing investigation and discussion, and in that most despotic manner endeavouring to compel its adoption by the people, with such precipitancy as to preclude the possibility of a due consideration, and then say whether the motives of these men can be pure.

My fellow citizens, such false detestable *patriots* in every nation, have led their blind confiding country, shouting their applauses, into the jaws of *despotism* and *ruin*. May the wisdom and virtue of the people of America, save them from the usual fate of nations.

# 5.4   Letters from the 'Federal Farmer,' December 25, 1787

*Perhaps the most eloquent and persuasive exposition of Anti-Federalist thought was provided in a series of letters published in the Poughkeepsie Country Journal, in New York, from November 1787 through January 1788. Many of these letters were republished and circulated widely. The author, known as the "Federal Farmer," has long been thought to be Richard Henry Lee (1732–1794), a Virginia delegate to the Continental Congress then sitting in New York, but many scholars later came to think the author was more likely to be Melancton Smith (1744–1798) of New York. The following excerpt, from the sixth letter, stresses the principle of government by the consent of the people and warns that the proposed Constitution is inconsistent with that fundamental principle of the American regime.*

My former letters to you, respecting the constitution proposed, were calculated merely to lead to a fuller investigation of the subject; having more extensively considered it, and the opinions of others relative to it, I shall, in a few letters, more particularly endeavour to point out the defects, and propose amendments. . . .

The gentlemen who oppose the constitution, or contend for amendments in it, are frequently, and with much bitterness, charged with wantonly attacking the men who framed it. The unjustness of this charge leads me to make one observation upon the conduct of parties, &c. Some of the advocates are only pretended federalists; in fact they wish for an abolition of the state governments. Some of them I believe to be honest federalists, who wish to preserve *substantially* the state governments united under an efficient federal head; and many of them are blind tools without any object. Some of the opposers also are only pretended federalists,—who want no federal government, or one merely advisory. Some of them are the true federalists, their object, perhaps, more clearly seen, is the same with that of the honest federalists; and some of them, probably, have no distinct object. We might as well call the advocates and opposers tories and whigs, or any thing else, as federalists and anti-federalists. To be for or against the constitution, as it stands, is not much evidence of a federal disposition; if any names are applicable to the parties, on account of their general politics, they are those of republicans and anti-republicans. The opposers are gen-

erally men who support the rights of the body of the people, and are properly republicans. The advocates are generally men not very friendly to those rights, and properly anti republicans. . . .

Good government is generally the result of experience and gradual improvements, and a punctual execution of the laws is essential to the preservation of life, liberty, and property. Taxes are always necessary, and the power to raise them can never be safely lodged without checks and limitation, but in a full and substantial representation of the body of the people; the quantity of power delegated ought to be compensated by the brevity of the time of holding it, in order to prevent the possessors increasing it. The supreme power is in the people, and rulers possess only that portion which is expressly given them; yet the wisest people have often declared this is the case on proper occasions, and have carefully formed stipulation to fix the extent, and limit the exercise of the power given.

The people by Magna Charta, &c. did not acquire powers, or receive privileges from the king, they only ascertained and fixed those they were entitled to as Englishmen; the title used by the king "we grant," was mere form. Representation, and the jury trial, are the best features of a free government ever as yet discovered, and the only means by which the body of the people can have their proper influence in the affairs of government.

In a federal system we must not only balance the parts of the same government, as that of the state, or that of the union; but we must find a balancing influence between the general and local governments—the latter is what men or writers have but very little or imperfectly considered.

A free and mild government is that in which no laws can be made without the formal and free consent of the people, or of their constitutional representatives; that is, of a substantial representative branch. Liberty, in its genuine sense, is security to enjoy the effects of our honest industry and labours, in a free and mild government, and personal security from all illegal restraints.

Of rights, some are natural and unalienable, of which even the people cannot deprive individuals: Some are constitutional or fundamental; these cannot be altered or abolished by the ordinary laws; but the people, by express acts, may alter or abolish them.—These, such as the trial by jury, the benefits of the writ of habeas corpus, &c. individuals claim under the solemn compacts of the people, as constitutions, or at least under laws so strengthened by long usuage as not to be repealable by the ordinary legislature—and some are common or mere legal rights, that is, such as individuals claim under laws which the ordinary legislature may alter or abolish at pleasure.

The confederation is a league of friendship among the states or sovereignties for the common defence and mutual welfare—Each state expressly retains its sovereignty, and all powers not expressly given to congress—All federal powers are lodged in a congress of delegates annually elected by the state legislatures, except in Connecticut and Rhode-Island, where they are chosen by the people—Each state has a vote in congress, pays its delegates, and may instruct or recall them; no delegate can hold any office of profit, or serve more than three years in any six years—Each state may be represented by not less than two, or more than seven delegates.

Congress (nine states agreeing) may make peace and war, treaties and alliances, grant letters of marque and reprisal, coin money, regulate the alloy and value of the coin, require men and monies of the states by fixed proportions, and appropriate monies, for armies and navies, emit bills of credit, and borrow monies.

Congress (seven states agreeing) may send and receive ambassadors, regulate captures, make rules for governing the army and navy, institute courts for the trial of piracies and felonies committed on the high seas, and for settling territorial disputes between the individual states, regulate weight and measures, post-offices, and Indian affairs.

No state, without the consent of congress, can send or receive embassies, make any agreement with any other state, or a foreign state, keep up any vessels of war or bodies of forces in time of peace, or engage in war, or lay any duties which may interfere with the treaties of congress—Each state must appoint regimental officers, and keep up a well regulated militia—Each state may prohibit the importation or exportation of any species of goods.

The free inhabitants of one state are intitled to the privileges and immunities of the free citizens of the other states—Credit in each state shall be given to the records and judicial proceedings in the others.

Canada, acceding, may be admitted, and any other colony may be admitted by the consent of nine states.

Alterations may be made by the agreement of congress, and confirmation of all the state legislatures.

The following, I think, will be allowed to be unalienable or fundamental rights in the United States:—

No man, demeaning himself peaceably, shall be molested on account of his religion or mode of worship—The people have a right to hold and enjoy their property according to known standing laws, and which cannot be taken from them without their consent, or the consent of their representatives; and whenever taken in the pressing urgencies of government, they are to receive a reasonable compensation for it.—Individual security consists in having free recourse to the laws—The people are subject to no laws or taxes not assented to by their representatives constitutionally assembled—They are at all times intitled to the benefits of the writ of habeas corpus, the trial by jury in criminal and civil causes—They have a right, when charged, to a speedy trial in the vicinage; to be heard by themselves or counsel, not to be compelled to furnish evidence against themselves, to have witnesses face to face, and to confront their adversaries before the judge—No man is held to answer a crime charged upon him till it be substantially described to him; and he is subject to no unreasonable searches or seizures of his person, papers or effects—The people have a right to assemble in an orderly manner, and petition the government for a redress of wrongs—The freedom of the press ought not to be restrained—No emoluments, except for actual service—No hereditary honors, or orders of nobility, ought to be allowed—The military ought to be subordinate to the civil authority, and no soldier be quartered on the citizens without their consent—The militia ought always to be armed and disciplined, and the usual defence of the country—The supreme power is in the people, and power delegated ought to return to them at stated periods, and frequently—The legislative, executive, and judicial powers, ought always to be kept distinct—others perhaps might be added.

The organization of the state governments—Each state has a legislature, an executive, and a judicial branch—In general legislators are excluded from the important executive and judicial offices—Except in the Carolinas there is no constitutional distinction among Christian sects—The constitutions of New York, Delaware, and Virginia, exclude the clergy from offices civil and military—the other states do nearly the same in practice.

Each state has a democratic branch elected twice a-year in Rhode-Island and Connecticut, biennially in South Carolina, and annually in the other states—There are about 1500 representatives in all the states, or one to each 1700 inhabitants, reckoning five blacks for three whites—The states do not differ as to the age or moral characters of the electors or elected, nor materially as to their property.

Pennsylvania has lodged all her legislative powers in a single branch, and Georgia has done

the same; the other eleven states have each in their legislatures a second or senatorial branch. In forming this they have combined various principles, and aimed at several checks and balances. It is amazing to see how ingenuity has worked in the several states to fix a barrier against popular instability. In Massachusetts the senators are apportioned on districts according to the taxes they pay, nearly according to property. In Connecticut the freemen, in September, vote for twenty counsellers, and return the names of those voted for in the several towns; the legislature takes the twenty who have the most votes, and give them to the people, who, in April, chuse twelve of them, who, with the governor and deputy governor, form the senatorial branch. In Maryland the senators are chosen by two electors from each county; these electors are chosen by the freemen, and qualified as the members in the democratic branch are: In these two cases checks are aimed at in the mode of election. Several states have taken into view the periods of service, age, property, &c. In South-Carolina a senator is elected for two years, in Delaware three, and in New-York and Virginia four, in Maryland five, and in the other states for one. In New-York and Virginia one-fourth part go out yearly. In Virginia a senator must be twenty-five years old, in South Carolina thirty. In New-York the electors must each have a freehold worth 250 dollars, in North-Carolina a freehold of fifty acres of land; in the other states the electors of senators are qualified as electors of representatives are. In Massachusetts a senator must have a freehold in his own right worth 1000 dollars, or any estate worth 2000, in New-Jersey any estate worth 2666, in South Carolina worth 1300 dollars, in North-Carolina 300 acres of land in fee, &c. The numbers of senators in each state are from ten to thirty-one, about 160 in the eleven states, about one of 14000 inhabitants.

Two states, Massachusetts and New-York, have each introduced into their legislatures a third, but incomplete branch. In the former, the governor may negative any law not supported by two-thirds of the senators, and two-thirds of the representatives: in the latter, the governor, chancellor, and judges of the supreme court may do the same.

Each state has a single executive branch. In the five eastern states the people at large elect their governors; in the other states the legislatures elect them. In South Carolina the governor is elected once in two years; in New-York and Delaware once in three, and in the other states annually. The governor of New-York has no executive council, the other governors have. In several states the governor has a vote in the senatorial branch—the governors have similar powers in some instances, and quite dissimilar ones in others. The number of executive counsellers in the states are from five to twelve. In the four eastern states, New-Jersey, Pennsylvania, and Georgia, they are of the men returned legislators by the people. In Pennsylvania the counsellers are chosen triennially, in Delaware every fourth year, in Virginia every three years, in South-Carolina biennially, and in the other states yearly.

Each state has a judicial branch; each common law courts, superior and inferior; some chancery and admiralty courts: The courts in general sit in different places, in order to accommodate the citizens. The trial by jury is had in all the common law courts, and in some of the admiralty courts. The democratic freemen principally form the juries; men destitute of property, of character, or under age, are excluded as in elections. Some of the judges are during good behaviour, and some appointed for a year, and some for years; and all are dependant on the legislatures for their salaries—Particulars respecting this department are too many to be noticed here.

## 6.1   The Declaration and the Structure of Government

*The Declaration of Independence is typically understood to provide guidance only on the basic principles of government. The following excerpts reveal that the Declaration also offers insight into the proper structure and operation of government.*

We hold these truths to be self-evident, that all men are created equal, that they are endowed by their Creator with certain unalienable Rights; that among these are Life, Liberty and the pursuit of Happiness. That to secure these rights, Governments are instituted among Men, deriving their just powers from the consent of the governed. That whenever any Form of Government becomes destructive of these ends, it is the Right of the People to alter or to abolish it, and to institute new Government, laying its foundation on such principles and organizing its powers in such form, as to them shall seem most likely to effect their Safety and Happiness. . . .

[On the necessity for an elected legislature:] He has refused for a long time, after such dissolutions, to cause others to be elected; whereby the Legislative powers, incapable of Annihilation, have returned to the People at large for their exercise; the State remaining in the meantime exposed to all the dangers of invasion from without, and convulsions within. . . .

[On the judiciary:] He has obstructed the Administration of Justice, by refusing his Assent to Laws for establishing Judiciary Powers. . . .

[On consent:] He has kept among us, in time of peace, Standing Armies without the Consent of our legislatures. . . .

[On the necessity for consent expressed through periodic elections:] [The king and Parliament are guilty of] suspending our own Legislatures, and declaring themselves invested with power to legislate for us in all cases whatsoever.

# 6.2   The Constitution of the United States, 1787

*The U.S. Constitution is usually read separate and apart from the Declaration of Independence. The following excerpts suggest the presence of the principles of the Declaration in the Constitution.*

[Preamble:] We the People of the United States, in Order to form a more perfect Union, establish Justice, insure domestic Tranquility, provide for the common defence, promote the general Welfare, and secure the Blessings of Liberty to ourselves and our Posterity, do ordain and establish this Constitution for the United States of America. . . .

[The Bill of Rights, 1791:]

Amendment I. Congress shall make no law respecting an establishment of religion, or prohibiting the free exercise thereof; or abridging the freedom of speech, or of the press; or the right of the people peaceably to assemble, and to petition the government for a redress of grievances.

Amendment II. A well regulated militia, being necessary to the security of a free state, the right of the people to keep and bear arms, shall not be infringed.

Amendment III. No soldier shall, in time of peace be quartered in any house, without the consent of the owner, nor in time of war, but in a manner to be prescribed by law.

Amendment IV. The right of the people to be secure in their persons, houses, papers, and effects, against unreasonable searches and seizures, shall not be violated, and no warrants shall issue, but upon probable cause, supported by oath or affirmation, and particularly describing the place to be searched, and the persons or things to be seized.

Amendment V. No person shall be held to answer for a capital, or otherwise infamous crime, unless on a presentment or indictment of a grand jury, except in cases arising in the land or naval forces, or in the militia, when in actual service in time of war or public danger; nor shall any person be subject for the same offense to be twice put in jeopardy of life or limb; nor shall be compelled in any criminal case to be a witness against himself, nor be deprived of life, liberty, or property, without due process of law; nor shall private property be taken for public use, without just compensation.

Amendment VI. In all criminal prosecutions, the accused shall enjoy the right to a speedy and public trial, by an impartial jury of the state and district wherein the crime shall have been committed, which district shall have been previously ascertained by law, and to be informed of the nature and cause of the accusation; to be confronted with the witnesses against him; to have compulsory process for obtaining witnesses in his favor, and to have the assistance of counsel for his defense.

Amendment VII. In suits at common law, where the value in controversy shall exceed twenty dollars, the right of trial by jury shall be preserved, and no fact tried by a jury, shall be otherwise reexamined in any court of the United States, than according to the rules of the common law.

Amendment VIII. Excessive bail shall not be required, nor excessive fines imposed, nor cruel and unusual punishments inflicted.

Amendment IX. The enumeration in the Constitution, of certain rights, shall not be construed to deny or disparage others retained by the people.

Amendment X. The powers not delegated to the United States by the Constitution, nor prohibited by it to the states, are reserved to the states respectively, or to the people. . . .

[The Civil War Amendments, 1865, 1868, 1870, respectively:]

Amendment XIII [Section 1]. Neither slavery nor involuntary servitude, except as a punishment for crime whereof the party shall have been duly convicted, shall exist within the United States, or any place subject to their jurisdiction. . . .

Amendment XIV [Section 1]. All persons born or naturalized in the United States and subject to the jurisdiction thereof, are citizens of the United States and of the State wherein they reside. No State shall make or enforce any law which shall abridge the privileges or immunities of citizens of the United States; nor shall any State deprive any person of life, liberty, or property, without due process of law; nor deny to any person within its jurisdiction the equal protection of the laws. . . .

Amendment XV [Section 1]. The right of citizens of the United States to vote shall not be denied or abridged by the United States or by any State on account of race, color, or previous condition of servitude.

---

## 6.3 Delegates to the Constitutional Convention, Selected Remarks, 1787

*The Constitutional Convention was called to amend the Articles of Confederation, but the delegates quickly decided to create a new form of government. However, the following excerpts from the convention deliberations reveal that delegates were aware that the purpose of the Constitution, like that of the Articles, was to effectuate the principles of the Declaration of Independence.*

[George Mason of Virginia had] "for his primary object, for the pole star of his political conduct, the preservation of the rights of the people."

[James Madison of Virginia stated that his principal aim was to secure the] "rights of the people."

[Roger Sherman of Connecticut maintained that] "the question [faced by the Convention] is not what rights naturally belong to men, but how they may be most equally and effectually guarded in society."

[Edmund Randolph of Virginia insisted that] "this . . . display of theory, howsoever proper in the first formation of state governments, . . . is unfit here; since we are not working on the natural rights of men not yet gathered into society, but upon those rights, modified by society, and . . . interwoven with what we call . . . the rights of states."

[Robert Yates of New York said that] "the first principle of government is founded on the natural rights of individuals, and in perfect equality. Locke, Vattel, Lord Somers, and Dr. Priestly, all confirm this principle."

---

## 6.4 James Wilson, Speech at the Pennsylvania Ratifying Convention, December 4, 1787

*James Wilson (1742–1798) is generally regarded as second only to James Madison in terms of contributions made to the framing of the Constitution. The following excerpt from one of Wilson's speeches urging that the Constitution be ratified explicitly addresses the connection between the Declaration of Independence and the Constitution.*

I consider the people of the United States as forming one great community; and I consider the people of the different states as forming communities, again, on a lesser scale. From this great division of the people into distinct communities, it will be found necessary that different proportions of legislative powers should be given to the governments, according to the nature, number, and magnitude of their objects.

Unless the people are considered in these two views, we shall never be able to understand the principle on which this system was constructed. I view the states as made *for* the people, as well as by them, and not the people as made for the states; the people, therefore, have a right, whilst enjoying the undeniable powers of society, to form either a general government, or state governments, in what manner they please, or to accommodate them to one another, and by this means preserve them all. This, I say, is the inherent and unalienable right of the people; and as an illustration of it, I beg to read a few words from the Declaration of Independence, made by the representatives of the United States, and recognized by the whole Union.

"We hold these truths to be self-evident, that all men are created equal; that they are endowed by their Creator with certain unalienable rights; that among these are life, liberty, and the pursuit of happiness; that, to secure these rights, *governments* are instituted among men, *deriving their just powers from the consent of the governed;* that, whenever any form of government becomes destructive of these ends, it is the right of the people to alter or abolish it, and institute new government, laying its foundation on such principles, and organizing its powers in such forms, as to them shall seem most likely to effect their safety and happiness."

This is the broad basis on which our independence was placed: on the same certain and solid foundation this system is erected.

---

# 6.5   *The Federalist*, No. 10, November 22, 1787

The Federalist *papers are a series of newspaper essays written by Alexander Hamilton (1755–1804), James Madison (1751–1836), and John Jay (1745–1829) to persuade the people of New York to ratify the Constitution. They are generally regarded as the best insight into the framers' understanding of the Constitution. The following excerpt is from Madison's famous discussion of faction, and it outlines the fundamental problem of republican government: how to reconcile the consent of the governed with security of the natural rights of all the people.*

By a faction I understand a number of citizens, whether amounting to a majority or minority of the whole, who are united and actuated by some common impulse of passion, or of interest, adverse to the rights of other citizens, or to the permanent and aggregate interests of the community.

There are two methods of curing the mischiefs of faction: the one, by removing its causes; the other, by controling its effects.

There are again two methods of removing the causes of faction: the one by destroying the liberty which is essential to its existence; the other, by giving to every citizen the same opinions, the same passions, and the same interests.

It could never be more truly said than of the first remedy, that it is worse than the disease. Liberty is to faction, what air is to fire, an aliment without which it instantly expires. But it could not be a less folly to abolish liberty, which is essential to political life, because it nourishes faction, than it would be to wish the annihilation of air, which is essential to animal life, because it imparts to fire its destructive agency.

The second expedient is as impracticable, as the first would be unwise. As long as the reason of man continues fallible, and he is at liberty to exercise it, different opinions will be formed. As long as the connection subsists between his reason and his self-love, his opinions and his passions will have a reciprocal influence on each other; and the former will be objects to which the latter will attach themselves. The diversity in the faculties of men from which the rights of property originate, is not less an insuperable obstacle to a uniformity of interests. The protection of these faculties is the first object of Government. From the protection of different and unequal faculties of acquiring property, the possession of different degrees and kinds of property immediately results: and from the influence of these on the sentiments and views of the respective proprietors, ensues a division of the society into different interests and parties.

---

## 6.6    *The Federalist*, No. 22, December 14, 1787

*The following excerpt from an essay written by Alexander Hamilton highlights one of the major defects of the Articles of Confederation: the fact that it was never ratified by representatives of the people elected for that specific purpose.*

It has not a little contributed to the infirmities of the existing federal system, that it never had a ratification by the PEOPLE. Resting on no better foundation than the consent of the several Legislatures; it has been exposed to frequent and intricate questions concerning the validity of its powers; and has in some instances given birth to the enormous doctrine of a right of legislative repeal. Owing its ratification to the law of a State, it has been contended, that the same authority might repeal the law by which it was ratified. However gross a heresy it may be, to maintain that a party to a compact has a right to revoke that compact, the doctrine itself has had respectable advocates. The possibility of a question of this nature, proves the necessity of laying the foundations of our national government deeper than in the mere sanction of delegated authority. The fabric of American Empire ought to rest on the solid basis of THE CONSENT OF THE PEOPLE. The streams of national power ought to flow immediately from that pure original fountain of all legitimate authority.

---

## 6.7    *The Federalist*, No. 40, January 18, 1788

*In this selection, James Madison invokes the fundamental principles of the Declaration of Independence as the ultimate reason why the Articles of Confederation must be replaced.*

Let us view the ground on which the Convention stood. It may be collected from their proceedings, that they were deeply and unanimously impressed with the crisis which had led their country almost with one voice to make so singular and solemn an experiment, for correcting the errors of a system by which this crisis had been produced; that they were no less deeply and unanimously convinced, that such a reform as they have proposed, was absolutely necessary to effect the purposes of their appointment. It could not be unknown to them, that the hopes and expectations of the great body of citizens, throughout this great empire, were turned with the keenest anxiety, to the event of their deliberations. They had every reason to believe that the contrary sentiments agitated the minds and bosoms of every external and internal foe to the liberty and prosperity of the United States. They had seen in the origin and progress of the experiment, the alacrity with which the proposition made by a single State (Virginia) towards a partial amendment of the confederation, had been attended to and promoted. They had seen the liberty assumed by a very few deputies, from a very few States, convened at Annapolis, of recommending a great and critical object, wholly foreign to their commission, not only justified by the public opinion, but actually carried into effect, by twelve out of the thirteen States. They had seen in a variety of instances, assumptions by Congress, not only of recommendatory, but of operative powers, warranted in the public estimation, by occasions and objects infinitely less urgent than those by which their conduct was to be governed. They must have reflected, that in all great changes of established governments, forms ought to give way to substance; that a rigid adherence in such cases to the former, would render nominal and nugatory, the transcendent and precious right of the people to "abolish or alter their governments as to them shall seem most likely to effect their safety and happiness;"* since it is impossible for the people spontaneously and universally, to move in concert towards their object; and it is therefore essential, that such changes be instituted by some informal and unauthorised propositions, made by some patriotic and respectable citizen or number of citizens. They must have recollected that it was by this irregular and assumed privilege of proposing to the people

plans for their safety and happiness, that the States were first united against the danger with which they were threatened by their antient government; that Committees and Congresses, were formed for concentrating their efforts, and defending their rights; and that Conventions were elected in the several States, for establishing the constitutions under which they are now governed; nor could it have been forgotten that no little ill-timed scruples, no zeal for adhering to ordinary forms, were any where seen, except in those who wished to indulge under these masks, their secret enmity to the substance contended for. They must have borne in mind, that as the plan to be framed and proposed, was to be submitted to the people themselves, the disapprobation of this supreme authority would destroy it for ever; its approbation blot out all antecedent errors and irregularities. It might even have occurred to them, that where a disposition to cavil prevailed, their neglect to execute the degree of power vested in them, and still more their recommendation of any measure whatever not warranted by their commission, would not less excite animadversion, than a recommendation at once of a measure fully commensurate to the national exigencies.

---

*Declaration of Independence.

---

## 6.8   *The Federalist*, No. 43, January 23, 1788

*James Madison frankly admits that the Articles of Confederation were not fully legitimate, according to the principles of the Declaration of Independence. In the final paragraph of this excerpt, he indicates that the "rights of humanity" exist and must be respected, whether or not there is a Constitution in place to secure them.*

Two questions of a very delicate nature present themselves on this occasion. 1. On what principle the confederation, which stands in the solemn form of a compact among the States, can be superseded without the unanimous consent of the parties to it? 2. What relation is to subsist between the nine or more States ratifying the Con-

stitution, and the remaining few who do not become parties to it.

The first question is answered at once by recurring to the absolute necessity of the case; to the great principle of self preservation; to the transcendent law of nature and of natures God, which declares that the safety and happiness of society are the objects at which all political institutions aim, and to which all such institutions must be sacrificed. PERHAPS also an answer may be found without searching beyond the principles of the compact itself. It has been heretofore noted among the defects of the Confederation, that in many of the States, it had received no higher sanction than a mere legislative ratification. The principle of reciprocality seems to require, that its obligation on the other States should be reduced to the same standard. A compact between independent sovereigns, founded on ordinary acts of legislative authority, can pretend to no higher validity than a league or treaty between the parties. It is an established doctrine on the subject of treaties, that all the articles are mutually conditions of each other; that a breach of any one article is a breach of the whole treaty; and that a breach committed by either of the parties absolves the others; and authorises them, if they please, to pronounce the treaty violated and void. Should it unhappily be necessary to appeal to these delicate truths for a justification for dispensing with the consent of particular States to a dissolution of the federal pact, will not the com-

plaining parties find it a difficult task to answer the MULTIPLIED and IMPORTANT infractions with which they may be confronted? The time has been when it was incumbent on us all to veil the ideas which this paragraph exhibits. The scene is now changed, and with it, the part which the same motives dictate.

The second question is not less delicate; and the flattering prospect of its being merely hypothetical, forbids an overcurious discussion of it. It is one of those cases which must be left to provide for itself. In general it may be observed, that although no political relation can subsist between the assenting and dissenting States, yet the moral relations will remain uncancelled. The claims of justice, both on one side and on the other, will be in force, and must be fulfilled; the rights of humanity must in all cases be duly and mutually respected; whilst considerations of a common interest, and above all the remembrance of the endearing scenes which are past, and the anticipation of a speedy triumph over the obstacles to re-union, will, it is hoped, not urge in vain MODERATION on one side, and PRUDENCE on the other.

---

## 6.9    *The Federalist,* No. 51, February 6, 1788

*Written by James Madison, No. 51 is an excellent summary of how the Constitution was designed to secure rights on the basis of consent. All the major constitutional themes are covered: separation of powers, division of legislative authority, federalism, multiplicity of factions, the framers' willingness to make use of selfish motives for the public good, and the ultimate limitation of government in its dependence on the people in elections.*

To what expedient then shall we finally resort for maintaining in practice the necessary partition of power among the several departments, as laid down in the constitution? The only answer that can be given is, that as all these exterior provisions are found to be inadequate, the defect must be supplied, by so contriving the interior structure of the government, as that its several constituent parts may, by their mutual relations, be the means

of keeping each other in their proper places. Without presuming to undertake a full development of this important idea, I will hazard a few general observations, which may perhaps place it in a clearer light, and enable us to form a more correct judgment of the principles and structure of the government planned by the convention.

In order to lay a due foundation for that separate and distinct exercise of the different powers of government, which to a certain extent, is admitted on all hands to be essential to the preservation of liberty, it is evident that each department should have a will of its own; and consequently should be so constituted, that the members of each should have as little agency as possible in the appointment of the members of the others. Were this principle rigorously adhered to, it would require that all the appointments for the supreme executive, legislative, and judiciary magistracies, should be drawn from the same fountain of authority, the people, through channels, having no communication whatever with one another. Perhaps such a plan of constructing the several departments would be less difficult in practice than it may in contemplation appear. Some difficulties however, and some additional expence, would attend the execution of it. Some deviations therefore from the principle must be admitted. In the constitution of the judiciary department in particular, it might be inexpedient to insist rigorously on the principle; first, because peculiar qualifications being essential in the members, the primary consideration ought to be to select that mode of choice, which best secures these qualifications; secondly, because the permanent tenure by which the appointments are held in that department, must soon destroy all sense of dependence on the authority conferring them.

It is equally evident that the members of each department should be as little dependent as possible on those of the others, for the emoluments annexed to their offices. Were the executive magistrate, or the judges, not independent of the legislature in this particular, their independence in every other would be merely nominal.

But the great security against a gradual concentration of the several powers in the same department, consists in giving to those who administer each department, the necessary constitutional means, and personal motives, to resist encroachments of the others. The provision for defence must in this, as in all other cases, be made commensurate to the danger of attack. Ambition must be made to counteract ambition. The interest of the man must be connected with the con-

stitutional rights of the place. It may be a reflection on human nature, that such devices should be necessary to controul the abuses of government. But what is government itself but the greatest of all reflections on human nature? If men were angels, no government would be necessary. If angels were to govern men, neither external nor internal controuls on government would be necessary. In framing a government which is to be administered by men over men, the great difficulty lies in this: You must first enable the government to controul the governed; and in the next place, oblige it to controul itself. A dependence on the people is no doubt the primary controul on the government; but experience has taught mankind the necessity of auxiliary precautions.

This policy of supplying by opposite and rival interests, the defect of better motives, might be traced through the whole system of human affairs, private as well as public. We see it particularly displayed in all the subordinate distributions of power; where the constant aim is to divide and arrange the several offices in such a manner as that each may be a check on the other; that the private interest of every individual, may be a centinel over the public rights. These inventions of prudence cannot be less requisite in the distribution of the supreme powers of the state.

But it is not possible to give to each department an equal power of self defence. In republican government the legislative authority, necessarily, predominates. The remedy for this inconvenience is, to divide the legislature into different branches; and to render them by different modes of election, and different principles of action, as little connected with each other, as the nature of their common functions, and their common dependence on the society, will admit. It may even be necessary to guard against dangerous encroachments by still further precautions. As the weight of the legislative authority requires that it should be thus divided, the weakness of the executive may require, on the other hand, that it should be fortified. An absolute negative, on the legislature, appears at first view to be the natural defence with which the executive magistrate should be armed. But perhaps it would be neither altogether safe, nor alone sufficient. On ordinary occasions, it might not be exerted with the requisite firmness; and on extraordinary occasions, it might be perfidiously abused. May not this defect of an absolute negative be supplied, by some qualified connection between this weaker department, and the weaker branch of the stronger department, by which the latter may be led to support the constitutional rights of the former, without being too much detached from the rights of its own department?

If the principles on which these observations are founded be just, as I persuade myself they are, and they be applied as a criterion, to the several state constitutions, and to the federal constitution, it will be found, that if the latter does not perfectly correspond with them, the former are infinitely less able to bear such a test.

There are moreover two considerations particularly applicable to the federal system of America, which place that system in a very interesting point of view.

First. In a single republic, all the power surrendered by the people, is submitted to the administration of a single government; and usurpations are guarded against by a division of the government into distinct and separate departments. In the compound republic of America, the power surrendered by the people, is first divided between two distinct governments, and then the portion allotted to each, subdivided among distinct and separate departments. Hence a double security arises to the rights of the people. The different governments will controul each other; at the same time that each will be controlled by itself.

Second. It is of great importance in a republic, not only to guard the society against the oppression of its rulers; but to guard one part of the society against the injustice of the other part. Different interests necessarily exist in different classes of citizens. If a majority be united by a common interest, the rights of the minority will be insecure. There are but two methods of providing against this evil: The one by creating a will in the community independent of the majority, that is,

of the society itself; the other by comprehending in the society so many separate descriptions of citizens, as will render an unjust combination of a majority of the whole, very improbable, if not impracticable. The first method prevails in all governments possessing an hereditary or self appointed authority. This at best is but a precarious security; because a power independent of the society may as well espouse the unjust views of the major, as the rightful interests, of the minor party, and may possibly be turned against both parties. The second method will be exemplified in the federal republic of the United States. Whilst all authority in it will be derived from and dependent on the society, the society itself will be broken into so many parts, interests and classes of citizens, that the rights of individuals or of the minority, will be in little danger from interested combinations of the majority. In a free government, the security for civil rights must be the same as for religious rights. It consists in the one case in the multiplicity of interests, and in the other, in the multiplicity of sects. The degree of security in both cases will depend on the number of interests and sects; and this may be presumed to depend on the extent of country and number of people comprehended under the same government. This view of the subject must particularly recommend a proper federal system to all the sincere and considerate friends of republican government: Since it shews that in exact proportion as the territory of the union may be formed into more circumscribed confederacies or states, oppressive combinations of a majority will be facilitated, the best security under the republican form, for the rights of every class of citizens, will be diminished; and consequently, the stability and independence of some member of the government, the only other security, must be proportionally increased. Justice is the end of government. It is the end of civil society. It ever has been, and ever will be pursued, until it be obtained, or until liberty be lost in the pursuit. In a society under the forms of which the stronger faction can readily unite and oppress the weaker, anarchy may as truly be said to reign, as in a state of nature where the weaker individual is not secured against the violence of the stronger: And as in the latter state even the stronger individuals are prompted by the uncertainty of their condition, to submit to a government which may protect the weak as well as themselves: So in the former state, will the more powerful factions or parties be gradually induced by a like motive, to wish for a government which will protect all parties, the weaker as well as the more powerful. It can be little doubted, that if the state of Rhode Island was separated from the confederacy, and left to itself, the insecurity of rights under the popular form of government within such narrow limits, would be displayed by such reiterated oppressions of factious majorities, that some power altogether independent of the people would soon be called for by the voice of the very factions whose misrule had proved the necessity of it. In the extended republic of the United States, and among the great variety of interests, parties and sects which it embraces, a coalition of a majority of the whole society could seldom take place on any other principles than those of justice and the general good; and there being thus less danger to a minor from the will of the major party, there must be less pretext also, to provide for the security of the former, by introducing into the government a will not dependent on the latter; or in other words, a will independent of the society itself. It is no less certain than it is important, notwithstanding the contrary opinions which have been entertained, that the larger the society, provided it lie within a practicable sphere, the more duly capable it will be of self government. And happily for the republican cause, the practicable sphere may be carried to a very great extent, by a judicious modification and mixture of the federal principle.

---

# 7.1   State Constitutions, Enabling Acts, Admission Acts, and Presidential Proclamations of Admission

*Often overlooked in constitutional jurisprudence is the significant role played by state constitutions, several of which were enacted even before the united colonies declared their independence. As the following excerpts from 1776 to 1907 suggest, many state constitutions employed language drawn from the Declaration of Independence, while others ignored the Declaration's principles—until forced to include them following the Civil War—to avoid slavery's stark contradiction with those principles. Also included are excerpts from state enabling acts (federal laws defining the terms upon which new states were to be admitted to the Union). Most of the enabling acts followed one of three models: the Ohio model, mandating compliance with the provisions of the Northwest Ordinance; the Mississippi model, exempting from that requirement the prohibition on slavery; and the Nebraska model, substituting conformity to the principles of the Declaration for compliance with the Northwest Ordinance.*

## ALABAMA

1819 ENABLING ACT
[See Mississippi model]

1819 CONSTITUTION
- Preamble: "[I]n order to establish justice, insure tranquility, provide for the common defence, promote the general welfare, and secure to ourselves and our posterity the rights of life, liberty, and property, do or-

dain and establish the following constitution or form of government."
- Article I, Section 1: "That all freemen, when they form a social compact, are equal in rights; and that no man or set of men are entitled to exclusive, separate public emoluments or privileges, but in consideration of public services."
- Article I, Section 2: "All political power is inherent in the people, and all free govern-

ments are founded on their authority, and instituted for their benefit: and, therefore, they have at all times an inalienable and indefeasible right to alter, reform, or abolish their form of government, in such manner as they may think expedient."

- Article I, Section 30: "This enumeration of certain rights shall not be construed to deny or disparage others retained by the people; and to guard against any encroachments on the rights herein retained, or any transgression of any of the high powers herein delegated, we declare, that everything in this article is excepted out of the general powers of government, and shall forever remain inviolate; and that all laws contrary thereto, or to the following provisions, shall remain void."

- Article VI, Section 1: "The general assembly shall have no power to pass laws for the emancipation of slaves, without the consent of their owners, or without paying their owners, previous to such emancipation, a full equivalent in money for the slaves so emancipated. They shall have no power to prevent emigrants to this State from bringing with them such persons as are deemed slaves by the laws of any one of the United States, so long as any person of the same age or description shall be continued in slavery by the laws of this State: *Provided,* That such person or slave be the *bona-fide* property of such emigrants: *And provided, also,* That laws may be passed to prohibit the introduction into this State of slaves who have committed high crimes in other States or Territories. They shall have power to pass laws to permit the owners of slaves to emancipate them, saving the rights of creditors, and preventing them from becoming a public charge. They shall have full power to prevent slaves from being brought into this State as merchandise, and also to oblige the owners of slaves to treat them with humanity, to provide for them necessary food and clothing, to abstain from all injuries to them extending to life or limb, and, in case of their neglect, or refusal to comply with the directions of such laws, to have such slave or slaves sold for the benefit of the owner or owners."

1865 CONSTITUTION

- Preamble: "We, the people of the State of Alabama, by our representatives in convention assembled; in order to establish justice, insure domestic tranquility, provide for the common defence, promote the general welfare, and secure to ourselves and to our posterity the rights of life, liberty, and property; invoking the favor and guidance of Almighty God, do ordain and establish the following constitution and form of government for the State of Alabama—that is to say:"

- Article I, Section 1: "That no man, and no set of men, are entitled to exclusive separate public emoluments or privileges, but in consideration of public services."

- Article I, Section 2: "That all political power is inherent in the people, and all free governments are founded on their authority, and instituted for their benefit; and that, therefore, they have at all times an inalienable and indefeasible right to alter, reform, or abolish their form of government, in such manner as they may deem expedient."

- Article I, Section 34: "That hereafter there shall be in this State neither slavery, nor involuntary servitude, otherwise than for the punishment of crime, whereof the party shall have been duly convicted."

- Article I, Section 36: "This enumeration of certain rights shall not be construed to deny or disparage others retained by the people; and to guard against any encroachment on the rights hereby retained, or any transgression of any of the high powers by this constitution delegated, we declare, that everything in this article is excepted out of the general powers of government, and shall forever remain inviolate, and that all laws contrary thereto, or to the following provisions, shall be void."

1867 CONSTITUTION
- Preamble: [Same as 1865 Alabama Constitution]
- Article I, Section 1: "That all men are created equal; that they are endowed by their Creator with certain inalienable rights; that among these are life, liberty, and the pursuit of happiness."
- Article I, Sections 3, 35: [Similar to 1865 Alabama Constitution, Article I, Sections 2 and 34]
- Article I, Section 37: "That this State has no right to sever its relation to the Federal Union, or to pass any law in derogation of the paramount allegiance of the citizens of this State to the Government of the United States."
- Article I, Section 38: "That this enumeration of certain rights shall not impair or deny others retained by the people."

1875 CONSTITUTION
- Article I, Section 1: "That all men are equally free and independent; that they are endowed by their Creator with certain inalienable rights; that among these are life, liberty, and the pursuit of happiness."
- Article I, Section 3: [Similar to 1865 Alabama Constitution, Article I, Section 2]
- Article I, Sections 33, 39: [Same as 1867 Alabama Constitution, Article I, Sections 35, 38]

## ARIZONA

1906 ENABLING ACT
[See Nebraska model]

## ARKANSAS

1836 CONSTITUTION
- Preamble: "We, the people of the Territory of Arkansas, . . . in order to secure to ourselves and our posterity the enjoyment of all the rights of life, liberty, and property, and the free pursuit of happiness, do mutually agree with each other to form ourselves into a free and independent State, by the name and style of 'The State of Arkansas,' and do ordain and establish the following constitution for the government thereof:"
- Article II, Section 1: "That all freemen, when they form a social compact, are equal, and have certain inherent and indefeasible rights, among which are those of enjoying and defending life and liberty; of acquiring, possessing and protecting property and reputation; and of pursuing their own happiness."
- Article II, Section 2: "That all power is inherent in the people; and all free governments are founded on their authority, and instituted for their peace, safety and happiness. For the advancement of these ends, they have at all times, an unqualified right to alter, reform or abolish their government, in such manner as they may think proper."
- Article II, Section 24: "This enumeration of rights shall not be construed to deny or disparage others retained by the people; and, to guard against any encroachments on the rights herein retained, or any transgression of any of the higher powers herein delegated, we declare that everything in this article is excepted out of the general powers of the government, and shall forever remain inviolate; and that all laws contrary thereto, or to the other provisions herein contained, shall be void."
- Article VII, Section 1: "The general assembly shall have no power to pass laws for the emancipation of slaves, without the consent of the owners. They shall have no power to prevent emigrants to this State from bringing with them such persons as are deemed slaves by the laws of any one of the United States. They shall have power to pass laws to permit owners of slaves to emancipate them, saving the right of creditors, and preventing them from becoming a public charge. They shall have power to prevent slaves from being brought to this State as merchandise, and also to oblige the owners of slaves to treat them with humanity."

**1864 Constitution**

- Preamble: "And we, the people of the State of Arkansas, in order to establish therein a State government, loyal to the Government of the United States—to secure to ourselves and our posterity, the protection and blessings of the Federal Constitution, and the enjoyment of all the rights of liberty and the free pursuit of happiness, do agree to continue ourselves as a free and independent State, by the name and style of 'the State of Arkansas,' and do ordain and establish the following Constitution for the government thereof:"
- Article II, Section 1: [Same as 1836 Arkansas Constitution, Article II, Section 1, except "men" substituted for "freemen"]
- Article II, Sections 2, 24: [Same as 1836 Arkansas Constitution, Article II, Sections 2, 24]

**1868 Constitution**

- Bill of Rights, Article I, Section 1: "All political power is inherent in the people. Government is instituted for the protection, security and benefit of the people, and they have the right to alter or reform the same whenever the public good may require it. But the paramount allegiance of every citizen is due to the Federal Government in the exercise of all its constitutional powers as the same may have been or may be defined by the Supreme Court of the United States, and no power exists in the people of this or any other State of the Federal Union to dissolve their connection therewith, or perform any act tending to impair, subvert or resist the supreme authority of the United States. The Constitution of the United States confers full powers on the Federal Government to maintain and perpetuate its existence; and whensoever any portion of the States, or the people thereof, attempt to secede from the Federal Union, or forcibly resist the execution of its laws, the Federal Government may, by warrant of the Constitution, employ armed force in compelling obedience to its authority."

- Article I, Section 3: "The equality of all persons before the law is recognized and shall ever remain inviolate; nor shall any citizen ever be deprived of any right, privilege, or immunity, nor exempted from any burden or duty, on account of race, color, or previous condition."
- Article V, Section 37: "No citizen of this State shall be disfranchised, or deprived of any of the rights or privileges secured to any citizen thereof, unless the same is done by the law of the land, or the judgment of his peers, except as hereinafter provided. There shall be neither slavery nor involuntary servitude, either by indentures, apprenticeships or otherwise, in the State, except for the punishment of crime, whereof the party shall have been duly convicted."

**1874 Constitution**

- Article II, Section 1: [Similar to 1836 Arkansas Constitution, Article II, Section 2]
- Article II, Section 2: "All men are created equally free and independent, and have certain inherent and inalienable rights; amongst which are those of enjoying and defending life and liberty; of acquiring, possessing, and protecting property and reputation; and of pursuing their own happiness. To secure these rights governments are instituted among men, deriving their just powers from the consent of the governed."
- Article II, Section 3: [Same as 1868 Arkansas Constitution, Article I, Section 3]
- Article II, Section 27: "There shall be no slavery in this State, nor involuntary servitude, except as a punishment for crime."
- Article II, Section 29: [Same as 1836 Arkansas Constitution, Article II, Section 24]

## CALIFORNIA

**1849 Constitution**

- Article I, Section 1: "All men are by nature free and independent, and have certain inalienable rights, among which are those of enjoying and defending life and liberty, acquiring, possessing, and protecting property, and pursuing and obtaining safety and happiness."

- Article I, Section 2: "All political power is inherent to the people. Government is instituted for the protection, security, and benefit of the people; and they have the right to alter or reform the same whenever the public good may require it."
- Article I, Section 18: "Neither slavery, nor involuntary servitude, unless for the punishment of crimes, shall ever be tolerated in this State."
- Article I, Section 21: "This enumeration of rights shall not be construed to impair or deny others retained by the people."

1879 CONSTITUTION

- Article I, Sections 1, 2, 18, 23: [Same as 1849 California Constitution, Article I, Sections 1, 2, 18, 21]

## COLORADO

1875 ENABLING ACT
[See Nebraska model]

1876 CONSTITUTION

- Bill of Rights, Article II, Section 1: "That all political power is vested in and derived from the people; that all government, of right, originates from the people, is founded upon their will only, and is instituted solely for the good of the whole."
- Article II, Section 2: "That the people of this State have the sole and exclusive right of governing themselves, as a free, sovereign, and independent State, and to alter and abolish their constitution and form of government whenever they may deem it necessary to their safety and happiness, provided such change be not repugnant to the Constitution of the United States."
- Article II, Section 3: "That all persons have certain natural, essential, and inalienable rights, among which may be reckoned the right of enjoying and defending their lives and liberties; that of acquiring, possessing,

and protecting property, and of seeking and obtaining their safety and happiness."

- Article II, Section 26: "That there shall never be in this State either slavery or involuntary servitude, except as a punishment for crime, whereof the party shall have been duly convicted."
- Article II, Section 28: "The enumeration in this constitution of certain rights shall not be construed to deny, impair, or disparage others retained by the people."

## CONNECTICUT

1818 CONSTITUTION

- Article I, Section 1: "That all men, when they form a social compact, are equal in rights; and that no man or set of men are entitled to exclusive public emoluments or privileges from the community."

## DELAWARE

1776 CONSTITUTION

- Article XXVI: "No person hereafter imported into this State from Africa ought to be held in slavery under any pretence whatever; and no Negro, Indian, or mulatto slave ought to be brought into this State, for sale, from any part of the world."

1792 CONSTITUTION

- Preamble: "Through divine goodness all men have, by nature, the rights of worshipping and serving their Creator according to the dictates of their consciences; of enjoying and defending life and liberty, of acquiring and protecting reputation and property, . . . and, therefore, all just authority in the institutions of political society is derived from the people, and established with their consent, to advance their happiness. And they may, for this end, as circumstances require, from time to time, alter their constitution of government."

1831 CONSTITUTION

- Preamble: [Same as 1792 Delaware Constitution]

## 1897 Constitution

- Preamble: [Same as 1792 Delaware Constitution]

## FLORIDA

### 1838 Constitution

- Article I, Section 1: "That all freemen, when they form a social compact, are equal, and have certain inherent and indefeasible rights, among which are those of enjoying and defending life and liberty; of acquiring, possessing, and protecting property and reputation, and of pursuing their own happiness."
- Article I, Section 2: "That all political power is inherent in the people, and all free governments are founded on their authority, and established for their benefit; and, therefore, they have at all times an inalienable and indefeasible right to alter or abolish their form of government in such manner as they may deem expedient."
- Article XVI, Section 1: "The general assembly shall have no power to pass laws for the emancipation of slaves."
- Article XVI, Section 2: "They shall have no power to prevent emigrants to this State from bringing with them such persons as may be deemed slaves by the laws of any one of the United States: *Provided*, They shall have power to enact laws to prevent the introduction of any slaves who may have committed crimes in other States."

### 1865 Constitution

- Article I, Sections 1, 2: [Similar to 1838 Florida Constitution, Article I, Sections 1, 2]
- Article XVI, Section 1: "Whereas slavery has been destroyed in this State by the Government of the United States, therefore neither slavery nor involuntary servitude shall in future exist in this State, except as a punishment for crimes whereof the party shall have been convicted by the courts of the State; and all the inhabitants of the State, without distinction of color, are free, and shall enjoy the rights of person and property, without distinction of color."

### 1868 Constitution

- Article I, Section 1: "All men are by nature free and equal, and have certain inalienable rights, among which are those of enjoying and defending life and liberty, acquiring, possessing, and protecting property, and pursuing and obtaining safety and happiness."
- Article I, Section 2: "All political power is inherent in the people. Government is instituted for the protection, security, and benefit of its citizens, and they have the right to alter or amend the same whenever the public good may require it; but the paramount allegiance of every citizen is due to the Federal Government, and no power exists with the people of this State to dissolve its connection therewith."
- Article I, Section 19: "Neither slavery or involuntary servitude, unless for the punishment of crime, shall ever be tolerated in this State."

### 1885 Constitution

- Declaration of Rights, Section 1: "All men are equal before the law, and have certain inalienable rights, among which are those of enjoying and defending life and liberty, acquiring, possessing, and protecting property, and pursuing happiness and obtaining safety."
- Sections 2, 19: [Same as 1868 Florida Constitution, Article I, Sections 2, 19]
- Section 24: "The enunciation of rights shall not be construed to impair or deny others retained by the people."

## GEORGIA

### 1777 Constitution

- Preamble: "Whereas the conduct of the legislature of Great Britain for many years past has been so oppressive on the people of America that of late years they have plainly declared and asserted a right to raise taxes upon the people of America, and to make laws to bind them in all cases whatsoever, without their consent; which conduct, being repugnant to the common rights of mankind, hath obliged the Americans, as freemen, to oppose such oppressive measures, and to assert the rights and privileges they are entitled to by the laws of nature and reason; . . ."

1798 CONSTITUTION

- Article IV, Section 11: "There shall be no future importation of slaves into this State, from Africa or any foreign place, after the first day of October next. The legislature shall have no power to pass laws for the emancipation of slaves without the consent of each of their respective owners, previous to such emancipation. They shall have no power to prevent emigrants from either of the United States to this State from bringing with them such persons as may be deemed slaves by the laws of any one of the United States."

1865 CONSTITUTION

- Article I, Section 20: "The Government of the United States having, as a war-measure, proclaimed all slaves held or owned in this State emancipated from slavery, and having carried that proclamation into full practical effect, there shall henceforth be, within the State of Georgia, neither slavery nor involuntary servitude, save as a punishment for crime, after legal conviction thereof: *Provided,* This acquiescence in the action of the Government of the United States is not intended to operate as a relinquishment, waiver, or estoppel of such claim for compensation of loss sustained by reason of the emancipation of his slaves as any citizen of Georgia may hereafter make upon the justice and magnanimity of that Government."
- Article I, Section 21: "The enumeration of rights herein contained is a part of this constitution, but shall not be construed to deny to the people any inherent rights which they have hitherto enjoyed."

1868 CONSTITUTION

- Article I, Section 1: "Protection to person and property is the paramount duty of government, and shall be impartial and complete."
- Article I, Section 4: "There shall be within the State of Georgia neither slavery nor involuntary servitude, save as a punishment for crime after legal conviction thereof."

1877 CONSTITUTION

- Article I, Section 1, paragraph 1: "All government, of right, originates with the people, is founded upon their will only, and is instituted solely for the good of the whole."
- Article I, Section 1, paragraph 17: [Same as 1868 Georgia Constitution, Article I, Section 4]
- Article I, Section 5, paragraph 1: "The people of this State have the inherent, sole and exclusive right of regulating their internal government, and the police thereof, and of altering and abolishing their Constitution whenever it may be necessary to their safety and happiness."

## IDAHO

1889 CONSTITUTION

- Declaration of Rights, Article I, Section 1: "All men are by nature free and equal and have certain inalienable rights, among which are enjoying and defending life and liberty, acquiring, possessing, and protecting property, pursuing happiness, and securing safety."
- Article I, Section 2: "All political power is inherent in the people. Government is instituted for their equal protection and benefit, and they have the right to alter, reform, or abolish the same whenever they may deem it necessary, and no special privileges or immunities shall ever be granted that may not be altered, revoked, or repealed by the legislature."
- Article I, Section 3: "The State of Idaho is an inseparable part of the American Union, and the Constitution of the United States is the supreme law of the land."

- Article I, Section 21: "This enumeration of rights shall not be construed to impair or deny other rights retained by the people."

## ILLINOIS

1818 ENABLING ACT
[See Ohio model]

1818 CONSTITUTION

- Article VI, Section 1: "Neither slavery nor involuntary servitude shall hereafter be introduced into this State, otherwise than for the punishment of crimes, whereof the party shall have been duly convicted; nor shall any male person, arrived at the age of twenty-one years, nor female person arrived at the age of eighteen years, be held to serve any person as a servant, under any indenture hereafter made, unless such person shall enter into such indenture while in a state of perfect freedom, and on condition of a *bona-fide* consideration received or to be received for their service. Nor shall any indenture of any Negro or mulatto, hereafter made and executed out of this State, or if made in this State, where the term of service exceeds one year, be of at least validity, except those given in cases of apprenticeship."
- Article VIII, Section 1: "That all men are born equally free and independent, and have certain inherent and indefeasible rights; among which are those of enjoying and defending life and liberty, and of acquiring, possessing, and protecting property and reputation, and of pursuing their own happiness."
- Article VIII, Section 2: "That all power is inherent in the people, and all free governments are founded on their authority, and instituted for their peace, safety, and happiness."

1848 CONSTITUTION

- Article XIII, Sections 1, 2: [Same as 1818 Illinois Constitution, Article VIII, Sections 1, 2]
- Article XIV: "The general assembly shall, at its first session under the amended constitu-

tion, pass such laws as will effectually prohibit free persons of color from immigrating to and settling in this State; and to effectually prevent the owners of slaves from bringing them into this State, for the purpose of setting them free."

1870 CONSTITUTION

- Article II, Section 1: "All men are by nature free and independent, and have certain inherent and inalienable rights—among these are life, liberty and the pursuit of happiness. To secure these rights and the protection of property, governments are instituted among men, deriving their just powers from the consent of the governed."

## INDIANA

1816 ENABLING ACT
[See Ohio model]

1816 CONSTITUTION

- Article I, Section 1: "That the general, great and essential principles of liberty and free Government may be recognized and unalterably established; we declare, that all men are born equally free and independent, and have certain natural inherent, and unalienable rights; among which are the enjoying and defending life and liberty, and of acquiring, possessing and protecting property and pursuing and obtaining happiness and safety."
- Article I, Section 2: "That all power is inherent in the people; and all free Governments are founded on their authority, and instituted for their peace, safety and happiness. For the advancement of these ends, they have at all times an unalienable and indefeasible right to alter or reform their Government in such manner as they may think proper."
- Article XI, Section 7: "There shall be neither slavery nor involuntary servitude in this State, otherwise than for the punishment of crimes, whereof the party shall have been duly convicted, nor shall any indenture of any Negro or mulatto, hereafter made and

executed out of the bounds of this State be of any validity within the State."

1851 CONSTITUTION

- Article I, Section 1: "We declare that all men are created equal; that they are endowed by their Creator with certain unalienable rights; that among these are life, liberty, and the pursuit of happiness; that all power is inherent to the people; and that all free governments are, and of right ought to be, founded on their authority, and instituted for their peace safety, and well being. For the advancement of these ends, the people have at all times an indefeasible right to alter and reform their government."
- Article I, Section 37: [Similar to 1816 Indiana Constitution, Article XI, Section 7, except the word "hereafter" has been deleted]
- Article XIII, Section 1: "No Negro or mulatto shall come into, or settle in the State, after the adoption of this constitution."

## IOWA

1846 CONSTITUTION

- Bill of Rights, Article I, Section 1: "All men are, by nature, free and independnt, and have certain unalienable rights—among which are those of enjoying and defending life and liberty, acquiring, possessing and protecting property, and pursuing and obtaining safety and happiness."
- Article I, Section 2: "All political power is inherent in the people. Government is instituted for the protection, security, and benefit of the people, and they have the right, at all times, to alter or reform the same, whenever the public good may require it."
- Article I, Section 23: "Neither slavery nor involuntary servitude, unless for the punishment of crimes, shall ever be tolerated in this State."
- Article I, Section 24: "This enumeration of rights shall not be construed to impair or deny others, retained by the people."

1857 CONSTITUTION

- Bill of Rights, Article I, Section 1: [Same as 1847 Iowa Constitution, except "equal" substituted for "independent"]
- Article I, Sections 2, 23, 25: [Same as 1847 Iowa Constitution, Article I, Sections 2, 23, 24]

## KANSAS

Competing free-soil and slave factions in Kansas held several different constitutional conventions, resulting in several different proposed constitutions before Congress finally admitted Kansas to statehood.

1855 CONSTITUTION (TOPEKA)

- Bill of Rights, Article I, Section 1: "All men are by nature free and independent, and have certain inalienable rights, among which are those of enjoying and defending life and liberty, acquiring, possessing, and protecting property, and seeking and obtaining happiness and safety."
- Article I, Section 2: "All political power is inherent in the people. Government is instituted for their equal protection and benefit; and they have the right to alter, reform, or abolish the same whenever they may deem it necessary; and no special privileges or immunities shall ever be granted that may not be altered, revoked, or repealed by the general assembly."
- Article I, Section 21: "No indenture of any Negro, or mulatto, made and executed out of the bounds of the State shall be valid within the State."
- Article I, Section 22: "This enumeration of rights shall not be construed to impair or deny others retained by the people; and all powers not herein delegated shall remain with the people."

1857 CONSTITUTION (LECOMPTON)

- Article VII, Section 1: "The right of property is before and higher than any constitutional sanction, and the right of the owner of a slave to such slave and its increase is the same, and as inviolable as the right of the owner of any property whatever."

- Article VII, Section 2: "The legislature shall have no power to pass laws for the emancipation of slaves without the consent of the owners, or without paying the owners previous to their emancipation a full equivalent in money for the slaves so emancipated. They shall have no power to prevent emigrants to the State from bringing with them such persons as are deemed slaves by the laws of any one of the United States or Territories, so long as any person of the same age or description shall be continued in slavery by the laws of this State:"
- Bill of Rights, Article XV, Section 1: "That all freemen, when they form a social compact, are equal in rights, and that no man or set of men are entitled to exclusive separate public emoluments or privileges but in consideration of public services."
- Article XV, Section 2: "All political power is inherent in the people, and all free governments are founded on their authority, and instituted for their benefit; and therefore they have at all times an inalienable and indefeasible right to alter, reform, or abolish their form of government in such manner as they may think proper."
- Article XV, Section 23: "Free Negroes shall not be permitted to live in this State under any circumstances."
- Article XV, Section 24: "This enumeration of rights shall not be construed to deny or disparage others retained by the people; and to guard against any encroachments on the rights herein retained, or any transgression of any of the higher power herein delegated, we declare that everything in this article is excepted out of the general powers of government, and shall forever remain inviolate, and that all laws contrary thereto, or to the other provisions herein contained, shall be void."

1858 CONSTITUTION (LEAVENWORTH)
- Bill of Rights, Article I, Section 1: "All men are by nature equally free and independent, and have certain inalienable rights, among which are those of enjoying and defending life and liberty, acquiring, possessing, and protecting property, and seeking and obtaining happiness and safety; and the right of all men to the control of their persons exists prior to law, and is inalienable."
- Article I, Section 2: "All political power is inherent in the people, and all free governments are founded on their authority, and are instituted for their equal protection and benefit, and they alone have the right at all times to alter, reform, or abolish their form of government in such manner as they may think proper. No special privileges or immunities shall ever be granted by the general assembly which may not be altered, revoked, or repealed by the same authority."
- Article I, Sections 2, 21, 22: [Similar to 1855 Kansas Constitution, Article I, Sections 2, 21, 22]

1859 CONSTITUTION (WYANDOTTE)
- Bill of Rights, Section 1: "All men are possessed of equal and inalienable natural rights, among which are life, liberty, and the pursuit of happiness."
- Sections 2, 20: [Similar to 1855 Kansas Constitution, Article I, Sections 2, 20]

## KENTUCKY

1790 TERRITORIAL GOVERNMENT
- Section 1: "*Be it enacted by the Senate and House of Representatives of the United States of America in Congress* assembled, That the territory of the United States south of the river Ohio, for the purposes of temporary government, shall be one district; the inhabitants of which shall enjoy all the privileges, benefits, and advantages set forth in the ordinance of the late Congress for the government of the territory of the United States northwest of the river Ohio. And the

government of the said territory south of the Ohio shall be similar to that which is now exercised in the territory northwest of the Ohio; except so far as is otherwise provided in the conditions expressed in an act of Congress of the present session, entitled 'An act to accept a cession of the claims of the State of North Carolina to a certain district of western territory.' "

1792 CONSTITUTION

- Article IX, Section 1: "The legislature shall have no power to pass laws for the emancipation of slaves without the consent of their owners, previous to such emancipation, and a full equivalent in money for the slaves so emancipated. They shall have no power to prevent emigrants to this State from bringing with them such persons as are deemed slaves by the laws of any one of the United States, so long as any person of the same age or description shall be continued in slavery by the laws of this State."
- Article XII, Section 1: "That the general, great, and essential principles of liberty and free government may be recognized and unalterably established, we declare that all men, when they form a social compact, are equal, and that no man or set of men are entitled to the exclusive or separate public emoluments or privileges from the community, but in consideration of public services."
- Article XII, Section 2: "That all power is inherent in the people, and all free governments are founded on their authority and instituted for their peace, safety, and happiness. For the advancement of those ends, they have at all times an unalienable and indefeasible right to alter, reform, or abolish their government, in such manner as they may think proper."
- Article XII, Section 28: "To guard against the high powers which have been delegated, we declare that everything in this article is excepted out of the general powers of government, and shall forever remain inviolate;

and that all laws contrary thereto, or contrary to this constitution, shall be void."

1799 CONSTITUTION

- Article VII, Section 1: [Similar to 1792 Kentucky Constitution, Article IX, Section 1]
- Article X, Section 1: [Similar to 1792 Kentucky Constitution, Article XII, Section 1, except "free men" substituted for "men"]
- Article X, Sections 2, 28: [Same as 1792 Kentucky Constitution, Article XII, Sections 2, 28]

1850 CONSTITUTION

- Article X, Section 1: "The general assembly shall have no power to pass laws for the emancipation of slaves without the consent of their owners, or without paying their owners, previous to such emancipation, a full equivalent in money for the slaves so emancipated, and providing for their removal from the State. They shall have no power to prevent immigrants to this State from bringing with them such persons as are deemed slaves by the laws of any of the United States, so long as any person of the same age or description shall be continued in slavery by the laws of this State. They shall pass laws to permit owners of slaves to emancipate them, saving the rights of creditors, and to prevent them from remaining in this State after they are emancipated. They shall have full power to prevent slaves being brought into this State as merchandise. They shall have full power to prevent slaves being brought into this State who have been, since the first day of January, one thousand seven hundred and eighty-nine, or may hereafter be, imported into any of the United States from a foreign country. And they shall have full power to pass such laws as may be necessary to oblige the owners of slaves to treat them with humanity; to provide for them necessary clothing and provisions; to abstain from all injuries to them extending to life or limb; and in case of their neglect or refusal to comply with the directions of such laws, to have such slave or slaves sold for the benefit of their owner or owners."

- Article XIII, Section 1: [Same as 1799 Kentucky Constitution, Article X, Section 1]
- Article XIII, Section 2: "That absolute, arbitrary power over the lives, liberty, and property of freemen exists nowhere in a republic, not even in the largest majority."
- Article XIII, Section 3: "The right of property is before and higher than any constitutional sanction; and the right of the owner of a slave to such slave, and its increase, is the same, and as inviolable as the right of the owner of any property whatever."
- Article XIII, Sections 4, 30: [Same as 1792 Kentucky Constitution, Article XII, Sections 2, 28]

1890 CONSTITUTION

- Bill of Rights, Section 1: "All men are, by nature, free and equal, and have certain inherent and inalienable rights, among which may be reckoned: *First:* The right of enjoying and defending their lives and liberties. *Second:* The right of worshiping Almighty God according to the dictates of their consciences. *Third:* The right of seeking and pursuing their safety and happiness. *Fourth:* The right of freely communicating their thoughts and opinions. *Fifth:* The right of acquiring and protecting property. *Sixth:* The right of assembling together in a peaceable manner for their common good, and of applying to those invested with the power of government for redress of grievances or other proper purposes, by petition, address or remonstrance. *Seventh:* The right to bear arms in defense of themselves and of the State, subject to the power of the General Assembly to enact laws to prevent persons from carrying concealed weapons."
- Section 3: "All men, when they form a social compact, are equal; and no grant of exclusive, separate public emoluments or privileges shall be made to any man or set of men, except in consideration of public services; but no property shall be exempt from taxation except as provided in this Constitution; and every grant of a franchise, privilege or exemption, shall remain subject to revocation, alteration or amendment."
- Sections 4, 26: [Similar to 1792 Kentucky Constitution, Article XII, Sections 2, 28]
- Section 25: "Slavery and involuntary servitude in this State are forbidden, except as a punishment for crime, whereof the party shall have been duly convicted."

## LOUISIANA

1805 TERRITORIAL GOVERNMENT FOR ORLEANS DISTRICT

- Section 1: "*Be it enacted by the Senate and House of Representatives of the United States of America in Congress assembled,* That the President of the United States be, and he is hereby, authorized to establish with the territory of Orleans a government in all respects similar (except as is herein otherwise provided) to that now exercised in the Mississippi territory; and shall, in the recess of the Senate, but to be nominated at their next meeting, for their advice and consent, appoint all the officers necessary therein, in conformity with the ordinance of Congress, made on the thirteenth day of July, one thousand seven hundred and eighty-seven; and that from and after the establishment of the said government, the inhabitants of the territory of Orleans shall be entitled to and enjoy all the rights, privileges, and advantages secured by the said ordinance, and now enjoyed by the people of the Mississippi territory."
- Section 5: "*And be it further enacted,* That the second paragraph of the said ordinance, which regulates the descent and distribution of estates; and also the sixth article of compact which is annexed to and makes part of said ordinance, are hereby declared not to extend to but are excluded from all operation within the said territory of Orleans."

1812 CONSTITUTION

- Preamble: "In order to secure to all the citizens thereof the enjoyment of *the right of life, liberty and property,* do ordain and establish the following constitution or form of government, and do mutually agree with each other to form ourselves into a free and independent State, by the name of the State of Louisiana."

1864 CONSTITUTION

- Title I, Article 1: "Slavery and involuntary servitude, except as a punishment for crime, whereof the party shall have been duly convicted, are hereby forever abolished and prohibited throughout the State."
- Title I, Article 2: "The legislature shall make no law recognizing the right of property in man."

1868 CONSTITUTION

- Bill of Rights, Title I, Article 1: "All men are created free and equal, and have certain inalienable rights; among these are life, liberty, and the pursuit of happiness. To secure these rights, governments are instituted among men, deriving their just powers from the consent of the governed."
- Title I, Article 3: "There shall be neither slavery nor involuntary servitude in this State, otherwise than for the punishment of crime, whereof the party shall have been duly convicted."
- Title I, Article 14: "The rights enumerated in this title shall not be construed to limit or abridge other rights of the people not herein expressed."

1879 CONSTITUTION

- Bill of Rights, Article I: "All government of right originates with the people, is founded on their will alone, and is instituted solely for the good of the whole, deriving its just powers from the consent of the governed. Its only legitimate end is to protect the citizen in the enjoyment of life, liberty and property. When it assumes other functions it is usurpation and oppression."
- Articles V, XIII: [Similar to 1868 Louisiana Constitution, Title I, Articles III, XIV]

1898 CONSTITUTION

- Bill of Rights, Article I: "All government, of right, originates with the people, is founded on their will alone and is instituted solely for the good of the whole. Its only legitimate end is to secure justice to all, preserve peace and promote the interest and happiness of the people."
- Article XV: [Same as 1868 Louisiana Constitution, Title I, Article XIV]

## MAINE

1819 CONSTITUTION

- Article I, Section 1: "All men are born equally free and independent, and have certain natural, inherent and unalienable rights, among which are those of enjoying and defending life and liberty, acquiring, possessing and protecting property, and of pursuing and obtaining safety and happiness."
- Article I, Section 2: "All power is inherent in the people; all free governments are founded in their authority and instituted for their benefit; they have therefore an unalienable and indefeasible right to institute government, and to alter, reform, or totally change the same, when their safety and happiness require it."
- Article I, Section 24: "The enumeration of certain rights shall not impair nor deny others retained by the people."

## MARYLAND

1776 CONSTITUTION

- Declaration of Rights, Article I: "That all government of right originates from the people, is founded in compact only, and instituted solely for the good of the whole."
- Article IV: "That all persons invested with the legislative or executive powers of government are the trustees of the public, and, as such, accountable for their conduct; wherefore, whenever the ends of government are perverted, and public liberty man-

ifestly endangered, and all other means of redress are ineffectual, the people may, and of right ought, to reform the old or establish a new government. The doctrine of non-resistance, against arbitrary power and oppression, is absurd, slavish, and destructive of the good and happiness of mankind."

1851 CONSTITUTION

- Declaration of Rights, Article I: "That all government of right originates from the people, is founded in compact only, and instituted solely for the good of the whole; and they have at all times, according to the mode prescribed in this constitution, the unalienable right to alter, reform, or abolish their form of government, in such manner as they may deem expedient."
- Article XXI: "That no freeman ought to be taken or imprisoned, or disseized of his freehold, liberties, or privileges, or outlawed, or exiled, or in any manner destroyed, or deprived of his life, liberty, or property, but by the judgment of his peers, or by the law of the land: *Provided,* That nothing in this article shall be so construed as to prevent the legislature from passing all such laws for the government, regulation, and disposition of the free colored population of this State as they may deem necessary."
- Article XLII: "This enumeration of rights shall not be construed to impair or deny others retained by the people."

1864 CONSTITUTION

- Declaration of Rights, Article I: "That we hold it to be self-evident that all men are created equally free; that they are endowed by their Creator with certain unalienable rights, among which are life, liberty, the enjoyment of the proceeds of their own labor, and the pursuit of happiness."
- Articles II, XLIV: [Same as 1851 Maryland Constitution, Declaration of Rights, Articles I, XLII]
- Article XXIV: "That hereafter, in this State, there shall be neither slavery nor involuntary servitude, except in punishment of

crime, whereof the party shall have been duly convicted; and all persons held to service or labor as slaves are hereby declared free."

1867 CONSTITUTION

- Declaration of Rights, Articles I, XLV: [Same as 1851 Maryland Constitution, Declaration of Rights, Articles I, XLII]
- Article XXIV: "That slavery shall not be re-established in this State; but having been abolished, under the policy and authority of the United States, compensation in consideration thereof, is due from the United States."

## MASSACHUSETTS

1780 CONSTITUTION

- Preamble: "The end of the institution, maintenance, and administration of government, is to secure the existence of the body politic, to protect it, and to furnish the individuals who compose it with the power of enjoying in safety and tranquility their natural rights, and the blessings of life: and whenever these great objects are not obtained, the people have a right to alter the government, and to take measures necessary for their safety, prosperity, and happiness."
- Preamble: "The body politic is formed by a voluntary association of individuals: it is a social compact, by which the whole people covenants with each citizen, and each citizen with the whole people, that all shall be governed by certain laws for the common good. It is the duty of the people, therefore, in framing a constitution of government, to provide for an equitable mode of making laws, as well as for an impartial interpretation and a faithful execution of them; that every man may, at all times, find his security in them."
- Part the First, Article I: "All men are born free and equal, and have certain natural, essential, and unalienable rights; among which may be reckoned the right of enjoy-

ing and defending their lives and liberties; that of acquiring, possessing, and protecting property; in fine, that of seeking and obtaining their safety and happiness."

## MICHIGAN

1835 CONSTITUTION
- Article I, Section 1: "All political power is inherent in the people."
- Article I, Section 2: "Government is instituted for the protection, security, and benefit of the people; and they have the right at all times to alter or reform the same, and to abolish one form of government and establish another, whenever the public good requires it."
- Article XI: "Neither slavery nor involuntary servitude shall ever be introduced into this State, except for the punishment of crimes of which the party shall have been duly convicted."

## MINNESOTA

1857 CONSTITUTION
- Bill of Rights, Article I, Section 1: "Government is instituted for the security, benefit and protection of the people, in whom all political power is inherent, together with the right to alter, modify or reform such government, whenever the public good may require it."
- Article I, Section 2: "No member of this State shall be disfranchised, or deprived of any of the rights or privileges secured to any citizen thereof, unless by the law of the land, or the judgment of his peers. There shall be neither slavery nor involuntary servitude in the State otherwise than in the punishment of crime, whereof the party shall have been duly convicted."
- Article I, Section 16: "The enumeration of rights in this constitution shall not be construed to deny or impair others retained by and inherent in the people."

## MISSISSIPPI

1817 ENABLING ACT
- Section 1: "*Be it enacted by the Senate and House of Representatives of the United States of America in Congress assembled,* That the inhabitants of the western part of the Mississippi Territory be, and they hereby are, authorized to form for themselves a constitution and State government, and to assume such name as they shall deem proper; and the said State, when formed, shall be admitted into the Union upon the same footing with the original States, in all respects whatever."
- Section 4: "Provided, That the same, when formed, shall be republican, and not repugnant to the principles of the ordinance of the thirteenth of July, one thousand seven hundred and eighty-seven, between the people and States of the territory northwest of the river Ohio, so far as the same has been extended to the said territory by the articles of agreement between the United States and the State of Georgia, or of the Constitution of the United States."

1817 ACT OF ADMISSION
- "Whereas, in pursuance of an act of Congress passed on the first day of March, one thousand eight hundred and seventeen, entitled 'An act to enable the people of the western part of the Mississippi Territory to form a constitution and State government, and for the admission of such State into the Union on an equal footing with the original States,' the people of the said Territory did, on the fifteenth day of August, in the present year, by a convention called for that purpose, form for themselves a constitution and State government, which constitution and State government so formed is republican, and in conformity to the principles of the articles of compact between the original States and the people and States in the Territory northwest of the river Ohio, passed on the thirteenth day of July, one thousand seven hundred and eighty-seven."

- *"Resolved by the Senate and House of Representatives of the United States of America in Congress assembled,* That the State of Mississippi shall be one, and is hereby declared to be one, of the United States of America, and admitted into the Union on an equal footing with the original States, in all respects whatever."

1817 CONSTITUTION

- Article I, Section 1: "That all *freemen*, when they form a social compact, are equal in rights; and that no man or set of men are entitled to exclusive, separate public emoluments or privileges, from the community, but in consideration of public services."
- Article 1, Section 2: "That all political power is inherent in the people, and all free governments are founded on their authority, and instituted for their benefit; and, therefore, they have at all times an unalienable and indefeasible right to alter or abolish their form of government, in such manner as they may think expedient."
- Article I, Conclusion: "To guard against transgressions of the high powers herein delegated, we declare that everything in this article is excepted out of the general powers of government, and shall forever remain inviolate; and that all laws contrary thereto, or to the following provisions, shall be void."
- Article VI, Section 1: "The general assembly shall have no power to pass laws for the emancipation of slaves, without the consent of their owners, unless where a slave shall have rendered to the State some distinguished service, in which case the owner shall be paid a full equivalent for the slaves so emancipated. They shall have no power to prevent immigrants to this State from bringing with them such persons as are deemed slaves by the laws of any one of the United States, so long as any person of the same age or description shall be continued in slavery by the laws of this State:"

1832 CONSTITUTION

- Article I, Sections 1, 2: [Same as 1817 Mississippi Constitution, Article I, Sections 1, 2]
- Article VII, Slaves, Section 1: [Similar to 1817 Mississippi Constitution, Article VI, Section 1]

1865 AMENDMENT

- First. "That the constitution shall be amended by abolishing and striking out sections one, two and three of article seven, under the title 'slaves,' and amendment number one, approved February second, eighteen hundred and forty-six, relative to slaves."
- Second. "That a provision in the following language shall be inserted in the constitution as article eight, to wit: 'The institution of slavery having been destroyed in the State of Mississippi, neither slavery nor involuntary servitude, otherwise than in the punishment of crimes, whereof the party shall have been duly convicted, shall hereafter exist in this State; and the legislature at its next session, and thereafter as the public welfare may require, shall provide by law for the protection and security of the person and property of the freedmen of this State, and guard them and the State against any evils that may arise from their sudden emancipation.' "

1868 CONSTITUTION

- Article I, Section 19: "There shall be neither slavery nor involuntary servitude in this State, otherwise than in the punishment of crime, whereof the party shall have been duly convicted."
- Article I, Section 20: "The right to withdraw from the Federal Union on account of any real or supposed grievances shall never be assumed by this State, nor shall any law be passed in derogation of the paramount allegiance of the citizens of this State to the government of the United States."
- Article I, Section 32: "The enumeration of rights in this constitution shall not be construed to deny or impair others retained by and inherent in the people."

1890 CONSTITUTION
- Article III, Section 5: "All political power is vested in, and derived from, the people; all government of right originates with the people, is founded upon their will only, and is instituted solely for the good of the whole."
- Article III, Section 6: "The people of this State have the inherent, sole and exclusive right to regulate the internal government and police thereof, and to alter and abolish their constitution and form of government whenever they may deem it necessary to their safety and happiness; provided, such change be not repugnant to the constitution of the United States."
- Article III, Sections 7, 15, 32: [Same as 1868 Mississippi Constitution, Article I, Sections 19, 20, 32]

## MISSOURI

1820 ENABLING ACT
- Section 4: "*Provided,* That the [constitution], whenever formed, shall be republican, and not repugnant to the Constitution of the United States; . . ."

1820 CONSTITUTION
- Article III, Section 26, "The general assembly shall not have power to pass laws— 1. For the emancipation of slaves without the consent of their owners; or without paying them, before such emancipation, a full equivalent for such slaves so emancipated; and, 2. To prevent *bona-fide* immigrants to this State, or actual settlers therein, from bringing from any of the United States, or from any of their Territories, such persons as may there be deemed to be slaves so long as any persons of the same description are allowed to be held as slaves by the laws of this State."
- They shall have power to pass laws— . . . 2. To prohibit the introduction of any slave for the purpose of speculation, or as an article of trade or merchandise."

- Article XIII, Section 1: "That all political power is vested in, and derived from, the people."
- Article XIII, Section 2: "That the people of this State have the inherent, sole, and exclusive right of regulating the internal government and police thereof, and of altering and abolishing their constitution and form of government whenever it may be necessary to their safety and happiness."

1821 ACT OF ADMISSION
- "*Resolved by the Senate and House of Representatives of the United States of America, in Congress assembled,* That Missouri shall be admitted into this union on an equal footing with the original states, in all respects whatever, upon the fundamental condition, that the fourth clause of the twenty-sixth section of the third article of the constitution submitted on the part of said state to Congress, shall never be construed to authorize the passage of any law, and that no law shall be passed in conformity thereto, by which any citizen, of either of the states in this Union, shall be excluded from the enjoyment of any of the privileges and immunities to which such citizen is entitled under the constitution of the United States."

1865 CONSTITUTION
- Article I, Section 1: "That we hold it to be self-evident that all men are endowed by their Creator with certain inalienable rights, among which are life, liberty, the enjoyment of the fruits of their own labor, and the pursuit of happiness."
- Article I, Section 2: "That there cannot be in this State either slavery or involuntary servitude, except in punishment of crime, whereof the party shall have been duly convicted."
- Article I, Section 4: "That all political power is vested in and derived from the people; that all government of right originates from the people, is founded upon their will only, and is instituted solely for the good of the whole."

- Article I, Section 5: "That the people of this State have the inherent, sole, and exclusive right of regulating the internal government and police thereof and of altering and abolishing their constitution and form of government whenever it may be necessary to their safety and happiness, but every such right should be exercised in pursuance of law and consistently with the Constitution of the United States."

1875 CONSTITUTION
- Article II, Sections 1, 32: [Same as 1865 Missouri Constitution, Article I, Sections 2, 4]
- Article II, Section 2: [Similar to 1865 Missouri Constitution, Article I, Section 5]
- Article II, Section 32: "The enumeration in this Constitution of certain rights shall not be construed to deny, impair or disparage others retained by the people."

## MONTANA

1889 ENABLING ACT
[See Nebraska model]

1889 CONSTITUTION
- Declaration of Rights, Article III, Section 1: "All political power is vested in and derived from the people; all government of right originates with the people; is founded upon their will only and is instituted solely for the good of the whole."
- Article III, Section 2: "The people of the State have the sole and exclusive right of governing themselves, as a free, sovereign and independent State, and to alter and abolish their constitution and form of government, whenever they may deem it necessary to their safety and happiness, provided such change be not repugnant to the Constitution of the United States."

## NEBRASKA

1864 ENABLING ACT
- Section 4: "*Provided*, That the Constitution, when formed, shall be republican, and not repugnant to the Constitution of the United States and the principles of the Declaration of Independence: *And provided further,* That said constitution shall provide, by an article forever irrevocable, without the consent of the Congress of the United States— First. That slavery or involuntary servitude shall be forever prohibited in said State."

1866 CONSTITUTION
- Declaration of Rights, Article I, Section 1: "All men are born equally free and independent, and have certain inherent rights; among these are life, liberty, and the pursuit of happiness. To secure these rights, governments are instituted among men, deriving their just powers from the consent of the governed."
- Article I, Section 2: "There shall be neither slavery nor involuntary servitude in this State, otherwise than for the punishment of crime, whereof the party shall have been duly convicted."
- Article I, Section 20: "This enumeration of rights shall not be construed to impair or deny others retained by the people; and all powers not herein delegated remain with the people."

1875 CONSTITUTION
- Bill of Rights, Article I, Sections 1, 2, 26: [Similar to 1866 Nebraska Constitution, Article I, Sections 1, 2, 20]

## NEVADA

1864 ENABLING ACT
[See Nebraska model]

1864 CONSTITUTION
- Ordinance Section 3: "In obedience to the requirements of an Act of the Congress of the United States, approved March twenty-first, A. D. eighteen hundred and sixty-four, to enable the people of Nevada to form a Constitution and State Government, this Convention, elected and convened in obedience to said enabling Act, do ordain as follows, and this ordinance shall be irrevocable, without the consent of the United States and the people of the State of Nevada:"

- Declaration of Rights, Article I, Section 1: "All men are, by nature, free and equal, and have certain inalienable rights, among which are those of enjoying and defending life and liberty; acquiring, possessing and protecting property, and pursuing and obtaining safety and happiness."
- Article I, Section 2: "All political power is inherent in the people. Government is instituted for the protection, security, and benefit of the people; and they have the right to alter or reform the same whenever the public good may require it."
- Article I, Section 17: "Neither slavery nor involuntary servitude, unless for the punishment of crimes, shall ever be tolerated in this State."
- Article I, Section 20: "This enumeration of rights shall not be construed to impair or deny others retained by the people."

## NEW HAMPSHIRE

1776 CONSTITUTION
- Preamble: "We, the members of the Congress of New Hampshire, chosen and appointed by the free suffrages of the people of said colony, . . . Have taken into our serious consideration the unhappy circumstances, into which this colony is involved by means of many grievous and oppressive acts of the British Parliament, depriving us of our natural and constitutional rights and privileges; . . ."

1784 CONSTITUTION
- Part I, Article I, Section 1: "All men are born equally free and independent; therefore, all government of right originates from the people, is founded in consent, and instituted for the general good."
- Part I, Article I, Section 2: "All men have certain natural, essential, and inherent rights; among which are—the enjoying and defending life and liberty—acquiring, possessing and protecting property—and in a word, of seeking and obtaining happiness."

- Part I, Article I, Section 3: "When men enter into a state of society, they surrender up some of their natural rights to that society, in order to insure the protection of others; and, without such an equivalent, the surrender is void."
- Part I, Article I, Section 4: "Among the natural rights, some are in their very nature unalienable, because no equivalent can be given or received for them. Of this kind are the RIGHTS OF CONSCIENCE."
- Part I, Article I, Section 10: "Government being instituted for the common benefit, protection, and security of the whole community, and not for the private interest or emolument of any one man, family or class of men; therefore, whenever the ends of government are perverted, and public liberty manifestly endangered, and all other means of redress are ineffectual, the people may, and of right ought, to reform the old, or establish a new government."

1792 CONSTITUTION
- Bill of Rights, Articles I, II, III, IV, X: [Similar to 1784 New Hampshire Constitution, Article I, Sections 1, 2, 3, 4, 10 ]

1902 CONSTITUTION
- Bill of Rights, Articles 1, 2, 3, 4, 10: [Same as 1792 New Hampshire Constitution, Bill of Rights, Articles I, II, III, IV, X]

## NEW JERSEY

1776 CONSTITUTION
- Preamble: "WHEREAS all the constitutional authority ever possessed by the kings of Great Britain over these colonies, or their other dominions, was, by compact, derived from the people, and held of them, for the common interest of the whole society; allegiance and protection are, in the nature of things, reciprocal ties, each equally depending upon the other, and liable to be dissolved by the others being refused or withdrawn."

1844 CONSTITUTION
- Article I, Section 1: "All men are by nature free and independent, and have certain nat-

ural and inalienable rights, among which are those of enjoying and defending life and liberty; acquiring, possessing and protecting property, and of pursuing and obtaining safety and happiness."

- Article I, Section 2: "All political power is inherent in the people. Government is instituted for the protection, security and benefit of the people, and they have the right at all times to alter or reform the same, whenever the public good may require it."

- Article I, Section 21: "The enumeration of rights and privileges shall not be construed to impair or deny others retained by the people."

## NEW MEXICO

1906 ENABLING ACT
[See Nebraska model]

## NEW YORK

1777 CONSTITUTION

- "And whereas the Delegates of the United American States, in general Congress convened, did, on the fourth day of July now last past, solemnly publish and declare, in the words following, viz: [reprints the Declaration of Independence in its entirety]."

## NORTH CAROLINA

1775 MECKLENBURG RESOLUTION

- Article II: "*Resolved:* That we do hereby declare ourselves a free and independent people; are, and of right ought to be a sovereign and self-governing association, under the control of no power, other than that of our God and the General Government of the Congress: To the maintenance of which Independence we solemnly pledge to each other our mutual co-operation, our Lives, our Fortunes, and our most Sacred Honor."

1776 CONSTITUTION

- Declaration of Rights, Section 1: "That all political power is vested in and derived from the people only."

1865 ORDINANCE

- "*Be it declared and ordained by the delegates of the people of the State of North Carolina in convention assembled, and it is hereby declared and ordained,* That slavery and involuntary servitude, otherwise than for crimes, whereof the parties shall have been duly convicted, shall be, and is hereby, forever prohibited within the State."

1868 CONSTITUTION

- Article I, Section 1: "That we hold it to be self-evident that all men are created equal; that they are endowed by their Creator with certain unalienable rights; that among these are life, liberty, the enjoyment of the fruits of their own labor, and the pursuit of happiness."

- Article I, Section 2: "That all political power is vested in and derived from the people; all government of right originates from the people, is founded upon their will only, and is instituted solely for the good of the whole."

- Article I, Section 3: "That the people of this State have the inherent, sole, and exclusive right of regulating the internal government and police thereof and of altering and abolishing their constitution and form of government whenever it may be necessary to their safety and happiness; but every such right should be exercised in pursuance of law and consistently with the Constitution of the United States."

- Article I, Section 4: "That this State shall ever remain a member of the American Union; that the people thereof are part of the American nation; that there is no right on the part of this State to secede, and that all attempts, from whatever source or upon whatever pretext, to dissolve said Union or to sever said nation ought to be resisted with the whole power of the State."

- Article I, Section 33: "Slavery and involuntary servitude, otherwise than for crime whereof the parties shall have been duly convicted, shall be, and are hereby, forever prohibited within this State."

- Article I, Section 37: "This enumeration of rights shall not be construed to impair or deny others retained by the people; and all powers, not herein delegated, remain with the people."

1876 CONSTITUTION

- Article I, Sections 1, 2, 3, 4, 33, 37: [Same as 1868 North Carolina Constitution, Article I, Sections 1, 2, 3, 4, 33, 37]

## NORTH DAKOTA

1889 ENABLING ACT
[See Nebraska model]

1889 CONSTITUTION

- Declaration of Rights, Article 1, Section 1: "All men are by nature equally free and independent and have certain inalienable rights, among which are those of enjoying and defending life and liberty; acquiring, possessing and protecting property and reputation; and pursuing and obtaining safety and happiness."
- Article 1, Section 2: "All political power is inherent in the people. Government is instituted for the protection, security and benefit of the people, and they have a right to alter or reform the same whenever the public good may require."
- Article 1, Section 3: "The State of North Dakota is an inseparable part of the American union and the constitution of the United States is the supreme law of the land."
- Article 1, Section 17: "Neither slavery nor involuntary servitude, unless for the punishment of crime, shall ever be tolerated in this state."

## OHIO

1802 ENABLING ACT

- Section 1: "*Be it enacted by the Senate and House of Representatives of the United States of America in Congress assembled,* That the inhabitants of the eastern division of the territory northwest of the river Ohio be, and they are hereby, authorized to form

for themselves a constitution and State government, and to assume such name as they shall deem proper, and the said State, when formed, shall be admitted into the Union upon the same footing with the original States in all respects whatever."

- Section 5: "*And be it further enacted,* That the members of the convention, thus duly elected, be, and they are hereby, authorized to meet at Chillicothe on the first Monday in November next; which convention, when met, shall first determine, by a majority of the whole number elected, whether it be or be not expedient at that time to form a constitution and State government for the people within the said territory, and if it be determined to be expedient, the convention shall be, and hereby are, authorized to form a constitution and State government, or, if it be deemed more expedient, the said convention shall provide by ordinance for electing representatives to form a constitution or frame of government; which said representative shall be chosen in such manner and in such proportion, and shall meet at such time and place, as shall be prescribed by the said ordinance; and shall form for the people of the said State a constitution and State government, provided the same shall be republican, and not repugnant to the ordinance of the thirteenth of July, one thousand seven hundred and eighty-seven, between the original States and the people and States of the territory northwest of the river Ohio."

1802 CONSTITUTION

- Preamble: "We, the people of [Ohio], having the right of admission into the General Government as a member of the Union, consistent with the Constitution of the United States, the ordinance of Congress of one thousand seven hundred and eighty-seven, and the law of Congress entitled 'An act to enable the people of the eastern division of the territory of the United States northwest of the river Ohio to form a constitution and State government, and for the admission of such State into the Union on an equal footing with the original States, and for other purposes,' in order to establish justice, promote the welfare and secure the blessings of liberty to ourselves and our posterity, do ordain and establish the following constitution or form of government, and do mutually agree with each other to form ourselves into a free and independent State by the name of the State of Ohio."

- Article VIII: "That the general, great, and essential principles of liberty and free government may be recognized, and forever unalterably established, we declare—"
- Article VIII, Section 1: "That all men are born equally free and independent, and have certain natural, inherent, and unalienable rights, amongst which are the enjoying and defending life and liberty, acquiring, possessing, and protecting property, and pursuing and obtaining happiness and safety; and every free republican government being founded on their sole authority, and organized for the great purpose of protecting their rights and liberties and securing their independence; to effect these ends, they have at all times a complete power to alter, reform, or abolish their government, whenever they may deem it necessary."
- Article VIII, Section 2: "There shall be neither slavery nor involuntary servitude in this State, otherwise than for the punishment of crimes, whereof the party shall have been duly convicted; . . ."
- Article VIII, Section 4: "Private property ought to and shall ever be held inviolate, but always subservient to the public welfare; provide a compensation in money be made to the owner."

1851 CONSTITUTION
- Article I, Section 1: "All men are, by nature, free and independent, and have certain inalienable rights, among which are those of enjoying and defending life and liberty, acquiring, possessing, and protecting property, and seeking and obtaining happiness and safety."

- Article I, Section 2: "All political power is inherent in the people. Government is instituted for their equal protection and benefit, and they have the right to alter, reform, or abolish the same, whenever they may deem it necessary; and no special privileges or immunities shall ever be granted, that may not be altered, revoked, or repealed by the General Assembly."
- Article I, Section 6: [Same as 1802 Ohio Constitution, Article VIII, Section 2]
- Article I, Section 20: "This enumeration of rights shall not be construed to impair or deny others retained by the people; and all powers, not herein delegated, remain with the people."

## OKLAHOMA

1906 ENABLING ACT
[See Nebraska model]

1907 CONSTITUTION
- Bill of Rights, Article II, Section 1: "All political power is inherent in the people; and government is instituted for their protection, security, and benefit, and to promote their general welfare; and they have the right to alter or reform the same whenever the public good may require it: *Provided,* Such change be not repugnant to the Constitution of the United States."
- Article II, Section 2: "All persons have the inherent right to life, liberty, the pursuit of happiness, and the enjoyment of the gains of their own industry."
- Article II, Section 33: "The enumeration in this constitution of certain rights shall not be construed to deny, impair, or disparage others retained by the people."

## OREGON

1857 CONSTITUTION
- Bill of Rights, Article I, Section 1: "We declare that all men, when they form a social compact, are equal in rights; that all power

is inherent in the people, and all free governments are founded on their authority and instituted for their peace, safety, and happiness; and they have at all times a right to alter, reform, or abolish the government in such manner as they may think proper."

- Article I, Section 34: "This enumeration of rights and privileges shall not be construed to impair or deny others retained by the people."
- Article I, Section 35: "There shall be neither slavery nor involuntary servitude in the State, otherwise than as a punishment for crime, whereof the party shall have been duly convicted."

## PENNSYLVANIA

1776 CONSTITUTION

- Declaration of Rights, Article I: "That all men are born equally free and independent, and have certain natural, inherent, and inalienable rights, amongst which are, the enjoying and defending life and liberty, acquiring, possessing and protecting property, and pursuing and obtaining happiness and safety."
- Article IV: "That all power being originally inherent in, and consequently derived from, the people; therefore all officers of government, whether legislative or executive, are their trustees and servants, and at all times accountable to them."
- Article V: "That government is, or ought to be, instituted for the common benefit, protection and security of the people, nation or community; and not for the particular emolument or advantage of any single man, family, or sett of men, who are a part only of that community; And that the community hath an indubitable, unalienable and indefeasible right to reform, alter, or abolish government in such manner as shall be by that community judged most conducive to the public weal."

1790 CONSTITUTION

- Article IX, Section 1: [Similar to 1776 Pennsylvania Constitution, Declaration of Rights, Article I]
- Article IX, Section 2: "That all power is inherent in the people, and all free governments are founded on their authority and instituted for their peace, safety, and happiness. For the advancement of those ends, they have at all times an unalienable and indefeasible right to alter, reform, or abolish their government, in such manner as they may think proper."

1838 CONSTITUTION

- Article IX, Sections 1, 2: [Same as 1790 Pennsylvania Constitution, Article IX, Sections 1, 2]

1873 CONSTITUTION

- Article I, Sections 1, 2: [Same as 1790 Pennsylvania Constitution, Article IX, Sections 1, 2]

## RHODE ISLAND

1842 CONSTITUTION

- Article I, Section 1: "In the words of the Father of his Country, we declare, that 'the basis of our political systems is the right of the people to make and alter their constitutions of government; but that the constitution which at any time exists, till changed by an explicit and authentic act of the whole people, is sacredly obligatory upon all.' "
- Article I, Section 4: "Slavery will not be permitted in this state."
- Article I, Section 23: "The enumeration of the foregoing rights shall not be construed to impair or deny others retained by the people."

## SOUTH CAROLINA

1776 CONSTITUTION

- "Whereas the British Parliament, claiming of late years a right to bind the North American colonies by law in all cases whatsoever, have enacted statutes for raising a revenue in those colonies and disposing of such revenue as they thought proper, without the consent and against the will of the colonists. And whereas it appearing to them that (they not being represented in Parliament) such claim was altogether unconstitutional, and, if admitted, would at once reduce them from the rank of freeman to a state of the most abject slavery;"

1778 CONSTITUTION

- Preamble: "Whereas the constitution or form of government agreed to and resolved upon by the freemen of this country, met in congress, the twenty-sixth day of March, one thousand seven hundred and seventy-six, was temporary only, and suited to the situation of their public affairs at that period, looking forward to an accommodation with Great Britain, and event then desired; and whereas the United Colonies of America have been since constituted independent States, and the political connection heretofore subsisting between them and Great Britain entirely dissolved by the declaration of the honorable the Continental Congress, dated the fourth day of July, one thousand seven hundred and seventy-six, for the many great and weighty reasons therein particularly set forth: It therefore becomes absolutely necessary to frame a constitution suitable to that great event."

1790 CONSTITUTION

- Article IX, Section 1: "All power is originally vested in the people; and all free governments are founded on their authority, and are instituted for their peace, safety, and happiness."
- Article IX, Section 2: "No freemen of this State shall be taken, or imprionsed, or disseized of his freehold, liberties, or privileges, or outlawed, or exiled, or in any manner destroyed, or deprived of his life, liberty or property, but by the judgment of his peers, or by the law of the land; nor shall any bill of attainder, *ex post facto* law, or law im-

pairing the obligation of contracts, ever be passed by the legislature of this State."

1860 DECLARATION OF SECESSION

- "A struggle for the right of self-government ensued, which resulted, on the 4th of July, 1776, in a Declaration, by the colonies, 'that they are, and of right ought to be, *free and independent states . . .*' They further solemnly declared that whenever any 'form of government becomes destructive of the ends for which it was established, it is the right of the people to alter or abolish it, and to institute a new government. . . .' Thus were established the two great principles asserted by the colonies, namely, the right of a state to govern itself; and the right of a people to abolish a government when it becomes destructive of the ends for which it was instituted."

1865 CONSTITUTION

- Article IX, Section 1: [Same as 1790 South Carolina Constitution, Article IX, Section 1]
- Article IX, Section 2: [Similar to 1790 South Carolina Constitution, Article IX, Section 2, except "person" substituted for "freemen"]
- Article IX, Section 11: "The slaves in South Carolina having been emancipated by the action of the United States authorities, neither slavery nor involuntary servitude, except as a punishment for crime, whereof the party shall have been duly convicted, shall ever be reestablished in this State."

1868 CONSTITUTION

- Article I, Section 1: "All men are born free and equal, endowed by their Creator with certain inalienable rights, among which are the rights of enjoying and defending their lives and liberties, of acquiring, possessing, and protecting property, and of seeking and obtaining their safety and happiness."
- Article I, Section 2: "Slavery shall never exist in this State; neither shall involuntary servitude, except as a punishment for crime, whereof the party shall have been duly convicted."
- Article I, Section 3: "All political power is vested in and derived from the people only;

therefore they have the right at all times to modify their form of government in such manner as they may deem expedient, when the public good demands."

- Article I, Section 41: "The enumeration of rights in this constitution shall not be construed to impair or deny others retained by the people, and all powers not herein delegated remain with the people."

1895 CONSTITUTION

- Article I, Section 1: "All political power is vested in and derived from the people only, therefore they have the right at all times to modify their form of government."
- Article I, Section 5: "The privileges and immunities of citizens of this State and of the United States under this Constitution shall not be abridged, nor shall any person be deprived of life, liberty or property without due process of law, nor shall any person be denied the equal protection of the laws."

## SOUTH DAKOTA

1889 ENABLING ACT
[See Nebraska model]

1889 CONSTITUTION

- Bill of Rights, Article VI, Section 1: "All men are born equally free and independent, and have certain inherent rights, among which are those of enjoying and defending life and liberty, of acquiring and protecting property and the pursuit of happiness. To secure these rights governments are instituted among men, deriving their just powers from the consent of the governed."
- Article VI, Section 26: "All political power is inherent in the people and all free government is founded on their authority, and is instituted for their equal protection and benefit, and they have the right in lawful and constituted methods to alter or reform their forms of government in such manner as they may think proper."

## TENNESSEE

1790 NORTH CAROLINA CESSION ACT

- "Congress shall . . . assume the government of the said ceded territory, which they shall execute in a manner similar to that which they support in the territory west of the Ohio; shall protect the inhabitants against enemies, and shall never bar or deprive them of any privileges which the people in that territory west of the Ohio enjoy: *Provided always,* That no regulations made or to be made by Congress shall tend to emancipate slaves."

1790 TERRITORIAL GOVERNMENT

- "*Be it enacted by the Senate and House of Representatives of the United States of America in Congress assembled,* That the territory of the United States south of the river Ohio, for the purposes of temporary government, shall be one district; the inhabitants of which shall enjoy all the privileges, benefits, and advantages set forth in the ordinance of the late Congress for the government of the territory of the United States northwest of the river Ohio. And the government of the said territory south of the Ohio shall be similar to that which is now exercised in the territory northwest of the Ohio; except so far as is otherwise provided in the conditions expressed in an act of Congress of the present session, entitled 'An act to accept a cession of the claims of the State of North Carolina to a certain district of western territory.' "

1796 CONSTITUTION

- Article XI, Section 1: "That all power is inherent in the people, and all free governments are founded on their authority, and instituted for their peace, safety, and happiness; for the advancement of those ends, they have at all times an unalienable and indefeasible right to alter, reform, or abolish the government in such manner as they may think proper."

1834 CONSTITUTION

- Article I, Sections 1, 8: [Same as 1796 Tennessee Constitution, Article XI, Section 1]

1866 AMENDMENT

- Article I, Section 1: "That slavery and involuntary servitude, except as a punishment for crime, whereof the party shall have been duly convicted, are hereby forever abolished and prohibited throughout the State."
- Article I, Section 2: "The legislature shall make no law recognizing the right of property in man."

1870 CONSTITUTION

- Article I, Section 1: [Same as 1796 Tennessee Constitution, Article XI, Section 1]
- Article I, Sections 33, 34: [Same as 1866 Tennessee Constitution, Article I, Sections 1, 2]
- Article XI, Section 16: *Bill of Rights to remain* inviolate.—The declaration of rights, hereto prefixed, is declared to be a part of the Constitution of this State, and shall never be violated on any pretense whatever. And to guard against transgression of the high powers we have delegated, we declare that everything in the Bill of Rights contained is excepted out of the general powers of the government, and shall forever remain inviolate."

## TEXAS

1836 DECLARATION OF INDEPENDENCE

- "When a government has ceased to protect the lives liberty and property of its people, from whom its legitimate powers are derived, and for the advancement of whose happiness it was instituted, and so far from being a guarantee for the enjoyment of those inestimable and inalienable rights, becomes an instrument in the hands of evil rulers for their oppression: When the Federal Republican Constitution of their country, which they have sworn to support, no longer has a substantial existence, and the whole nature of their government has been forcibly changed without their consent, from a restricted federative republic, composed of sovereign states to a consolidated central military despotism in which every interest is disregarded but that of the army and the priesthood—both the eternal enemies of civil liberty, the ever-ready minions of power, and the usual instruments of tyrants."

- "When, long after the spirit of the constitution has departed, moderation is at length so far lost by those in power that even the semblance of freedom is removed, and the forms, themselves, of the constitution discontinued; and so far from their petitions and remonstrances being regarded, the agents who bear them are thrown into dungeons; and mercenary armies sent forth to force a new government upon them at the point of the bayonet: When, in consequence of such acts of malfeasance and abdication, on the part of the government, anarchy prevails, and Civil Society is dissolved into its original elements. In such a crisis, the first law of nature, the right of self-preservation—the inherent and unalienable right of the people to appeal to first principles and take their political affairs into their own hands in extreme cases enjoins it as a right towards themselves and a sacred obligation to their posterity to abolish such government and create another in its stead, calculated to rescue them from impending dangers, and to secure their future welfare and happiness."

- "Nations, as well as individuals, are amenable for their acts to the public opinion of mankind. Statement of a part of our grievance is, therefore, submitted to an impartial world, in justification of the hazardous but unavoidable step now taken of severing our political connection with the Mexican people, and assuming an independent attitude among the nations of the earth."

1836 CONSTITUTION

- General Provisions, Article VI, Section 9: "All persons of color who were slaves for life previous to their emigration to Texas, and who are now held in bondage, shall remain in the like state of servitude: *Provided,* The said slave shall be the *bona-fide* property of the person so holding said slave as aforesaid. Congress shall pass no laws to prohibit emigrants from bringing their slaves into the republic with them, and holding them by the same tenure by which such slaves were held in the United States; nor shall congress have power to emancipate slaves; nor shall any slaveholder be allowed to emancipate his or her slave or slaves without the consent of congress, unless he or she shall send his or her slave or slaves without the limits of the republic. No free person of African descent, either in whole or in part, shall be permitted to reside permanently in the republic without the consent of congress; and the importation or admission of Africans or Negroes into this republic, excepting from the United States of America, is forever prohibited, and declared to be piracy."

- Declaration of Rights, Section 1: "All men, when they form a social compact, have equal rights; and no men or set of men are entitled to exclusive public privileges or emoluments from the community."
- Section 2: "All political power is inherent in the people, and all free governments are founded on their authority and instituted for their benefit; and they have at all times an inalienable right to alter their government in such manner as they may think proper."

1845 CONSTITUTION
- Article I, Section 1: [Similar to 1836 Texas Constitution, Declaration of Rights, Section 2]
- Article I, Section 2: [Similar to 1836 Texas Constitution, Declaration of Rights, Section 1, but "freemen" substituted for "men"]
- Article VIII, Section 1: "The legislature shall have no power to pass laws for the emancipation of slaves, without the consent of their owners; nor without paying their own-

ers, previous to such emancipation, a full equivalent in money for the slaves so emancipated. They shall have no power to prevent emigrants to this State from bringing with them such persons as are deemed slaves by the laws of any of the United States, so long as any person of the same age or description shall be continued in slavery by the laws of this State: *Provided,* That such slave be the *bona-fide* property of such emigrants:"

1866 CONSTITUTION
- Article I, Sections 1, 2: [Same as 1845 Texas Constitution, Article I, Sections 1, 2]
- Article VIII, Section 1: "African slavery, as it heretofore existed, having been terminated within this State by the Government of the United States, by force of arms, and its reestablishment being prohibited by the amendment to the Constitution of the United States, it is declared that neither slavery nor involuntary servitude, except as a punishment for crime, whereof the party shall have been duly convicted shall exist in this State; and Africans and their descendants shall be protected in their rights of person and property by appropriate legislation; they shall have the right to contract and be contracted with; to sue and be sued; to acquire, hold, and transmit property; and all criminal prosecutions against them shall be conducted in the same manner as prosecutions for like offences against the white race, and they shall be subject to like penalties."

1868 CONSTITUTION
- Article I, Section 2: [Same as 1845 Texas Constitution, Article I, Section 2]
- Article I, Section 22: "Importations of persons under the name of 'coolies,' or any other name or designation, or the adoption of any system of peonage, whereby the helpless and unfortunate may be reduced to practical bondage, shall never be authorized or tolerated by the laws of this State; and neither slavery nor involuntary servitude, except as a punishment for crime, whereof

the party shall have been duly convicted, shall ever exist in this State."

## UTAH

1894 ENABLING ACT
[See Nebraska model]

1895 CONSTITUTION
- Declaration of Rights, Article I, Section 1: "All men have the inherent and inalienable right to enjoy and defend their lives and liberties; to acquire, possess, and protect property; to worship according to the dictates of their consciences; to assemble peaceably, protest against wrongs, and petition for redress of grievances; to communicate freely their thoughts and opinions, being responsible for the abuse of that right."
- Article I, Section 2: "All political power is inherent in the people, and all free governments are founded on their authority for their equal protection and benefit, and they have the right to alter or reform their government as the public welfare may require."
- Article I, Section 3: "The State of Utah is an inseparable part of the Federal Union, and the Constitution of the United States is the supreme law of the land."
- Article I, Section 21: "Neither slavery nor involuntary servitude, except as a punishment for crime, whereof the party shall have been duly convicted, shall exist within this State."
- Article I, Section 25: "This enumeration of rights shall not be construed to impair or deny others retained by the people."

## VERMONT

1777 CONSTITUTION
- "Whereas, all government ought to be instituted and supported, for the security and protection of the community, as such, and to enable the individuals who compose it, to enjoy their natural rights, and the other blessings which the Author of existence has bestowed upon man; and whenever those great ends of government are not obtained, the people have a right, by common consent, to change it, and take such measures as to them may appear necessary to promote their safety and happiness."
- Chapter 1, Section 1: "That all men are born equally free and independent, and have certain, inherent and unalienable rights, amongst which are the enjoying and defending life and liberty; acquiring, possessing and protecting property, and pursuing and obtaining happiness and safety."
- Chapter 1, Section 6: "That government is, or ought to be, instituted for the common benefit, protection, and security of the people, nation or community; and not for the particular emolument or advantage of any single man, family or set of men, who are a part only of that community; and that the community hath an indubitable, unalienable and indefeasible right to reform, alter, or abolish, government, in such manner as shall be, by that community, judged most conducive to the public weal."
- Chapter 2, Section 42: "The declaration of rights is hereby declared to be a part of the Constitution of this State, and ought never to be violated, on any pretense whatsoever."

1786 CONSTITUTION
- Chapter 1, Sections 1, 7, 39 : [Similar to 1777 Vermont Constitution, Chapter 1, Sections 1, 6, 42]

1793 CONSTITUTION
- Chapter 1, Articles I, VII, XLII: [Same as 1786 Vermont Constitution, Chapter 1, Sections 1, 7, 39 ]

## VIRGINIA

1776 DECLARATION OF RIGHTS
- Bill of Rights, Section 1: "That all men are by nature equally free and independent, and have certain inherent rights, of which, when they enter into a state of society, they cannot, by any compact, deprive or divest their

posterity; namely, the enjoyment of life and liberty, with the means of acquiring and possessing property, and pursuing and obtaining happiness and safety."

- Section 2: "That all power is vested in, and consequently derived from, the people; that magistrates are their trustees and servants, and at all times amenable to them."

- Section 3: "That government is, or ought to be, instituted for the common benefit, protection, and security of the people, nation, or community; of all the various modes and forms of government, that is best which is capable of producing the greatest degree of happiness and safety, and is most effectually securing against the danger of maladministration; and that, when any government shall be found inadequate or contrary to these purposes, a majority of the community hath an indubitable, inalienable, and indefeasible right to reform, alter, or abolish it, in such manner as shall be judged most conducive to the public weal."

1830 CONSTITUTION

- Article I: "The declaration of rights made on the 12th June, 1776, by the representatives of the good people of Virginia, assembled in full and free convention, which pertained to them and their posterity, as the basis and foundation of government, requiring in the opinion of this convention no amendment, shall be prefixed to this constitution, and have the same relation thereto as it had to the former constitution of this commonwealth."

1850 CONSTITUTION

- Bill of Rights, Sections 1, 2, 3: [Same as 1776 Virginia Declaration of Rights, Sections 1, 2, 3]

- Article IV, Section 19: "Slaves hereafter emancipated shall forfeit their freedom by remaining in the commonwealth more than twelve months after they become actually free, and shall be reduced to slavery under such regulation as may be prescribed by law."

- Article IV, Section 20: "The general assembly may impose such restrictions and conditions as they shall deem proper on the power of slave-owners to emancipate their slaves; and may pass laws for the relief of the commonwealth from the free negro population, by removal or otherwise."

- Article IV, Section 21: "The general assembly shall not emancipate any slave, or the descendant of any slave, either before or after the birth of such descendant."

1864 CONSTITUTION

- Bill of Rights, Sections 1, 2, 3: [Same as 1776 Virginia Declaration of Rights, Sections 1, 2, 3]

- Article IV, Section 19: "Slavery and involuntary servitude (except for crime) is hereby abolished and prohibited in the State forever."

- Article IV, Section 21: "The general assembly shall make no law establishing slavery or recognizing property in human beings."

1870 CONSTITUTION

- Article I, Bill of Rights, Sections 1, 4, 5: [Same as 1776 Virginia Declaration of Rights, Sections 1, 2, 3]

- Article I, Section 2: "That this State shall ever remain a member of the United States of America, and that the people thereof are part of the American nation, and that all attempts, from whatever source or upon whatever pretext, to dissolve said Union or to sever said nation, are unauthorized and ought to be resisted with the whole power of the State."

- Article I, Section 3: "That the Constitution of the United States, and the laws of Congress passed in pursuance thereof, constitute the supreme law of the land, to which paramount allegiance and obedience are due from every citizen, anything in the constitution, ordinances, or laws of any State to the contrary notwithstanding."

- Article I, Section 19: "That neither slavery nor involuntary servitude, except as lawful imprisonment may constitute such, shall exist within this State."

- Article I, Section 20: "That all citizens of the State are hereby declared to possess equal civil and political rights and public privileges."
- Article I, Section 21: "The rights enumerated in this bill of rights shall not be construed to limit other rights of the people not therein expressed."

1902 CONSTITUTION
- Article I, Bill of Rights, Sections 1, 2, 3: [Same as 1776 Virginia Declaration of Rights, Sections 1, 2, 3]
- Article I, Section 17: [Same as 1870 Virginia Constitution, Article I, Section 21]

## WASHINGTON

1853 CONSTITUTION
- Declaration of Rights, Article I, Section 1: "All political power is inherent in the people, and governments derive their just powers from the consent of the governed, and are established to protect and maintain individual rights."

## WEST VIRGINIA

1872 CONSTITUTION
- Article III, Section 1: "All men are, by nature, equally free and independent, and have certain inherent rights, of which, when they enter into a state of society, they cannot, by any compact, deprive or divest their posterity, namely; the enjoyment of life and liberty, with the means of acquiring and possessing property, and of pursuing and obtaining happiness and safety."
- Article III, Section 3: "Government is instituted for the common benefit, protection and security of the people, nation or community. Of all its various forms that is the best, which is capable of producing the greatest degree of happiness and safety, and is most effectually secured against the danger of maladministration; and when any government shall be found inadequate or contrary to these purposes, a majority of the community has an indubitable, inalienable, and indefeasible right to reform, alter or abolish it in such a manner as shall be judged most conducive to the public weal."

## WISCONSIN

1848 CONSTITUTION
- Declaration of Rights, Article I, Section 1: "All men are born equally free and independent, and have certain inherent rights; among these are life, liberty, and the pursuit of happiness: to secure these rights governments are instituted among men, deriving their just powers from the consent of the governed."
- Article I, Section 2: "There shall be neither slavery, nor involuntary servitude in this State, otherwise than for the punishment of crime, whereof the party shall have been duly convicted."

## WYOMING

1889 CONSTITUTION
- Declaration of Rights, Article I, Section 1: "All power is inherent in the people, and all free governments are founded on their authority, and instituted for their peace, safety and happiness; for the advancements of these ends they have at all times an inalienable and indefeasible right to alter, reform or abolish the government in such manner as they may think proper."
- Article I, Section 2: "In their inherent right to life, liberty and the pursuit of happiness, all members of the human race are equal."

# 7.2  Virginia Act of Cession, December 20, 1783

*The lands in the Northwest Territory—present-day Illinois, Indiana, Michigan, Ohio, and Wisconsin— were originally claimed by Virginia. When Virginia ceded those lands to the United States, it did so on the condition that any new states formed from the territory would be "republican" and would enjoy the same rights as existing states.*

*Be it enacted by the general assembly,* That . . . the delegates of this State to the Congress of the United States . . . are hereby fully authorized and empowered, for and on behalf of this State, by proper deeds or instrument in writing, under their hands and seals, to convey, transfer, assign, and make over unto the United States, in Congress assembled, for the benefit of the said States, all right title, and claim, as well of soil as jurisdiction, which this commonwealth hath to the territory or tract of country within the limits of the Virginia charter situate, lying, and being to the northwest of the river Ohio, subject to the terms and conditions contained in the before-recited act of Congress of the 13th day of September last, that is to say: Upon condition that the territory so ceded shall be laid out and formed into States . . . ; and that the States so formed shall be distinct republican States, and admitted members of the Federal Union, having the same rights of sovereignty, freedom, and independence as the other States.

# 7.3  Northwest Ordinance, July 13, 1787

*One of the founders' most significant accomplishments was the provision of government in the territories offering the same guarantees of equality and liberty to the inhabitants of those territories as was enjoyed by the inhabitants of the original states. The Northwest Ordinance of 1787 banned slavery as inconsistent with the "fundamental principles" on which the original states were formed, arguably mandated by the requirement in the 1783 Virginia Act of Cession that the new states were to be "republican" in nature. Later acts establishing territorial governments in the south omitted that important provision.*

Section 13. And for extending the fundamental principles of civil and religious liberty, which form the basis whereon these republics, their laws and constitutions, are erected; to fix and establish those principles as the basis of all laws, constitutions, and governments, which forever hereafter shall be formed in the said territory; to provide, also, for the establishment of States, and permanent government therein, and for their admission to a share in the Federal councils on an equal footing with the original States, at as early periods as may be consistent with the general interest:

Section 14. It is hereby ordained and declared, by the authority aforesaid, that the following articles shall be considered as articles of compact, between the original States and the people and States in the said territory, and forever remain unalterable, unless by common consent, to wit: . . .

**Article V**

There shall be formed in the said territory not less than three nor more than five States; and the boundaries of the States, as soon as Virginia shall alter her act of cession and consent to the same, shall become fixed and established as follows. . . . And whenever any of the said States shall have sixty thousand free inhabitants therein, such State shall be admitted by its delegates, into the Congress of the United States, on an equal footing with the original States, in all respects whatever; and shall be at liberty to form a permanent constitution and State government: Provided, The constitution and government, so to be formed, shall be republican, and in conformity to the principles contained in these articles, and, so far as it can be consistent with the general interest of the confederacy, such admission shall be allowed at an earlier period, and when there may be a less number of free inhabitants in the State than sixty thousand.

### Article VI

There shall be neither slavery nor involuntary servitude in the said territory, otherwise than in the punishment of crimes, whereof the party shall have been duly convicted: Provided always, That any person escaping into the same, from whom labor or service is lawfully claimed in any one of the original States, such fugitive may be lawfully reclaimed, and conveyed to the person claiming his or her labor or service as aforesaid.

## 7.4 North Carolina Act of Cession, April 2, 1790

*In stark contrast to the 1783 Virginia Act of Cession and the 1787 Northwest Ordinance, North Carolina ceded its western lands to the United States on the condition that Congress could not emancipate slaves in the ceded territory. Consequently, when the territory petitioned for admission as the State of Tennessee, Congress was without power to impose on it the antislavery conditions that it would later impose on the states in the Northwest Territory. The Georgia Act of Cession of April 24, 1820, included a condition similar to that of North Carolina, and it resulted in similar consequences for the subsequent statehoods of Alabama and Mississippi.*

*Be it enacted by the General Assembly of the State of North Carolina, and it is hereby enacted by the authority of the same,* That the Senators of this state, in the Congress of the United States, . . . are hereby authorized, empowered and required to execute a deed or deeds on the part and behalf of this state, conveying to the United States of America, all right, title and claim which this state has to the sovereignty and territory of the lands situated within the chartered limits of this state, west of a line beginning on the extreme height of the Stone Mountain . . . upon the following express conditions, and subject thereto—that is to say: . . . That the territory so ceded, shall be laid out and formed into a state or states, containing a suitable extent of territory, the inhabitants of which shall enjoy all the privileges, benefits and advantages set forth in the ordinance of the late Congress, for the government of the western territory of the United States, that is to say; whenever the Congress of the United States shall cause to be officially transmitted to the executive authority of this state, an authenticated copy of the act to be passed by the Congress of the United States, accepting the cession of territory made by virtue of this act, under the express conditions hereby certified; the said Congress shall at the same time assume the government of the said ceded territory, which they shall execute in a manner similar to that which they support in the territory west of the Ohio; shall protect the inhabitants against enemies, and shall never bar or deprive them from any privileges which the people in the territory west of the Ohio enjoy: *Provided always,* That no regulations made or to be made by Congress, shall tend to emancipate slaves.

# 8.1   Charles Sumner, U.S. Senate Speech, January 31, 1872

*Charles Sumner (1811–1874) represented Massachusetts in the U.S. Senate from 1851 to 1874. On May 19, 1856, he was battered on the floor of the Senate by U.S. representative Preston Smith Brooks of South Carolina for an alleged affront to Southern honor: the delivery of a particular anti-slavery speech in the Senate. In the wake of the American Civil War, Sumner advocated interpreting the U.S. Constitution in light of the principles articulated in the Declaration of Independence.*

When I allude to the Declaration I know well the way with which such an allusion is received on this floor. I have lived through a period of history, and do not forget that I here heard that great title deed arraigned as a "self-evident lie." There are Senators now who, while hesitating to adopt that vulgar extravagance of dissent, are willing to trifle with it as a rule of interpretation. I am not frightened. Sir, I insist that the Constitution must be interpreted by the Declaration. I insist that the Declaration is or equal and coordinate authority with the Constitution itself. I know, sir, the ground on which I stand. I need no volume of law, no dog-eared book, no cases to sustain me. Every lawyer is familiar with the great fundamental beginning of the British constitution, *Magna Charta*. But what is *Magna Charta*? Simply certain concessions wrung by barons of England from an unwilling monarch; not an act of Parliament, nothing constitutional, in our sense of the term; simply a declaration of rights; and such, sir, was the Declaration of Independence. And now, sir, I am prepared to insist that, whenever you are considering the Constitution, so far as it concerns human rights, you must bring it always to that great touchstone; the two must go together, and the Constitution can never be interpreted in any way inconsistent with the Declaration. Show me any words in the Constitution applicable to human rights, and I invoke at once the great truths of the Declaration as the absolute guide in determining their meaning. Is it a question of power? Then must every word in the Constitution be interpreted so that Liberty and Equality do not fail.

# 8.2   Rutherford B. Hayes, Speech in Sacramento, California, September 22, 1880

*Rutherford B. Hayes (1822–1893) was the nineteenth president of the United States. In 1880, as he was considering his prospects for reelection, he completed the first transcontinental trip by a president. On the steps of the California capitol, he delivered a speech in which he described the future of the United States in terms of the Declaration of Independence's affirmation of fairness and opportunity, the command of the Golden Rule, and the national ideal of equal legal rights for all.*

What is to be the future of this beautiful land? . . . Our fathers . . . began one hundred years ago to build up a nation upon new principles. They stood upon three great principles, set forth in three great charters. It seems to me that if we shall regard those charters—if we shall embody in our own, in our institutions, those principles, we shall be able to go forward conquering and to conquer. . . . First, then, the Declaration of Independence. It embodies the sentiment expressed by Lincoln: "Let every man have a fair start and an equal chance in the race of life." It expressed the sentiment of the Divine Master: "Do unto others as ye would they should do unto you." It is the great corner-stone—"Equal rights of all men before the law." That is the very foundation-stone of our institutions. My friends, that victory is alone worth having—that victory which causes the soldier the greatest delight—which is won after a long and stubborn fight—victory snatched out of the very jaws of defeat."

---

## 8.3  Calvin Coolidge, 'The Inspiration of the Declaration of Independence,' July 5, 1926

*Calvin Coolidge (1872–1933) was elected vice president of the United States in 1920. Upon the death of President Warren G. Harding in 1923, Coolidge became the thirtieth president. He was elected president in 1924 but did not seek reelection in 1928. He is best known for his observation that the business of America is business, but he found the Declaration of Independence a more profound reference point for understanding the nation and its development, turning to it often in his presidential speeches. The following excerpt is from a speech he delivered in Philadelphia, Pennsylvania, commemorating the 150th anniversary of the Declaration.*

We meet to celebrate the birthday of America. The coming of a new life always excites our interest. Although we know in the case of the individual that it has been an infinite repetition reaching back beyond our vision, that only makes it the more wonderful. But how our interest and wonder increase when we behold the miracle of the birth of a new nation. It is to pay our tribute of reverence and respect to those who participated in such a mighty event that we annually observe the fourth day of July. Whatever may have been the impression created by the news which went out from this city on that summer day in 1776, there can be no doubt as to the estimate which is now placed upon it. At the end of 150 years the four corners of the earth unite in coming to Philadelphia as to a holy shrine in grateful acknowledgment of a service so great, which a few inspired men here rendered to humanity, that it is still the preeminent support of free government throughout the world.

. . . Amid all the clash of conflicting interests, amid all the welter of partisan politics, every American can turn for solace and consolation to the Declaration of Independence and the Constitution of the United States with the assurance and confidence that those two great charters of freedom and justice remain firm and unshaken. . . .

It was not because it was proposed to establish a new nation, but because it was proposed to establish a nation on new principles, that July 4, 1776, has come to be regarded as one of the greatest days in history. Great ideas do not burst upon the world unannounced. They are reached by a gradual development over a length of time usually proportionate to their importance. This is especially true of the principles laid down in the Declaration of Independence. Three very definite propositions were set out in its preamble regarding the nature of mankind and therefore of government. These were the doctrine that all men are created equal, that they are endowed with certain inalienable rights, and that therefore the source of the just powers of government must be derived from the consent of the governed. . . .

Placing every man on a plane where he acknowledged no superiors, where no one possessed any right to rule over him, he must inevitably choose his own rulers through a system of self-government. This was their theory of democracy. In those days such doctrines would scarcely have been permitted to flourish and spread in any other country. This was the purpose which the fathers cherished. In order that they might have freedom to express these thoughts and opportunity to put them into action, whole congregations with their pastors had migrated to the colonies. These great truths were in the air that our people breathed. Whatever else we may say of it, the Declaration of Independence was profoundly American.

. . . In its main features the Declaration of Independence is a great spiritual document. It is a declaration not of material but of spiritual conceptions. Equality, liberty, popular sovereignty, the rights of man these are not elements which we can see and touch. They are ideals. They have their source and their roots in the religious convictions. They belong to the unseen world. Unless the faith of the American people in these religious convictions is to endure, the principles of our Declaration will perish. We can not continue to enjoy the result if we neglect and abandon the cause. . . .

About the Declaration there is a finality that is exceedingly restful. It is often asserted that the world has made a great deal of progress since 1776, that we have had new thoughts and new experiences which have given us a great advance over the people of that day, and that we may therefore very well discard their conclusions for something more modern. But that reasoning can not be applied to this great charter. If all men are created equal, that is final. If they are endowed with inalienable rights, that is final. If governments derive their just powers from the consent of the governed, that is final. No advance, no progress can be made beyond these propositions. If anyone wishes to deny their truth or their soundness, the only direction in which he can proceed historically is not forward, but backward toward the time when there was no equality, no

rights of the individual, no rule of the people. Those who wish to proceed in that direction can not lay claim to progress. They are reactionary. Their ideas are not more modern, but more ancient, than those of the Revolutionary fathers.

In the development of its institutions America can fairly claim that it has remained true to the principles which were declared 150 years ago. In all the essentials we have achieved an equality which was never possessed by any other people. Even in the less important matter of material possessions we have secured a wider and wider distribution of wealth. The rights of the individual are held sacred and protected by constitutional guaranties, which even the Government itself is bound not to violate. If there is any one thing among us that is established beyond question, it is self government; the right of the people to rule. If there is any failure in respect to any of these principles, it is because there is a failure on the part of individuals to observe them. We hold that the duly authorized expression of the will of the people has a divine sanction. But even in that we come back to the theory of John Wise that "Democracy is Christ's government. . . ."

The ultimate sanction of law rests on the righteous authority of the Almighty.

. . . Ours is a government of the people. It represents their will. Its officers may sometimes go astray, but that is not a reason for criticizing the principles of our institutions. The real heart of the American Government depends upon the heart of the people. It is from that source that we must look for all genuine reform. It is to that cause that we must ascribe all our results.

## 8.4   Franklin D. Roosevelt, State of the Union Address, January 11, 1944

*Franklin D. Roosevelt (1882–1945), the thirty-second president of the United States, was the first and only four-term president. In his first two terms, Roosevelt, along with Congress, combated the economic hardships of the Great Depression. In his latter two terms, he led the nation through the trials of World War II. By 1944, Roosevelt and the rest of America were looking toward the end of the war and to the long hoped for return of American soldiers from Europe and Asia. In this historic State of the Union Address, the president envisions a new national economic and political future, one in which the ideal of individual freedom expressed in the Declaration of Independence is understood in terms of economic security and independence.*

It is our duty now to begin to lay the plans and determine the strategy for the winning of a lasting peace and the establishment of an American standard of living higher than ever before known. We cannot be content, no matter how high that general standard of living may be, if some fraction of our people—whether it be one-third or one-fifth or one-tenth—is ill-fed, ill-clothed, ill-housed, and insecure.

This Republic had its beginning, and grew to its present strength, under the protection of certain inalienable political rights—among them the right of free speech, free press, free worship, trial by jury, freedom from unreasonable searches and seizures. They were our rights to life and liberty.

As our Nation has grown in size and stature, however—as our industrial economy expanded—these political rights proved inadequate to assure us equality in the pursuit of happiness.

We have come to a clear realization of the fact that true individual freedom cannot exist without economic security and independence. "Necessitous men are not free men." People who are hungry and out of a job are the stuff of which dictatorships are made.

In our day these economic truths have become accepted as self-evident. We have accepted, so to speak, a second Bill of Rights under which a new basis of security and prosperity can be established for all—regardless of station, race, or creed.

Among these are: The right to a useful and remunerative job in the industries or shops or farms or mines of the Nation; The right to earn enough to provide adequate food and clothing and recreation; The right of every farmer to raise and sell his products at a return which will give him and his family a decent living; The right of every businessman, large and small, to trade in an atmosphere of freedom from unfair competition and domination by monopolies at home or abroad; The right of every family to a decent home; The right to adequate medical care and the opportunity to achieve and enjoy good health; The right to adequate protection from the economic fears of old age, sickness, accident, and unemployment; The right to a good education.

All of these rights spell security. And after this war is won we must be prepared to move forward, in the implementation of these rights, to new goals of human happiness and well-being.

America's own rightful place in the world depends in large part upon how fully these and similar rights have been carried into practice for our citizens. For unless there is security here at home there cannot be lasting peace in the world. . . .

I ask the Congress to explore the means for implementing this economic bill of rights—for it is definitely the responsibility of the Congress so to do. . . .

Each and every one of us has a solemn obligation under God to serve this Nation in its most critical hour—to keep this Nation great—to make this Nation greater in a better world.

## 8.5  Gerald R. Ford, U.S. Bicentennial Speech, Independence Hall, Philadelphia, Pennsylvania, July 4, 1976

*The bicentennial of the Declaration of Independence was celebrated with unparalleled fanfare in 1976. Gerald R. Ford, who became the nation's thirty-eighth president of the United States in 1974 when Richard M. Nixon resigned from office, offered the following reflection on what the Declaration meant to him.*

The Declaration was not a protest against government, but against the excess of government. It prescribed the proper role of government, to secure the rights of individuals and to effect their safety and happiness. In modern society, no individual can do this alone. So government is not a necessary evil but a necessary good.

## 9.1  Supreme Court Cases That Invoke the Declaration of Independence

*The U.S. Supreme Court, the nation's highest court, was created by Article III of the U.S. Constitution. Supreme Court cases through the 2000 term that invoke the Declaration of Independence are summarized below, in reverse chronological order.*

*United States v. Hatter,* 532 U.S. 557, 568 (2001). (Justice Stephen G. Breyer, for the Court, cites and quotes the Declaration to support his argument that the founders wanted an independent judiciary.)

*Troxel v. Granville,* 530 U.S. 57, 91 (2000). (Justice Antonin Scalia, dissenting, argues that the right of parents to direct the upbringing of their children is among the "unalienable rights" with which "all men . . . are endowed by their Creator." However, he explicitly rejects the idea that the Declaration confers power on any court.)

*Alden v. Maine,* 527 U.S. 706, 764, 778 (1999). (Justice David H. Souter, dissenting, quotes Justice Joseph Story's claim that "antecedent to the Declaration of Independence, none of the colonies were, or pretended to be, sovereign states," and writes in a footnote that Charles Pinckney believed that the Declaration was an act of the Union, not individual states.)

*Neder v. United States,* 527 U.S. 1, 30–31 (1999). (Justice Scalia, concurring in part and dissenting in part, cites the Declaration as evidence that the founders valued trial by jury.)

*Jones v. United States,* 526 U.S. 227, 246 (1999). (Justice Souter, in his opinion for the Court, notes that Americans complained in the Declaration about Great Britain's attempt to diminish the power of juries.)

*United States v. Cabrales,* 524 U.S. 1, 6 (1998). (Justice Ruth Bader Ginsburg, for the Court, quotes from the Declaration to help demonstrate that the founders were concerned with having jury trials in local venues.)

*Seminole Tribe of Florida v. Florida,* 517 U.S. 44, 95 (1996). (Justice John Paul Stevens, dissenting, notes that the Declaration helps demonstrate that the founders rejected the idea that "the King can do no wrong.")

*Rosenberger v. Rector and Visitors of University of Virginia,* 515 U.S. 819, 823 (1995). (Justice Anthony M. Kennedy, for the Court, notes that Thomas Jefferson ranked his founding of the University of Virginia with his authorship of the

Declaration and the Virginia Statute of Religious Freedom as his most important accomplishments.)

*Sandin v. Conner,* 515 U.S. 472, 489 (1995). (Justice Ginsburg, dissenting, argues that the Due Process Clause of the Fourteenth Amendment protects the " 'Liberty' enshrined among 'unalienable Rights' with which all persons are 'endowed by their Creator.' ")

*Adarand Constructors, Inc. v. Peña,* 515 U.S. 200, 240 (1995). (Justice Clarence Thomas, concurring, appeals to the Declaration's statement that "We hold these truths to be self-evident, that all men are created equal, that they are endowed by their Creator with certain unalienable Rights, that among these are Life, Liberty, and the pursuit of Happiness" as evidence of "the principle of inherent equality that underlies and infuses our Constitution.") (See Chapter 4.)

*McIntyre v. Ohio Elections Commission,* 514 U.S. 334, 343 (1995). (Justice Stevens, for the Court, notes that Richard Henry Lee was a signer of the Declaration.)

*Plaut v. Spendthrift Farm, Inc.,* 514 U.S. 211, 221 (1995). (Justice Scalia, for the Court, cites an article by Edward Corwin that includes the Declaration in its title.)

*Weiss v. United States,* 510 U.S. 163, 198 (1994). (Justice Scalia, in his concurring opinion, cites the Declaration to emphasize the importance the founders placed on an independent judiciary.)

*Lee v. Weisman,* 505 U.S. 577, 633, 641, 645 (1992). (Justice Scalia, dissenting, quotes from the Declaration to support his assertion that "[f]rom our nation's origin, prayer has been a prominent part of governmental ceremonies and proclamations." Specifically, he notes that Americans " 'appeal[ed] to the Supreme Judge of the world for the rectitude of our intentions' and avowed " 'a firm reliance on the protection of divine Providence.' ")

*Griffin v. United States,* 502 U.S. 46, 49 (1991). (Justice Scalia, for the Court, uses the Declaration to mark independence.)

*Harmelin v. Michigan,* 501 U.S. 957, 969 (1991). (Justice Scalia, for the Court, refers to the Declaration in passing.)

*Chisom v. Roemer,* 501 U.S. 380, 403 (1991). (Justice Stevens, for the Court, quotes from Justice William O. Douglas's opinion in *Gray v. Sanders* (1963), which uses the Declaration to support his understanding of political equality.)

*Metropolitan Washington Airports Authority v. Citizens for Abatement of Aircraft Noise, Inc.,* 501 U.S. 252, 273 (1991). (Justice Stevens, for the Court, argues that the "abuses by the monarch recounted in the Declaration of Independence provide dramatic evidence of the threat to liberty posed by a too powerful executive.")

*Cruzan by Cruzan v. Director, Missouri Dept. of Health,* 497 U.S. 261, 330, 345, 355 (1990). (Justice Stevens, dissenting, argues that interpreting the Fourteenth Amendment in light of the Declaration should lead the Court to allow individuals (or guardians acting on their behalf) to refuse life-sustaining medical procedures.)

*Texas Monthly, Inc. v. Bullock,* 489 U.S. 1, 29 (1989). (Justice Scalia, dissenting, appeals to the Declaration and other public documents to show that Americans have long mixed religion and politics.)

*Solorio v. United States,* 483 U.S. 435, 459 (1987). (Justice Thurgood Marshall, dissenting, quotes from the Declaration to support his assertion that the founders were wary of granting the military broad authority in courts-martial.)

*Northern Pipeline Construction Co. v. Marathon Pipe Line Co.,* 458 U.S. 50, 60 (1982). (Justice William J. Brennan Jr., for the Court, quotes from the Declaration to show that the founders desired an independent judiciary.)

*Dames & Moore v. Regan,* 453 U.S. 654, 661–662 (1981). (Justice William H. Rehnquist, for the Court, quotes from Justice Robert H. Jackson's opinion in *Youngstown Sheet & Tube Co. v. Sawyer* (1952) appealing to the Declaration to support the argument that the founders wanted an executive with limited power.)

*United States v. Will,* 449 U.S. 200, 219 (1980). (Chief Justice Warren E. Burger, for the Court, quotes from the Declaration to show that the founders valued an independent judiciary.)

*Fullilove v. Klutznick,* 448 U.S. 448, 531, 533 (1980). (Justice Potter Stewart, dissenting, argues that the Fourteenth Amendment was intended to enact "a fundamental principle upon which this Nation had been founded—that the law would honor no preference based on lineage." In making this claim he acknowledges that many founders were concerned primarily with protecting the rights of white men, but he also suggests that "[t]he words Thomas Jefferson wrote in 1776 in the Declaration of Independence . . . contained the seeds of a far broader principle: 'We hold these truths to be self-evident: that all men are created equal.' " Likewise, Justice Stevens, in his dissenting opinion, quotes from his opinion in *Mathews v. Lucas* (1976) relying on the Declaration to support his argument that "the Federal Government has been directed" from its inception "to treat all its citizens as having been 'created equal' in the eyes of the law.")

*City of Mobile v. Bolden,* 446 U.S. 55, 104, 128 (1980). (Justice Marshall, dissenting, argues that "[t]he American ideal of political equality, conceived in the earliest days of our colonial existence and fostered by the egalitarian language of the Declaration of Independence, could not forever tolerate the limitation of the right to vote to white propertied males." He also quotes from Justice Douglas's opinion in *Gray v. Sanders* (1963), which uses the Declaration to support his understanding of political equality.)

*Secretary of Navy v. Huff,* 444 U.S. 453, 454 (1980). (Per curiam opinion that simply mentions the Declaration in the Court's discussion of the facts.)

*Nevada v. Hall,* 440 U.S. 410, 415 (1979). (Justice Stevens, for the Court, cites and quotes

from the Declaration as evidence that the colonists rejected the fiction that "the King could do no wrong.")

*Vance v. Bradley,* 440 U.S. 93, 94 (1979). (Justice Byron R. White, for the Court, quotes a member of Congress who helped pass the Fourteenth Amendment and argued that "all of section 1 of the Fourteenth Amendment is already within the spirit of the Declaration of Independence.")

*Washington v. Confederated Bands and Tribes of Yakima Indian Nation,* 439 U.S. 463, 481 (1979). (Justice Stewart, for the Court, quotes from the state of Washington's Enabling Act, which requires the state to adopt a constitution not repugnant to the "principles of the Declaration of Independence.")

*Parklane Hosiery Co., Inc. v. Shore,* 439 U.S. 322, 340, 354 (1979). (Justice Rehnquist, dissenting, cites and quotes from the Declaration to help demonstrate that the founders valued highly the right to trial by jury in civil cases.)

*Regents of University of California v. Bakke,* 438 U.S. 265, 388–389 (1978). (Justice Marshall, concurring in part and dissenting in part, argues that the "self-evident truths and unalienable rights" of the Declaration were meant by their authors to apply only to white men. He also suggests that the removal from Jefferson's original draft of his condemnation of the slave trade is evidence that the Declaration implicitly protected slavery.)

*McDaniel v. Paty,* 435 U.S. 618, 625 (1978). (Chief Justice Burger, for the Court, mentions in passing that John Witherspoon was the only clergyman to sign the Declaration.)

*Mathews v. Lucas,* 427 U.S. 495, 516, 520 (1976). (Justice Stevens, dissenting, argues that "[f]rom its inception, the Federal government has been directed to treat all its citizens as having been 'created equal' in the eyes of the law." As evidence, he offers the following quotation from the Declaration: "We hold these truths to be self-evident, that all men are created equal, that they are endowed by their Creator with certain unalienable Rights, that among these are Life, Liberty and the pursuit of Happiness.")

*Massachusetts Board of Retirement v. Murgia,* 427 U.S. 307, 322 (1976). (Justice Marshall, dissenting, quotes from Justice Joseph P. Bradley's opinion in *Butchers' Union Co. v. Crescent City Co.* (1884) to support his argument that the right of an individual to engage in an occupation "is an inalienable right; it was formulated as such under the phrase 'pursuit of happiness' in the declaration of independence. . . . This right is a large ingredient in the civil liberty of the citizen." As such, it should be protected by the Fourteenth Amendment.)

*Faretta v. California,* 422 U.S. 806, 829 (1975). (Justice Stewart, in his opinion for the Court, uses the Declaration to mark America's independence.)

*Schlesinger v. Reservists Committee to Stop the War,* 418 U.S. 208, 233 (1974). (Justice Douglas, dissenting, quotes the Declaration to support his argument that "the people, not the bureaucracy, are sovereign" and that "Our Federal Government was created for the security and happiness of the people.")

*Committee for Public Education and Religious Liberty v. Nyquist,* 413 U.S. 756, 772 (1973). (Justice Lewis F. Powell Jr., in his opinion for the Court, mentions that Thomas Jefferson was as proud of his authorship of the Virginia Statute of Religious Freedom as he was his authorship of the Declaration and the founding of the University of Virginia.)

*Branzburg v. Hayes,* 408 U.S. 665, 716 (1972). (Justice Douglas, dissenting in No. 70–57, *United States v. Caldwell,* refers to the case of *In re Anastaplo* (1961), in which he notes that the government's interest in "regulating membership of bar" was found to outweigh "protection of the applicant's belief in Declaration of Independence that citizens should revolt against an oppressive government.")

*Laird v. Tatum,* 408 U.S. 1, 19 (1972). (Justice Douglas, dissenting, quotes from the Declara-

tion to support his claim that the founders desired civilian control of the military.)

*McKeiver v. Pennsylvania,* 403 U.S. 528, 571 (1971). (Justice Douglas, dissenting, quotes a lower court judge's opinion that juveniles should have trials because the Declaration speaks of the equality of all citizens.)

*Whitcomb v. Chavis,* 403 U.S. 124, 166 (1971). (Justice White, for the Court, cites someone who uses the Declaration to mark independence. Justice John Marshall Harlan, in a concurring opinion, attacks Justice Douglas's simple majoritarianism, which he finds best represented in Douglas's opinion in *Gray v. Sanders* (1963), where the Declaration is cited.)

*Perkins v. Matthews,* 400 U.S. 379, 407 (1971). (Justice Hugo L. Black, dissenting, makes an analogy between federal interference in state laws and the king's interference in colonial laws complained of in the Declaration.)

*Oregon v. Mitchell,* 400 U.S. 112, 144, 194 (1970). (Justice Douglas, dissenting, quotes from his opinion in *Gray v. Sanders* (1963) that uses the Declaration to support his view of political equality. Justice Harlan, concurring in part and dissenting in part, mentions the Declaration in his discussion of the congressional debate over the Fourteenth Amendment.)

*Welsh v. United States,* 398 U.S. 333, 350 (1970). (Justice Harlan, concurring, uses the Declaration to illustrate his point that "it is common practice to use various synonyms for the Deity. The Declaration of Independence refers to 'Nature's God,' 'Creator,' 'Supreme Judge of the World,' and 'divine Providence.' ")

*Powell v. McCormack,* 395 U.S. 486, 580 (1969). (Chief Justice Earl Warren, for the Court, uses the Declaration to mark independence.)

*Ferrell v. Dallas Independent School District,* 393 U.S. 856 (1968). (Justice Douglas, dissenting from a denial of certiorari, argues that "the ideas of 'life, liberty, and the pursuit of happiness,' expressed in the Declaration of Independence, later found specific definition in the

Constitution itself, including of course freedom of expression and a wide zone of privacy." Based on these rights a person should not be denied an education in a public school because of the length of his hair.)

*Board of Education of Central School Dist. No. 1 v. Allen,* 392 U.S. 236, 260 (1968). (Justice Douglas, dissenting, complains that texts loaned to religious schools might contain religious content. As an example, he points to a history text that notes that "one of the men who signed the Declaration of Independence and two who attended the Constitutional Convention were Catholic.")

*Duncan v. Louisiana,* 391 U.S. 145, 152 (1968). (Justice White, for the Court, quotes from the Declaration to help demonstrate the importance of jury trials in the American legal system.)

*Berger v. New York,* 388 U.S. 41, 58 (1967). (Justice Tom C. Clark, for the Court, cites the Declaration's criticism of "general warrants" in his opinion striking down a New York law that made it too easy for police to get warrants to conduct electronic searches.)

*Curtis Publishing Co. v. Butts,* 388 U.S. 130, 149 (1967). (Justice Harlan, for the Court, argues that "[t]he dissemination of the individual's opinions on matters of public interest is for us, in the historic words of the Declaration of Independence, an 'unalienable right' that 'governments are instituted among men to secure.' ")

*Keyishian v. Board of Regents of University of State of New York,* 385 U.S. 589, 600 (1967). (Justice Brennan, for the Court, strikes down a law prohibiting teaching that governments may be overthrown. In his opinion he asks, rhetorically, "Does the teacher who informs his class about the precepts of Marxism or the Declaration of Independence violate this prohibition?")

*Fortson v. Morris,* 385 U.S. 231, 240 (1966). (Justice Douglas, for the Court, quotes from his opinion in *Gray v. Sanders* (1963) that uses the Declaration to help define the American conception of political equality.)

*Adderley v. Florida,* 385 U.S. 39, 51 (1966). (Justice Douglas, dissenting, cites the Declaration to support his argument that Americans value highly their right to petition the government.)

*South Carolina v. Katzenbach,* 383 U.S. 301, 359 (1966). (Justice Black, concurring in part and dissenting in part, cites and quotes from the Declaration to support his claim that the founders objected to having legislative and judicial proceedings in "inconvenient and distant places.")

*Bell v. Maryland,* 378 U.S. 226, 286, 342 (1964). (Justice Arthur J. Goldberg, concurring, contends that "[t]he Declaration of Independence states the American creed." Justice Black, dissenting, cites the Declaration as evidence that English common law was not always considered "good" in America.)

*Reynolds v. Sims,* 377 U.S. 533, 558 (1964). (Chief Justice Warren, for the Court, quotes from Justice Douglas's opinion in *Gray v. Sanders* (1963), which uses the Declaration to support his understanding of political equality.)

*School District of Abington Township, Pennsylvania v. Schempp,* 374 U.S. 203, 307 (1963). (Justice Goldberg, concurring, quotes a passage from Justice Black's opinion in *Engel v. Vitale* (1962) to emphasize that the Court's opinion does not forbid "reciting historical documents such as the Declaration of Independence which contain references to the Deity.")

*Gray v. Sanders,* 372 U.S. 368, 381, 384 (1963). (Justice Douglas, for the Court, writes, "The conception of political equality from the Declaration of Independence, to Abraham Lincoln's Gettysburg Address, to the Fifteenth, Seventeenth, and Nineteenth Amendments can mean only one thing—one person, one vote." Justice Harlan, dissenting, repeats and criticizes Justice Douglas's claim.)

*Engel v. Vitale,* 370 U.S. 421, 435, 450 (1962). (Justice Black, for the Court, emphasizes that the Court's decision prohibiting teacher-led prayer in public schools does not forbid "reciting historical documents such as the Declaration of Independence which contain references to the Deity." Justice Stewart, dissenting, argues that school prayer is no different from the many public appeals to God by U.S. officials such as those found in the Declaration.)

*Scales v. United States,* 367 U.S. 203, 268–269 (1961). (Justice Black, dissenting, cites and quotes from the Declaration to support his contention that "[b]elief in the principle of revolution is deep in our traditions.")

*McGowan v. Maryland,* 366 U.S. 420, 563 (1961). (Justice Douglas, dissenting, argues that "[t]he Declaration of Independence stated the now familiar theme: 'We hold these Truths to be self-evident, that all Men are created equal, that they are endowed by their Creator with certain unalienable Rights, that among these are Life, Liberty and the Pursuit of Happiness.' And the body of the Constitution as well as the Bill of Rights enshrined those principles.")

*In re Anastaplo,* 366 U.S. 82, 102, 104, 112 (1961). (Justice Black, dissenting, argues that the Illinois bar improperly refused to admit George Anastaplo because of his commitment to the principles promulgated in the Declaration of Independence.)

*Cooper v. Aaron,* 358 U.S. 1, 23 (1958). (Justice Felix Frankfurter, concurring, cites the Declaration as evidence that the founders desired a government of laws, not of men.)

*Perez v. Brownell,* 356 U.S. 44, 64 (1958). (Chief Justice Warren, dissenting, quotes the Declaration to support his argument that governments are made by and for the people.)

*Green v. United States,* 356 U.S. 165, 209 (1958). (Justice Black, dissenting, cites the Declaration to help show that the founders valued trial by jury.)

*Reid v. Covert,* 354 U.S. 1, 29, 58 (1957). (Justice Black, for the Court, cites the Declaration to help show that the founders valued trial by jury. Justice Frankfurter, concurring, quotes John Quincy Adams's assertion that the Decla-

ration recognized that the colonies were bound by international law.)

*Konigsberg v. State Bar of California,* 353 U.S. 252, 272 (1957). (Justice Black, for the Court, mentions the title of a pamphlet written by the defendant that discusses the Declaration.)

*United States v. Twin City Power Co.,* 350 U.S. 222, 246 (1956). (Justice Harold H. Burton, dissenting, quotes from Justice David J. Brewer's opinion in *Monongahela Navigation Co. v. United States* (1893), where he defends the importance of "those rights of persons and property which by the Declaration of Independence were affirmed to be unalienable rights.")

*United States ex rel. Toth v. Quarles,* 350 U.S. 11, 16 (1955). (Justice Black, for the Court, cites the Declaration to support his argument that the right to trial by jury was important to the founders.)

*Youngstown Sheet & Tube Co. v. Sawyer,* 343 U.S. 579, 641 (1952). (Justice Jackson, concurring, refers to the Declaration's attack on King George III's use of the executive prerogative to support his argument that the founders did not create an executive with unlimited power.)

*Tenney v. Brandhove,* 341 U.S. 367, 375 (1951). (Justice Frankfurter, for the Court, cites a journal article by Edward Corwin with the Declaration in the title.)

*American Communications Association, C.I.O., v. Douds,* 339 U.S. 382, 425, 428, 442 (1950). (Justice Jackson, concurring and dissenting, argues that the Communist movement is designed to undo the Declaration of Independence, the Constitution, and the Bill of Rights. He also notes that Jefferson risked his life to sign the Declaration and quotes from the Declaration's assertion that people have the right to rebel.)

*Bute v. Illinois,* 333 U.S. 640, 651 (1948). (Justice Burton, for the Court, argues that "[t]he Constitution was conceived in large part in the spirit of the Declaration of Independence which declared that to secure such 'unalienable Rights' as those of 'Life, Liberty and the pursuit of Happiness.' ")

*United States v. United Mine Workers of America*, 330 U.S. 258, 308 (1947). (Justice Frankfurter, concurring, cites the Declaration as evidence that the founders desired a government of laws, not of men.)

*Duncan v. Kahanamoku*, 327 U.S. 304, 320, 325 (1946). (Justice Black, for the Court, cites the Declaration to help show that the founders did not want "civilian government and especially the courts [to be] interfered with by the exercise of military power." Justice Frank Murphy, in his concurring opinion, cites the language of the Declaration to make the same point.)

*Cramer v. United* States, 325 U.S. 1, 14 (1945). (Justice Jackson, for the Court, mentions and quotes from the Declaration in his discussion of the history of treason law in America. He also notes that the signers of the Declaration all could have been hung for treason.)

*Schneiderman v. United States*, 320 U.S. 118, 140 (1943). (Justice Murphy, for the Court, quotes from the U.S. Government's brief that mentions the Declaration.)

*Adams v. United States ex rel. McCann*, 317 U.S. 269, 276 (1942). (Justice Frankfurter, for the Court, cites the Declaration to help demonstrate that the founders wanted to protect the right to trial by jury.)

*O'Malley v. Woodrough*, 307 U.S. 277, 284 (1939). (Justice Pierce Butler, dissenting, cites and quotes the Declaration to support his argument that the founders were very concerned with protecting the independence of the judiciary.)

*Senn v. Tile Layers Protective Union, Local No. 5*, 301 U.S. 468, 487 (1937). (Justice Butler, dissenting, quotes from Justice Bradley's opinion in *Butchers' Union Co. v. Crescent City Co.* (1884) to support his argument that the right of an individual to engage in an occupation "is an inalienable right.")

*United States v. Curtiss-Wright Export Corp.*, 299 U.S. 304, 316 (1936). (Justice George Sutherland, for the Court, argues that the colonies were independent prior to the Declaration and that sovereignty clearly passed from the Crown to the colonies as a whole with the separation from Great Britain.)

*Milwaukee County v. M.E. White Co.*, 296 U.S. 268, 271 (1935). (Justice Harlan Fiske Stone, for the Court, uses the Declaration to mark independence.)

*New Jersey v. Delaware*, 291 U.S. 361, 371 (1934). (Justice Benjamin N. Cardozo, for the Court, argues that the Declaration made Delaware a state and fixed her boundaries at that time.)

*O'Donoghue v. United States*, 289 U.S. 516, 531 (1933).(Justice Sutherland, for the Court, cites the Declaration to support his argument that the founders valued an independent judiciary.)

*Powell v. Alabama*, 287 U.S. 45, 65 (1932). (Justice Sutherland, for the Court, uses the Declaration to mark independence.)

*New State Ice Co. v. Liebmann*, 285 U.S. 262, 305 (1932). (Justice Louis D. Brandeis, dissenting, uses the Declaration to mark independence.)

*McCarthy v. Arndstein*, 266 U.S. 34, 41 (1924). (Justice Brandeis, for the Court, uses the Declaration to mark independence.)

*Weems v. United States*, 217 U.S. 349, 393 (1910). (Justice Edward D. White, dissenting, uses the Declaration to mark independence.)

*Twining v. New Jersey*, 211 U.S. 78, 119 (1908). (Justice John Marshall Harlan, dissenting, cites the Declaration in his discussion of the importance of the right against self-incrimination to the American revolutionaries.)

*Carter v. McClaughry*, 183 U.S. 365, 384 (1902). (Chief Justice Melville W. Fuller, for the Court, quotes from an opinion that uses the Declaration to mark independence.)

*Cotting v. Kansas City Stock Yards Co. and the State of Kansas*, 183 U.S. 79, 107 (1901). (Justice Brewer, for the Court, quotes from his opinion in *Gulf, C. & S.F. Ry. Co. v. Ellis* (1897), where he argues that "it is always safe to read the letter of the Constitution in the spirit of the Declaration of Independence.")

*Downes v. Bidwell,* 182 U.S. 244, 272, 302 (1901). (Justice Henry B. Brown, for the Court, mentions the Declaration in passing when discussing Chief Justice Roger B. Taney's argument in *Dred Scott v. Sandford* (1857). Justice White, concurring, quotes from the last paragraph of the Declaration to help show that the founders assumed the nation could acquire new territory.)

*French v. Barber Asphalt Pavement Co.,* 181 U.S. 324, 331 (1901). (Justice George Shiras Jr., for the Court, uses the Declaration to mark independence.)

*Missouri v. Illinois,* 180 U.S. 208, 219 (1901). (Justice Shiras, for the Court, uses the Declaration to mark independence.)

*Maxwell v. Dow,* 176 U.S. 581, 609 (1900). (Justice Harlan, dissenting, cites the Declaration to support his argument that the founders valued trial by jury.)

*Capital Traction Co. v. Hof,* 174 U.S. 1, 17 (1899). (Justice Horace Gray, for the Court, uses the Declaration to mark independence.)

*Merrill v. National Bank of Jacksonville,* 173 U.S. 131, 172 (1899). (Justice Horace Gray, dissenting, uses the Declaration to mark independence.)

*Missouri, K. & T. Trust Co. v. Krumseig,* 172 U.S. 351, 360 (1899). (Justice Shiras, for the Court, quotes from an opinion that uses the Declaration to mark independence.)

*Magoun v. Illinois Trust & Savings Bank,* 170 U.S. 283, 301 (1898). (Justice Brewer, dissenting in a case involving a graduated tax, argues, "Equality in right, in protection, and in burden is the thought which has run through the life of this nation, and its constitutional enactments, from the Declaration of Independence to the present hour.")

*United States v. Wong Kim Ark,* 169 U.S. 649, 658–660, 706, 711 (1898). (Justice Gray, for the Court, and Chief Justice Fuller, concurring, use the Declaration to mark independence.)

*Allgeyer v. Louisiana,* 165 U.S. 578, 589 (1897). (Justice Rufus W. Peckham, for the Court, quotes from Justice Bradley's opinion in *Butchers' Union Co. v. Crescent City Co.* (1884) to support his argument that " 'the right to follow any of the common occupations of life is an inalienable right. It was formulated as such under the phrase "pursuit of happiness" in the Declaration of Independence.' ")

*Gulf, Colorado & Santa Fe Railway v. Ellis,* 165 U.S. 150, 159–160 (1897). (Justice Brewer, for the Court, argues that the Declaration was the "first official action of this nation" and that although it "may not have the force of organic law, or be made the basis of judicial decision as to the limits of right and duty," it is an important statement of principles and "it is always safe to read the letter of the Constitution in the spirit of the Declaration of Independence.")

*Warner v. Texas & Pacific Railway Co.,* 164 U.S. 418, 422 (1896). (Justice Gray, for the Court, uses the Declaration to mark independence.)

*Lowe v. Kansas,* 163 U.S. 81, 85 (1896). (Justice Gray, for the Court, uses the Declaration to mark independence.)

*Hamilton v. Brown,* 161 U.S. 256, 263 (1896). (Justice Gray, for the Court, uses the Declaration to mark independence.)

*Hilton v. Guyot,* 159 U.S. 113, 150, 160 (1895). (Justice Gray, for the Court, uses the Declaration to mark independence.)

*Sparf v. United States,* 156 U.S. 51, 142–143 (1895). (Justice Gray, dissenting, uses the Declaration to mark independence.)

*Scott v. McNeal,* 154 U.S. 34, 39 (1894). (Justice Gray, for the Court, uses the Declaration to mark independence.)

*Shively v. Bowlby,* 152 U.S. 1, 24 (1894). (Justice Gray, for the Court, quotes an opinion that uses the Declaration to mark independence.)

*Hill v. United States,* 149 U.S. 593, 596 (1893). (Justice Gray, for the Court, uses the Declaration to mark independence.)

*Monongahela Navigation Co. v. United States,* 148 U.S. 312, 324–325 (1893). (Justice Brewer, for the Court, argues that the Bill of Rights was adopted to prevent the government from trespassing "upon those rights of persons and property which by the Declaration of Independence were affirmed to be unalienable rights." He proceeds to argue that, in this case, "we need not have recourse to this natural equity, nor is it necessary to look through the Constitution to the affirmations lying behind it in the Declaration of Independence, for in this Fifth Amendment there is stated the exact limitation on the power of the government to take private property for public uses.")

*United States v. Sanges,* 144 U.S. 310, 312 (1892). (Justice Gray, for the Court, uses the Declaration to mark independence.)

*Holy Trinity Church v. United States,* 143 U.S. 457, 467–468 (1892). (Justice Brewer, for the Court, cites the Declaration, along with other documents, to support his argument that America is a Christian nation.)

*Boyd v. Nebraska,* 143 U.S. 135, 163 (1892). (Chief Justice Fuller, for the Court, uses the Declaration to mark independence.)

*Claassen v. United States,* 142 U.S. 140, 146 (1891). (Justice Gray, for the Court, uses the Declaration to mark independence.)

*Manchester v. Massachusetts,* 139 U.S. 240, 260 (1891). (Justice Samuel Blatchford, for the Court, quotes an earlier opinion that uses the Declaration to mark independence.)

*In re Palliser,* 136 U.S. 257, 265 (1890). (Justice Gray, for the Court, uses the Declaration to mark independence.)

*Liverpool & Great Western Steam Co. v. Phenix Ins. Co.,* 129 U.S. 397, 439, 445, 447 (1889). (Justice Gray, for the Court, uses the Declaration to mark independence.)

*Powell v. Pennsylvania,* 127 U.S. 678, 692 (1888). (Justice Stephen J. Field, dissenting, argues that "[t]he right to pursue one's happiness is placed by the Declaration of Independence among the inalienable rights of man, with which all men are endowed, not by the grace of emperors or kings, or by force of legislative or constitutional enactments, but by their Creator; and to secure them, not to grant them, governments are instituted among men. The right to procure healthy and nutritious food, by which life may be preserved and enjoyed, and to manufacture it, is among these inalienable rights, which, in my judgment, no state can give, and no state can take away, except in punishment for crime. It is involved in the right to pursue one's happiness.")

*In re Sawyer,* 124 U.S. 200, 210 (1888). (Justice Gray, for the Court, uses the Declaration to mark independence.)

*Mackin v. United States,* 117 U.S. 348, 350 (1886). (Justice Gray, for the Court, uses the Declaration to mark independence.)

*Smith v. Whitney,* 116 U.S. 167, 174 (1886). (Justice Gray, for the Court, uses the Declaration to mark independence.)

*Kurtz v. Moffitt,* 115 U.S. 487, 502 (1885). (Justice Gray, for the Court, uses the Declaration to mark independence.)

*Ex parte Wilson,* 114 U.S. 417, 421 (1885). (Justice Gray, for the Court, uses the Declaration to mark independence.)

*Head v. Amoskeag Mfg. Co.,* 113 U.S. 9, 16 (1885). (Justice Gray, for the Court, uses the Declaration to mark independence.)

*Lamar v. Micou,* 112 U.S. 452, 465 (1884). (Justice Gray, for the Court, uses the Declaration to mark independence.)

*Butchers' Union Slaughter-House & Live-Stock Landing Co. v. Crescent City Live-Stock Landing & Slaughter-House Co.,* 111 U.S. 746, 762, 756–757 (1884). (Justices Bradley and Field, in separate concurring opinions, argue that the "right to follow any of the common occupations of life" is one of the inalienable rights described in the Declaration that governments may not restrict except as punishment for a crime.)

*Civil Rights Cases,* 109 U.S. 3, 31 (1883). (Justice Harlan, dissenting, mentions the Declaration in his discussion of Chief Justice Taney's opinion in *Dred Scott v. Sandford* (1857).)

*Cushing v. Laird,* 107 U.S. 69, 79 (1883). (Justice Gray, for the Court, uses the Declaration to mark independence.)

*United States v. Lee,* 106 U.S. 196, 238 (1882). (Justice Gray, for the Court, uses the Declaration to mark independence.)

*Ex parte Virginia,* 100 U.S. 339, 365–366 (1879). (Justice Field, dissenting, argues that the Privileges or Immunities Clause of the Fourteenth Amendment should be held to prohibit "the denial or abridgment by any State of those fundamental privileges and immunities which of right belong to citizens of all free governments; and with which the Declaration of Independence proclaimed that all men were endowed by their Creator, and to secure which governments were instituted among men.")

*Brine v. Hartford Fire Ins. Co.,* 96 U.S. 627, 633 (1877). (Justice Samuel F. Miller, for the Court, rejects an argument by counsel that uses the Declaration to mark independence.)

*Williams v. Bruffy,* 96 U.S. 176, 186 (1877). (Justice Field, for the Court, refers to the Declaration when making an analogy between the Revolutionary War and the Civil War.)

*United States v. Cruikshank,* 92 U.S. 542, 554 (1875). (Chief Justice Morrison R. Waite, for the Court, argues that "[t]he rights of life and personal liberty are natural rights of man. 'To secure these rights,' says the Declaration of Independence, 'governments are instituted among men, deriving their just powers from the consent of the governed.' The very highest duty of the States, when they entered into the Union under the Constitution, was to protect all persons within their boundaries in the enjoyment of these 'unalienable rights with which they were endowed by their Creator.' Sovereignty, for this purpose, rests alone with the States.")

*Minor v. Happersett,* 88 U.S. 162, 166 (1874). (Chief Justice Waite, for the Court, notes that the Declaration released the American people from the "political bands which connected them with Great Britain.")

*Slaughter-House Cases,* 83 U.S. 36, 105, 115–116 (1872). (Justice Field, dissenting, argues that the Fourteenth Amendment "was intended to give practical effect to the declaration of 1776 of inalienable rights, rights which are the gift of the Creator, which the law does not confer, but only recognizes." Justice Bradley, dissenting, argues that the "Declaration of Independence, which was the first political act of the American people in their independent sovereign capacity, lays the foundation of our National existence upon this broad proposition: 'That all men are created equal; that they are endowed by their Creator with certain inalienable rights; that among these are life, liberty, and the pursuit of happiness.' ")

*Ware v. United States,* 71 U.S. 617, 630 (1866). (Justice Nathan Clifford, for the Court, cites the Declaration as a historical reference point.)

*Kentucky v. Dennison,* 65 U.S. 66, 101 (1860). (Chief Justice Taney, for the Court, contends that "by the Declaration of Independence" the colonies "bec[a]me separate and independent sovereignties.")

*Jackson v. The Magnolia,* 61 U.S. 296, 323, 327 (1857). (Justice John A. Campbell, dissenting, cites the Declaration to mark independence.)

*Dred Scott v. Sandford,* 60 U.S. 393, 407–412, 574–578 (1857). (Chief Justice Taney, for the Court, argues that "the language used in the Declaration of Independence," as well as the legislation and history of the time, show that "Negroes" were not considered to be part of "the people" or citizens of the United States in 1776. Because this sentiment had not changed among the framers of the Constitution, "Negroes" were not, and cannot be, considered citizens of the United States. Justice Campbell, concurring, cites an earlier opinion by Justice Samuel Chase that used the Declaration to argue the states were sovereign. Justice Benjamin R. Curtis, dissenting, offers a rebuttal to Taney, maintaining that the principles of the Declaration advocate freedom for all men and that freed slaves have been, and could be, considered citizens of the United States.)

*Den ex dem. Murray v. Hoboken Land & Imp. Co.*, 59 U.S. 272, 278 (1855). (Justice Curtis, for the Court, cites the Declaration to mark independence).

*Smith v. Maryland*, 59 U.S. 71, 74 (1855). (Justice Curtis, for the Court, uses the Declaration to mark independence.)

*United States v. Ritchie*, 58 U.S. 525, 539–540 (1854). (Justice Samuel Nelson, for the Court, argues that the 1821 Mexican declaration of independence had the same effect with respect to Mexico that the U.S. Declaration had with respect to the colonies.)

*Howard v. Ingersoll*, 54 U.S. 381, 398 (1851). (Justice James M. Wayne, for the Court, argues that it is well known that the Declaration dissolved ties with Great Britain, fixed the boundaries of the colonies, and committed unsettled land to the union of the colonies.)

*United States v. Reid*, 53 U.S. 361, 364 (1851). (Chief Justice Taney, for the Court, uses the Declaration to mark independence.)

*Luther v. Borden*, 48 U.S. 1, 35, 39, 58 (1849). (Chief Justice Taney, for the Court, argues that state governments in existence when the Declaration was issued are legitimate and that Congress and the president get to decide the legitimacy of changes to state constitutions made after this time. Justice Levi Woodbury, dissenting, cites the Declaration to support his argument that de facto government should be considered to be the legitimate government in the eyes of the law.)

*Smith v. Turner*, 48 U.S. 283, 440, 521 (1849). (Justice John Catron, for the Court, supporting

his opinion striking down state taxes on immigrants, notes that the colonists complained in the Declaration that the king interfered with immigration. He also suggests that it was in the "spirit of the Declaration of Independence" that Congress passed liberal immigration laws. Justice Woodbury, dissenting, cites the Declaration in the course of praising immigration but would uphold the state law on technical grounds.)

*Waring v. Clarke*, 46 U.S. 441, 484 (1847). (Justice Woodbury, dissenting, cites the Declaration to support his argument that the founders valued trial by jury.)

*Groves v. Slaughter*, 40 U.S. 449, 513 (1841). (Justice Henry Baldwin, concurring, cites the Declaration in the course of arguing that slaves were considered property subject to the laws of the states before the adoption of the Constitution.)

*Rhode Island v. Massachusetts*, 37 U.S. 657, 737, 743, 745, 748 (1838). (Justice Baldwin, for the Court, cites the Declaration several times to mark independence. He contends that the states became independent with the Declaration, but that they "surrendered to Congress, and its appointed Court, the right and power of settling their mutual controversies" when they agreed to the Articles of Confederation in 1781.)

*Mayor, Aldermen and Commonalty of City of New York v. Miln*, 36 U.S. 102, 153 (1837). (Justice Baldwin, concurring, cites the Declaration to support his argument that the states were completely sovereign from independence until they gave up part of their sovereignty when they agreed to Articles of Confederation.)

*Charles River Bridge v. Warren Bridge*, 36 U.S. 420, 582 (1837). (Justice Baldwin, concurring, to support his argument regarding the importance of charters notes that "one of the grievances set forth in the declaration of independence is, 'for taking away our charters' &c.")

*Shanks v. Dupont*, 28 U.S. 242, 244, 251, 255 (1830). (Justice Story, for the Court, uses the

Declaration to mark independence in this citizenship case. Justice William Johnson, dissenting, points out the anomaly that "the courts of this country all consider th[e] transfer of allegiance as resulting from the Declaration of Independence; the British from its recognition by the treaty of peace.")

*Inglis v. Trustees of Sailor's Snug Harbor,* 28 U.S. 99, 121, 123, 158, 161–162, 164, 166 (1830). (Justice Smith Thompson, for the Court, and Justice Story, dissenting, use the Declaration to mark independence in this citizenship case.)

*Harcourt v. Gaillard,* 25 U.S. 523, 525–527 (1827). (Justice Johnson, for the Court, uses the Declaration to mark independence in this state boundary case.)

*Kirk v. Smith ex dem Penn,* 22 U.S. 241, 276, 289 (1824). (Chief Justice John Marshall, for the Court, uses the Declaration and, in a separate passage, the date "4th of July, 1776," to mark independence in this boundary case.)

*Johnson v. McIntosh,* 21 U.S. 543, 584 (1823). (Chief Justice Marshall, for the Court, uses the Declaration to mark independence in this case involving the regulation of lands occupied by Native Americans.)

*Dawson's Lessee v. Godfrey,* 8 U.S. 321, 322 (1808). (Justice Johnson, for the Court, uses the Declaration to mark independence.)

*M'Ilvaine v. Coxe's Lessee,* 8 U.S. 209, 211 (1808). (Justice William Cushing, for the Court, uses the Declaration to mark independence.)

*M'Ilvaine v. Coxe's Lessee,* 6 U.S. 280, 332 (1804). (The Court's opinion uses the Declaration to mark independence in this citizenship case.)

*Ware v. Hylton,* 3 U.S. 199, 224–225, 281 (1796). (Justice Chase, in his seriatim opinion, uses the Declaration to mark the independence of thirteen "sovereign and independent state[s]." Justice James Wilson, in his seriatim opinion, argues that when the United States declared independence, they were bound to receive the law of nations.")

*Penhallow v. Doane's Adm'rs,* 3 U.S. 54, 91, 110–111 (1795). (Justices James Iredell and John Blair Jr., in their seriatim opinions, use the Declaration to mark independence.)

*Chisholm v. Georgia,* 2 U.S. 419, 471 (1793). (Chief Justice John Jay, in his seriatim opinion, uses the Declaration to mark independence and notes that unappropriated lands at the time passed to the American people as a whole.)

---

## 10.1  Frederick Douglass, 'What to the Slave Is the Fourth of July?,' July 5, 1852

*Frederick Douglass (1817–1895) was born a slave. He escaped from slavery in 1838 and became active in antislavery circles. The following speech, his most famous oration, was delivered in Rochester, New York.*

Pardon me, and allow me to ask, why am I called upon to speak here to-day? What have I, or those I represent, to do with your national independence? Are the great principles of political freedom and of natural justice, embodied in that Declaration of Independence, extended to us? and am I, therefore, called upon to bring our humble offering to the national altar, and to confess the bene-

fits, and express devout gratitude for the blessings, resulting from your independence to us?

Would to God, both for your sakes and ours, that an affirmative answer could be truthfully returned to these questions! Then would my task be light, and my burden easy and delightful. For who is there so cold that a nation's sympathy could not warm him? Who so obdurate and dead to the claims of gratitude, that would not thankfully acknowledge such priceless benefits? Who so stolid and selfish, that would not give his voice to swell the hallelujahs of a nation's jubilee, when the chains of servitude had been torn from his limbs? I am not that man. In a case like that, the dumb might eloquently speak, and the "lame man leap as an hart."

But, such is not the state of the case. I say it with a sad sense of the disparity between us. I am not included within the pale of this glorious anniversary! Your high independence only reveals the immeasurable distance between us. The blessings in which you this day rejoice, are not enjoyed in common. The rich inheritance of justice, liberty, prosperity, and independence, bequeathed by your fathers, is shared by you, not by me. The sunlight that brought life and healing to you, has brought stripes and death to me. This Fourth of July is *yours,* not *mine. You* may rejoice, *I* must mourn. To drag a man in fetters into the grand illuminated temple of liberty, and call upon him to join you in joyous anthems, were inhuman mockery and sacrilegious irony. Do you mean, citizens, to mock me, by asking me to speak to-day? If so, there is a parallel to your conduct. And let me warn you that it is dangerous to copy the example of a nation whose crimes, towering up to heaven, were thrown down by the breath of the Almighty, burying that nation in irrecoverable ruin! I can to-day take up the plaintive lament of a peeled and woe-smitten people.

"By the rivers of Babylon, there we sat down. Yea! we wept when we remembered Zion. We hanged our harps upon the willows in the midst thereof. For there, they that carried us away captive, required of us a song; and they who wasted us required of us mirth, saying, Sing us one of the songs of Zion. How can we sing the Lord's song in a strange land? If I forget thee, O Jerusalem, let my right hand forget her cunning. If I do not remember thee, let my tongue cleave to the roof of my mouth."

Fellow-citizens, above your national, tumultuous joy, I hear the mournful wail of millions, whose chains, heavy and grievous yesterday, are to-day rendered more intolerable by the jubilant shouts that reach them. If I do forget, if I do not faithfully remember those bleeding children of sorrow this day, "may my right hand forget her cunning, and may my tongue cleave to the roof of my mouth!" To forget them, to pass lightly over their wrongs, and to chime in with the popular theme, would be treason most scandalous and shocking, and would make me a reproach before God and the world. My subject, then, fellow-citizens, is AMERICAN SLAVERY. I shall see this day and its popular characteristics from the slave's point of view. Standing there, identified with the American bondman, making his wrongs mine, I do not hesitate to declare, with all my soul, that the character and conduct of this nation never looked blacker to me than on this Fourth of July. Whether we turn to the declarations of the past, or to the professions of the present, the conduct of the nation seems equally hideous and revolting. America is false to the past, false to the present, and solemnly binds herself to be false to the future. Standing with God and the crushed and bleeding slave on this occasion, I will, in the name of humanity which is outraged, in the name of liberty which is fettered, in the name of the constitution and the bible, which are disregarded and trampled upon, dare to call in question and to denounce, with all the emphasis I can command, everything that serves to perpetuate slavery—the great sin and shame of America! "I will not equivocate; I will not excuse;" I will use the severest language I can command; and yet not one word shall escape me that any man, whose judgment is not blinded by prejudice, or who is not at heart a slaveholder, shall not confess to be right and just.

But I fancy I hear some one of my audience say, it is just in this circumstance that you and your brother abolitionists fail to make a favorable impression on the public mind. Would you argue more, and denounce less, would you persuade more and rebuke less, your cause would be much more likely to succeed. But, I submit, where all is plain there is nothing to be argued. What point in the antislavery creed would you have me argue? On what branch of the subject do the people of this country need light? Must I undertake to prove that the slave is a man? That point is conceded already. Nobody doubts it. The slaveholders themselves acknowledge it in the enactment of laws for their government. They acknowledge it when they punish disobedience on the part of the slave. There are seventy-two crimes in the state of Virginia, which, if committed by a black man, (no matter how ignorant he be,) subject him to the punishment of death; while only two of these same crimes will subject a white man to the like punishment. What is this but the acknowledgment that the slave is a moral, intellectual, and responsible being. The manhood of the slave is conceded. It is admitted in the fact that southern statute books are covered with enactments forbidding, under severe fines and penalties, the teaching of the slave to read or write. When you can point to any such laws, in reference to the beasts of the field, then I may consent to argue the manhood of the slave. When the dogs in your streets, when the fowls of the air, when the cattle on your hills, when the fish of the sea, and the reptiles that crawl, shall be unable to distinguish the slave from a brute, then will I argue with you that the slave is a man!

For the present, it is enough to affirm the equal manhood of the negro race. Is it not astonishing that, while we are plowing, planting, and reaping, using all kinds of mechanical tools, erecting houses, constructing bridges, building ships, working in metals of brass, iron, copper, silver, and gold; that, while we are reading, writing and cyphering, acting as clerks, merchants, and secretaries, having among us lawyers, doctors, ministers, poets, authors, editors, orators, and teachers; that, while we are engaged in all manner of enterprises common to other men—digging gold in California, capturing the whale in the Pacific, feeding sheep and cattle on the hillside, living, moving, acting, thinking, planning, living in families, as husbands, wives, and children, and above all confessing and worshiping the christian's God, and looking hopefully for life and immortality beyond the grave,—we are called upon to prove that we are men!

Would you have me argue that man is entitled to liberty? that he is the rightful owner of his own body? You have already declared it. Must I argue the wrongfulness of slavery? Is that a question for republicans? Is it to be settled by the rules of logic and argumentation, as a matter beset with great difficulty, involving a doubtful application of the principle of justice, hard to be understood? How should I look to-day in the presence of Americans, dividing and subdividing a discourse, to show that men have a natural right to freedom, speaking of it relatively and positively, negatively and affirmatively? To do so, would be to make myself ridiculous, and to offer an insult to your understanding. There is not a man beneath the canopy of heaven that does not know that slavery is wrong *for him*.

What! am I to argue that it is wrong to make men brutes, to rob them of their liberty, to work them without wages, to keep them ignorant of their relations to their fellow-men, to beat them with sticks, to flay their flesh with the lash, to load their limbs with irons, to hunt them with dogs, to sell them at auction, to sunder their families, to knock out their teeth, to burn their flesh, to starve them into obedience and submission to their masters? Must I argue that a system, thus marked with blood and stained with pollution, is wrong? No; I will not. I have better employment for my time and strength than such arguments would imply.

What, then, remains to be argued? Is it that slavery is not divine; that God did not establish it; that our doctors of divinity are mistaken? There is blasphemy in the thought. That which is inhuman cannot be divine. Who can reason on such a proposition! They that can, may; I cannot. The time for such argument is past.

At a time like this, scorching irony, not convincing argument, is needed. Oh! had I the ability, and could I reach the nation's ear, I would to-day pour out a fiery stream of biting ridicule, blasting reproach, withering sarcasm, and stern rebuke. For it is not light that is needed, but fire; it is not the gentle shower, but thunder. We need the storm, the whirlwind, and the earthquake. The feeling of the nation must be quickened; the conscience of the nation must be roused; the propriety of the nation must be startled; the hypocrisy of the nation must be exposed; and its crimes against God and man must be proclaimed and denounced.

What to the American slave is your Fourth of July? I answer, a day that reveals to him, more than all other days in the year, the gross injustice and cruelty to which he is the constant victim. To him, your celebration is a sham; your boasted liberty, an unholy license; your national greatness, swelling vanity; your sounds of rejoicing are empty and heartless; your denunciations of tyrants, brass-fronted impudence; your shouts of liberty and equality, hollow mockery; your prayers and hymns, your sermons and thanksgivings, with all your religious parade and solemnity, are to him mere bombast, fraud, deception, impiety, and hypocrisy—a thin veil to cover up crimes which would disgrace a nation of savages. There is not a nation on the earth guilty of practices more shocking and bloody, than are the people of these United States, at this very hour.

Go where you may, search where you will, roam through all the monarchies and despotisms of the old world, travel through South America, search out every abuse, and when you have found the last, lay your facts by the side of the every-day practices of this nation, and you will say with me, that, for revolting barbarity and shameless hypocrisy, America reigns without a rival.

---

# 10.2   Martin Luther King Jr., 'I Have a Dream,' August 28, 1963

*The Rev. Dr. Martin Luther King Jr. (1929–1968) is widely regarded as the most influential figure of the modern civil rights movement. He delivered the following speech on the steps of the Lincoln Memorial in Washington, D.C. The speech is almost certainly the most important speech about the Declaration of Independence delivered during the twentieth century.*

I am happy to join with you today in what will go down in history as the greatest demonstration for freedom in the history of our nation.

Five score years ago a great American in whose symbolic shadow we stand today signed the Emancipation Proclamation. This momentous decree came as a great beacon light of hope to millions of Negro slaves who had been seared in the flames of withering injustice. It came as a joyous daybreak to end the long night of their captivity.

But one hundred years later the Negro is not free.

One hundred years later the life of the Negro is still sadly crippled by the manacles of segregation and the chains of discrimination.

One hundred years later the Negro lives on a lonely island of poverty in the midst of a vast ocean of material prosperity.

One hundred years later the Negro is still languished in the corners of American society and finds himself in exile in his own land.

So we've come here today to dramatize a shameful condition.

In a sense we've come to our nation's capital to cash a check. When the architects of our Republic wrote the magnificent words of the Constitution and the Declaration of Independence, they were signing a promissory note to which every American was to fall heir. This note was a promise that all men—yes, black men as well as white men—would be guaranteed the unalienable rights of life, liberty and the pursuit of happiness. It is obvious today that America has defaulted on this promissory note insofar as her citizens of color are concerned. Instead of honoring this sacred obligation, America has given the Negro people a bad check, a check which has come back marked "insufficient funds."

But we refuse to believe that the bank of justice is bankrupt. We refuse to believe that there are insufficient funds in the great vaults of opportunity of this nation. So we've come to cash this check, a check that will give us upon demand the riches of freedom and the security of justice.

We have also come to this hallowed spot to remind America of the fierce urgency of now. This is no time to engage in the luxury of cooling off or to take the tranquilizing drug of gradualism.

Now is the time to make real the promises of democracy.

Now is the time to rise from the dark and desolate valley of segregation to the sunlit path of racial justice.

Now is the time to lift our nation from the quicksands of racial injustice to the solid rock of brotherhood.

Now is the time to make justice a reality for all of God's children.

It would be fatal for the nation to overlook the urgency of the moment. This sweltering summer of the Negro's legitimate discontent will not pass until there is an invigorating autumn of freedom and equality—nineteen sixty-three is not an end but a beginning. Those who hope that the Negro needed to blow off steam and will now be content will have a rude awakening if the nation returns to business as usual.

There will be neither rest nor tranquility in America until the Negro is granted his citizenship rights. The whirlwinds of revolt will continue to shape the foundations of our nation until the bright day of justice emerges.

But there is something that I must say to my people who stand on the worn threshold which leads into the palace of justice. In the process of gaining our rightful place we must not be guilty of wrongful deeds. Let us not seek to satisfy our thirst for freedom by drinking from the cup of bitterness and hatred.

We must forever conduct our struggle on the high plane of dignity and discipline. We must not allow our creative protests to degenerate into physical violence. Again and again we must rise to the majestic heights of meeting physical force with soul force. The marvelous new militancy which has engulfed the Negro community must not lead us to a distrust of all white people, for many of our white brothers, as evidenced by their presence here today, have come to realize that their destiny is tied up with our destiny. They have come to realize that their freedom is inextricably bound to our freedom. We cannot walk alone. And as we walk we must make the pledge that we shall always march ahead. We cannot turn back.

There are those who are asking the devotees of civil rights, "When will you be satisfied?"

We can never be satisfied as long as the Negro is the victim of the unspeakable horrors of police brutality.

We can never be satisfied as long as our bodies, heavy with the fatigue of travel, cannot gain lodging in the motels of the highways and the hotels of the cities.

We cannot be satisfied as long as the Negro's basic mobility is from a smaller ghetto to a larger one.

We can never be satisfied as long as our children are stripped of their selfhood and robbed of their dignity by signs stating "For Whites Only."

We cannot be satisfied as long as the Negro in Mississippi cannot vote and the Negro in New York believes he has nothing for which to vote.

No, no, we are not satisfied, and we will not be satisfied until justice rolls down like waters and righteousness like a mighty stream.

I am not unmindful that some of you have come here out of great trials and tribulations. Some of you have come fresh from narrow jail cells. Some of you have come from areas where your quest for freedom left you battered by the storms of persecution and staggered by the winds of police brutality. You have been the veterans of creative suffering.

Continue to work with the faith that unearned suffering is redemptive.

Go back to Mississippi.

Go back to Alabama.

Go back to South Carolina.

Go back to Georgia.

Go back to Louisiana.

Go back to the slums and ghettos of our Northern cities, knowing that somehow this situation can and will be changed. Let us not wallow in the valley of despair.

I say to you today, my friends, so even though we face the difficulties of today and tomorrow, I still have a dream. It is a dream deeply rooted in the American dream.

I have a dream that one day this nation will rise up, live out the true meaning of its creed: "We hold these truths to be self-evident, that all men are created equal."

I have a dream that one day on the red hills of Georgia sons of former slaves and the sons of former slave-owners will be able to sit down together at the table of brotherhood.

I have a dream that one day even the state of Mississippi, a state sweltering with the heat of injustice, sweltering with the heat of oppression, will be transformed into an oasis of freedom and justice.

I have a dream that my four little children will one day live in a nation where they will not be judged by the color of their skin but by the content of their character.

I have a dream today!

I have a dream that one day down in Alabama, with its vicious racists, with its governor having his lips dripping with the words of interposition and nullification, one day right there in Alabama little black boys and black girls will be able to join hands with little white boys and white girls as sisters and brothers.

I have a dream today.

I have a dream that one day every valley shall be exalted, every hill and mountain shall be made low. The rough places will be made plain, and the crooked places will be made straight. And the glory of the Lord shall be revealed, and all flesh shall see it together. This is our hope. This is the faith that I go back to the South with.

With this faith we will be able to hew out of the mountain of despair a stone of hope. With this faith we will be able to transform the jangling discords of our nation into a beautiful symphony of brotherhood.

With this faith we will be able to work together, to pray together, to struggle together, to go to jail together, to stand up for freedom together, knowing that we will be free one day.

This will be the day, this will be the day when all of God's children will be able to sing with new meaning,

My country, 'tis of thee, sweet land of liberty, of thee I sing.

Land where my fathers died, land of the pilgrim's pride,

From every mountainside, let freedom ring.

And if America is to be a great nation, this must become true.

So let freedom ring from the prodigious hilltops of New Hampshire.

Let freedom ring from the mighty mountains of New York.

Let freedom ring from the heightening Alleghenies of Pennsylvania.

Let freedom ring from the snowcapped Rockies of Colorado.

Let freedom ring from the curvaceous slopes of California.

But not only that.

Let freedom ring from Stone Mountain of Georgia.

Let freedom ring from Lookout Mountain of Tennessee.

Let freedom ring from every hill and molehill of Mississippi.

From every mountainside, let freedom ring.

And when this happens, when we allow freedom [to] ring—when we let it ring from every village and every hamlet, from every state and every city, we will be able to speed up that day when all of God's children, black men and white men, Jews and Gentiles, Protestants and Catholics, will be able to join hands and sing in the words of the old Negro spiritual, "Free at last, Free at last, Thank God a-mighty, We are free at last."

## *10.3*    Malcolm X, 'Black Revolution,' April 8, 1964

*Malcolm X (1925–1965), born Malcolm Little, was a black militant leader of the Nation of Islam who articulated concepts of race pride and black nationalism in the early 1960s. After his assassination, the widespread distribution of his life story—The Autobiography of Malcolm X (1965)—made him an ideological hero, especially among black youth. The following excerpts are from a speech he delivered at a meeting sponsored by the Militant Labor Forum at Palm Gardens in New York.*

Friends and enemies, tonight I hope that we can have a little fireside chat with as few sparks as possible being tossed round, especially because of the very explosive condition that the world is in today. Sometimes, when a person's house is on fire and someone comes in yelling fire, instead of the person who is awakened by the yell being thankful, he makes the mistake of charging the one who awakened him with having set the fire. I hope that this little conversation tonight about the Black revolution won't cause any of you to accuse us of igniting it when you find it at your doorstep. . . .

The seriousness of this situation must be faced up to. You should not feel that I am inciting someone to violence. I'm only warning of a powder-keg situation. You can take it or leave it. If you take the warning perhaps you can still save yourself. But if you ignore it or ridicule it, well death is already at your doorstep. There are 22 million African-Americans who are ready to fight for independence right here, and I don't mean any nonviolent fight, or turn-the-other-cheek fight. Those days are gone. Those days are over.

If George Washington didn't get independence for this country nonviolently, and if Patrick Henry didn't come up with a nonviolent statement, and you taught me to look upon them as patriots and heroes, then it's time for you to realize that I have studied your books as well.

Our people, 22 million African-Americans, are fed up with America's hypocritical democracy, and today we care nothing about the odds that are against us. Every time a Black man gets ready to defend himself, some Uncle Tom tries to tell us, how can you win? That's Tom talking. Don't listen to him. This is the first thing we hear: the odds are against you. You're dealing with Black people who don't care anything about odds. We care nothing about odds.

Again I go right back to the people who founded and secured the independence of this country from the colonial power of England. When George Washington and the others got ready to declare or come up with the Declaration of Independence, they didn't care anything about the odds of the British Empire. They were fed up with taxation without representation. And you've got 22 million Black people in this country today, 1964, who are fed up with taxation without representation and will do the same thing, who are ready, willing, and justified to do the same thing today to bring about independence for our people that your forefathers did to bring about independence for your people.

And I say your people because I certainly couldn't include myself among those for whom independence was fought in 1776. How in the world can a Negro talk about the Declaration of Independence when he is still singing "We Shall Overcome"? Our people are increasingly developing the opinion that we just have nothing to lose but the chains of segregation and the chains of second-class citizenship. . . .

All of our people have the same goals. The same objective. That objective is freedom, justice, equality. All of us want recognition and respect as human beings. We don't want to be integrationists. Nor do we want to be separationists. We want to be human beings. Integration is only a method that is used by some groups to obtain freedom, justice, equality, and respect as human beings. Separation is only a method that is used by other groups to obtain freedom, justice, equality, or human dignity. . . .

Revolutions are fought to get control of land, to remove the absentee landlord and gain control of the land and the institutions that flow from that land. The Black man had been in a very low condition because he has had no control whatsoever over any land. He has been a beggar economically, a beggar politically, a beggar socially, a beggar even when it comes to trying to get some education. So that in the past, the type of mentality that was developed in this colonial system among our people, today is being overcome.

And as the young ones come up they know what they want. And as they listen to your beautiful preaching about democracy and all those other flowery words, they know what they're supposed to have.

So you have a people today who not only know what they want, but also know what they are supposed to have. And they themselves are creating another generation that is coming up that not only will know what it wants and know what it should have, but also will be ready and willing to do whatever is necessary to see that what they should have materializes immediately.

Thank you.

---

# 11.1   Letters of Abigail Adams to John Adams, 1776

*Abigail Adams (1744–1818) was married to John Adams (1735–1826), one of the leading figures of America's founding period as well as the second president of the United States. She was a gifted letter writer, confidante of her husband in his long public career, and mother of the most important family dynasty in American public life. The following excerpts reveal her concern with women's unequal status in American society.*

### MARCH 31

That your Sex are Naturally Tyrannical is a Truth so thoroughly established as to admit of no dispute, but such of you as wish to be happy willingly give up the harsh title of Master for the more tender and endearing one of Friend. Why then, not put it out of the power of the vicious and the Lawless to use us with cruelty and indignity with impunity. Men of Sense in all Ages abhor these customs which treat us only as the vassals of your Sex. Regard us then as Beings placed by providence under your protection and in imitation of the Supreme Being make use of that power only for our happiness.

### APRIL 14

I cannot say that I think you are very generous to the ladies; for whilst you are proclaiming peace and good-will to men, emancipating all nations, you insist upon retaining an absolute power over wives. But you must remember that arbitrary power is like most other things which are very hard, very liable to be broken; and, notwithstanding all your wise laws and maxims, we have it in our power not only to free ourselves, but to subdue our masters, and without violence, throw both your natural and legal authority at our feet.

# 11.2 Declaration of Sentiments, Seneca Falls, New York, 1848

*The following excerpts are from what is perhaps the most famous document in the history of the women's rights movement. It was adopted at the first conference to address women's rights and is modeled directly on the Declaration of Independence.*

When, in the course of human events, it becomes necessary for one portion of the family of man to assume among the people of the earth a position different from that which they have hitherto occupied, but one to which the laws of nature and of nature's God entitle them, a decent respect to the opinions of mankind requires that they should declare the causes that impel them to such a course.

We hold these truths to be self-evident: that all men and women are created equal; that they are endowed by their Creator with certain inalienable rights; that among these are life, liberty, and the pursuit of happiness; that to secure these rights governments are instituted, deriving their just powers from the consent of the governed. Whenever any form of Government becomes destructive of these ends, it is the right of those who suffer from it to refuse allegiance to it, and to insist upon the institution of a new government, laying its foundation on such principles, and organizing its powers in such form as to them shall seem most likely to effect their safety and happiness. Prudence, indeed, will dictate that governments long established should not be changed for light and transient causes; and accordingly, all experience hath shown that mankind are more disposed to suffer, while evils are sufferable, than to right themselves by abolishing the forms to which they are accustomed. But when a long train of abuses and usurpations, pursuing invariably the same object, evinces a design to reduce them under absolute despotism, it is their duty to throw off such government, and to provide new guards for their future security. Such has been the patient sufferance of the women under this government, and such is now the necessity which constrains them to demand the equal station to which they are entitled.

The history of mankind is a history of repeated injuries and usurpations on the part of man toward woman, having in direct object the establishment of an absolute tyranny over her. To prove this, let facts be submitted to a candid world.

He has never permitted her to exercise her inalienable right to the elective franchise.

He has compelled her to submit to laws, in the formation of which she had no voice.

He has withheld from her rights which are given to the most ignorant and degraded men—both natives and foreigners.

Having deprived her of this first right of a citizen, the elective franchise, thereby leaving her without representation in the halls of legislation, he has oppressed her on all sides.

He has made her, if married, in the eye of the law, civilly dead.

He has taken from her all right in property, even to the wages she earns.

He has made her, morally, an irresponsible being, as she can commit many crimes with impunity, provided they be done in the presence of her husband. In the covenant of marriage, she is compelled to promise obedience to her husband, he becoming, to all intents and purposes, her master—the law giving him power to deprive her of her liberty, and to administer chastisement.

He has so framed the laws of divorce, as to what shall be the proper causes of divorce; in case of separation, to whom the guardianship of the children shall be given; as to be wholly regardless of the happiness of women—the law, in all cases, going upon the false supposition of the supremacy of man, and giving all power into his hands.

After depriving her of all rights as a married woman, if single and the owner of property, he has taxed her to support a government which recognizes her only when her property can be made profitable to it.

He has monopolized nearly all the profitable employments, and from those she is permitted to follow, she receives but a scanty remuneration.

He closes against her all the avenues to wealth and distinction, which he considers most honorable to himself. As a teacher of theology, medicine, or law, she is not known.

He has denied her the facilities for obtaining a thorough education—all colleges being closed against her.

He allows her in Church as well as State, but a subordinate position, claiming Apostolic authority for her exclusion from the ministry, and, with some exceptions, from any public participation in the affairs of the Church.

He has created a false public sentiment, by giving to the world a different code of morals for men and women, by which moral delinquencies which exclude women from society, are not only tolerated but deemed of little account in man.

He has usurped the prerogative of Jehovah himself, claiming it as his right to assign for her a sphere of action, when that belongs to her conscience and her God.

He has endeavored, in every way that he could, to destroy her confidence in her own powers, to lessen her self-respect, and to make her willing to lead a dependent and abject life.

Now, in view of this entire disfranchisement of one-half the people in this country, their social and religious degradation—in view of the unjust laws above mentioned, and because women do feel themselves aggrieved, oppressed, and fraudulently deprived of their most sacred rights, we insist that they have immediate admission to all the rights and privileges which belong to them as citizens of these United States.

In entering upon the great work before us, we anticipate no small amount of misconception, misrepresentation, and ridicule; but we shall use every instrumentality within our power to effect our object. We shall employ agents, circulate tracts, petition the State and national Legislatures, and endeavor to enlist the pulpit and the press in our behalf. We hope this Convention will be followed by a series of Conventions, embracing every part of the country. Firmly relying upon the final triumph of the Right and the True, we do this day affix our signatures to this declaration.

## 11.3   Carrie Chapman Catt, 'Address to the United States Congress,' 1917

*Carrie Chapman Catt (1859–1947) was one of the best known leaders of the women's suffrage movement. The following excerpts are from a speech to the National American Woman Suffrage Association. The speech influenced the U.S. Congress to enact the Nineteenth Amendment (women's suffrage), and it is replete with references to the Declaration of Independence.*

Ours is a nation born of revolution; of rebellion against a system of government so securely entrenched in the customs and traditions of human society that in 1776 it seemed impregnable. From the beginning of things nations had been ruled by kings and for kings, while the people served and paid the cost. The American Revolutionists boldly proclaimed the heresies:

'Taxation without representation is tyranny.'

'Governments derive their just powers from the consent of the governed.'

The colonists won and the nation which was established as a result of their victory has held unfailingly that these two fundamental principles of democratic government are not only the spiritual source of our national existence but have been our chief historic pride and at all times the sheet anchor of our liberties. . . .

Not one American has arisen to question their logic in the one hundred and forty-one years of our national existence. . . . Not only has it unceasingly upheld the THEORY but it has carried these theories into PRACTICE whenever men made application. . . . The United States opened wide its gates to men of all the nations of earth. . . . [While] it has been the custom in our country for three generations that any male immigrant accepted by the national government as a citizen, automatically becomes a voter in any State in which he chooses to reside, [Uncle Sam] . . . denies that fundamental right of democracy to thousands of women public school teachers from whom many of these men learn all they know of citizenship and patriotism, to women college presidents, to women who preach in our pulpits, interpret law in our courts, preside over our hospitals, write books and magazines and serve in every uplifting moral and social enterprise.

Is there a single man who can justify such inequality of treatment, such outrageous discriminations? Not one.

Woman suffrage became an assured fact when the Declaration of Independence was written. It matters not at all whether Thomas Jefferson and his compatriots thought of women when they wrote that immortal document. They conceived and voiced a principle greater than any man. 'A power not of themselves which makes for righteousness' gave them the vision and they proclaimed truisms as immutable as the multiplication table, as changeless as time. The Hon. Champ Clark announced that he had been a woman suffragist ever since he 'got the hang of the Declaration of Independence.' So it must be with every other American. The amazing thing is that it has required so long a time for a people, most of whom know how to read, 'to get the hang of it.'

---

## 11.4   Equal Rights Amendment, 1972

*The Equal Rights Amendment (ERA) was written in 1923 by Alice Paul (1885–1985), a suffragist leader and founder of the National Woman's Party (NWP). She and the NWP considered the ERA to be the next necessary step after the Nineteenth Amendment, which gave women the vote, in guaranteeing "equal justice under law" to all citizens. The ERA was introduced into every session of Congress between 1923 and 1972, when it was passed and sent to the states for ratification. The seven-year time limit in the ERA's proposing clause was extended by Congress to June 30, 1982, but at the deadline, the ERA had been ratified by thirty-five states, three states short of the thirty-eight required for ratification. It has been reintroduced into every Congress since that time.*

Section 1. Equality of Rights under the law shall not be denied or abridged by the United States or any state on account of sex.

Section 2. The Congress shall have the power to enforce, by appropriate legislation, the provisions of this article.

Section 3. This amendment shall take effect two years after the date of ratification.

# 12.1 Interpreting the Declaration of Independence by Translation

*The following six excerpts resulted from a March 1999 roundtable assembled by the Journal of American History on translations of the Declaration of Independence. Professor David Thelen, the editor of the Journal of American History from 1985 to 1999, and Professor Willi Paul Adams of the Kennedy Institute of the Free University of Berlin, coordinated the roundtable. The translations were retranslated back to English. The excerpts (which in each case are the first two paragraphs of the Declaration of Independence) illustrate how both the cultural possibilities offered by different languages and the choices made by individual translators shape the reception of the Declaration in foreign languages. The retranslations were made or supervised by Joaquim Oltra (Spanish), Willi Paul Adams (German), and Tadashi Aruga (Japanese).*

## Declaration of Independence in Spanish: Retranslation Back to English (1821)

When in the course of human events it becomes necessary for one people to dissolve the political ties which have connected them with another and assume among the powers of the earth the separate and equal station for which the laws of nature and its Author entitle them, a decent respect to the opinions of mankind requires that they declare the causes which impel them to the separation.

We hold these truths to be self-evident, that all men are born equal and are endowed by their Creator with certain inalienable rights: that among these the principal ones are the security of liberty and life, which constitute human happiness; that to secure these rights governments were instituted among men, deriving their just powers from the consent of the governed; that whenever any form of government becomes destructive to these ends, it is the right of the society to alter it, or to abolish it and institute a new one, laying its foundations on such principles, and organizing its powers in a manner it judges most conducive to effect its security and happiness. Prudence, indeed, dictates that established governments should not change for light and transient causes; and experience has shown that mankind is more disposed to suffer, while the evils are sufferable, than to right itself by abolishing the forms of government to which it has been accustomed. But when a train of abuses and usurpations, contin-

uing invariably towards the same end, makes it clear that it is the will of the rulers to oppress the people with absolute despotism, it is their right and their duty to throw away such a government and provide new guards for their future security.

## Declaration of Independence in German: Retranslation Back to English (1776)

When in the course of human conditions it becomes necessary for a people to sever the Political Bonds with which it has been linked to another, and to assume under the powers of the earth a separate and equal position, to which the laws of Nature and of the God of Nature entitle it, propriety and respect for the opinions of the human race require that it give notice of the grounds upon which it was driven to the separation.

We hold these truths to be universally accepted, that all people have been created equal, that they have been endowed by their Creator with certain inalienable rights, among which are life, liberty and the pursuit of happiness. That to guarantee these rights governments have been instituted among men which derive their lawful power from the assent of the governed; that when some form of government becomes injurious to these purposes, it is the right of the people to alter or abolish it, and to install a new government which is established on such principles, and whose authority and power is constructed in such a way as appears to them to be most appropriate for guaranteeing their security and happiness. To be sure, prudence requires that governments which have been long established should not be changed for trivial or transitory reasons; and accordingly, experience has at all times shown that men prefer to suffer and be patient, as long as the grievance is bearable, than to procure justice and relief by overthrowing such forms of government to which they are accustomed. But when a long series of abuses and violent encroachments directed unremittingly toward one and the same object makes evident a plot to subject them to absolute rule, then it is their right, indeed their duty, to cast off such a government and to obtain new guarantees for their future security.

## Declaration of Independence in German: Retranslation Back to English (1950)

When in the course of the development of mankind it becomes necessary for a people to sever the political bonds that have tied it to another people and to assume among the powers of the earth the independent and equal status to which natural law and the law of God entitle it, a due respect for the opinion of mankind requires that it set forth the reasons which induce it to effect the separation.

We consider the following truths to be self-evident: that all people are created equal, that they are endowed by their Creator with certain inalienable rights to which belong life, liberty and the pursuit of happiness; that for insuring these rights governments are installed among people which derive their lawful authority from the consent of the governed; that, whenever any form of government proves to be harmful to these objectives, it is the right of the people to change it or to abolish it and install a new government, and to erect the latter according to such principles and to organize its powers in such a way as seems necessary for the preservation of the people's security and good fortune. Wisdom no doubt requires that long-existing governments should not be altered on insignificant and transitory grounds;

and correspondingly all experience has shown that people are more inclined to be patient as long as the grievances are bearable than to take the law into their hands by removing long-familiar forms. But when a long series of abuses and infringements which always pursue the same aim reveals the intention of subjecting them to absolute despotism, then it is their right and their duty to abolish such a government and to appoint new guardians for their future security.

## Declaration of Independence in Japanese: Retranslation Back to English (partial retranslation of Fukuzawa Yukichi's translation) (1866)

When it becomes inevitable for one kin group of people, compelled by the course of events in human life, to leave the government of another nation, to join the rank of the nations of the world and establish a separate nation in accordance with the nature of the reason of the physical world and that of the way of heaven, they must explain the reasons for establishing a new nation and let them be known widely by a declaration out of consideration for [other] peoples' sentiments.

Heaven created all persons in the same rut and endowed them with unremovable rights. These rights are, for instance, rights to preserve one's own life, to seek liberty and to wish to enjoy happiness, and they cannot be taken away from one by others. The reason to institute governments among persons was to make these rights secure, and a government can truly claim its legitimacy only when it satisfies its subjects. If the measures of a government betray the purpose of instituting governments, the people can alter or abolish it and institute a new government on the basis of this great principle to secure their safety and happiness. This, too, is a right of the people. All of this should be quite evident without our argument. To a timid conservative mind, it may seem that a government established long ago cannot be changed easily and lightly. But when a government repeatedly practices willful usurpations, always making the same people their target, however, such evil practice ought to be stopped. Otherwise, the government will eventually exercise absolutely arbitrary power over the whole country. To abolish such a government and secure the future safety of the people is also their right and duty.

## Declaration of Independence in Japanese: Retranslation Back to English (partial retranslation of Takagi Yasaka's translation) (1952)

When it becomes necessary, in the course of development of humankind, for one national people to dissolve the political bands which have placed them under another national people, and assume among the powers of the world the independent and equal status to which they are entitled by the law of nature and the law of nature's god, they declare as a natural manifestation of their respect for the opinion of mankind the causes which have impelled them to the separation.

We believe as self-evident truths that all persons are created equal and are endowed by the Creator with certain unalienable heavenly-given rights, including life, liberty, and the pursuit of happiness. Likewise, we believe that governments are instituted among the humankind to secure these rights and that their just powers are derived from the consent of the governed. We also believe that whenever any form of government becomes destructive of these purposes, the people have the right to alter and abolish it and organize a new government which is based on the principle, and provided with powers, that will bring them safety and happiness.

Prudence indeed dictates that governments which have existed long should not be changed for light and transient causes. All past experience therefore has shown the tendency of humankind to suffer, while evils are sufferable, rather than to abolish the forms to which they are accustomed. But when continual abuses and usurpations are committed clearly with a persistence aim, revealing the design to reduce the people under absolute despotism, it is their right and duty to abolish such government and create a new guaranteeing organization for their future security.

## Declaration of Independence in Japanese: Retranslation Back to English (partial retranslation of Saito Makoto's translation) (1998)

As it happens in the human world, a group of people find it necessary to dissolve the political bands which have connected the[m] with other people, and to claim, among the powers of the earth, the independent and equal station to which the law of nature and the law of nature's god entitle them. In such a case, if they want to pay a decent respect to the opinions of humankind, they are required to declare the causes which have impelled them to the separation.

We believe the following truths too obvious to require any proof: That all persons are created equal; That all persons are endowed by the creator with certain rights inalienable to anyone; that in these rights, life, liberty, and the pursuit of happiness are included; That to secure these rights, governments are instituted, the powers of which are justified only when the governed give their consent to it; that when any government, regardless of its form, becomes destructive of the proper ends of government, the people always have the right to alter or to abolish such a government; That they have the right to institute a new government and make its principle and the organizational form of its powers most likely to effect the safety and happiness of the people. Of course, governments long established should not be changed lightly for transient causes, and that is indeed dictated by prudence. As a matter of fact, all human experience indicates that humankind are more disposed to suffer, while evils are sufferable, than to restore their rights by abolishing the form of government to which they are accustomed. But when abuses of power and usurpations of rights are practiced for long years with a consistent aim, clearly intending to reduce them under absolute despotism, it is the right and also the duty of the people to throw off such a government and create a new organization to safeguard their own future safety.

---

# 12.2   'The Working Men's Declaration of Independence,' December 26, 1829

*The following document was published in the* Working Men's Advocate *in New York in the hopes of restoring rights employers allegedly "have robbed" from workers. It is patterned on the Declaration of Independence.*

"When, in the course of human events, it becomes necessary" for one class of a community to assert their natural and unalienable rights in opposition to other classes of their fellow men, "and to assume among" them a political "station of equality to which the laws of nature and of nature's God," as well as the principles of their political compact, "entitle them; a decent respect to the opinions of mankind," and the more paramount duty they owe to their own fellow citizens, "requires that they should declare the causes which impel them" to adopt so painful, yet so necessary, a measure.

"We hold these truths to be self evident, that all men are *created equal;* that they are endowed by their creator with certain unalienable rights; that among these are *life, liberty,* and the *pursuit of happiness;* that to secure these rights" against the undue influence of other classes of society, prudence, as well as the claims of self defence, dictates the necessity of the organization of a party, who shall, by their representatives, prevent dangerous combinations to subvert these indefeasible and fundamental privileges. "All experience hath shown, that mankind" in general, and *we as a class in particular,* "are more disposed to suffer, while evils are sufferable, than to right themselves," by an opposition which the pride and self interest of unprincipled political aspirants, with more unprincipled zeal or religious bigotry, will wilfully misrepresent. "But when a long train of abuses and usurpations" take place, all invariably tending to the oppression and degradation of one class of society and to the un-

natural and iniquitous exaltation of another by political leaders, "it is their right, it is their duty," to use every constitutional means to *reform* the abuses of such a government, and to provide new guards for their future security. The history of the political *parties* in this state, is a history of political *iniquities,* all tending to the enacting and enforcing oppressive and unequal laws. To prove this, let facts be submitted to the candid and impartial of our fellow citizens of all parties.

1. The laws for levying taxes are all based on erroneous principles in consequence of their operating most oppressively on one class of society, and being scarcely felt by the other.
2. The laws regarding the duties of jurors, witnesses, and militia trainings, are still more unequal and oppressive.
3. The laws for private incorporations are all partial in their operations; favoring one class of society to the expense of the other, who have no equal participation.
4. The laws incorporating religious societies have a pernicious tendency by promoting the erection of magnificent places of public worship, by the rich, excluding others, and which others cannot imitate: consequently engendering spiritual pride in the clergy and people, and thereby creating odious distinctions in society, destructive to its social peace and happiness.
5. The laws establishing and patronizing seminaries of learning are unequal, favoring

the rich, and perpetuating imparity, which natural causes have produced, and which judicious laws ought, and can remedy.

6. The laws and municipal ordinances and regulations, generally, besides those specially enumerated, have heretofore been ordained on such principles, as have deprived nine tenths of the members of the body politic, who are *not* wealthy, of the *equal means* to enjoy *"life, liberty, and the pursuit of happiness,"* which the *rich* enjoy exclusively; but the federative compact intended to secure to all, indiscriminately. The lien law in favor of landlords against tenants, and all other honest creditors, is one illustration among innumerable others which can be adduced to prove the truth of these allegations.

We have trusted to the influence of the justice and good sense of our political leaders, to prevent the continuance of these abuses, which destroy the natural bands of equality so essential to the attainment of moral happiness, "but they have been deaf to the voice of justice and consanguinity."

*Therefore, we, the working class of society, of the city of New York,* "appealing to the supreme judge of the world," and to the reason, and consciences of the impartial of all parties, "for the rectitude of our intentions, do, in the spirit, and by the authority," of that political liberty which has been promised to us equally with our fellow men, solemnly publish and declare, and invite all under like pecuniary circumstances, together with every liberal mind, to join us in the declaration, "that we are, & of right ought to be," entitled to EQUAL MEANS to obtain equal moral happi-ness, and social enjoyment, and that all lawful and constitutional measures ought to be adopted to the attainment of those objects. "And for the support of this declaration, we mutually pledge to each other" our faithful aid to the end of our lives.

# Case Index

*See also the Supreme Court case summaries starting on page 303.*

# Subject Index

*Page numbers in italics indicate references to the documents section, which starts on page 213. For court cases, see the Case Index (page 331) as well as the Supreme Court case summaries starting on page 303.*

Abolitionists. *See* Slavery
Adams, Abigail, 175, 205, *321*
Adams, John
  author of Massachusetts Constitution of 1780, 73
  copy of Declaration of Independence in handwriting of, 7, 8, *215*
  death on July 4, 1826, 127
  defender of Declaration to Congress, 10–11
  later recollections of drafting process, 3, 8, 13–14
  recruiting overseas supporters for American Revolution, 193
  role in drafting Declaration of Independence, 3, 4, 5, 7, 8–9, 136
  on setting up a republican government, 73
  on sovereignty, 63
  on women's role, 174–176
Adams, John Quincy, 127–128, 144
Adams, Samuel, 61
Adams, Willi Paul, 199, 201, 203, 204, *325*
Addams, Jane, 185
Admission Acts, *267. See also specific states*
Affirmative action
  constitutionality of, 155
  Thomas's views on, 45, 52–53
African Americans. *See also* Civil rights movement; Discrimination; Slavery
  Black Arts Movement, 171
  Black Nationalism, 166
  Black Panther Party, 171
  Black Power Movement, 171
  Declaration of Independence and "Negroes," 32–33, 39–40
  Fourth of July, refusal to celebrate, 162, 171, 208

  lawsuit by Sojourner Truth, 177
  post–Civil War history of, 162–163
  pre–Civil War views of "Negroes," 30–33, 37
  women, 174, 177
Alabama
  Act of Admission, 107
  Constitution, *267*
    antebellum constitution and right to alter or abolish government, 113
    post–Civil War Constitution, 112, 114
  Enabling Act, 106
  Selma civil rights protest, 165
  statehood and slavery, 106, 107, 109
American Woman Suffrage Association, 182, 184
Americans putting into practice the Declaration of Independence, 203–210
Anderson, Richard Clough, Jr., 110
Anthony, Susan B., 181, 182, 183, 184, 208
Appleby, Joyce, 210
Argument by Trajectory, 165, 170, 172. *See also* Promise/Failure/Fulfillment jeremiads
Aristotle, 16, 18, 19–20, 42, 74, 128, 232
Arizona statehood, 114, *269*
Arkansas
  Constitution, *269*
    post–Civil War Constitution, 112, 113, 114
  statehood and slavery, 112
Arms, right to bear, 91
Arthur, Chester A., 133
Articles of Association (1774), 129, 130
Articles of Confederation, 56–71, *248*
  Article II, 64
  Article IV, 65
  Article XIII, 64
  constituting the American government, 64–67